New Directions in German Studies

Vol. 30

Series Editor:
IMKE MEYER
Professor of Germanic Studies, University of Illinois at Chicago

Editorial Board:

KATHERINE ARENS
Professor of Germanic Studies, University of Texas at Austin

ROSWITHA BURWICK
Distinguished Chair of Modern Foreign Languages Emerita,
Scripps College

RICHARD ELDRIDGE
Charles and Harriett Cox McDowell Professor of Philosophy,
Swarthmore College

ERIKA FISCHER-LICHTE
Professor Emerita of Theater Studies, Freie Universität Berlin

CATRIONA MACLEOD
Frank Curtis Springer and Gertrude Melcher Springer Professor in
the College and the Department of Germanic Studies, University
of Chicago

STEPHAN SCHINDLER
Professor of German and Chair, University of South Florida

HEIDI SCHLIPPHACKE
Associate Professor of Germanic Studies,
University of Illinois at Chicago

ANDREW J. WEBBER
Professor of Modern German and Comparative Culture,
Cambridge University

SILKE-MARIA WEINECK
Professor of German and Comparative Literature,
University of Michigan

DAVID WELLBERY
LeRoy T. and Margaret Deffenbaugh Carlson University
Professor, University of Chicago

SABINE WILKE
Joff Hanauer Distinguished Professor for Western Civilization and
Professor of German, University of Washington

JOHN ZILCOSKY
Professor of German and Comparative Literature, University of Toronto

Volumes in the series:

Vol. 1. *Improvisation as Art: Conceptual Challenges, Historical Perspectives*
by Edgar Landgraf

Vol. 2. *The German Pícaro and Modernity: Between Underdog and Shape-Shifter*
by Bernhard Malkmus

Vol. 3. *Citation and Precedent: Conjunctions and Disjunctions of German Law and Literature*
by Thomas O. Beebee

Vol. 4. *Beyond Discontent: "Sublimation" from Goethe to Lacan*
by Eckart Goebel

Vol. 5. *From Kafka to Sebald: Modernism and Narrative Form*
edited by Sabine Wilke

Vol. 6. *Image in Outline: Reading Lou Andreas-Salomé*
by Gisela Brinker-Gabler

Vol. 7. *Out of Place: German Realism, Displacement, and Modernity*
by John B. Lyon

Vol. 8. *Thomas Mann in English: A Study in Literary Translation*
by David Horton

Vol. 9. *The Tragedy of Fatherhood: King Laius and the Politics of Paternity in the West*
by Silke-Maria Weineck

Vol. 10. *The Poet as Phenomenologist: Rilke and the New Poems*
by Luke Fischer

Vol. 11. *The Laughter of the Thracian Woman: A Protohistory of Theory*
by Hans Blumenberg, translated by Spencer Hawkins

Vol. 12. *Roma Voices in the German-Speaking World*
by Lorely French

Vol. 13. *Vienna's Dreams of Europe: Culture and Identity beyond the Nation-State*
by Katherine Arens

Vol. 14. *Thomas Mann and Shakespeare: Something Rich and Strange*
edited by Tobias Döring and Ewan Fernie

Vol. 15. *Goethe's Families of the Heart*
by Susan E. Gustafson

Vol. 16. *German Aesthetics: Fundamental Concepts from Baumgarten to Adorno*
edited by J. D. Mininger and Jason Michael Peck

Vol. 17. *Figures of Natality: Reading the Political in the Age of Goethe*
by Joseph D. O'Neil

Vol. 18. *Readings in the Anthropocene: The Environmental Humanities, German Studies, and Beyond*
edited by Sabine Wilke and Japhet Johnstone

Vol. 19 *Building Socialism: Architecture and Urbanism in East German Literature, 1955–1973*
by Curtis Swope

Vol. 20. *Ghostwriting: W. G. Sebald's Poetics of History*
by Richard T. Gray

Vol. 21. *Stereotype and Destiny in Arthur Schnitzler's Prose: Five Psycho-Sociological Readings*
by Marie Kolkenbrock

Vol. 22. *Sissi's World: The Empress Elisabeth in Memory and Myth*
edited by Maura E. Hametz and Heidi Schlipphacke

Vol. 23. *Posthumanism in the Age of Humanism: Mind, Matter, and the Life Sciences after Kant*
edited by Edgar Landgraf, Gabriel Trop, and Leif Weatherby

Vol. 24. *Staging West German Democracy: Governmental PR Films and the Democratic Imaginary, 1953–1963*
by Jan Uelzmann

Vol. 25. *The Lever as Instrument of Reason: Technological Constructions of Knowledge around 1800*
by Jocelyn Holland

Vol. 26. *The Fontane Workshop: Manufacturing Realism in the Industrial Age of Print*
by Petra McGillen

Vol. 27. *Gender, Collaboration, and Authorship in German Culture: Literary Joint Ventures, 1750–1850*
edited by Laura Deiulio and John B. Lyon

Vol. 28. *Kafka's Stereoscopes: The Political Function of a Literary Style*
by Isak Winkel Holm

Vol. 29. *Ambiguous Aggression in German Realism and Beyond: Flirtation, Passive Aggression, Domestic Violence*
by Barbara N. Nagel

Vol. 30. *Thomas Bernhard's Afterlives*
edited by Stephen Dowden, Gregor Thuswaldner, and Olaf Berwald

Thomas Bernhard's Afterlives

Edited by
Stephen Dowden,
Gregor Thuswaldner, and
Olaf Berwald

BLOOMSBURY ACADEMIC
NEW YORK • LONDON • OXFORD • NEW DELHI • SYDNEY

BLOOMSBURY ACADEMIC
Bloomsbury Publishing Inc
1385 Broadway, New York, NY 10018, USA
50 Bedford Square, London, WC1B 3DP, UK

BLOOMSBURY, BLOOMSBURY ACADEMIC and the Diana logo
are trademarks of Bloomsbury Publishing Plc

First published in the United States of America 2020
This paperback edition published 2022

Volume Editors' Part of the Work © Stephen Dowden, Gregor Thuswaldner, and Olaf Berwald, 2020
Each chapter © of Contributor

Excerpt(s) from THE LIME WORKS by Thomas Bernhard, translated
by Sophie Wilkins, translation copyright © 1973 by Penguin Random House LLC. Used by permission of
Vintage Books, an imprint of the
Knopf Doubleday Publishing Group, a division of Penguin Random
House LLC. All rights reserved.

Excerpts from "The Nature and Aim of Fiction" from MYSTERY AND MANNERS by
Flannery O'Connor. Reprinted by permission of Farrar, Straus and Giroux.

Cover design: Andrea F. Bucsi
Cover photograph © ANL / Vienna, HW vp 4654

All rights reserved. No part of this publication may be reproduced
or transmitted in any form or by any means, electronic or mechanical,
including photocopying, recording, or any information storage or
retrieval system, without prior permission in writing from the publishers.

Bloomsbury Publishing Inc does not have any control over, or
responsibility for, any third-party websites referred to or in this book.
All internet addresses given in this book were correct at the time of
going to press. The author and publisher regret any inconvenience
caused if addresses have changed or sites have ceased to exist, but can
accept no responsibility for any such changes.

Library of Congress Cataloging-in-Publication Data
Names: Berwald, Olaf, editor. Dowden, Stephen D., editor. | Thuswaldner, Gregor, editor.
Title: Thomas Bernhard's afterlives / edited by Olaf Berwald, Stephen D. Dowden, and Gregor Thuswaldner.
Description: New York : Bloomsbury Academic, 2020. | Series: New directions in German studies; vol. 30
| Includes bibliographical references and index. | Summary: "Explores and assesses the impact of Thomas
Bernhard on writers around the world since his death in 1989"– Provided by publisher.
Identifiers: LCCN 2020013046 | ISBN 9781501351518 (hardback) | ISBN 9781501351532 (pdf) | ISBN
9781501351525 (ebook)
Subjects: LCSH: Bernhard, Thomas–Influence. | Bernhard, Thomas–Criticism and interpretation.
Classification: LCC PT2662.E7 Z8976 2020 | DDC 833/.914 [B]–dc23
LC record available at https://lccn.loc.gov/2020013046

ISBN:	HB:	978-1-5013-5151-8
	PB:	978-1-5013-6926-1
	ePDF:	978-1-5013-5153-2
	eBook:	978-1-5013-5152-5

Series: New Directions in German Studies

Typeset by Integra Software Services Pvt. Ltd.

To find out more about our authors and books visit www.bloomsbury.com and sign up for our newsletters.

Contents

Introduction: The Master of Understatement, or Remembering Schermaier
Stephen Dowden   1

1 The Afterlife of Thomas Bernhard in Contemporary Austrian Literature
 Katya Krylova   23

2 Writing Failure: Geoff Dyer, Thomas Bernhard, and the Inability to Begin
 Kata Gellen   45

3 Bernhard, Sebald, and Photography in Holocaust Memory
 Agnes Mueller   71

4 Radical Style: Bernhard, Sontag, Kertész
 Stephen Dowden   81

5 The Stains of Cultural Inheritance: Thomas Bernhard and Philip Roth
 Byron Spring   97

6 Gaddis before Bernhard before Gaddis
 Martin Klebes   117

7 Thomas Bernhard, a Writer for Spain
 Heike Scharm   137

8 Immersions into Bernhard's Works in Recent Francophone Literature
 Olaf Berwald   157

9 Thomas Bernhard's Influence on Gabriel Josipovici's Monologue Novels
 Gregor Thuswaldner   169

10 Thomas Bernhard, Italo Calvino, Elena Ferrante, and
   Claudio Magris: From Postmodernism to Anti-Semitism
   Saskia Elizabeth Ziolkowski 183

11 Thomas Bernhard's *Extinction*: Variations/Variazioni/
   Variaciones
   Juliane Werner 207

   Bibliography 233
   Notes on Contributors 246
   Index 250

Introduction: The Master of Understatement, or Remembering Schermaier

Stephen Dowden

> *The basis of art is truth, both in matter and in mode. The person who aims after art in his work aims after truth, in an imaginative sense, no more and no less.*
>
> —Flannery O'Connor

According to Jean Améry—Austrian critic, writer, and Holocaust survivor—Thomas Bernhard stands in a line of Austrian writers infected by what he called *morbus austriacus*: the Austrian disease. Alluding to Kierkegaard's description of despair as a "sickness unto death," Améry offers *morbus austriacus* as the characteristic malady of other Austrian writers, too.[1] He had in mind Franz Kafka, Otto Weininger, Hugo von Hofmannsthal, Ernst Weiß, and Joseph Roth. In Améry's view this condition presents as a passionate hatred for Austria.

The disease metaphor addresses the life and works of Thomas Bernhard accurately and productively. His characters often suffer from mental or physical illnesses or both, and the condition is usually congenital, because it arises from the pathology of his historical era. To be born Austrian in Bernhard's world means to suffer from a debility from which no recovery is possible, a sickness unto death. His own poor health is germane. For decades, Bernhard lived with a terminal pulmonary illness, and that condition—as much spiritual as somatic—spilled over into his writing. Moreover, his prose style and its characteristic motifs have proved to be highly contagious to other writers. As early as 1963, with the appearance of his first novel, *Frost*, reviews were

---

1   Jean Améry, "Morbus Austriacus," *Merkur* 30.1 (1976), 91–94.

already affected, or afflicted, with the style that Bernhard made use of in his work. Bernhard's circulatory, highly repetitive, and therefore also musical style, his facility with monstrously long compound words, his offensive generalizations, meandering digressions, and abusive tirades were often imitated, adopted, adapted, and—later on, as the essays in the book will show—reconfigured and developed in imaginative ways.

But the German and Austrian context is not the only way of placing Bernhard's contagious effect. Thomas Bernhard belongs to a minuscule tradition of cosmopolitan modern writers whose foremost European figures are Kafka and Beckett. What links his works with theirs is above all the international impact of their seemingly small ambition. Beckett's aim was to write less and less. Kafka's ambition was to belong to a small (or minor) literature. Bernhard's ambition was to call attention to and mercilessly deride the brokenness of the provincial postwar country he inhabited. In the most immediate terms this brokenness refers to Austria in particular, heartland of Nazi anti-Semitism and of crimes whose infamy outstrips all possible description. Rather than describe them in the weary and wearisome realistic prose of his German contemporaries, Bernhard's characters harp cantankerously on a handful of themes, lacking all nuance or pretense of impartiality: Austria's wartime guilt, its postwar amnesia, its betrayal of its own tradition, the assent and collaboration of Catholics in the degradation of Austrian culture, the hardy survival of the fascist mentality into its postwar life and institutions, the decline of quality in all things after the apocalypse that he never calls by name. Like the writing of Kafka and Beckett in Europe and Flannery O'Connor in the United States, Bernhard's prose foregoes all uplift. It has no use for compassionate or tragic plots and offers no respite other than the one indirect, gestural moment that is the art itself. This, too, his works have in common with those of Kafka, Beckett, and O'Connor. He gives up all hope. But, as in the case of his great colleagues, he also gives up hopelessness—which is evident from the fact that he keeps on writing and that his protagonists keep on talking.

Like Kafka, O'Connor, and Beckett, too, Bernhard created his own uniquely distinctive style, ultimately comic, that is tailored to the needs of his imagination and its grasp of the true. He writes long, looping, repetitive sentences, largely monologues, page after page of print unrelieved by paragraph breaks. His minimal plots recur from novel to novel, if indeed his books can be called novels at all. They are tidal waves of prose that have the effect of carrying the reader away on a tsunami of manic loquacity from the perspective of an irascible outsider.

Finally, like O'Connor, Kafka, and Beckett, Bernhard's imagination has turned out to have an extraordinary reach and appeal, far beyond his immediate context. What Bernhard has in common with them and a handful of the other greatest twentieth-century writers is above all this: a willingness to look at the worst without looking away and, in a feat of dialectical reversal, to transform that gaze at horror and failure and corruption into supremely affecting prose.

After the Second World War—when Bernhard, Beckett, and O'Connor were writing, and when Kafka emerged as the epitome of modern style—cities, cultures, and entire traditions lay in ruins, those of Austria not least of all—but not only Austria. Whole peoples vegetated on as survivors of a disaster that allowed of no survivors: the living cannot flourish in the true sense of the word, according to Bernhard's tales, in the spiritual wasteland of squandered tradition and a moral catastrophe that Austria had brought on itself. This world is so damaged, so lacking in spiritual nourishment that even those who seem to be alive have no idea that their lives are posthumous, zombie-like parodies of life. This specific variety of despair—the not-knowing that one is in a state of despair—is one that Kierkegaard and Bernhard depict. People in this condition are unaware that their new cars, custom homes, ever faster internet speeds, and luxury vacations are not expressions of success but much more just flimsy material substitutes for the right life. They dress up the underlying nihilism as a reassuring display of conspicuous consumption. Only Bernhard's obnoxiously garrulous protagonists—from Strauch in *Frost* to Franz-Josef Murau in *Extinction* and Reger of *Old Masters* (the last book Bernhard completed)—have the self-awareness to see how matters really stand with us.

Their animadversions, which are also Bernhard's, feel true and satisfying because only in rhetorically heightened elaboration does the horror underlying our supposed normalcy find proper expression. "You have to make your vision apparent by shock," wrote Flannery O'Connor in a similar spirit. "To the hard of hearing you shout, and for the almost blind you draw large and startling figures."[2] So it is in Bernhard's prose, in his larger-than-life figures: "The traces of the war are not yet wiped out," blusters the reclusive ex-painter Strauch in *Frost*. "This war will never be forgotten. People will continue to encounter it wherever they go."[3] The undead spirit of wartime devastation is omnipresent, not hidden: "Even today you keep encountering skulls or entire skeletons, covered over by a thin layer of pine needles," says the painter.[4] Though never invoked by name, the Shoah haunts the whole of Bernhard's writing as the ultimate but not exclusive source of Austrian guilt and shame—and not only Austrian. There is plenty of failure to go around. Bernhard's prose insists on wartime suffering and the presence of the

---

2 Flannery O'Connor, "The Fiction Writer and His Country" (1957), *Collected Works* (New York: Library of America, 1988), 805–6.
3 Thomas Bernhard, *Frost*, trans. Michael Hofmann (New York: Knopf, 2006), 150.
4 Bernhard, *Frost*, 149.

dead as its legacy, even a perverse birthright, which—like some grave genetic defect—cannot be corrected except by obliterating the bloodline in which it occurs.

Still, it would be a mistake to take Bernhard's fiction literally. Despite what he may have said he believed about the emptiness and futility of life, the work itself is not ultimately nihilistic. That he continued to make art at all—instead of retiring from life and art (as Strauch does) or committing suicide (as Roithamer does)—is neither hypocrisy nor a logical flaw but an aesthetic clue. Bernhard chooses a backhanded affirmation by way of total negation. He is always concerned in his novels and plays to achieve a style that will best intervene in society, a style that provokes critical attention. He is fundamentally an ironist and a moralist, as were Swift and Rabelais, Nestroy and Karl Kraus.[5]

The eleven essays collected here demonstrate that *morbus austriacus* has infected and affected writers across the world. Let us not speak narrowly of "influence." For one thing, influence implies a single direction of pressure, from Bernhard to those who have felt and responded to the challenge of his creativity. What really is happening, rather, is that a conversation has been expanding and developing. As Bernhard's admirers explore the avenues he has opened, a new understanding of Bernhard will develop. He is no longer just an off-piste Austrian anomaly of postwar German prose, but a phenomenon of world literature. Moreover, like the singularity of Kafka and Beckett and O'Connor, Bernhard's uniqueness is untouchable. To imitate these writers too closely is to miscarry the standards they set, to be an epigone. But like them he has shown the way to new expressive possibilities in prose form that other writers have explored in various original ways over the last thirty years.

In his native land Bernhard, of course, has made a lasting impact, and Katya Krylova documents it in her contribution to this volume. She focuses on four figures. Robert Schindel and Gerhard Roth have Bernhard appear as a character in novels of their own. Alexander Schimmelbusch and Thomas Mulitzer both satirize Austria's posthumous retooling of Bernhard into a benign classic: Mulitzer imagines, along the lines of Austria's chocolate Mozartkugeln, a parallel "Bernhard torte," which a Viennese confectioner invents to celebrate the dead writer by turning him into an object of popular consumption—sweet and easy to digest.

Outside of Austria, the most conspicuous Bernhard acolyte in the German world is W. G. Sebald. Himself a writer of international

---

5 W. G. Sebald, "Wo die Dunkelheit den Strick zuzieht: Zu Thomas Bernhard," *Die Beschreibung des Unglücks: Zur österreichischen Literatur von Stifter bis Handke* (Frankfurt am Main: Fischer Taschenbuch, 1994), 103–14, here 110–14.

Introduction: The Master of Understatement   5

stature, Sebald credits Bernhard as mentor and model. Agnes Mueller in her chapter demonstrates that the question of influence gives way to something more like a conversation between these two writers of immense imaginative resource. She brings Bernhard's *Extinction* and Sebald's *Austerlitz* into productive dialogue with each other regarding their visual dynamics and their narrative performance of correlations between writing and art, trauma and memory. A key feature in the prose writings of Bernhard and Sebald is the sense of the incommensurability between lived fact and written fiction, between truth and memory, reality and image. The things we think we know may be, perhaps largely are, stories we make up to reinforce or critique our beliefs, fears, hopes, and plans. Owing to this gap of uncertainty, Bernhard and Sebald write stories that unsettle our sense of how things are rather than endorse the settled conventions we take as true. Hence both of their works feature narrators who say outrageous or ambiguous or contingent things.

Some fail to say anything at all, despite great effort: a prominent Bernhard theme is the blocked writer or artist or scientist. Two essays in this volume deal with its afterlife in later fiction. Kata Gellen takes up the theme in Geoff Dyer's memoir, *Out of Sheer Rage: Wrestling with D. H. Lawrence*. She finds Dyer absorbed in conversation with Bernhard's *Lime Works*, in which the scientist-protagonist Konrad continuously fails to get his great study of hearing off the ground. Dyer likewise, in full Bernhardian regalia, fails to get his study of D. H. Lawrence off the ground, but he also fails his way into spectacular artistic success. Similarly, Martin Klebes takes up the protagonists and narrators of Bernhard's novels *Concrete* and *The Loser*, vis-à-vis the novels of William Gaddis. The protagonists of *Agapē Agape* and *J.R.* are consumed by an obsession with their (failed) writing projects.

In a chapter on Bernhard and Philip Roth, Byron Spring discovers unexpected affinities between two writers who at first seem far apart. No radical stylist himself, Roth coincides with Bernhard on the unreliability of language. Always we are writing fictitious versions of our lives, for which no final, authoritative text is even possible. Always there is a void between words and reality. The stories we tell ourselves about ourselves necessarily get tangled up in each other and can't help but create contradictions, confusion, and falsehoods. These narrated versions of our lives, no matter whether they are obvious embellishments or unintentional misrepresentations, nevertheless constitute the best hold on reality we have and must stand as the provisory truth in place of any final truth.

It is similar with Susan Sontag. In a chapter focusing attention on the importance of radical style, I investigate the way that Bernhard's prose informs Susan Sontag's illness narrative "The Way We Live Now" and certain of Imre Kertész's works. Sontag was drawn to radical writers, including Bernhard, and she modifies his stylistic radicalism for her own purposes. Both Bernhard and Sontag battled terminal illnesses for decades. While Bernhard struggled with lung disease, Sontag fought cancer. Written at the height of the AIDS crisis in the mid-1980s, "The Way We Live Now" tells the story—or, in a variation on Gellen's and Klebe's failure theme, manages pointedly to *not* tell the story—of a terminally ill man named Max, who never even gets to appear in the tale. He is the crucial void at the center. He himself, in his specificity and suffering, is beyond representation, as indeed any crisis is as a whole or any individual's fate. "Language is inadequate when it comes to communicating the truth," says Bernhard, "and the best the writer can offer is an approximation to the truth ... Language can only falsify and distort whatever is authentic."[6] What Sontag captures instead of the truth about Max, in wave after wave of Bernhardian digression, is the aspiration to truth expressed and the social repercussions surrounding a friend's severe illness.

Imre Kertész, in his own aspiration to telling the truth about Auschwitz, is also known for radical style. He felt a strong kinship with Bernhard and was attracted to his Austrian counterpart's way of writing. A survivor of Auschwitz, Kertész in his *Kaddish for an Unborn Child* was directly motivated by Bernhard's *Yes*. Though a native of Budapest, Kertész identified not so much as a provincial Hungarian writer but rather as a cosmopolitan European Jew with a special affinity for the Austrian tradition of German prose. Similarly, it seems fair to say that Bernhard, like Kertész, has become a cosmopolitan European writer who happens to be an Austrian provincial, much as Kertész just happens to be a native of Hungary.

In a similar vein, Heike Scharm shows that Thomas Bernhard found a ready audience among Spanish novelists in a conscious effort to free themselves of Franco-era conventions and leave behind what they conceived to be a cultural and political provincialism. His writing about Austria rang true and seemed familiar to them. Reading about Bernhard's presence in post-Franco Spain, one could come to the conclusion that Bernhard was indeed grounded in the literary and cultural context of twentieth-century Spain. Bernhard's influence on a young generation of disillusioned and skeptical writers, including Javier Marías and Félix de Azúa, was profound. In addition to reflecting on Bernhard's meaning for Marías and Azúa, Scharm finds telling affinities between the Austrian writer and Pío Baroja, a representative of the generation of 1898. Scharm suspects that especially Baroja's widely read novel *El árbol de la ciencia* (*The Tree of Knowledge*, 1911) paved the way for Bernhard's

---

6 Thomas Bernhard, *Gathering Evidence: A Memoir*, trans. David McLintock (New York: Knopf, 1985), 314.

Introduction: The Master of Understatement   7

reception in Spain seven decades later. That both Spain and Austria have roots in the Habsburg baroque may also be significant.

Olaf Berwald hears echoes of Bernhard's voice in francophone prose. He takes up works by Hervé Guibert, Gemma Salem, Israel Eliraz, Linda Lê, and Cyril Huot. These writers have found a range of creative ways to carry out and expand on the purport of Bernhard's topoi and style. While Guibert's protagonist in À l'ami qui ne m'a pas sauvé la vie (To the Friend Who Didn't Save my Life, 1990) wrestles with Bernhard's oeuvre and likens the Austrian author to a virus, Nicolas Stakhovitch's novel, Les Aphorismes de Gralph (1991), was initially thought in France to be the translation of a posthumously published book by Bernhard, as its themes and language so closely resemble those of Bernhard. Gemma Salem was drawn to and drew on the ethical dimension of Bernhard's works, and Linda Lê's works engage in an ongoing dialogue with Bernhard's characters.

Saskia Ziolkowski explores both the role of Italy in Bernhard's works and the effect he exerted on Italo Calvino, Claudio Magris, and Elena Ferrante. Some of Bernhard's protagonists escape to Italy because they find living in Austria unbearable. Murau in Auslöschung (Extinction) lives in Rome because he cannot abide his homeland and particularly the family estate, Wolfsegg. Calvino discovered Bernhard in the 1960s, urging his publisher to translate his works, which did not happen until the late 1970s. For Calvino, Bernhard was something of an alter ego. Magris, both an influential scholar of Austrian literature and culture and a novelist in his own right, organized the first academic conference on Bernhard's works in the 1970s. Magris's recent novel Non luogo a procedere (Blameless, 2015) explores Bernhard's ambivalent view of victimizer and victimhood. Likewise, the mysteriously elusive novelist Elena Ferrante has responded creatively to Bernhard's use of language.

In her essay for this volume, Juliane Werner takes a different tack. She focuses on three variations of just one novel, Bernhard's Extinction, in different languages: Tim Parks's Destiny (1999), Horacio Castellanos Moya's El asco: Thomas Bernhard en San Salvador (1997), and Vitaliano Trevisan's Il ponte: Un crollo (2007). These books offer variations of Bernhard's topoi, style, and language that recall his last published novel. Set in three distinct cultural and linguistic contexts, the three novels under investigation reveal fascinating similarities to Extinction.

The ninth chapter analyzes Gabriel Josipovici's imaginative response to Bernhard in three monologue novels, Moo Pak (1986), The Big Glass (1991), and Infinity: The Story of a Moment (2012). Gregor Thuswaldner rejects the notion that Josipovici is "the English Thomas Bernhard," as Suhrkamp advertised the German translation of Moo Pak. Instead, Thuswaldner shows Josipovici's sophistication in appropriating and revising Bernhard's linguistic and literary strategies to suit his own purposes.

The musicality of Bernhard's works, and the acidity of his protagonists' comments on Austria and the human condition, continue to infuse world literature with vibrant possibilities. His style and topoi will remain viral, and many afterlives of Bernhard are yet to emerge. But what might account for the extraordinary appeal of Bernhard outside the German-language context, and for that matter in a context that is beyond any national language?

In an introduction such as this, it is tempting to provide helpful "context," to ease the newcomer into the topic via historical facts, biographical information, and literary background. The obliging editor could expound on Bernhard's harsh childhood, his suffering as a schoolboy at the hands of Nazi and Catholic schoolmasters, his mother's sharp tongue, his adoration of his despotic grandfather, his thwarted desire to be a singer, his degrading experiences as a tubercular teenager in the Austrian public health system that as good as handed him a death sentence. It was there, in Grafenhof sanatorium between 1949 and 1951, under threat of death, that he discovered literature. He took refuge in reading and then in writing. Bernhard covered this ground himself in his five very fine memoirs, collected in English under a single title, *Gathering Evidence*. Most famously we could emphasize his caustic insults at the official ceremonies that honored him with many writing awards. However, academic contextualizing entails not only explaining but also almost inevitably some "explaining away," as if biography could unlock his art. This introduction seeks to avoid that trap.

In life Bernhard was a divisive figure. His rancorous, unnuanced, and scalding contempt for Austrian life, Austrian Catholics, and Austrian cultural pretensions stems from his categorical rejection of the Austro-German Nazi past and its denial by many, as well as the nation's consequently unredeemable present. "The destruction and annihilation of our country," opines Franz-Josef Murau in a characteristic passage,

> has been encompassed by *National Socialism* and *pseudosocialism*, aided and abetted by Austrian *Catholicism*, which has always cast its blight upon Austria. Today Austria is a country governed by unscrupulous profiteers belonging to parties devoid of all conscience. In the last few centuries, Gambetti, Austria has been cheated of everything and had all its sense knocked out of it by Catholicism, National Socialism, and pseudosocialism. In the Austria of today, Gambetti, vulgarity is the watchword, baseness the motive, and mendacity the key. Every morning when we wake up we ought to be utterly ashamed of today's Austria.[7]

---

7 Thomas Bernhard, *Extinction*, trans. David McLintock (New York: Knopf, 1995), 325.

Bernhard's behavior in both his art and his public utterances reveals an artist who refused to engage the reasoned argumentation and virtue-signaling that is otherwise so characteristic of postwar German fiction: these refusals earned him both intense hatred and fervent admiration in Austria of the 1960s, 1970s, and 1980s. Krylova's account in her chapter contextualizes this reception, and we may be tempted to find a biographical reason for the specificity of his persona vis-à-vis Austria. But the writer's work should be allowed to speak for itself, too, as art rather than personal animus.

Often it is not allowed to. Now that Bernhard has been safely dead since 1989, a new, less troublesome simulacrum has replaced him as a culture hero in Austria. The writer's house in Ohlsdorf has become a public shrine. Salzburg, cruel to him formerly, celebrates "Bernhard Days." A scholarly organization devoted to his work has been formed. Once a hateful scourge beyond all possible reconciliation with the status quo, Bernhard has now been styled an endearingly grumpy eccentric—and therefore a true Austrian after all. He is now a national treasure embalmed—like Lenin lying pickled and harmless in his mausoleum—in fancy coffee-table photo books, online videos, popular publications, and academic seminars. He has become a monument to a once virulent affliction that it's now safe to ignore, like the Pestsäule in the middle of Vienna's first district. The baroque column memorializes the Black Plague that ravaged the city in 1679, but now is so familiar that it has become all but invisible.

One symptom of this faux-Bernhard reduced to a housebroken likeness of himself is an epithet frequently attached to him: *Übertreibungskünstler*, or "exaggeration artist." The currency of this refrain derives perhaps from a much-quoted collection of academic essays so titled.[8] The comforting platitude is only partly true, and true in only a trivial way that clichés are always true. Despite being drawn from a rant in *Extinction* ("The art of exaggeration is in fact the secret of all mental endeavor," says Murau to Gambetti), it falsifies Bernhard because it downplays the authentically destructive force of his anarchic comedy and his no-holds-barred relationship to the truth.[9] It implies that Bernhard was "only" exaggerating—just kidding around—that in fact things in Austria and in postwar life generally just are not all that bad. It insinuates that his own public rants and those of the protagonists are all just subjective anyway—entertaining, of course, but ultimately no more than the subjective exaggerations of a prose virtuoso.

---

8 Wendelin Schmidt-Dengler, *Der Übertreibungskünstler: Studien zu Thomas Bernhard*, 4th ed., ed. Martin Huber and Wolfgang Straub (Vienna: Sonderzahl, 2010). Originally published in 1986.
9 Bernhard, *Extinction*, 308.

To saddle Bernhard with the label "Übertreibungskünstler" diminishes him as an artist because it minimizes the earnest, abiding, and authentic negativity that is the essence of his art. Bernhard obviously intended to give offense, and this offense is part of the art, its *irreconcilable otherness*. His writing sides with the outcasts, not with comfortable intellectuals in academic lockstep. Its aggression toward the status quo is not to be overlooked, domesticated, or toned down as "exaggeration." It is instead what in his "Meridian" speech of 1960 Paul Celan calls a *Gegenwort*, a "counterword," a speaking *against*: against exhausted narrative ploys and poetic forms, against inherited cultural norms, against unthinking or forgetful complacency, against Austrian complicity in the horrors of the twentieth century.[10] Consequently, Bernhard's enemies probably have a better grasp of his aesthetic power than his supposed defenders do. Bernhardian negativity may well be grotesque and offensive, but it is no exaggeration. Like the kindred negations of Kafka, Beckett, O'Connor, and Paul Celan too, Bernhard's negativity epitomizes and reveals what affirmative culture refuses to accept or even see about itself. Encroaching darkness and debilitating cold draw Bernhard like a magnet. He takes pleasure in, delights in his rescue of endangered truths.

It's not that Bernhard endorses Konrad's barbaric behavior toward his disabled wife in *The Lime Works*, or Roithamer's lethal veneration for his sister in *Correction*, or Wertheimer's abusive relationship with his sister in *The Loser*. Rather, Bernhard endorses a frank acknowledgment of the negative energy that permeates and supercharges modern culture as a whole—even as it eats away at it from within. Art is not excepted from negation either. A basic Bernhard theme, as Gellen and Klebes observe, is the failure to complete artistic and scholarly projects. But there is more: the failure of even completed projects to offer transcendence is a basic theme too; for example, the utopian Cone in which Roithamer's beloved sister not only fails to experience the "supreme happiness" that he had planned for her but which in fact kills her.

Art is lethal: his fictional Glenn Gould, a supremely inhuman artist in Bernhard's novel *The Loser*, drops dead while playing Bach's *Goldberg Variations*. This variation on the failure theme emerges as early as the first novel with Strauch, a painter who has incinerated all his own paintings as misbegotten. Artists, he says,

---

10 Paul Celan, *The Meridian: Final Version—Drafts—Materials*, ed. Bernhard Böschenstein and Heino Schmull, trans. Pierre Joris (Stanford: Stanford University Press, 2011), 10. On the importance of the poetic "Gegenwort" for Celan, see Amir Eshel, *Poetic Thinking Today: An Essay* (Stanford: Stanford University Press, 2020), 45–8.

are the sons and daughters of loathsomeness, of paradisiac shamelessness, the original sons and daughters of lewdness; artists, painters, writers, and musicians are the compulsive masturbators on the planet, its disgusting cramps, its peripheral puffings and swellings, its pustular secretions ... I want to say: artists are the great emetic agents of the time, they were always the great, the very greatest emetics ... Artists, are they not a devastating army of absurdity, of scum?[11]

Bernhard's despair, not different from Strauch's, is all-devouring and includes four simple points to be made about this self-contradiction.

The first could be described as its Dostoevskian moment. Reading Dostoevsky, wrote Bernhard, made him strong at a time in his life when all indications were that he would die of tuberculosis in a squalid welfare sanatorium.[12] It also pointed him in the direction of writing. As in Dostoevsky's *Notes from Underground* (where the Underground Man, a figure as perverse as Strauch, insists on his right to declare that two plus two equal five), self-contradiction and even self-negation stand as a paradoxically effective form of self-assertion. That doesn't mean the absurd claim is true, but it does voice the self's defining, if also negative, freedom. Moreover, it embodies the spirit of resistance (the *Gegenwort*) that is central to all Bernhard's writing. Similarly, Bernhard readers should not allow themselves to get snagged on the factuality of this or that seeming exaggeration. Truth is to be sought in the constellation of the work, and especially of his works altogether, as the detail relates to the whole, and what that larger constellation opens up to view.

Second is a Kierkegaardian moment, which distinguishes among different varieties of the sickness unto death. A key variant is what Kierkegaard calls demonic despair. Its defining feature is defiance. The Bernhard protagonist embodies this defiance. He carries on out of spite.[13] Strauch clings to his melancholia as if it were a raft in a storm. He revels in despair. It generates endless reflection and language in him. But suicide never tempts him: This sort of despairing person— Strauch, Reger, Murau, Saurau—does not really want release from his agony. Rather than seek help or commit suicide, he chooses to be himself amid and at least partly because of all imaginable torment. This being is expressed verbally and indirectly, in and as the striking musicality of Bernhard's prose.

---

11 Bernhard, *Frost*, 143.
12 Bernhard, *Gathering Evidence*, 335–36.
13 Mikkel Frantzen, "The Demonic Comedy of Thomas Bernhard," *Journal of Austrian Studies* 50 (2018), 89–108, here 93.

Third is what might be described as his Arendtian moment of thinking poetically rather than discursively. According to Hannah Arendt, *poetic thinking* is a rare gift. What guides it, she writes, is the conviction that even when such a thinker has been subjected to the "ruin of the time, the process of decay is at the same time a process of crystallization."[14] Bernhard has this strange gift. His prose works and theater plays are just such crystallizations that the energy released by decay has caused to form. Elaborating on the importance of Arendt's insight, Amir Eshel writes that "poetic thinking refers to artworks that open up *spaces of* and *spaces for* open-ended thinking."[15] Thomas Bernhard's works do precisely this. They are provocations that forcefully break open spaces for thought—hard-edged, sharp, clear crystals that draw the eye and invite response. The works that the contributors of this volume explore are themselves crystallizations formed from the energy that Bernhard's writing gives off.

Fourth is the question of why all this hate and pain should be written about to the exclusion of any kindness and love that might be expressed in a positive way. I don't think Bernhard was cynical about kindness and love. What interested him was not the denial of love but the ascendancy—outrageous and unacceptable—of its opposite. He does not celebrate cruelty or sanction misery. Instead, he calls them out so that he can rail against them. Note, too, the spiritual kinship of his celebrated publications to Walter Benjamin's famous remark that "there is no document of civilization which is not at the same time a document of barbarism."[16] Bernhard's writing recognizes itself as being embedded in the unresolved and unresolvable struggle to reconcile the two, and it implicates the reader in that struggle too.

This is not to suggest that Bernhard acquiesces in barbarism. The opposite is true. However, his protest against barbarism does not come from an intellectual's logically reasoned point of view. Indeed, Bernhard's heroes and Bernhard himself—as Thuswaldner writes in his contribution—are not intellectuals but *Geistesmenschen*, human beings driven by mind and by spirit, but not only or necessarily by instrumental reason. An intellectual's protest against barbarity would come from a moral high ground that is rational, argued, measured, tasteful, judicious, socially respectable, and in general acceptable from the discursive point of view that governs conventional novel writing and academic

---

14 Hannah Arendt, "Walter Benjamin," trans. Harry Zohn, *Men in Dark Times* (Orlando: Mariner, 1970), 153–206, here 206.
15 Eshel, *Poetic Thinking Today*, 6.
16 Walter Benjamin, "Theses on the Philosophy of History," *Illuminations: Essays and Reflections*, ed. Hannah Arendt, trans. Harry Zohn (New York: Harcourt Brace Jovanovich, 1968), 256.

scholarship. In his poetic thinking, Bernhard, the instinctive artist akin to other *Geistesmenschen* such as Beckett, Celan, Kafka, and O'Connor, takes an approach that is audaciously *mimetic* rather than discursive. As we will see in all of the essays in the volume, the mimetic dimension of Bernhard's writing has proved immensely attractive to other writers. His prose (like his protagonists' speech) has something monstrous and tyrannical about it. It has absorbed into itself the epoch's negativity and barbarism. The spirit of destruction and ruin has seeped into its very syntax and its narrative form. That is its mimetic moment, as is his refusal to resolve the most dissonant of his insults into the tonic key of common sense. Bernhard does not trust common sense. He grew up in an environment in which common sense dictated it would be best to be rid of Jews and homosexuals for good, to get shut of Roma and Sinti, to sterilize and euthanize the mentally and physically disabled. All this should be accomplished by the authorities for the greater social good and in the name of order.

Consequently, order's reputation is in question too. His protagonists' monologues seem always to teeter on the brink of chaos. The torrent of words never lets up or eases off. He never offers any merry wink of the authorial eye to signal ironic intent. There is no mitigating gesture to suggest it's all, so to speak, in good fun. This prose achievement is as monomaniacal as the murderous Konrad is in *The Lime Works* and as are Bernhard's other obsessives, those who are unable or unwilling to un-know the violent, unstable foundations of modern, postwar well-being. Its darkness inhabits them. It drives them. While it may be comforting to minimize Bernhard's insistence on negation as mere exaggeration, it is also misleading. It obscures what makes Bernhard an artist instead of a garden-variety crank.

The clinching indication that he is not quite taken seriously by at least some of his admirers, most obviously in his homeland, came shortly after his death. Bernhard's testamentary attempt to block the performance of his plays in Austria after his death was easily circumvented.[17] Presumably that ban, too, is to be seen as just another of his quirky exaggerations. In death, then, Bernhard has been reigned in, normalized, and domesticated by his advocates. (The fate of Randle McMurphy at the end of *One Flew over the Cuckoo's Nest* comes to mind. He, too, was a victim of normalization.)

Has Bernhard been irrevocably normalized and mainstreamed? Bernhard broke taboos, fearlessly and ferociously. Has that writer

---

17 Stephen D. Dowden, "A Testament Betrayed: Thomas Bernhard and His Legacy," in *A Companion to the Works of Thomas Bernhard*, ed. Matthias Konzett (Rochester, NY: Camden House, 2002), 51–68.

become a literary-historical monument effectively as remote from the present as, say, Rabelais and Swift or Vienna's Pestsäule? The essays gathered in this collection suggest otherwise. Bernhard's work continues to draw other writers, including and especially writers not connected with his immediate Austrian and German context. Possibly they are attracted to his penchant for the entertaining rant, a genre that has become ubiquitous in an era of "post-truth" or "truthiness." However, the more likely context of appeal may be the powerful, relentless, and compelling relationship of his fiction and drama to the true truth.

That relationship is guided by the Bernhardian sense that postwar Austrian and German life—and by extension the postwar world in general—is grotesquely false, smug, cold-hearted, and self-deceived. This world's prosperity, its progress, its faith in technological fixes for all problems, its obliviousness to atrocity past and present, the overall collapse of values that once had been self-evident: all these rest on foundations of ruin that have been concentrated into the signifier "Auschwitz." The overused word stands, inadequately but indispensably, for unimaginable cruelty and, by extension, for an irreversible and historically unexampled transformation that occurred in the twentieth century. It stands for an atrocity among countless atrocities that we cannot un-see, a boundary we cannot un-cross, a historical experience that mere writers cannot overstate. Exaggeration falls short.

Here we again veer toward Byron Spring's view of Philip Roth as a Bernhardian spirit. "The American writer in the middle of the twentieth century," said Roth to Stanford students in 1960, "has his hands full trying to understand, describe, and make *credible* much of American reality. It stupefies, it sickens, it infuriates, and finally it is even a kind of embarrassment to one's own meager imagination."[18] Another overexcitable exaggerator? No, Roth soberly corroborates the fundamental gesture of Bernhard's prose by his own parallel experience. And he is not even considering the more profoundly sickened condition of Europe in the aftermath of Nazi atrocities.

Given the radically altered world after Auschwitz, the postwar novel required a new language. Imre Kertész, novelist, Auschwitz prisoner, and Bernhard admirer, puts it this way:

> the unbearable burden of the Holocaust has over time given rise to the forms of language that appear to talk about the Holocaust, while never even touching the reality of it. [...] Most people—and this is psychologically quite understandable—want to reconstruct

---

18 Philip Roth, "Writing American Fiction," *Why Write? Collected Nonfiction 1960–2014* (New York: Library of America, 2017), 27.

what happened at Auschwitz in a pre-Auschwitz language and with pre-Auschwitz ideas, as though the humanistic world of the nineteenth century were still relevant and had only broken down for a single historical moment under the pressure of incomprehensible barbarism.[19]

We must connect this thought not only to language alone but also to the form of the novel, or to the novel as a form of language. Kertész discovered in Thomas Bernhard a post-Auschwitz narrative form adequate to his own needs as novelist of Auschwitz. He speaks not of "exaggeration," though, but of dissonance and atonality in the novel's form. Tonality, a uniform key, was once a universally accepted convention. But gradually its authority eroded and came to seem confining, coercive, and false to lived experience. Atonality declares that this agreement or tradition no longer stands as absolute. In literature, too, a tonic keynote once existed, a seemingly absolute set of values based upon a generally accepted morality and ethics that defined the system of relationships among statements and ideas. The European catastrophe of 1914–45 demonstrated, if by then such was still necessary, that the unthinkable can simply happen, that what once seemed like moral certainties can simply fail. Once again, the shorthand for this descent from an orderly universe into moral chaos is "Auschwitz." In the degraded world of Bernhard's fiction and drama, no universal certainties exist anymore, and that would include the predictable structures of traditional novel writing, structures both formal and moral. Uncertainty emerges as a major theme for the tormented souls in his plays and novels.

There is in fact a modest parallel between Bernhard and the death camp survivors who became writers, people such as Tadeusz Borowski, Imre Kertész, and Jean Améry. Though not as extreme as their actual survivor experiences, Bernhard's stories bear a family resemblance to theirs. His own wartime childhood in Salzburg was saturated with death and shock that defined his later life as a writer. Like the Holocaust novelists who returned to "normal life" with stories that seemed like preposterous exaggerations to the few willing to listen, Bernhard too found that his memories and stories lacked what people thought of as real-life legitimacy. In his memoir he writes of his bafflement in postwar Salzburg:

> When I visit the city today, I always ask people what they recall of that terrible period, but they react by shaking their heads. To

---

19 Imre Kertész, "Language in Exile," trans. Lewis P. Hinchman, *Hannah Arendt Newsletter* 4 (2001): 5–11, here 7.

me these shocking experiences are as vivid now as if they had happened only yesterday. Whenever I visit the city, I suddenly remember sounds and smells which they, it seems, have blotted out of their memories. When I speak to people who are old inhabitants of the city who must have been through what I went through, I meet only with extreme annoyance, ignorance, and forgetfulness. It's like being confronted with a concerted determination not to know, and I find this offensive—offensive to the spirit.[20]

The spirit of Auschwitz and the many other catastrophes of the twentieth century—including the carpet bombing of German cities, the nuclear obliteration of Japanese civilians, the mass slaughters in the Soviet Union, Rwanda, Bosnia, and on and on—have saturated Bernhard's protagonists, figures such as Franz-Josef Murau, Roithamer, Prince Saurau, and Strauch. They have been steeped in its poison. Small wonder that they appear to be demented.

In order to get a purchase on the truth of this spiritual situation, then, Bernhard needed a new language for the novel, a *Gegenwort*. His oeuvre might best be regarded as an arena or a theater in which the language is not referential but gestural, which is to say, mimetic. It signals: *This is art*, a space in which unpredictable encounters are probable, encounters that will give pause, pull us up short, and invite reflection. Thus the Bernhard narrative's relation to the world, its claim to truth-telling, is not one of factual representation (and seeming exaggeration) but instead the imaginatively exact expression of a spiritual climate in which chaos, anxiety, and uncertainty predominate. It would be similarly unhelpful, by way of comparison, to say that van Gogh exaggerates the colors of the landscape in Provence or of the people's faces there. What counts instead is the gesture of his style, its poetic thinking, the mimetic force of brushstroke and color choice, which mimic not the factual look of a thing but its spiritual dynamism. It would not be surprising to learn that some of van Gogh's sitters felt insulted by the way their images turned out. By the same token, it is not surprising that so many of Bernhard's countrymen have felt ill used by his fiction. Bernhard's style is radical and not designed to flatter his subject but to express something that cannot be directly represented without also being thereby grossly *mis*represented.

The more conventional, more comforting novels of Bernhard's many West and East German contemporaries—Grass, Böll, Lenz, Walser, Wolf, and many more—raked through the still smoking crater of the

---

20 Bernhard, *Gathering Evidence*, 95.

German devastation in fictional forms drawn from the pre-Auschwitz past. Not for nothing was Hemingway a mentor to that generation of writers. They are more comforting because the tried-and-true conventions of novel-writing imply, by their structural certainties, that reality has remained just as stable as it always has been, that novels still simply mirror the universal certainties that underlie outward fluctuations of circumstance. If the novel had not changed much after the catastrophe, then it must mean that the world, despite everything that had happened, was still pretty much the same too. Auschwitz could then be set to one side as a historical glitch, terrible and sad of course, but still we can and must now get back to the reality of how things always have been and still are.

In the late 1950s, Bernhard sensed this fraudulence in the novels being written by his colleagues, consumed by the reading public, celebrated by reviewers and critics. The secret power of contemporary novels written in the tradition of the nineteenth century, says Gabriel Josipovici, is this: "they look like mirrors held up to the world but what they are is machines that secrete spurious meaning into the world and so muddy the waters of genuine understanding of the human condition."[21] The formal certainties of conventional fiction make the world appear to be solid, not the other way around. Familiar structures reassure readers that the world has meaning, even after historical experience has offered a good deal of evidence to the contrary. Bernhard was not so sure that fiction ought to continue on its normal path. He went a different way, the opposite way. In a rich and strange access of spontaneous artistic combustion, Bernhard instinctively thrust novelistic conventions aside. With his imagination on fire, he created a bracing new form that functions not in accordance with the orderly laws of respectable fiction but molds itself directly to the disorderly contours of his era's lived reality. "To find a form that accommodates the mess, that is the task of the artist now," Beckett said in an interview in 1961.[22] Beckett found one way to do that. Bernhard found another.

It is as if Bernhard were the survivor of some nameless catastrophe that has left him in a landscape littered with frozen corpses, which he sees, though no one else does. Note, too, that the word "Auschwitz" never falls in his writing (just as the main character of Sontag's story never appears), though its chilling presence is felt everywhere in Bernhard's fiction, like an all-devouring wintery blast that coats everything

---

21 Gabriel Josipovici, *What Ever Happened to Modernism?* (New Haven, CT and London: Yale University Press, 2010), 70.
22 Tom Driver, "Beckett by the Madeleine," *Columbia University Forum* 4 (1961): 21–5, here 23.

in ice: "The frost eats everything up," says the painter Strauch in 1963, when the war was still a fresh memory, "trees, humans, animals, and whatever is in the trees and the humans and the animals. The blood stalls, and at great speed. You can break apart a frozen human like a piece of stale bread."[23] This resort to figurative indirection—the image of a debilitating frost that immobilizes the spirit of postwar European life—is a typical example of Bernhardian understatement and tact. This *poetic thinking* avoids language that is too direct in certain matters. For example, no one in his fiction ever swears or curses. Such "real-life" talk is a staple of conventional fiction. Nor does he use Austrian vernacular in his art, though in his recorded interviews he hams it up for the camera with his I'm-just-a-country-boy-from-Salzburg routine. There is no such ingratiating hokum in his art.

Most significantly, though, he avoids naming or describing those horrors that would be diminished, falsified, cheapened through being pinned down in words at all, because words—as he repeatedly pointed out—inevitably miss the mark even in the best of circumstances. To talk about Auschwitz or the Shoah too directly would be tactless. He approaches these matters obliquely and with the utmost tact. Sometimes the approach is figurative, as in the frost metaphor. It coats and kills everything, which is an oblique way of pointing at the effect exerted by the cruelty, horror, and waste of Nazi Austria without naming it. To name it would reduce it.

Note that not even the vilely misanthropic Prince Saurau of *Gargoyles*, in his otherwise unsparing harangue, ever falls into anti-Semitic invective. There are in Bernhard's works many Jewish figures, beginning with the Bloch in *Gargoyles*. Bloch has remained in Austria even though his father was murdered by Nazis. But these characters are marginal, understated, even a bit ghostly since they are living out a posthumous existence.[24] Even Wertheimer, in *The Loser*, never appears. Circumspection with regard to this open wound in Austrian and German culture is also an expression of tact on Bernhard's part rather than a bow to political correctness. This is because anti-Semitism, Auschwitz, is the blight that brought about Austrian degradation and not a result of that degradation.

What is *not* said in Bernhard can be more crucial than what *is* said. Saskia Ziolkowski observes the importance of gaps and absences in Bernhard, not least of all in *Heldenplatz*, a play that guides Claudio

---

23 Bernhard, *Frost*, 265.
24 For an overview of Jews and Jewish themes in Bernhard, see Karl Müller, "Über Jüdisches bei Bernhard," in *Bernhard-Handbuch: Leben – Werk – Wirkung*, eds. Martin Huber and Manfred Mittermayer (Stuttgart: Metzler, 2018), 427–32.

Magris's way of writing about Italian fascism and anti-Semitism. Rather than portray scenes of anti-Semitic violence, *Heldenplatz* features an accomplished Jewish émigré, Professor Josef Schuster of Oxford, driven into exile by Austrian anti-Semitism. He has returned to the homeland he has missed for fifty years only to find that anti-Semitism remains intact in the Vienna of 1988. The ongoing hatred drives him to suicide, and his surviving elderly mother keeps hearing the jubilant crowds of 1938 welcoming Hitler to Austria as he speaks from the balcony that looks out over nearby Heldenplatz. But the entire play takes place after the fact, as a function of Professor Schuster's conspicuous absence. The main event is not depicted.

Another characteristic understatement comes at the end of *Extinction* when, after the death of Franz-Josef Murau, we learn that the protagonist has bequeathed his family's ancient estate to the Jewish Community of Vienna. This gift is, of course, an inadequate gesture of restitution, but it is also an index to what matters most in Bernhard's moral universe. What matters most are those who are left behind and those who cannot speak for themselves—those who have been trampled on by the aggressors of history, by progress, by the spirit of restoration. The Jews of Austria are an obvious case in point. Consequently, it may well be that Bernhard is not really an exaggeration artist. Against all expectation, he is a master of understatement and restraint.

In her study *The Inability to Love*, Agnes Mueller gives compelling evidence that much of the most celebrated postwar German fiction is shot through with anti-Semitic presuppositions.[25] These prejudices are mostly tacit and structural, but they persist all the more doggedly for just that reason. Such is not the case with Thomas Bernhard, and here his lead is followed closely by Sebald, especially stylistically. He stands as a good example of how Bernhard's successors can sharpen our view of Bernhard's art. Like Sebald, Bernhard employs understatement at certain junctures, because it is oblique rather than explicit. Sebald makes clear the empowering and morally liberating innovation of Bernhard's formal, mimetic gesture at absence and apart from all representational content:

> What Thomas Bernhard did to postwar fiction writing in the German language was to bring to it a new radicality which didn't exist before, which wasn't compromised in any sense. Much of German prose fiction writing, of the fifties certainly, but of the sixties and seventies also, is severely compromised, morally compromised, and because of that, aesthetically frequently

---

25 Agnes C. Mueller, *The Inability to Love: Jews, Gender, and America in Recent German Literature* (Evanston: Northwestern University Press, 2014).

insufficient. And Thomas Bernhard was in quite a different league because he occupied a position which was absolute. Which had to do with the fact that he was mortally ill since late adolescence and knew that any day the knock could come at the door. And so he took the liberty which other writers shied away from taking. And what he achieved, I think, was also to move away from the standard pattern of the standard novel. He only tells you in his books what he heard from others. So he invented, as it were, a kind of periscopic form of narrative. You're always sure that what he tells you is related, at one remove, at two removes, at two or three. That appealed to me very much, because this notion of the omniscient narrator who pushes around the flats on the stage of the novel, you know, cranks things up on page three and moves them along on page four and one sees him constantly working behind the scenes, is something that I think one can't do very easily any longer. So Bernhard, single-handedly I think, invented a new form of narrating which appealed to me from the start.[26]

Bernhard's writing is concerned with the expression of truths that cannot be systematized conceptually. Hence the eternally deferred circulation of talk around a missing center is not just a narrative game or idiosyncratic tic. The so-called periscopic effect arises from Bernhard's profound sense that normal dialogue in normal novels occurs in bad faith. Sureness of plot, character, and dialogue produce clear meaning, which is *an effect* of such literature itself, one that is in short supply in lived experience. If a novel is to have a claim on truth-telling about that experience, then the sleight of hand whereby a conventional writer creates the illusion of reality must be alienated or "framed," so to speak. Bernhard refuses to engage in illusionism's parlor tricks. He may not be able to nail down a final truth either, but his way of writing embodies the nature of the failure that is inevitable. However, this narrative technique of his has nothing to do with the lazy idea that truth in Bernhard's world is always merely subjective, as if the novelist were illustrating his opinions in fictional guise.

Exaggeration implies a merely subjective point of view. Bernhard's periscopic language is not subjective because the novel can be no more certain about representing subjectivity than it can about representing outward reality. Bernhard's novels and plays, individually and taken as a whole, are not in principle a form of communication. They are aesthetic expression founded in the much-remarked, little-understood

---

26 Michael Silverblatt, "A Poem of an Invisible Subject," in *The Emergence of Memory: Conversations with W. G. Sebald*, ed. Sharon Lynn Schwartz (New York: Seven Stories Press, 2007), 77–86, here 82–83.

musical character of his prose. They do not primarily communicate the subjective thoughts and ideas of his demented protagonists and vouch for their veracity. Rather, they express the nature of a spiritual situation that is neither subjective nor objective. Bernhard is not so much communicating his ideas as channeling the disturbed moral spirit of his time and place. Expression lies more in the dissonant, unresolved music of his language itself than in the abusive rant of his characters. His protagonists' fulminations, with their notoriously apodictic pronouncements, do not point referentially toward the outward fact or inward toward the self, either. Instead they function negatively in the overall texture and expressivity of Bernhard's imaginative achievement, especially when taken as a whole and from the perspective of his tact (i.e., asking what or who is absent).

What is absent is, first, an authentic relation with the past. Bernhard struggles mightily against the Austrian kitschification of its own culture and history. Second, and above all, love is missing, the feature of postwar German writing that is key in Mueller's book. The absence of erotic passion or even just a little fleshly warmth in Bernhard's writing is highly significant.

The lacking *who* are those who have been oppressed, silenced, and marginalized: Jews obviously, but also women are robbed of all power to speak for themselves (Roithamer's sister or Konrad's wife or the Persian woman in *Yes* or Wertheimer's sister or Rudolf's sister in *Concrete*). Bernhard does not arrogate to himself the right to speak *for* them. His task is to allow us to catch a glimpse of them in their silence and to reach our own conclusions. Juliane Werner helps us catch sight of one such damaged soul in *Extinction*, Schermaier, a marginal nobody in Nazi Austria. The authorities packed him off to a concentration camp for a minor act of resistance: listening to Swiss radio broadcasts. Schermaier, says Murau, now lives a broken postwar life with no restitution from the government for his suffering, while ex-SS mass murderers have gone on to enjoy fat state pensions and live a life of luxury in beautiful postwar Austria. Spain's Félix de Azúa proposes, as Heike Scharm observes, that Bernhard writes for the excluded nobodies: for those who have been damaged, wounded, or handicapped, for those whose spirits have been mutilated and forgotten. This state of affairs may be grotesquely perverse, but it is no exaggeration.

Thomas Bernhard's unprecedented, magnetic, and strange originality has attracted and fired the imaginations of writers from all over the world, from Hungary to El Salvador, from Germany to the United States, from England to France and Italy and Spain. This volume will begin the work of taking account of this most cosmopolitan and far-reaching of provincial writers. Even as Bernhard sheds light on those in whom his work takes on its afterlives, the new works will begin to reveal fresh layers of Bernhard's own achievement as well.

One The Afterlife of Thomas Bernhard in Contemporary Austrian Literature

Katya Krylova

More than three decades after his death, Thomas Bernhard remains a powerful presence in the German-language literary landscape. This can be observed in the new posthumously published works from his literary estate,[1] as well as several recent compendia of Bernhard quotations and text extracts, detailing, for example, Bernhard's most vicious insults in a collection entitled *Bernhard für Boshafte* (Bernhard for the vicious), his views on marriage in *Die Ehehölle* (Marital hell), or his infamous *Städtebeschimpfungen* (City insults).[2] Arguably, these compendia, presenting text extracts taken out of context, reduce the anger and rage that permeates Bernhard's work to a mere gesture of revolt. Such compendia serve to sanitize Bernhard, making his work into a commodity, suitable to be given as presents. However, during Bernhard's lifetime, his publisher Siegfried Unseld famously chastised him for naming his second novel *Verstörung* (literally "Disturbance," published as *Gargoyles* in English): "(es sind 90% aller Bücherkäufer), die Bücher zu Geschenkzwecken kaufen. Diese Leute wollen eben keinen Titel, der

---

1   These include Bernhard's *Meine Preise* (Frankfurt am Main: Suhrkamp, 2009), *Argumente eines Winterspaziergängers. Und ein Fragment zu Frost: Leichtlebig* (Berlin: Suhrkamp, 2013), as well as the published correspondence with Siegfried Unseld and Gerhard Fritsch. For a comprehensive list of works by Bernhard published during his lifetime and posthumously, see Bernhard Judex, "Werke Thomas Bernhards," in *Bernhard Handbuch: Leben – Werk – Wirkung*, eds. Martin Huber and Manfred Mittermayer (Würzburg: Metzler, 2018), 531–35.
2   Thomas Bernhard, *Bernhard für Boshafte*, ed. Raimund Fellinger (Berlin: Insel, 2014); *Die Ehehölle: Acht Szenen*, ed. Raimund Fellinger (Frankfurt am Main: Suhrkamp, 2008); *Städtebeschimpfungen*, ed. Raimund Fellinger (Berlin: Suhrkamp, 2016).

'Verstörung' heißt" ([90% of all book buyers] buy books for the purpose of giving them as gifts. These people certainly don't want a book called "Disturbance").[3] Glossy photobooks of Bernhard portraits, the writer's houses, and the places he wrote about testify to Bernhard's continuing presence, as author and biographical person, on the Austrian literary market. His plays are regularly staged, with even the originally explosive *Heldenplatz* performed in culturally conservative theaters such as Vienna's Theater in der Josefstadt.[4]

In addition, more than three decades after his death, the shadow of Bernhard continues to loom large over contemporary Austrian literature. This chapter analyzes four recent examples in Austrian fiction, which use both the biographical figure of Bernhard and/or Bernhard's works for different purposes, whether for utilizing his voice to undertake a critique of a seemingly timeless Vienna and its institutions, revisiting the period of protest and revolt that characterized the Waldheim era in Austria, satirizing the culture industry, or illustrating what an enduring influence Bernhard remains for a new generation of (male) writers (Thomas Mulitzer and Alexander Schimmelbusch). The chapter will examine works by established Austrian writers and Bernhard contemporaries Gerhard Roth and Robert Schindel, as well as by Thomas Mulitzer and Alexander Schimmelbusch, who represent a younger generation of authors.

Roth and Schindel, in their epic novels *Der Kalte* (The cold one, 2013) and *Orkus* (Orcus, 2011) respectively, return in fiction to a time when Bernhard was still alive, interweaving episodes featuring the biographical figure of Bernhard in a wider sociocultural critique. While in Roth's and Schindel's novels Bernhard's presence is episodic, in Alexander Schimmelbusch's and Thomas Mulitzer's novels, Bernhard dominates the narrative. Schimmelbusch's *Die Murau Identität* (The Murau identity, 2014), set in the second decade of the twenty-first century, affords Bernhard both literary and physical immortality, with the narrative centered around the premise that the author faked his own death in 1989 and is, in fact, still alive. Thomas Mulitzer's *Tau* (Thaw, 2017) emulates the

---

3 Thomas Bernhard and Siegfried Unseld, *Der Briefwechsel Thomas Bernhard/Siegfried Unseld*, eds. Raimund Fellinger, Martin Huber, and Julia Ketterer (Frankfurt am Main: Suhrkamp, 2009), 47.
4 *Heldenplatz* was staged at Theater in der Josefstadt in 2010, under Philip Tiedemann's direction. See "Thomas Bernhard: *Heldenplatz*," Theater in der Josefstadt webpage, available online: https://www.josefstadt.org/programm/stuecke/archiv-19981999-20182019/action/show/stueck/heldenplatz.html (accessed July 28, 2019). The significantly abridged play, for example, cut out references to Olga having been spat at in the street, an incident presented in Bernhard's play as an anti-Semitic act.

detective work undertaken by the narrator in Thomas Bernhard's debut novel *Frost* with a student narrator who embarks on a fact-finding mission in his home village of Weng, which Bernhard immortalized in *Frost*. While three of the four novels listed above (*Der Kalte, Die Murau Identität, Tau*) were identified in the 2018 *Bernhard Handbuch*'s list of literary works that engage with the Bernhard legacy, under a concise subsection entitled "Bernhard lebt" (Bernhard lives),[5] this precise constellation of these recent works has not hitherto been examined together. Through the analysis of these diverse texts, I will trace how Bernhard is represented, what function he serves in the narrative, and how the various authors engage with Bernhard's literary image and legacy. Ultimately, this chapter argues that these recent literary engagements with Bernhard attest to his indispensability to Austrian cultural history, and to literature itself.

I

Robert Schindel's *Der Kalte* (2013),[6] part of his planned trilogy focusing on the legacy of the Second World War and the Holocaust in Austria,[7] may be called a *roman à clef* (although Schindel himself has contested this label) about the Waldheim affair of 1986–1988. In this epic novel, which Joseph Moser has described as constituting part of the writer's *comédie humaine*,[8] Schindel fictionalizes the events surrounding the candidacy and election to the Austrian presidency of former UN Secretary-General Kurt Waldheim, who was found to have lied about the extent of his involvement in the Nazi war machine. Schindel reconstructs the scandal, which was instrumental in facilitating a long-overdue discussion about Austrian complicity in the crimes of Nazism, and the emergence of a civil society through the movement that protested Waldheim's candidacy and election. In doing so, Schindel highlights the crucial role that Bernhard occupied in Austrian cultural life at this time, when the country's self-image with regard to its National Socialist past was undergoing a significant shift. Schindel identifies three "Kulturkämpfe" (culture wars) in total that were

---

5 Uwe Betz and Manfred Mittermayer, "Wirkung auf andere Autoren und Autorinnen," in *Bernhard Handbuch*, 512–13.
6 Robert Schindel, *Der Kalte* (Berlin: Suhrkamp, 2013).
7 The trilogy will be called *Die Vorläufigen*. Schindel has spoken about the project in numerous interviews. See, for example, Reinhold Reiterer, "Oft weit weg von der Originalfigur," *Kleine Zeitung*, April 8, 2013, https://www.kleinezeitung.at/kultur/4040095/Oft-weit-weg-von-der-Originalfigur (accessed July 28, 2019).
8 Joseph Moser, "Blurring Fiction with Reality: Robert Schindel's comédie humaine of 1980s Vienna in *Gebürtig* and *Der Kalte*," in *New Perspectives on Contemporary Austrian Literature and Culture*, ed. Katya Krylova (Oxford: Peter Lang, 2018), 373–91.

happening at this time: the Waldheim affair itself, the unveiling of Alfred Hrdlicka's controversial and problematic *Mahnmal gegen Krieg und Faschismus* (Monument against war and fascism) in November 1988,[9] and the premiere of Thomas Bernhard's play *Heldenplatz* in the same month, nearly to the day, as the fiftieth anniversary of the November pogroms.

In Schindel's depiction of his home city of Vienna, where the theater has traditionally been held in great esteem,[10] the various goings-on at the Burgtheater, Vienna's national stage, are afforded as much importance in Schindel's novel as the events unfolding around the character of Johann Wais (modeled on Kurt Waldheim). Here we encounter Dietger Schönn (unmistakably recognizable as legendary theater director, Claus Peymann), who stages a number of plays intended to draw the audience's attention to the country's political situation. As details of Wais's (Waldheim's) military record emerge, Dietger Schönn decides to visit the writer Raimund Muthesius in Upper Austria in order to commission a "Vergangenheitsbewältigungsstück" (reckoning-with-the-past play).[11] The figure of Muthesius is, again, a thinly veiled depiction of Thomas Bernhard, identifiable as such both from biographical features such as his predilection for living in rural isolation in the Austrian countryside, but also through the clear thematic similarities in the subject matter of Muthesius's and Bernhard's plays. Muthesius decides to write a play, entitled "Vom Balkon" (From the balcony), from the perspective of an exiled violinist, who returns to Austria after many years. This is strongly reminiscent of Bernhard's last play, *Heldenplatz* (1988), which centers upon a Viennese Jewish family, the Schusters, who emigrated to England in 1938 and then returned to Vienna in the 1960s. Throughout the play (set in March 1988), the Schuster family is coming to terms with the suicide of Josef Schuster, which takes place around the fiftieth anniversary of Hitler proclaiming the Nazi annexation of Austria on the Heldenplatz on March 15, 1938. The scandal that the premiere of *Heldenplatz* provoked is very faithfully reconstructed in *Der Kalte*, as is the censure previously levelled at Bernhard, and his reaction to it by writing ever more polemical works:

---

9 See Tobias Lindemann, "Robert Schindel—Interview zu seinem Roman 'Der Kalte' über die Waldheim-Jahre in Österreich," *freie-radios.net*, June 26, 2013, http://www.freie-radios.net/56812 (accessed July 28, 2019).
10 As can be gleaned from an oft-cited observation by Stefan Zweig that the first pages a Viennese resident would turn to in his morning newspaper would be the theater listings rather than the political news. Zweig, *Die Welt von Gestern: Erinnerungen eines Europäers* (Frankfurt am Main: Fischer, [1944] 2001), 30.
11 Schindel, *Der Kalte*, 223.

Ein widerliches Zeug über dieses widerliche Land. Es käme zum sogenannten Bedenkjahr zurecht, übrigens eine lächerliche Bezeichnung für die Hirnarbeit von Hohlkopfen, aus denen sich die alpenländische Politkaste seit je rekrutierte. Seit ihm ein Unterrichtsminister habe ausrichten lassen, er, Muthesius, gehöre zum Psychiater [...], seine Texte erleichterten die Psychiatrisierung seiner Person, auf der Bühne hätten sie nichts verloren, seither glückte ihm die Überzeichnung der österreichischen Seele auf besondere Weise.
(A disgusting thing about this disgusting country. That would be just right for the so-called year of reflection, incidentally a ridiculous term for the cognitive work of blockheads, from which the Alpine political caste has recruited itself since time immemorial. Ever since a Minister of Education had let it be known to him that, he, Muthesius, needs a psychiatrist [...], his texts facilitated the psychiatricization of his person, they had no business on the stage, since then his exaggerations of the Austrian soul came especially easily to him.)[12]

By reconstructing the biographical details of Bernhard's life so faithfully—including an allusion to Education Minister Herbert Moritz pointedly suggesting in 1985 that Bernhard was "ein Fall für die Wissenschaft" (worthy of scientific attention)[13]—Schindel reflects on the crucial role that Bernhard came to occupy in Austrian cultural life, particularly by the late 1980s. By this point, Bernhard's reputation as an "established outsider"[14] had become cemented through instances such as his infamous speech on accepting the *Österreichischer Staatspreis für Literatur* (Austrian state prize for literature) in 1968,[15] and the seizure by the Austrian police of his 1984 novel *Holzfällen* (*Woodcutters*) following a libel suit against Bernhard by his erstwhile friend Gerhard Lampersberg. Additionally, the above-cited quotation echoes sentiments expressed in Bernhard's *Heldenplatz*, for example, regarding the

---

12 Schindel, *Der Kalte*, 478.
13 As cited in Manfred Mittermayer, "Lächerlich, charakterlos, furchterregend. Zu Thomas Bernhards Rhetorik der Bezichtigung," in *Rhetorik und Sprachkunst bei Thomas Bernhard*, ed. Joachim Knape and Olaf Kramer (Würzburg: Königshausen & Neumann, 2011), 39.
14 Dagmar C. G. Lorenz, "The Established Outsider: Thomas Bernhard," in *A Companion to the Works of Thomas Bernhard*, ed. Matthias Konzett (Rochester, NY: Camden House, 2002), 29–51.
15 This scandal, which paved the way for subsequent ones, is reconstructed in Olaf Lahayne, *Beschimpft Österreich! Der Skandal um die Staatspreisrede Thomas Bernhards im März 1968* (Göttingen: V & R unipress, 2016).

prevalence of "nurmehr noch den alpenländischen Schwachsinn" (only Alpine idiocy now) in Austria.[16] Ultimately, there are only minor reworkings of the scandal surrounding the premiere of Bernhard's last play in *Der Kalte*, while other events surrounding the Waldheim affair do undergo interventions and reworkings by Schindel in his fictionalization.[17] Such interventions frequently constitute wish fulfilments in Schindel's novel, as in the case of his treatment of Alfred Hrdlicka's controversial *Mahnmal gegen Krieg und Faschismus* (*Monument against War and Fascism*), to which a temporary amendment of jeering Viennese onlookers is added to the figure of the "Straßenwaschender Jude" (Street-washing Jew), depicting anti- Semitic violence following the *Anschluss*.[18] It is clearly the case that any major literary reworkings or interventions in the historical chronology and unfolding of the *Heldenplatz* scandal are deemed unnecessary by Schindel. The date of the premiere of "Vom Balkon" (From the balcony) in *Der Kalte* is amended to November 9, 1988 (rather than November 4, as was the case with *Heldenplatz*), the exact anniversary of the 1938 November pogroms, to further underline the play's attention to the resonances of the past in the present. However, no missed opportunities are identified, as in the case of the Hrdlicka memorial.

In his portrait of Thomas Bernhard in *Der Kalte*, Schindel reaffirms Bernhard's position as one of the most significant Austrian postwar writers. As a figure of revolt, Bernhard's *sprechende Name* (descriptive name) in the novel is Muthesius, evoking associations with courage and audacity, while his first name, Raimund, is associated with the nineteenth-century Austrian dramatist Ferdinand Raimund, known for his *Volkstücke* (folk plays), thereby reaffirming Bernhard's status as a national playwright: "Das ganze Land erkennt sich in den Erzsätzen von Muthesius" (The whole nation recognizes itself in Muthesius's arch phrases.)[19] *Der Kalte* does not, in any way, challenge or go beyond the prevailing biographical image of Bernhard as a figure of revolt against "den Spießern, den Altnazis, den Ignoranten" (the spiffs, the old Nazis, the ignoramuses),[20] or the prevailing reception of his work as that of a *Nestbeschmutzer* (nest dirtier). But Schindel does reaffirm Bernhard's significance in Austrian cultural history—the key turning point of the Waldheim era in Austrian post-war history is presented as unimaginable without him.

---

16 Thomas Bernhard, *Heldenplatz* (Frankfurt am Main: Suhrkamp, 1988), 146.
17 Martin Huber also makes this observation with relation to the faithful reconstruction of the *Heldenplatz* scandal. Martin Huber, "'Gedächtnisarbeit': Robert Schindels Roman *Der Kalte*." In *Die Rampe—Porträt Robert Schindel*, edited by Bernhard Jude (Linz: Trauner, 2018), 166–76.
18 For a discussion of this see Katya Krylova, *The Long Shadow of the Past: Contemporary Austrian Literature, Film and Culture* (Rochester, NY: Camden House, 2017), 90–94.
19 Schindel, *Der Kalte*, 621.
20 Schindel, *Der Kalte*, 621.

II

Gerhard Roth's *Orkus: Reise zu den Toten* (*Orcus: Journey to the Dead*, 2011)[21] offers another fictionalized portrayal of Bernhard that, on the surface, does not appear to radically challenge established views of the writer. Forming the conclusion to Roth's eponymous eight-volume cycle of novels, essays, and autobiography, the semi-autobiographical novel, true to its title, undertakes a journey to the dead, where fictional characters from Roth's previous novels are mixed with famous figures from art, music, politics, and literature, including, among others, Joseph Roth, Franz Kafka, Ingeborg Bachmann, and Thomas Bernhard. In contrast to the rural seclusion in which Robert Schindel situates the Muthesius (Bernhard) figure in *Der Kalte*, here a fictional Thomas Bernhard is presented as expounding his worldview in his favorite Viennese café, the Café Bräunerhof, to a journalist called Razumovsky, who hangs on his every word. In this chapter, entitled "Die Wiener Paranoia" (Viennese paranoia), it is not Bernhard's attacks on the country's lack of *Vergangenheitsbewältigung* (reckoning with the past) that take center stage, but rather Bernhard's notorious *Hassliebe* (love-hate) for Vienna, as expressed, for example, by the narrator of *Holzfällen*: "daß ich dieses Wien hasse und doch lieben muß" (that I hate and yet am compelled to love this Vienna).[22] In Bernhard's works, Vienna is at once the "existenzentscheidende Stadt" (life-defining city) for the Austrian intellectual,[23] offering personal and intellectual growth, but also a place that, just as quickly, prompts disappointment and disillusionment. Gerhard Roth adopts for his fictional Bernhard the ranting, exaggerating tone for which Bernhard's work is known as a vehicle through which to articulate a critique of Vienna: "die ganze Stadt sei ein Sumpf aus Stänkerern, Raunzern, Maulhelden, Schmähführern und zugleich Duckmäusern, Kriechern und Unterwürfigen." (the whole city was a swamp of troublemakers, grouches, braggarts and, at the same time, moral cowards, sycophants and submissives.)[24] Roth's Bernhard proceeds to regale the attentive journalist with his views on the culture of scheming, maliciousness, defamation, and spying that he views as intrinsic to the Viennese cultural establishment. Many of these phenomena are presented as having their roots in the hierarchy and culture of surveillance in and around the Habsburg court: "In Wien werde, wie gesagt, ohnehin jeder zum Spitzel und Verleumder" (as I've mentioned already, in Vienna

---

21 Gerhard Roth, *Orkus: Reise zu den Toten* (Frankfurt am Main: Fischer, 2011).
22 *Thomas Bernhard: Werke*, eds. Martin Huber, et al.(Frankfurt am Main: Suhrkamp, 2003–2015), 7 [*Holzfällen*]: 199.
23 Bernhard, *Werke*, 9 [*Auslöschung*]: 182.
24 Roth, *Orkus*, 271.

everyone becomes a spy and defamer anyhow).[25] However, the chapter also concludes with Bernhard praising the beauty of Vienna, suffusing it with a nostalgic quality, and concluding that, despite all the city's flaws, it still presents the best alternative to the Austrian provinces:

> "Und welche Stadt, Razumovsky," fragte Thomas Bernhard jetzt mit einem schlauen Lächeln, "soll sich ein Österreicher, der überall im Land nur Provinz antrifft, der nirgendwo aus dem Provinziellen herausfindet und sich ein Leben lang im Hinterwald verirrt, sonst aussuchen, wenn er nicht überhaupt entschlossen ist, auszuwandern oder sich umzubringen?"
>
> ("And what other city, Razumovsky," Bernhard now asked with a sly smile, "should an Austrian—who meets with the provincial everywhere he goes in the country, who is unable to find his way out of the provincial anywhere, and who gets lost in the backwoods for a lifetime—choose, when he isn't intent on emigrating or committing suicide?")[26]

In the chapter's move from Bernhard's severe criticism of Vienna and the Viennese cultural establishment to a love of sorts for the city, Roth mirrors the narrative pattern of Bernhard's 1984 novel *Holzfällen* exactly, which ends with the narrator walking through central Vienna in the early hours, following the fateful *künstlerisches Abendessen* (artistic soirée) at the Auersbergers, and concluding that he still loves Vienna and its inhabitants, in spite of everything. Thereby, in Gerhard Roth's *Orkus*, we see the figure of Bernhard being used for a very specific purpose: to articulate an ambivalent and complex image of Vienna. Here Roth follows a tradition of writing on Vienna, for which Thomas Bernhard's work is emblematic, and, indeed, draws on many of the motifs prevalent in Bernhard's writing on the Austrian capital. In Roth's *Orkus*, this discussion is colored by a deeper attention to the underlying causes of the Viennese malaise than we typically find in Bernhard's work, as well as the precise diagnosis of its symptoms that we find in Bernhard. This is reflective of Roth's own archaeological attention to the resonances of the past in the present, which pervades both the *Orkus* cycle (1995–2011) as well as the earlier *Archive des Schweigens* (Archives of silence, 1980–91) cycle.

Roth draws on a particular facet of Thomas Bernhard's literary work and biography—in this case, the love-hate relationship with Vienna, which finds its expression in Bernhard's fiction—in order to present an

---

25 Roth, *Orkus*, 279.
26 Roth, *Orkus*, 281.

image of the city that is as unsavory as it is enchanting, which is echoed in other episodes of the novel and in the *Orkus* cycle as a whole. Much in the way that Schindel's inclusion of a fictionalized Thomas Bernhard in his novel about the Waldheim affair is emblematic of Bernhard's centrality in Austrian cultural life in the 1980s, Roth's fictionalization of Bernhard affords the writer the status of an authority on Vienna, through whom the city may be better understood. Both Schindel's and Roth's fictionalizations of Bernhard therefore reaffirm Bernhard's indispensable role in Austrian culture—and, by extension, in their own wide-ranging works treating Austrian culture and history—albeit in different ways. In Roth's depiction of Bernhard, his railing against Vienna's cultural establishment and its traditions is unmasked as a posture of revolt, with Bernhard ultimately revealing his underlying affection for the city.

III

While Roth and Schindel return, in fiction, to a time when Bernhard was still alive, Alexander Schimmelbusch's novel *Die Murau Identität* (The Murau identity, 2014),[27] set in the second decade of the twenty-first century, affords Bernhard both literary and physical immortality. The narrative begins with the narrator, a freelance cultural journalist working in Vienna, contemplating how to spend his evening on the twenty-fifth anniversary of Thomas Bernhard's death, an anniversary that provides ample opportunities for Vienna's culture industry:

> entweder ins Rathaus auf das *künstlerische Abendessen* von Mailath-Pokorny oder zum Demel auf die Weltpremiere der Bernhardtorte—Gerüchten zufolge, denn die Geheimhaltung bezüglich der Torte war außerordentlich streng gewesen, hatte die Torte die Form eines spitzen Kegels, wie das Bauwerk des suizidalen Protagonisten in Bernhards *Korrektur*, die offenbar den Genuss der Torte erheblich erschwerte, sodass dieser nicht allein das Verlangen nach schneller Befriedigung, sondern ein gewisses Maß an nachhaltigem Interesse voraussetzte, wie ja auch Bernhards Schriften, zumindest das Frühwerk—entweder auf den Bernhardrave in der Kirche am Steinhof oder zur intimen Handkelesung aus Bernhards *Verstörung* in einer Suite im Imperial [...].
>
> (either to the City Hall for the *artistic soirée* hosted by Mailath-Pokorny [City Councillor for Cultural Affairs, Vienna, 2001–2018] or to Demel for the world premiere of the Bernhard

---

27 Alexander Schimmelbusch, *Die Murau Identität* (Berlin: Metrolit, 2014).

torte—according to rumors, since the secrecy surrounding the torte had been very strictly guarded, the cake had the shape of a pointed cone, similar to the construction of the suicidal protagonist in Bernhard's *Correction*, which apparently precluded the enjoyment of the torte quite significantly, so that the torte necessitated not only a desire for quick gratification, but rather a certain amount of sustained interest, as in the case of Bernhard's writing, at least the early work—either to the Bernhard rave in the Steinhof Church or to a reading by Handke from Bernhard's *Gargoyles* in the intimate setting of a suite in the Imperial Hotel.)[28]

In Schimmelbusch's novel, the figure of Bernhard functions as an exemplary case study through which to satirize the culture industry, with locations and cultural practices referred to in Bernhard's works becoming fetishized and exploited. These range from the *künstlerisches Abendessen* (artistic soirée) in *Holzfällen*, to the Steinhof Church, designed by Otto Wagner, near the Steinhof hospital, which is referred to in several Bernhard works, notably *Wittgensteins Neffe* (*Wittgenstein's Nephew*) and *Heldenplatz*. The satire is intensified *ad absurdum* through the detailed description of the Bernhard torte, with the texture and shape of the culinary creation supposedly reflecting the challenges that Bernhard's works pose to the reader.

Instead of participating in one of the many diversions on offer on the twenty-fifth anniversary of Bernhard's death, that very day the narrator of *Die Murau Identität* makes a far more interesting cultural discovery. On opening an envelope mysteriously sent to him by a Frankfurt lawyer, the journalist learns that Bernhard is in fact alive and well. The envelope contains the "versiegelte Reiseberichte" (travel reports under seal) of Bernhard's editor,[29] written between 1992 and 2000. The travel reports, clearly modeled on legendary publisher Siegfried Unseld's *Reiseberichte* (travel reports),[30] describe meetings with "Bernhard," who we learn faked his own death in 1989, was successfully cured of an autoimmune disease by undergoing an antibody treatment in New York, and has taken on the alias Franz Josef Murau (the name of the protagonist in Bernhard's last published novel *Auslöschung* [*Extinction*]). The travel

---

28 Schimmelbusch, *Die Murau Identität*, 14.
29 Schimmelbusch, *Die Murau Identität*, 15.
30 Unseld's *Reiseberichte* (held in the Suhrkamp Verlag archives) pertaining to Bernhard were included in the published edition of the Bernhard/Unseld correspondence: Thomas Bernhard and Siegfried Unseld, *Der Briefwechsel*. Unseld's *Reiseberichte*, edited by Raimund Fellinger, will be published in their own right in late 2020. See https://www.suhrkamp.de/buecher/reiseberichte-siegfried_unseld_22451.html (accessed July 28, 2019).

reports contain details of meetings with the fictional Bernhard both in Mallorca (where he has married and had a son) and in Bernhard's farmhouse in Upper Austria, where Bernhard has no hesitation in visiting local inns under the guise of his half-brother, given that "kein Mensch würde annehmen, daß Thomas Bernhard von den Toten auferstanden sei, wenn viel näher liege, daß der Bruder sich Bernhard optisch immer mehr angleiche" (no one would assume that Thomas Bernhard had risen from the dead, when it was much more likely that his brother looked more and more like Bernhard).[31]

In the course of his travel journal, Bernhard's editor also reflects on the transformation that the reception of Bernhard's works has undergone since the author's death (or what is perceived as Bernhard's death by the public at large in the fictional world of *Die Murau Identität*):

> da in den letzten Jahren, Bernhard betreffend, ein typisch österreichischer Prozeß in Gang gekommen ist, eine Art Mozartisierung. Bernhard entwickelt sich vom Nestbeschmutzer zum Nationalheiligtum. Dieselben Leute, die ihn hatten deportieren lassen wollen, die mit Spazierstöcken auf der Straße auf ihn eingeprügelt hatten, die mit Geifer in den Mundwinkeln geschrien hatten, daß Bernhard als Vaterlandsverräter erschossen gehöre, huldigten ihm nun unterwürfig als Schatz des reichen Kulturlebens ihrer und seiner doch so schönen und stolzen Heimat, in einer Reihe mit Nockerln und Lipizzanern.
>
> (since, in recent years, a typically Austrian process had got underway in relation to Bernhard, a kind of Mozartization. Bernhard is evolving from a nest dirtier to a national treasure. The same people who had wanted him deported, who had beaten him with walking sticks in the street, who had shouted, foaming at the corners of their mouths, that Bernhard should be shot as a traitor to the fatherland, now revered him obsequiously as a jewel of their beautiful and proud nation and rich cultural life, up there with dumplings and Lipizzaner horses).[32]

For Schimmelbusch, Bernhard therefore functions as a case in point for the appropriation of writers whose work was once viewed as rebellious or radical. With reference to Bernhard, this process is given a specifically Austrian note, which may be encapsulated by the oft-cited aphorism by Helmut Qualtinger: "In Wien mußt' erst sterben, damit sie dich hochleben lassen. Aber dann lebst' lang" (In Vienna you first have

---

31 Schimmelbusch, *Die Murau Identität*, 87.
32 Schimmelbusch, *Die Murau Identität*, 81.

to die, before your life is celebrated, but then you live a long time).³³ Schimmelbusch's use of the word "Mozartisierung" (Mozartization) emphasizes both the pervasive cult status now enjoyed by Bernhard, as well as the process of posthumous transformation from a figure much maligned during his own lifetime to a national treasure, a process for which Mozart serves as an exemplary case study.

As if to underline the transformation in the reception of Bernhard's biographical person from rebellious outsider to innocuous insider, the figure of Bernhard that we encounter in Schimmelbusch's novel is very far removed from the *Nestbeschmutzer* image that he enjoyed during his lifetime. In his publisher's travel diaries from the 1990s, we learn that Bernhard has put writing on hold in favor of a quiet existence with his new family. When Bernhard later returns to writing, penning a novel about his marriage (entitled *Anima Negra*), its proposed publication poses a particular challenge to his publisher, who is unsure whether to present it as a sensational find from Bernhard's literary estate, or to have Bernhard suddenly rise from the dead.³⁴ In thematizing this publishing conundrum, Schimmelbusch satirizes the literary marketing strategies routinely undertaken upon the posthumous publication of works from authors' literary estates, for which Bernhard's *Meine Preise* (*My Prizes*, 2009) may serve as a case in point.³⁵

There are no reports in the publisher's travelogues of Bernhard criticizing his native Austria, or commenting on Austrian current affairs. Rather, Bernhard's interests seem to lie in his marriage (prior to its collapse), in continuing to extract money from his publisher, and in hosting secret birthday parties, years after his official death, to which the still very much alive Thomas Bernhard invites guests such as Salman Rushdie and the American literary agent, Andrew Wylie. The omnipresence of Bernhard in the contemporary German-speaking literary landscape is reflected in Schimmelbusch's novel, where he is presented as indispensable to the literary world, which is shown to be unimaginable without him, so much so that Bernhard is not allowed to die in Schimmelbusch's depiction. Additionally, this portrayal of a

---

33 As cited in Anon, "Nachruf: Helmut Qualtinger," *Der Spiegel*, October 6, 1986, 277, available online: https://www.spiegel.de/spiegel/print/d-13519800.html (accessed July 28, 2019).
34 Schimmelbusch, *Die Murau Identität*, 92–93.
35 See Clemens Götze's discussion of the publicity strategies employed by the Suhrkamp Verlag on the publication of Bernhard's *Meine Preise* (2009), to the extent of coordinating the publication date to exactly twenty years since Bernhard's projected date of spring 1989 (prior to his untimely death in February 1989). Clemens Götze, "Der geehrte Autor und die Kunst der Invektive: Zu Thomas Bernhards *Meine Preise*," *Studia austriaca* XX (2012): 56.

Bernhard content in following private pursuits challenges his clichéd one-dimensional public image of *Nestbeschmutzer*. Yet, ultimately, Bernhard is presented as having lost none of his radicality in his literary ambitions. Upon meeting Bernhard in New York, the narrator learns that the author is collaborating with Andrew Wylie on a program called iMind, a mind-reading program that would ostensibly make literature obsolete: "Die Menschen würden sich gegenseitig verstehen können, sagte Bernhard, was naturgemäß die Auslöschung der Literatur bedeuten werde" (People would be able to understand each other, Bernhard said, which would naturally mean the extinction of literature).[36] As during his lifetime, Bernhard is once again presented as a literary innovator, ahead of the curve, using the latest innovations in computer programming to facilitate a technology that would make him redundant. The concept of "Auslöschung," or extinction, functions as a motif throughout *Die Murau Identität*, an intertextual reference to Bernhard's last novel *Auslöschung*, to which the title of Schimmelbusch's novel, and the fictional Bernhard's new alias, also allude. It is understood by the fictional Bernhard as the idea of art necessitating sacrifice, the eradication of life and its sublimation into art—a problematic process, which, in the protagonist's view, has led to the disintegration of his marriage. Yet it can also be understood, particularly with reference to the above-mentioned iMind program, in the sense of eradicating an old literary tradition in favor of a radically new form of literature, intimated in *Auslöschung*: "das Alte auflösen, um es am Ende ganz und gar auslöschen zu können für das Neue" (to dissolve the old, in order to be able to extinguish it altogether for the new).[37] Bernhard also indicated this ambition for his own literary works in an interview with Krista Fleischmann: "Aber was heißt Auslöschung? Wiederbeginn des Neuen" (What is extinction? A beginning again of the new).[38] In Schimmelbusch's portrayal, it is the undead Bernhard who is leading a renewal of literature in the twenty-first century, once again being far more radical than his literary contemporaries, even in advanced age. *Die Murau Identität* contends that this is a mantle that Bernhard would continue to wear, were it not for his untimely death in 1989. For all the posthumous appropriation of Bernhard as a *Nationalheiligtum* (national treasure), which Schimmelbusch satirizes in his novel, *Die Murau Identität* reaffirms an image of a writer that is primarily characterized by its radicality and revolutionary nature, a writer whose own ambitions

---

36 Schimmelbusch, *Die Murau Identität*, 203.
37 Bernhard, *Werke*, 9 [*Auslöschung*]: 211.
38 Bernhard, *Eine Begegnung: Gespräche mit Krista Fleischmann*, pb. edn. (Frankfurt am Main: Suhrkamp, 2006).

for a literary renewal during his own lifetime may serve as a model for literary innovations in the present day.

IV

Thomas Mulitzer's debut novel *Tau* (Thaw, 2017),[39] like Schimmelbusch's *Die Murau Identität*, is a novel that is similarly dominated by the biographical figure of Bernhard. Where it differs from all the novels hitherto discussed is in the extent of the homage to Bernhard undertaken in the novel. *Tau* is a novel that in its plot, structure, and—to some extent—its style explicitly draws on Thomas Bernhard's debut *Frost* (1963), a groundbreaking anti-*Heimat* novel, about which Bernhard famously commented: "Es war erstmalig diese Art zu schreiben" (This manner of writing had never been seen before).[40] While Bernhard's novel, largely written in diary form, is narrated by a medical student who has been charged with the task of being a glorified private detective, observing his supervising surgeon's brother in Weng, the protagonist of *Tau* is a student of German literature and an aspiring writer, who travels to his home in Weng on the suggestion of his university tutor, Professor Lavie, to examine the intersections of his grandparents' lives, who ran a *Wirtshaus* (inn) in Weng, with those of their contemporary, Thomas Bernhard. In the course of his twenty-seven-day-long stay in Weng (the same duration as that of *Frost*'s narrator), the narrator conducts conversations with his grandfather about Bernhard, engages in love affairs with two women (including his childhood sweetheart, Julia, now married with children), and attends a festival and a conference dedicated to Thomas Bernhard in neighboring towns.

The literary homage to *Frost* begins with the first sentence of *Tau*, which mirrors Bernhard's opening meditations on medicine in *Frost*, where established clichés about the medical profession are challenged. Mulitzer applies a similar discourse to the challenges of being a writer, which are very far removed from public perceptions of the vocation: "es besteht wirklich nicht nur aus der stolzen Einsamkeit und dem Flüchten in eine Fantasiewelt" (it really doesn't only consist of proud solitude and an escape into a fantasy world).[41] The literary homage proceeds with the part-archaeological/part-detective framing of the

---

39 Thomas Mulitzer, *Tau* (Vienna: Kremayr & Scheriau, 2017).
40 See Kurt Hofmann, *Aus Gesprächen mit Thomas Bernhard* (Vienna: Locker, 1988), 26.
41 Mulitzer, *Tau*, 7. Compare with the first line of Bernhard's *Frost*: "Eine Famulatur besteht ja nicht nur aus dem Zuschauen bei komplizierten Darmoperationen, aus Bauchfellaufschneiden, Lungenflügelzuklammern und Fußabsägen, sie besteht wirklich nicht nur aus Totenaugenzudrücken und aus Kinderherausziehen in der Welt." Bernhard, *Werke*, 1 [*Frost*]: 7.

narrator's project as "Schichten freizulegen und die Funde sauber zu vermessen" (exposing layers and neatly surveying the findings),[42] echoing the narrator's ambition in *Frost* "Etwas Unerforschliches zu erforschen" (to investigate something unfathomable).[43] In order to facilitate the immersion in the universe that served as a literary model for *Frost*, the narrator of *Tau* makes the journey to Weng by train (on Professor Lavie's recommendation), in the manner of the protagonist in Bernhard's novel, to which the narrator makes implicit reference.[44] Unlike the prophetic "Blutspur" (trail of blood) from a dead bird on the train carriage floor in *Frost*,[45] *Tau*'s narrator struggles to find anything of note on his journey to Weng, or to detect any animalistic or National Socialist tendencies among the train passengers, which is emphasized with comic effect:

> Mir schräg gegenüber saß ein Mann, der eine Wurstsemmel aß. Ich versuchte eine Vulgarität in dieser scheinbar alltäglichen Handlung zu erkennnen [...] Kein viehisches, nationalsozialistisches, katholisches Gebaren trat hervor. Er war ein Mann, und er aß eine Wurstsemmel. Nichts weiter.
> (Opposite me sat a man who ate a sausage sandwich. I tried to detect a vulgarity in this seemingly trivial act [...] No animalistic, National Socialist, Catholic behavior stood out. He was a man and he was eating a sausage sandwich. Nothing more.)[46]

The narrative continues in the same vein, incorporating countless allusions to Bernhardian motifs. These include extensive explorations of Weng's National Socialist past, as *Frost*'s central image of snow covering over and facilitating forgetting of a still war-torn landscape is extended in *Tau*, with the snow described as now thawing, bringing the past to light, in the novel's central metaphor. As in *Frost*, violence and death, both present and historical, pervade the narrative of *Tau*. The narrator recalls tales of Wehrmacht deserters hiding out on the mountains nearby, a passerby alerts him to the news of two climbing fatalities (echoing a similar, but nonfatal, accident of two tourists in *Frost*), while the narrator himself is both brutally beaten up by Julia's jealous husband, and is witness to a boy dying in the forest, following a fatal injury from colliding with a tree (alluding to the incident of a woodcutter dying, following an injury sustained from his own sleigh, in *Frost*).

---

42 Mulitzer, *Tau*, 8.
43 Bernhard, *Werke*, 1 [*Frost*]: 7.
44 "Ich hatte das Buch dabei." Mulitzer, *Tau*, 9.
45 Bernhard, *Werke*, 1 [*Frost*]: 8.
46 Mulitzer, *Tau*, 10.

Other, less significant, Bernhardian motifs are also referenced, such as the narrator's penchant for the *Neue Zürcher Zeitung*, echoing the narrator of Bernhard's *Wittgensteins Neffe* (1982). Like Schimmelbusch's *Die Murau Identität*, *Tau*, specifically through the protagonist's excursion to a Thomas Bernhard festival in a neighboring town on the eighth and ninth days of his sojourn in Weng, contains many reflections on the literary industry per se and on the evolving literary reception of Bernhard in particular: "irgendwann wird jeder Rebell zum Heimatdichter" (eventually, every rebel becomes a national writer).[47] Similar to the commentary on the events accompanying notable Bernhard anniversaries in Schimmelbusch's novel, the trip provides an opportunity to critique the burgeoning tourism industry surrounding the writer, especially one marked by a pretentiousness out of keeping with the festival's down-to-earth rural setting, leading to the local population, and even the narrator himself, feeling "fehl am Platz" (out of place).[48] The narrator's initial expectations for the event are very low—with the festival attracting "die Schickeria des Ortes und selbstverliebte Möchtegernintellektuelle" (the smart set of the town and narcissistic wannabe intellectuals)[49]—expectations that are only confirmed as the event progresses, leading the narrator to conclude that the literary scene is akin to "ein Affenzirkus" (a three-ring circus).[50] The incidents the narrator observes at the event range from omnipresent commercial exploitation of the festival by local businesses, to sexual harassment by a renowned actor of one of the female students that the narrator befriends at the gathering. With regard to the former, the narrator's supposition that the staff in the hotel, where the festival is being held, refill expensive champagne bottles "mit minderwertigem Brausewasser" (with substandard soda water)[51] and soften the champagne corks with hot water in order to fit them back into the bottles, echoes the narrator's discovery in *Frost* that the landlady of the inn cooks with dog meat.

The self-reflexive critique of the Bernhard industry, of which both the narrator and Mulitzer himself are, of course, a part, is continued during another of the narrator's excursions, this time to an academic conference on Bernhard, focusing on "Orte, Räume, Werke" (Places, Spaces, Works).[52] Here the narrator becomes increasingly bored, perceiving the papers as too theoretical, and neglecting the subject at hand:

---

47 Mulitzer, *Tau*, 120.
48 Mulitzer, *Tau*, 117.
49 Mulitzer, *Tau*, 95.
50 Mulitzer, *Tau*, 131.
51 Mulitzer, *Tau*, 127.
52 Mulitzer, *Tau*, 174.

"Den Autor erwähnte er mit keinem Wort" (He didn't say a word about the author).[53] Only the reading aloud of quotations from the primary texts prompts the narrator to sit up and take notice. This allows the narrator to reflect on the evolving reception of the erstwhile *Nestbeschmutzer*, also thematized in Schimmelbusch's *Die Murau Identität*. The narrator contemplates that, thirty or forty years ago, Bernhard's statements, such as those referring to "die vertrottelten, o-beinigen Mädchen des Innergebirgs" (the idiotic, bowlegged girls of the Innergebirg region),[54] would have provoked outrage among the local population, but are nowadays "als Übertreibung oder Satire, als literarische Stilmittel abgetan" (dismissed as exaggeration or satire, as a literary stylistic device).[55] The narrator's reflections on the diminishment of Thomas Bernhard's once explosive literary voice are further underpinned by observations of a growing musealization of the writer. The narrator is dismayed by a paltry display on Bernhard in a (fictional) local museum, likely to be based on the Seelackenmuseum St. Veit/Pongau:[56] "Das Literarische wird heruntergebrochen auf zwei, drei Kalendersprüche und als Schauobjekt hineingepresst in eine schmutzige Vitrine" (The literary is broken down into two or three calendar mottos and pressed into a dirty display case as an exhibition object).[57] In a similar fashion, *Tau* also comments on the instrumentalization of Thomas Bernhard for the purposes of tourism in the area surrounding the museum, citing the example of streets, houses, and a "Ruheoase" (oasis of tranquillity) named after the author.[58]

While the excursions to the museum and literary events devoted to the author do not bring the narrator any closer in his vague aims to uncover the connections of his own family's life with that of Bernhard, much more illuminating discoveries are made closer to home. The narrator discovers that his grandfather, who, together with his wife, ran an inn that reportedly served as the model for the one in *Frost*, has several photographs of Bernhard in his possession; yet the mention of Bernhard's name provokes a strong reaction in his

---

53 Mulitzer, *Tau*, 177.
54 Mulitzer, *Tau*, 179.
55 Mulitzer, *Tau*, 179.
56 The description of the exhibits in the Seelackenmuseum on the museum's website, including a focus on the painter Rudolf Holz (reportedly the model for Strauch in *Frost*), coalesces with Mulitzer's depiction. http://www.seelackenmuseum.at/ (accessed July 28, 2019).
57 Mulitzer, *Tau*, 80.
58 Mulitzer, *Tau*, 83. The "Ruheoase" forms part of the "Thomas Bernhard Rundwanderweg" in the Salzburg region, but, in contrast to Mulitzer's depiction, is not named after the author. http://www.salzburg-reiseinfo.com/ausflugsziele/thomas-bernhard-rundwanderweg-alpin/ (accessed July 28, 2019).

grandfather. Later, it emerges that this strong dislike is due to feelings of jealousy and injury with regard to the fictional Bernhard's supposed attraction toward his late wife, which extended to the wish fulfillment of writing her husband, who was frequently away from Weng on odd jobs, out of the narrative of *Frost*. Moreover, the biographical transformation of the narrator's grandmother into a nymphomaniac who cooks with dog meat constitutes, according to the narrator's grandfather, an embittered reaction to his wife's rebuttal of the writer's advances:

> [E]r hat den Wirt einfach weggelassen, weil er ihn weghaben wollte, er wollte die Wirtin für sich allein haben, und weil sie ihn nicht wollte, hat er sie zum absoluten Gegenteil ihrer selbst gemacht, zur Hure. Und das alles nur aus Rache oder aus einem Minderwertigkeitskomplex heraus.
>
> ([H]e simply left the innkeeper out because he wanted him out of the way, he wanted the landlady all to himself, and because she did not want him, he made her the absolute opposite of herself, into a whore. And all this merely out of revenge or because of an inferiority complex.)[59]

A later discovery of a torn-out title page of the first edition of *Frost*, hidden in a collection of his grandparents' music records, complicates the grandfather's straightforward account of the family's relationship to Thomas Bernhard. The title page bears a dedication written and signed by the author: "In tiefer Sehnsucht, Ihr ergebener" (In deepest longing, your devoted).[60] As the narrator reflects, the intensity of feeling expressed in the dedication suggests that the page was not torn out because of the content of the book, but rather because of the content of the dedication, in order to hide a secret. Ultimately, however, the possibility of this love triangle between his grandparents and Bernhard is not explored further by the narrator. Akin to the narrative of *Frost*, several discoveries are made in the course of the narrator's sojourn in Weng, but these are not brought together into a coherent story. Both narrators become overwhelmed by their respective tasks of observing the painter Strauch or uncovering the biographical basis for a landmark text of post-war Austrian literature.

Like Bernhard's *Frost*, *Tau* concludes with the protagonist escaping Weng, no longer seeing any point in continuing his report. There is the same intimation that the Weng landscape is pathogenic, infecting the

---

59 Mulitzer, *Tau*, 91.
60 Mulitzer, *Tau*, 238.

protagonist with melancholy and madness.[61] In addition to the pathologizing nature of the Weng landscape, the sense of being increasingly overwhelmed or in thrall to Bernhard's writing is evident in the protagonist: "Die Worte eines anderen krochen in mich hinein und krallten sich an meinen Gehirnwindungen fest. Ich war infiziert. (The words of another crawled into me and clawed firmly at the convolutions of my brain. I was infected.)"[62] Instead of the classic Bernhardian device of having the narrator in thrall to a larger-than-life authority figure for whom the male protagonist acts as a spokesperson or ventriloquist, in *Tau* it is Bernhard himself who is increasingly dominating the narrator's thoughts and perception of his surroundings to such an extent that his experiences of Weng are ever more mediated through Bernhard's immortalization of the place in literature. While, on the train journey to Weng, the protagonist is still reluctant to view his fellow travelers as Bernhardian prototypes, increasingly his perceptions echo those of the author: "Das Lebensziel ist der Tod, immer" (Life's destination is always death).[63] Additionally, his thoughts are inflected by those of Bernhard's protagonists, specifically those of the narrator of *Frost*: "Mir ging der Frost durch den Mund und machte mich beinahe wahnsinnig" (the frost went through my mouth and almost drove me crazy).[64] While the word "Frost" is not italicized in this sentence, it is clear that both the novel and the unexpectedly early winter in Weng are implied here. Moreover, it is not only the narrator who is unwittingly becoming a Bernhardian figure, unable to complete letters to his professor, but the narrator also perceives echoes of Bernhard among his family members: "die Worte meines Großvaters, die klangen wie aus dem Mund des Autors" (my grandfather's words sounded like they came from the mouth of the author).[65] Ultimately, while the protagonist is unable to finish his report to Professor Lavie, his sojourn in Weng at least reaffirms his intention to become a writer.

---

61 Cf. Krylova, "'Eine den Menschen zerzausende Landschaft': Psychotopography and the Alpine landscape in Thomas Bernhard's *Frost*," *Austrian Studies* 18 (2010): 74–88.
62 Mulitzer, *Tau*, 242.
63 Mulitzer, *Tau*, 105. Cf. Bernhard's infamous statement upon accepting the Österreichischer Staatspreis für Literatur in 1968: "es ist alles lächerlich, wenn man an den Tod denkt." Bernhard, *Meine Preise*, 121.
64 Mulitzer, *Tau*, 279.
65 Mulitzer, *Tau*, 279.

Out of the four novels discussed in this chapter, *Tau* presents the most intensive engagement with Thomas Bernhard's biographical person and literary work, both on the narrative level and by Mulitzer himself, who has freely spoken about the autobiographical basis (including about his grandparents who ran an inn in Goldegg-Weng) for his debut novel.[66] *Tau* is the product of a long-standing engagement with a writer whose descriptions of Mulitzer's home region of Salzburg have undoubtedly left a lasting impact not only on Mulitzer, but on the local population as a whole, leading to a "Hassliebe" (love-hate) toward Bernhard.[67] Yet it is also an acknowledgment of Bernhard's long shadow over the inaugural writing project of a young male author (Mulitzer was aged twenty-nine at the time of *Tau*'s publication), originating from Goldegg in Pongau, an area not far from where Bernhard himself grew up, and to which he frequently returned in his writing. Mulitzer's indebtedness to Bernhard is further acknowledged in *Tau*'s epigraph from Thomas Bernhard: "In das erste Buch, da schreibt man alles hinein" (One writes everything into the first book).[68] Ultimately, *Tau* attests to the enduring and pervasive impact of Bernhard's works, which, for the narrator, exceed the appropriations of the literary and tourism industries surrounding the author, or indeed the narrator's own attempts to reconstruct their possible biographical underpinnings.

The various homages to Thomas Bernhard discussed in this chapter are testament to the writer's lasting impact on Austrian literature, and the fascination that his literary persona and work continue to exert on successive generations of writers. The biographical figure of Bernhard is resurrected in novels by his contemporaries Robert Schindel and Gerhard Roth, where he functions as an indispensable political and cultural commentator. At the same time, a younger generation of writers, in the shape of Schimmelbusch and Mulitzer, while thematizing the posthumous *Mozartisierung* (Mozartization) of Bernhard's legacy, reaffirm the radical impulse of his literary work, with Schimmelbusch presenting

---

66 "Meine Verbindung zu Thomas Bernhard ist eine persönliche und hat mit seinem Debütroman *Frost* zu tun, dessen Handlung in einem Ort namens Weng spielt. Meine Großeltern haben in Goldegg-Weng ein Gasthaus betrieben, in dem früher auch Thomas Bernhard zu Gast war. Die übertrieben negative Beschreibung der Bewohner in seinem Werk—besonders der Wirtin—wurde von manchen Lesern als Tatsachenbericht missverstanden und das hat auch in meiner Familie Spuren hinterlassen. Diesen Spuren geht mein Protagonist in *Tau* nach." Thomas Mulitzer, as cited in "Liebeserklärung an das Innergebirg," *meinbezirk.at*, September 18, 2017, available online: https://www.meinbezirk.at/pongau/c-lokales/liebeserklaerung-an-das-innergebirg_a2250475 (accessed July 28, 2019).
67 Mulitzer, *Tau*, as cited in "Liebeserklärung an das Innergebirg."
68 Mulitzer, *Tau*, 5.

the author as indispensable to literature altogether and thereby—in *Die Murau Identität*'s fictional universe—not permitted to die. Schindel's *Der Kalte* and Roth's *Orkus* reaffirm established images of the author for their own purposes, whether that is providing an epic portrait of the Waldheim affair or underlining a deeply ambivalent presentation of the Austrian capital. By contrast, Schimmelbusch and Mulitzer thematize the by-now-established clichés and burgeoning industry surrounding Bernhard, while presenting the author's literary project as being characterized by an enduring radical impulse. This proves inspirational for the continual evolution of literature (in the case of Schimmelbusch's novel), or indeed for a new generation of writers emerging from the Austrian countryside influenced by the anti-*Heimat* novels of a famous predecessor (as exemplified by the narrator of Mulitzer's *Tau*). As for the biographical figure of Bernhard, these latter two works, from the posthumous revelations in *Tau* to the revenant Bernhard in *Die Murau Identität*, offer an image of the writer, who, in spite of his elevation to Austrian national treasure, can still surprise us, even from beyond the grave.

Two Writing Failure: Geoff Dyer, Thomas Bernhard, and the Inability to Begin

Kata Gellen

> In failure lies ongoingness. In the collapse of the will lies the instinct to write.[1]
>
> —Wayne Koestenbaum

Geoff Dyer's memoir *Out of Sheer Rage: Wrestling with D. H. Lawrence* (1997) is a book about failing to write a book about D. H. Lawrence. Dyer chronicles the endless excuses, deferrals, frustrations, and obstacles to producing his academic study of the great English novelist. It is a book about procrastination, whose central mode is procrastination. Dyer takes the relentless, circular, maddening experience of trying and failing to find a path toward writing, and sets it down in writing.

We generally assume that a written work, especially a published one, reflects the successes of writing. This point is almost tautological: if it is written, especially if it gets published, it is because the author has succeeded at writing. The failed attempts have been discarded, if they ever existed, and the text we read is proof of success. The opposite of successful writing is simply not writing, or perhaps writing badly. But could it be that the *failure* to write also produces a kind of writing? I

All quotations from the German editions of Thomas Bernhard's and Peter Handke's works are used with the friendly permission of Suhrkamp Verlag. Excerpts from THE LIME WORKS by Thomas Bernhard, translated by Sophie Wilkins, translation copyright ©1973 by Penguin Random House LLC. Used by permission of Vintage Books, an imprint of the Knopf Doubleday Publishing Group, a division of Penguin Random House LLC. All rights reserved. Excerpts from OUT OF SHEER RAGE: WRESTLING WITH D.H. LAWRENCE by Geoff Dyer. Copyright ©1997 by Geoff Dyer. Reprinted by permission of Farrar, Straus and Giroux and Canongate Books Ltd.
1   Wayne Koestenbaum, "Thomas Bernhard's Virtues," *Review of Contemporary Fiction* 31, no. 1 (2011) 53.

don't mean discarded drafts and bad prose, but rather that the deferral of writing can itself generate writing. Procrastination and postponement can stand in the place of successful writing, and they can produce their own form of written expression—a failed writing that takes a certain form, has a certain style, and expresses certain thoughts and feelings. Where, how, and under what circumstances could this failure be recorded? Dyer's book is the product of a failure to write. It shows us what it could mean to produce a record of the inability to write.

If there are success stories, why shouldn't there be failure stories? In movies there are outtakes and bloopers, which are sometimes collected in gag reels for audiences to view. We enjoy seeing these blunders and bad takes not only because they are funny, but because they give us an inside view into the production of the film. They make the experience of creating art seem more human, more relatable. Similarly, records sometimes have B sides with secondary recordings of the songs being released. These are not good enough to play on the radio or count as the official version of a song, but they have other qualities—graininess, talking, background noises—which, again, remind the listener that the process of making art is messy and meandering, and produces quite a bit of detritus. Some of us derive comfort, even delight from seeing these cracks and fissures that disrupt the illusion of an apparently seamless, polished work of art—not because we are mean-spirited, but because we identify with the creative struggle.

Dyer's book on trying to write a study of Lawrence delivers the by-product of the struggle to write. It records the failure. There is also a five-page essay, "D. H. Lawrence: *Sons and Lovers*," from 1999, which arguably represents the fruits of his labor. It is the corresponding success story. The 240-page memoir contains the outtakes, or perhaps it is better to think of it as the "Making of ... " documentary that accompanies the feature film. In any event, *Out of Sheer Rage* takes the struggle of writing—indeed, the *failure* to write, the reality of *not writing*—and sets it down on the page for us to read.

In this chapter I explore Dyer's remarkable project of producing a record of the failure to write. My central claim is that his particular mode of failing to write, or writing failure, is deeply indebted to Thomas Bernhard, an author whose entire oeuvre could be said to adhere to this mode. Specifically, I will draw connections to the 1970 novel *Das Kalkwerk* (*The Lime Works*), whose protagonist Konrad also struggles and fails to write.[2] Not writing, if it is to avoid being pure absence or negation,

---

2   Another prime example is Bernhard's 1982 novel *Beton* (*Concrete*), in which a man tries and fails to write a study of his favorite composer, Felix Mendelssohn-Bartholdy, over the course of the novel. Much like the main characters in *The Lime Works* and *Out of Sheer Rage*, he cannot even begin, and yet he is convinced that if he could only set down the first sentence, the rest of it would pour out of him effortlessly.

must have its own content, style, form, and rhetoric. Bernhard offers Dyer a model of how not to write.

Before I continue, I will say a word about the approach and style of this chapter, which does not necessarily conform to current conventions of academic writing. Dyer is inspired by Bernhard, and I am inspired by Dyer being inspired by Bernhard. One could demand that I nevertheless assume "critical distance" and analyze their works in a sober, academic manner and tone. I choose not to do this for two reasons. First, Dyer and Bernhard would hate me for it, and I am desperate to please these two authors whom I admire so deeply and who have given me so many hours of reading pleasure. I certainly practice the critical-analytical type of literary scholarship elsewhere—I am, after all, a product of the academy and beholden to its norms—but I am taking the liberty to try out something else here. I feel that Dyer has not only given me license to do this, he has practically demanded it of me. In *Out of Sheer Rage*, he offers this comment on traditional academic literary scholarship:

> [W]riting like that kills everything it touches. That is the hallmark of academic criticism: it kills everything it touches. Walk around a university campus and there is an almost palpable smell of death about the place because hundreds of academics are busy killing everything they touch. I recently met an academic who said that he taught German literature. I was aghast: to think, this man who had been in universities all his life was teaching Rilke. *Rilke!* Oh, it was too much to bear. You don't teach Rilke, I wanted to say, you kill Rilke! You turn him to dust and then you go off to conferences where dozens of other academic-morticians gather with the express intention of killing Rilke and turning him to dust. Then, as part of the cover-up, the conference papers are published, the dust is embalmed and before you know it literature is a vast graveyard of dust, a dustyard of graves. I was beside myself with indignation. I wanted to maim and harm this polite, well-meaning academic who, for all I knew, was a brilliant teacher who had turned on generations of students to the *Duino Elegies*. Still, I thought to myself the following morning when I had calmed down, the general point still stands: how can you know anything about literature if all you've done is read books?[3]

Given my admiration for Dyer, it would be perverse, even spiteful of me to subject his own decidedly nonacademic work to academic criticism, a mode of interpretation that he vehemently rejects. Yet I have quoted this passage not only to justify my approach, but also as initial

---

3 Geoff Dyer, *Out of Sheer Rage: Wrestling with D. H. Lawrence* (London: Picador, 1997), 101.

evidence for Dyer's indebtedness to Bernhard. In *Das Kalkwerk*, Konrad also rages against writers who destroy their objects of analysis by writing about them. These authors, one real and one fictional, share the suspicion that literary criticism destroys literature:

> Sage man beispielsweise, soll Konrad zu Fro gesagt haben, einen Satz, gleich, welchen Satz, und sei dieser Satz, um ein großes Beispiel zu geben, von einem unserer sogenannten größeren oder gar großen Schriftsteller, so beschmutze man diesen Satz nur, weil man sich nicht beherrschen könne, diesen Satz nicht, einfach überhaupt nichts zu sagen, beschmutze man, so treffe man, wo man hingehe und wo man hinschaue, nur auf Beschmutzer, eine in die Millionen, und, genau genommen, in die Milliarden angewachsene Gesellschaft von Beschmutzern sei am Werk, das erschüttere, wenn man sich erschüttern lasse, der Mensch lasse sich aber gar nicht mehr erschüttern, das sei ja das Merkmal des Heutigen, daß er sich ganz und gar nicht mehr und durch nichts mehr erschüttern lasse.[4]

> (Suppose you make a statement, Konrad is supposed to have said to Fro, only one sentence, say, no matter what it is, and suppose this sentence is a quotation from one of our major writers, or even one of our greatest writers, all you would succeed in doing is to besmirch, to pollute that sentence, simply by failing to exercise the self-control it would take not to pronounce that sentence at all, to say nothing at all, you would be polluting it, and once you start polluting things, the chances are you will see everywhere you look, everywhere you go, nothing but other polluters, a whole world of polluters going into the millions, or, more precisely, into the billions, is at work everywhere, it is enough to shock a man out of his mind, if he will let himself be shocked, but people no longer let themselves be shocked, this is in fact what characterizes the man of today, that he refuses to be shocked by anything at all.)[5]

As is often the case, Bernhard's rants take things to a new level. For it is not just academic criticism, but *any* writing about writers that he deems impossible and unacceptable. To quote from a great writer is to kill that writer. To fail to exercise the restraint required simply to remain quiet is the greatest crime against literature. The claim is as breathtaking as it is insane.

---

4 Thomas Bernhard, *Das Kalkwerk* (Frankfurt: Suhrkamp, 2019), 136.
5 Thomas Bernhard, *The Lime Works*, trans. Sophie Wilkins (New York: Vintage, 1973), 152.

So, this is my first reason for refraining from traditional academic interpretation: I wish to please my literary idols, who are in agreement on this point. I don't want to turn them to dust, destroy them, deaden their writing. To write about them in a way that they would loathe and dismiss feels self-defeating, even treasonous. But I have an additional motivation: I want to try to write about literature in another key. I want to develop a different "thought style" with which to approach talking about literary art. Here I take inspiration from the literary scholar and English professor Rita Felski, who argues in *The Limits of Critique* (2015) that most literary scholarship is characterized by one particular "thought style," which we can broadly call critique: driven by a "hermeneutics of suspicion," critics assume their task is to discover hidden meanings, secret agendas, and counterintuitive insights in literary and other works. Their approach is premised on the idea that a work hides its true meanings and its mechanisms of meaning-making, and the job of the critic is to unearth and explain these. Without rejecting the tremendous accomplishments and many insights that critical interpretation has yielded, Felski wants to open our minds to the possibility that there are other ways to read and write about literature, ones not motivated by a principle of disenchantment.

For Felski, the alternative to critique is not surface reading. She identifies a first-order hermeneutics that is essentially Freudian—it is about plumbing the depths for secret hidden meanings—and a second-order hermeneutics that is essentially Foucauldian: it involves looking broadly at surfaces, asking not what something means but where it has come from, and how certain "truths" have become "naturalized." This involves tracing genealogies of thought: the critique lies not in hidden meanings but in hidden origins. Felski wants to distance herself from both tendencies. Her issue is not so much with depth versus surface, but rather with a kind of disposition or attitude that shapes the entire critical endeavor—the skepticism of the critic.[6] More than just a practice, skeptical criticism comes with a certain mindset of distrust, as well as a knowing tone that implies one is disabused of illusions to which the nonskeptical critic is subject. She takes issue with the notion that we should doubt the things that works of art seem to be telling us and ignore the things they make us feel. Probing our attachments is a worthwhile form of reading. This is her alternative to critique.

Felski devotes only one of the five chapters of her book to elucidating this alternative, and she is understandably guarded about being

---

6   Felski argues that her misgivings about critique are not just attitudinal but also methodological and theoretical. Rita Felski, *The Limits of Critique* (Chicago: University of Chicago Press, 2015), 188.

overly prescriptive. First, this would give her opponents an easy target of attack, when her main point is in fact to show the limits of critique. Second, and more importantly, she has no interest in dictating noncritical forms of engagement, since this would undermine the question of personal attachment. For Felski, a central concern is how an artwork survives, how it is "registered, acknowledged, and mediated" in one or more time and place. This is not a matter of contextualization, but of an artwork's "sociability"—how it is "made the object of new attachments and connections between actors. Art works must be sociable to survive [...] [and] an indispensable element of this sociability [...] is a work's dexterity in soliciting and sustaining attachments."[7] At the heart of what Felski calls "postcritical reading" is the simple question of what draws us to works of art. While she does not herself perform a noncritical reading of a work in her book, she gives a few examples of student papers that are rigorous and insightful despite not having been written "under the sign of suspicion"; moreover, she praises these students for finding "an analytical language for reflecting on, rather than repudiating, their aesthetic attachments."[8] In all her examples, students are investigating how a personal reaction to a work—empathy, enchantment, shock—is brought about, often through an analysis of aesthetic form.

Susan Sontag presents a related idea in her 1964 essay "Against Interpretation," where she advocates for experience over interpretation, erotics over hermeneutics. Her description of interpretation comes close to Felski's at times: "All observable phenomena are bracketed, in Freud's phrase, as *manifest content*. This manifest content must be probed and pushed aside to find the true meaning—the *latent content*—beneath."[9] For Sontag, it is pretty clear what the alternative

---

[7] Felski, *Limits of Critique*, 166. Felski uses ANT (actor network theory) to explain this claim: texts are seen as "non-human actors" that act upon humans—individually, collectively, institutionally, via technology, etc.—in various ways. According to ANT, "art's distinctive qualities do not rule out social connections but are the very reason that such connections are forged and sustained. There never was an isolated self-contained aesthetic object to begin with; left to its own devices, this object would have long since sunk into utter oblivion rather than coming to our attention. Art works can only survive and thrive by making friends, creating allies, attracting disciples, inciting attachments, latching on to receptive hosts. If they are not to fade quickly from view they must persuade people to hang them on walls, watch them in movie theaters, purchase them on Amazon, dissect them in reviews, recommend them to their friends. These networks of alliances, relations, and translations are just as essential to experimental art as to blockbuster fiction, even if what counts as success looks radically different" (Felski, *Limits of Critique*, 165–66).

[8] Felski, *Limits of Critique*, 181.

[9] Susan Sontag, "Against Interpretation," in *Against Interpretation and Other Essays* (London: Picador, 2001), 7.

to interpretation is: the sensuous immediacy of the work of art. She praises those "essays which reveal the sensuous surface of art without mucking about in it."[10] These are presumably scholarly works that give rich descriptions of the literature and film in question, ones that highlight and enhance the firsthand experience of these works. Sontag also advocates for an attention to form over content, and is particularly dismissive of works that draw pat messages out of literature. One can hardly quarrel with this critique, though it seems like a gross mischaracterization of literary interpretation to say that it has not, for hundreds if not thousands of years (Lessing's *Laokoon*? Aristotle's *Poetics*?), attended to questions of form.

I take inspiration from both Felski's and Sontag's essays, though ultimately I think that Felski's approach is more workable as a model for scholarship. Indeed, it fits well in the context of this chapter, since a large part of what is motivating me is to query my attachment to Bernhard: why am I so drawn to him? And why, in turn, am I drawn to writers who are explicitly and implicitly drawn to him, too? Are they getting the same thing out of him that I do? It might simply be that their writing contains many of the same qualities that draw me to Bernhard himself, but it might also be their own attachment intrigues and delights me for its own reasons. This is why it is doubly alluring to explore my attachment to Bernhard via Dyer's attachment to him. In keeping with Felski and Sontag, I reject the principle of critical distance. I want to achieve a kind of closeness with the work in order to get a better understanding of its appeal and its power.[11]

A crucial part of this intimacy is bringing the works in question to the eyes and ears of my reader. Though Felski does not herself state this, one might suppose that according to the ideology of critique the critic's voice should come through more clearly and forcefully than the author's, since it is the critic who "knows better," so to speak. This is why the norm

---

10 Sontag, "Against Interpretation," 13.
11 Perhaps Bernhard invites this type of "non-critical" reading, which allows for more creative, unconventional, and personal reflection on his work. See, for example, Koestenbaum's "Thomas Bernhard's Virtues," from whom the epigraph for this essay is taken, which takes the form of a series of insightful aphorisms about Bernhard's literary production and life. Another example is Leo Federmair's "Als ich *Das Kalkwerk* von Thomas Bernhard las," which is an essay about a reading experience, which in turn takes inspiration from Peter Handke's 1967 essay, "Als ich *Verstörung* von Thomas Bernhard las." Wayne Koestenbaum, "Thomas Bernhard's Virtues," *Review of Contemporary Fiction* 31, no. 1: 53–55. Leo Federmair, "Als ich *Das Kalkwerk* von Thomas Bernhard las," *Literatur und Kritik* 385/386 (2004): 46–60. Peter Handke,"Als ich *Verstörung* von Thomas Bernhard las," in *Meine Ortstafeln, Meine Zeittafeln, 1967–2007*(Frankfurt am Main: Suhrkamp, 2007): 283–88.

in literary scholarship is to avoid too many or overly long quotations from the texts under discussion. The critical voice should prevail, not the author's. We should "use" the text only insofar as we need it to demonstrate the points *we* want to make about it. But if my goal is to investigate how and why failing to write is a form of writing for both Dyer and Bernhard, then it seems that I can—indeed, must—give many lengthy examples of their not writing. I am not trying to "pierce through" this mode of writing; nor am I willing to accept that the fruits of failure are meaningless. I want to show what this kind of writing is and what it does, rather than focus on what it claims to fail to be. To accomplish this, I must put Dyer's and Bernhard's "not writing" on display.

This seems like a good place to return to my authors, since Dyer himself adopts a method related to my own when writing about D. H. Lawrence. He tells stories about Lawrence that illuminate Dyer's struggle to write. He quotes him. He invokes related authors and experiences. But he does not interpret or critically evaluate him. His approach is based on affinity and identification. One of the authors he mentions in the process of getting closer to Hardy is Thomas Bernhard. Lawrence and Bernhard are kindred spirits, Dyer suggests. I am not the one who discovered this link—remember, I am not in the business of unearthing hidden meanings and connections—but I do want to explore why it is so important to Dyer, and what it tells us about both authors.

> The resemblance between Lawrence's nerve-irritation, as revealed in his letters and Bernhard's fictional neurasthenic rambling, is as striking as it is, at first, surprising. Lawrence shares with Bernhard's narrators the same chronic prevarication ('Suddenly that I am on the point of coming to America I feel I *can't* come'), intermittently, at least, the same wild misanthropy, the same loathing of their country and countrymen. Both writers display the same abrupt surges and reversals of intent, the perpetual rages that accentuate the ill health – another shared theme – by which they are, in part, generated. Both suffered badly with their lungs and in both there is the same frayed-nerve, end-of-the-tether quality. Some of the classic Bernhard riffs – berating the world for exactly the characteristics he is displaying in the course of his tirades, for example – are prefigured in Lawrence who declared in 1929 that he hated 'people who rave with unreasonable antipathies'. My favourite example is when he denounces Robert Mountsier as 'one of those irritating people who have generalised detestation'. *One of those* …[12]

---

12 Dyer, *Out of Sheer Rage*, 159.

Ostensibly Dyer connects Lawrence to Bernhard because his mind is on Lawrence. He needs to write his study. He is thinking of associations, connections, affinities. He is trying to find a way in. But another reason, I propose, is that Dyer *himself* feels a fraternal bond with both of these authors. He does not so much assert this connection as perform it, repeatedly, over the course of the memoir: he is drawing Lawrence, Bernhard, and himself into the same orbit. Though Dyer explicitly connects only Lawrence and Bernhard, and makes no direct assertions about Bernhard's writing and his own, as soon as he mentions Bernhard it becomes impossible *not* to think about the influence of Bernhard on Dyer's own prose. One need only look to the opening of the work to discover a tortured, digressive, self-undermining act of deferral that is distinctly reminiscent of Bernhard:

> Looking back it seems, on the one hand, hard to believe that I could have wasted so much time, could have exhausted myself so utterly, wondering when I was going to begin my study of D. H. Lawrence; on the other, it seems equally hard to believe that I ever started it, for the prospect of embarking on this study of Lawrence accelerated and intensified the psychological disarray it was meant to delay and alleviate. Conceived as a distraction, it immediately took on the distracted character of that from which it was intended to be a distraction, namely myself. If, I said to myself, if I can apply myself to a sober – I can remember saying that word 'sober' to myself, over and over, until it acquired a hysterical, near-demented, ring – *if* I can apply myself to a sober, academic study of D. H. Lawrence then that will force me to pull myself together. I succeeded in applying myself but what I applied myself to – or so it seems to me now, now that I am lost in the middle of what is already a far cry from the sober academic study I had envisioned – was to pulling apart the thing, the book, that was intended to make me pull myself together.[13]

One could hardly imagine a more perfectly Bernhardian beginning: the act of recollection ("Looking back"), the speculative tone ("it seems"), the presentation of multiple possibilities ("on the one hand"), the incredulousness ("hard to believe"), the self-reproach ("that I could have wasted so much time"), the repetitions with slight additions and alterations ("could have exhausted myself so utterly"), and the delayed arrival of a crucial piece of information at the end of a long clause, which is not even the end of the sentence ("wondering when I was

---

13 Dyer, *Out of Sheer Rage*, 1.

going to begin my study of D. H. Lawrence"). I could go on with this kind of intensive scrutiny, but I think the point is clear: at every turn, with every phrase, Dyer is channeling Bernhard's rhetoric, mood, and style. It isn't parody, and it isn't derivative, and it isn't self-knowing postmodern pastiche—the sort that repeats and mixes known forms of expression because, after all, there is nothing new under the sun. Rather, it seems that Bernhard has captured a way of writing about certain experiences—what Dyer, referring to Bernhard later in the book, calls "the life-exhaustion feeling"—that Dyer finds apt for his current situation.[14]

In a sense, Dyer's whole book is about the struggle to begin his study of Lawrence—since once he manages to begin, the documentation of the failure can presumably end—but this theme is particularly pronounced in the first twenty to twenty-five pages. He goes on and on about not being able to write the book because he could not decide where to live, or because the weather was too hot to work, or because he could not settle on which books he needed to have with him and which he should leave behind or get from a library. For example:

> One of the reasons, in fact, that it was impossible to get started on either the Lawrence book or the novel was because I was so preoccupied with where to live. I could live anywhere, all I had to do was choose – but it was impossible to choose because I could live anywhere.[15]

Or:

> As soon as I arrived [in Rome] I knew I had made the right decision. My mind was made up: I was ready to begin my study of Lawrence. The only trouble was the heat. The heat was tremendous and nowhere in Rome was hotter than Laura's [his girlfriend's] apartment. […] My mind was made up, I was ready to work – but it was too hot to work.[16]

Or:

> I looked at the copy of *The Complete Poems* [of D. H. Lawrence] and felt suddenly sure that if I took it to Alonissos it would lie unopened for six weeks just as it had lain unopened in Paris for two months; but if I didn't take it to Alonissos I was equally sure that, once I was there, in Alonissos, I would decide that it was

---

14 Dyer, *Out of Sheer Rage*, 158–59.
15 Dyer, *Out of Sheer Rage*, 4–5.
16 Dyer, *Out of Sheer Rage*, 15.

indispensable and that, without it, I would be unable even to start my book on Lawrence. If I take it, I won't need it; if I don't take it I will not be able to get by without it, I said to myself as I packed and unpacked my bag, putting in my copy of *The Complete Poems* and taking it out again.[17]

There is great humor and self-awareness in these descriptions. Dyer is only mock-blaming his inability to write on these external factors; he knows, and he knows we will know, that it is not actually the weather, or the setting, or the presence or absence of books that determine whether or not he can write. Indeed, it is precisely the unfairness and unreasonableness of these excuses that make the passages so funny. We laugh at him, and we know he knows we are laughing at him, and he is sort of laughing at himself too. In other words, Dyer's blame game poignantly reflects the conviction he had, in the moment, that these things really *were* what was preventing him from writing, and the ironic distance he now has from this conviction. He does not blame the weather and his books in earnest, but he does capture the earnest feeling of the stalled writer who channels all his creative energies into blaming the outside world for his inability to write.

Bernhard's protagonist Konrad also grapples over the course of the novel with the impossibility of beginning, though Konrad is completely and utterly serious when he blames external factors for his inability to write. The novel begins with Konrad having murdered his wife and given an account of his life in the lime works to two other men, Fro and Wieser, whose testimonies are reported to us by an unnamed narrator, an insurance salesman. We learn that Konrad moved into the lime works with his disabled wife five and a half years earlier, in order to find a place of quiet seclusion to write his study on hearing ("Das Gehör"), the culmination of his life's work. Over and over Konrad insists that he has "das Ganze im Kopf" (the whole thing in his head). He is always on the brink of beginning when some interruption (a knock at the door, his wife ringing her bell, an outside noise) prevents him from doing so. What follows is just one of many passages in which Konrad describes the interferences that keep him from writing:

Zu Wieser: in dem Augenblick, in welchem er, Konrad, glaubte, sich mit der Studie beschäftigen zu können, hörte er plötzlich den Höller Holz hacken. Er stehe auf und gehe zum Fenster und schaue hinaus und sehe natürlich nichts, höre aber. Gerade habe er Lust, die Studie niederzuschreiben, alle Voraussetzungen für

---

17 Dyer, *Out of Sheer Rage*, 17.

eine rasche Niederschrift, denke er, fängt der Höller mit dem Holzhacken an. Als ob sich alles gegen die Niederschrift meiner Studie verschworen hätte, soll Konrad gesagt haben. Gestern ist es der Baurat gewesen, heute ist es der Höller, Tausende, aber Tausende von Winzigkeiten sind es, die mich daran hindern, meine Studie niederzuschreiben.[18]

(To Wieser: at the very moment when Konrad thought he could turn his attention to his work, he would suddenly hear Hoeller chopping wood. He would get up, go to look out the window, and of course see nothing; but he would hear it. It was always at the precise moment when he felt like starting to write, and everything seemed propitious to getting it all written down quickly, that Hoeller chose to start chopping wood. As though everything were in conspiracy against my writing the thing, Konrad is supposed to have said. Yesterday it was the public works inspector, today it's Hoeller, all sorts of trifles, thousands of them, keep getting in the way of my work.)[19]

And then, as if maybe we did not believe just how irritating these disruptions and obstacles were, and how persistently they intruded on his attempts to work, Konrad proceeds to elucidate them in excruciating detail:

Aber gestern machte mir der Baurat alles zunichte, soll Konrad zu Wieser gesagt haben, und heute fängt der Höller mit dem Holzhacken an und im Augenblick sei ihm einfach alles, die Studie betreffende unmöglich gemacht. Sei man von sich selber zu einer solchen Geistesarbeit wie der Studie verurteilt, soll Konrad zu Wieser gesagt haben, was wohl die lebenslängliche Beschäftigungshaft mit einer solchen Geistesarbeit bedeute, sei man mehr und mehr einer schließlich die ganze Welt und dann auch alles über die Welt hinaus Mögliche umfassenden Verschwörung gegen sich selbst ausgeliefert, denke er. Alles sei eine einzige Verschwörung gegen einen und das heiße, gegen die Geistesarbeit, die man verrichte. Und man könne dagegen nichts tun, man könne sich nur fortwährend des eigenen Kräfteverfalls vergewissern, um durch Erkenntnis daraus und aus nichts sonst die beinahe menschenunmögliche Anstrengung auf die Geistesarbeit zu intensivieren, in jedem Augenblick gleich alles zu überbrücken, denke er, was letzten Endes eine sehr hohe Kunst sei,

---

18 Bernhard, *Das Kalkwerk*, 52.
19 Bernhard, *The Lime Works*, 52–53.

die man durch nichts als durch Gehirnautomatismus beherrschen und in welcher man einzig und allein auf die Dauer Zuflucht und den Zweck des Existierens erhoffen und finden und schließlich erfinden könne. Die Welt, vor allem die Umwelt empfinde aber alles, was man in Richtung auf eine Geisteswissenschaft unternehme, als seine immer und in jedem Falle immer gegen die Welt und gegen diese Umwelt gerichtete Ungeheuerlichkeit, von welcher sie glaube, daß sie, obzwar nur dem einzelnen möglich, nur der Masse zustehe und der einzelne sei immer der radikalen Gegnerschaft der Masse ausgesetzt und allein durch die Konfrontation mit dem dadurch Verbrecherischen der Masse befähigt, das ihm von der Masse verbotene und lebenslänglich verweigerte Denken und Handeln dann doch in seinem Gehirn zu denken und zu beherrschen und zu vollenden. Die Masse verweigere dem einzelnen, was nur dem einzelnen und nicht der Masse möglich sei, der einzelne verweigere der Masse, was nur der Masse möglich sei, aber der einzelne kümmere sich nicht um die Masse, kümmere sich schließlich um nichts als um sich selbst zum Vorteil der Masse, wie die Masse sich schließlich nicht um den einzelnen kümmere zum Vorteil des einzelnen, der einzelne die Masse erst mit der Vernichtung der Masse, anerkenne und so fort. Einmal sei es der Baurat, dann sei es der Forstrat, dann der Höller, dann der Bäcker, dann sei es der Rauchfangkehrer, dann sei Wieser es, ich es, seine Frau sei es, alles sei es.[20]

(Unfortunately the public works inspector ruined everything for me yesterday, Konrad is supposed to have said to Wieser, and today Hoeller started with his wood chopping, and for the time being everything to do with his work had simply been wiped out. When a man had condemned himself to a scientific task such as his, Konrad said to Wieser, meaning a lifelong sentence at hard labor, it was tantamount to having surrendered himself as victim to a conspiracy that would ultimately involve the whole world and even whatever possibilities existed beyond the world. It was all part of a single conspiracy against a man, that is, against the intellectual labors he must perform. There was nothing one could do about it, except to be constantly aware of the wasting away of one's energies, an awareness that all by itself and unaided would have to fuel the intensification of a humanly almost impossible effort on behalf of his intellectual labors, to bridge all the gaps simultaneously each moment, he thought, ultimately a high art to be mastered only by brain automatism, an art that was

---

20 Bernhard, *Das Kalkwerk*, 53–54.

the only enduring refuge, the only purpose of one's existence one might hope for and find and, ultimately, invent. But the world, especially the part of it that constituted one's immediate environment, regarded every intellectual, scientific undertaking, though possible only for the individual, was considered to belong by right to the mass, and the individual was always exposed to the mass's radical opposition, which was in effect the criminality of the mass, a criminality that ended by empowering the individual to think and master and perfect precisely all the thought and action which the mass forbade and denied him all his life long. The mass denied to the individual what was possible only to the individual and not to the mass, the individual denied to the mass what was possible only to the mass, but the individual did not concern himself with the mass, ultimately he concerned himself only with himself to the advantage of the mass, just as the mass ultimately did not concern itself with the individual to the individual's advantage, the mass recognized the individual's achievement only after the destruction of the individual, as the individual recognized the achievement of the mass only after the destruction of the mass and so forth. If it wasn't the public works inspector then it was the forestry commissioner, or Hoeller, or the baker, or the chimney sweep, or Wieser, or myself, or his wife, it was everyone.)[21]

Bernhard really outdoes himself with Konrad, and he certainly outdoes Dyer. Perhaps this is the privilege of fiction. After all, Konrad really is a madman, whereas Dyer is just a frustrated writer taking inspiration from the hyperbolic affect of a fictional madman. Thus Konrad does not just find excuses for why he cannot write, a task he dramatically calls "a lifelong sentence at hard labor," but claims there is a massive conspiracy keeping him from writing, one that is part of a larger conspiracy of the mass against the individual creative genius. Konrad is clearly delusional, which means we cannot take at face value the reasons he gives for not being able to write, and yet his delusions generate absurd, hilarious streams of thought. As acts of creative literary expression, they are dramatic and virtuosic—indeed, they are inspirational to other writers. In describing his difficulties with writing, Dyer takes on aspects of Konrad's condition, makes use of some of his rhetorical flourishes, and expresses a degree of his emotional delusion—and yet he stops short of presenting himself as insane. Moreover, to get back to my earlier point, Dyer is careful to present his situation with a good dose of self-irony.

---

21 Bernhard, *The Lime Works*, 53–55.

The wild extremes of Konrad's thinking (the self-aggrandizement, the conspiracy theories, the complete abdication of personal responsibility) and behavior (the abuse and murder of his wife) come from the fact that he understands himself so poorly; he is utterly earnest about his sense of victimization, which means he is utterly self-deluded. Dyer is only pretending to blame the outside world, whereas Konrad does so without a shadow of self-doubt. We can laugh at him, but he is dead serious. Still, the parallels are striking, and the inspiration, whether direct or indirect, is unmistakable. Where Dyer obsesses for pages about finding the right *place* to begin writing, Konrad obsesses about finding the right *moment*:

> Diese Studie sei durchaus nicht lang, soll er zu Fro gesagt haben, vielleicht ist es die kürzeste Studie überhaupt, aber die Schwierigkeit, sie niederzuschreiben, ist die größte. Es sei vielleicht nur eine Frage der ersten Wörter, anzufangen mit den ersten Wörtern und so fort. Eine Frage des Augenblicks, wie ja alles eine Frage des Augenblicks sei. Monatelang, jahrelang, im Grunde jahrzentelang warte er auf diesen Augenblick, weil er aber auf diesen Augenblick warte, komme dieser Augenblick nicht. Und obwohl ihm das vollkommen klar sei, warte er doch immer auf diesen Augenblick, denn warte ich nicht auf diesen Augenblick, soll Konrad zu Fro gesagt haben, warte ich doch auf diesen Augenblick, undzwar immer noch, gleich, ob ich auf ihn warte oder nicht, mit noch größerem Energieaufwand, das sei wahrscheinlich sein Unglück. So präzisiere er, ändere er unaufhörlich und mache sich durch dieses fortwährende Ändern und Präzisieren und also durch das fortwährende unnachgiebige Beschäftigen, unnachgiebige Studium der Studie die Niederschrift der Studie unmöglich. Eine Studie, die man ganz und gar im Kopf habe, könne man wahrscheinlich nicht niederschreiben, soll er zu Fro gesagt haben, wie man auch eine Symphonie, die man zur Gänze durch und durch im Kopf habe, nicht niederschreiben könne und er habe die Studie zur Gänze durch und durch im Kopf. Er gebe aber nicht auf, wahrscheinlich muß die Studie in meinem Kopf wieder gänzlich zerfallen, damit ich sie auf einmal zur Gänze niederschreiben kann, soll er zu Fro gesagt haben, alles muß weg sein, damit es plötzlich vollkommen da ist, und zwar von einem Augenblick auf den anderen.[22]

(This book of his would not be a long one, he is supposed to have said to Fro, not at all, it might even be the shortest book

---

22 Bernhard, *Das Kalkwerk*, 117–18.

ever written, but it was the hardest of all to write. It might only be a question of the beginning, what words to begin with, and so forth. Perhaps it was a question of the right moment when to begin, as everything is a question of the right moment. He had been waiting for the right moment for months, for years, for decades, in fact; but because he was waiting for it, watching for it, the moment would not come. Although he understood this quite clearly, he nevertheless kept waiting for his moment, because even when I am not waiting for this moment, Konrad is supposed to have said to Fro, I nevertheless am waiting for this moment, still waiting for it, even now, regardless of whether I am waiting for it or not, I keep wearing myself out waiting, which is probably my real trouble. While waiting, he kept refining his points, he said, incessantly altering details, and by his endless alterations, refinements, unyielding pre-occupation, unyielding experiments in preparation for writing, he made the writing impossible. A book one had completely in one's head was probably the kind one couldn't write down, he is supposed to have said to Fro, just as one cannot write down a symphony one has entirely in one's head, and he did have his book entirely in his head. But he was not going to give up, he said, the book probably has to fall apart in my head before I can suddenly write it all down, he is supposed to have said to Fro, it has to be all gone, so that it can suddenly be back in its entirety, from one moment to the next.)[23]

By obsessing about perfecting the conditions for beginning to write, Konrad is able to defer indefinitely the act of writing. He thus tells a story about not writing, which at the same time functions as a further deferral of writing. Moreover, Konrad is clearly very creative when it comes to finding other people and things to blame for not being able to write. While he mostly complains about not being able to find the right moment to start writing, and largely blames the noise and disruptions from the outside world for this, at times Konrad also finds others to reproach for this failure:

> Es sei alles in allem, soll er zu Fro gesagt haben, alles in allen Eltern von der Natur in der Weise angelegt, daß es das Erstgeborene immer nur deprimieren und abstoßen und schließlich verkümmern und verkommen lassen und vernichten müsse. Welche ungeheuren Kräfte

---

23 Bernhard, *The Lime Works*, 131–32.

aber hätte es erfordert, mit dieser Ungerechtigkeit fertig zu warden, soll Konrad gesagt haben. Herauszukommen aus der Schwere und Schwüle einer völlig gedankenlosen Erziehung. In dieser, von ihm schließlich als skrupellos bezeichneten Erziehung sei die Ursache dafür zu suchen, habe er zu Fro gesagt, daß er die Studie, an welcher er zwei Jahrzente mehr oder weniger am intensivsten arbeite, nicht aufschreiben könne, immer sei er nur nahe daran, sie aufschreiben zu können, könne sie aber nicht aufschreiben, alles Folge dieser skrupellosen Erziehung, soll er zu Fro gesagt haben. Alles sei, und die Ursachen seien die frühesten, gegen die Niederschrift. Lauter entsetzensvolle Abschnitte, habe Konrad zu Fro gesagt, die sich jetzt unheilvoll gegen die Niederschrift seiner Studie auswirkten.[24]

(Nature seems to have designed parents to function in such a way, he told Fro, as to induce in the firstborn child acute depression and revulsion, so that it ends by pining away, going to seed, perishing. What superhuman energies I would have needed to cope with the unfairness of it! Konrad said. To get myself out from under the weight and swelter of such a wholly mindless upbringing. It was because of this upbringing, which ultimately he could regard as nothing less than unscrupulous, that he could not write his book, though he had been working on it most intently for two decades, more or less; he was always on the brink of writing it down, but unable to start writing it down, and all because of the unscrupulous way he had been brought up, as Fro tells it. Everything from his earliest beginnings conspired against his getting his work down on paper. One appalling phase of life after another, all adding up in the end to a catastrophic effect on his ability to write his book.)[25]

Konrad's rantings are so over-the-top that they make Dyer sound like a cranky but reasonable writer with a touch of writer's block. And while Dyer is indeed far tamer than Bernhard's protagonist, the parallels are striking. This is true not least because the problem of not being able to begin is the motivating idea of both works, as well as a leitmotif in each of them. Both digress from this problem at times, which constitutes a kind of double digression, but they always return to it. It is what binds each work to itself, and what binds them together. Thus the problem of not beginning is, on the one hand, a distraction from the work that needs to be done—the study on hearing, the study on D. H. Lawrence— but it is also, on the other hand, the basis of another work,

---

24 Bernhard, *Das Kalkwerk*, 48.
25 Bernhard, *The Lime Works*, 48–49.

the one we are given to read: Bernhard's novel and Dyer's memoir. The story of not being able to write is itself a story, even if it is not the one that the authors in these works think they should be writing. It has the character of a shadow story, the ghostly shadow emitted from an absent body. It seems, then, that distraction and deferral are forms of engagement, or at least forms of production. After all, *something* seems to come from not writing, even if it is hard to identify what these fictional and real authors are engaging with when they write about not being able to write.

This gets me to the question that I think Dyer wants to ask: What are the possible ways to engage with literature through writing? I think he wants to move away from the idea that engagement requires the kind of painstaking critical analysis that he detests and that he thinks kills the literary work. But the literary essay or review, which Dyer himself produces (he has published essays on Lawrence, Bernhard, and many other writers), is not the only other alternative. There is a form of engagement that comes with the struggle and failure to write about something, whether or not it is eventually followed by success. In the case of Konrad, he never produces his study on hearing, and yet clearly something has come of his struggle—the testimonies of Fro and Wieser, and the narrator's subsequent report, which constitutes Bernhard's novel. In the case of Dyer, he does write an essay on Lawrence, but he also produces the memoir of the struggle. This form of engagement consists of deferral, digression, and procrastination, which is not the same thing as complete avoidance or absence. That would seem to constitute a different form of not writing, one defined by actual nonengagement and by absence. Konrad moves into the lime works in order to be able to write his study, even if he never succeeds. Nevertheless it is his goal and intention to engage with the material and to write the study on hearing. He turns his attention to his object, but is constantly distracted from it. He wants to write but he cannot. Nor can he give up the struggle. Likewise, Dyer is committed to writing his study of Lawrence, which distinguishes his intentions and mindset from an earlier one in which he was truly *dis*engaged. He explains this early on:

> Then, after years of avoiding Lawrence, I moved into the phase of what might be termed pre-preparation. I visited Eastwood, his birthplace, I read biographies, I amassed a hoard of photographs which I kept in a once-new document wallet, blue, on which I had written 'D.H.L.: Photos' in determined black ink. I even built up an impressive stack of notes with Lawrence vaguely in mind but these notes, it is obvious to me now, actually served not to prepare for and facilitate the writing of a book about Lawrence but to defer and postpone doing so. There is nothing unusual

Writing Failure: Dyer and Inability to Begin 63

about this. All over the world people are taking notes as a way of postponing, putting off and standing in for. My case was more extreme for not only was taking notes about Lawrence a way of putting off writing a study of – and homage to – the writer who had made me want to become a writer, but this study I was putting off writing was itself a way of putting off and postponing another book.[26]

What Dyer gets from Bernhard is not just the hyperbole, the rage, the obsession, the cantankerousness, and the aspersions, but *the idea of not beginning as a mode of writing*: narrating the process of not writing becomes a form of engagement. In fact, he takes this idea from Bernhard but then carries it further than Bernhard himself ever does. Konrad, in ranting about not writing, reveals very little about what he intends to write. He tells us a bit about phonetics when he describes the experiments to which he subjects his wife, but overall we gain very little insight into his theories about sound and hearing. *Das Kalkwerk* is decidedly not about "Das Gehör." In contrast, we are given tidbits of insight into D. H. Lawrence throughout Dyer's work—tidbits that emerge in and through the act of deferral. Thus, in not writing about Lawrence, Dyer finds a way to write about Lawrence after all. For example:

> I didn't need *The Complete Poems* because once we were installed on Alonissos I had no impulse to begin my study of D. H. Lawrence anyway. It was not the availability or non-availability of books that was the problem, it was Alonissos itself. We always have this ideal image of being on an island but actually being on an island turns out to be hellish. For what it is worth, Lawrence wasn't too keen on islands either. "I don't care for islands, especially very small ones," he decided on Île de Port Cros. A week later, as if, first time around, he had simply been trying out an opinion, and had now made up his mind, he announced, definitively: "I *don't* like little islands."[27]

What starts out as yet another explanation of why he cannot start writing turns into a meaningful statement on Lawrence—first a biographical one, then one about his rhetorical mode. Dyer's way of describing this is not academic, and yet it is highly effective and insightful. He does not note the repetition or reinforcement of a preference, but instead finds a

---

26 Dyer, *Out of Sheer Rage*, 2.
27 Dyer, *Out of Sheer Rage*, 18.

casual and clever way to describe the mode of expression and the mood that accompanies it: "as if, first time around, he had simply been trying out an opinion." And he certainly does not read any deeper meaning or implication into Lawrence's distaste for small islands. Nevertheless we have learned something about Lawrence through this moment of distracted engagement.

It seems, then, that Dyer picks up where Bernhard leaves off. Or maybe he finds a way to modify Konrad's fanaticism, for whom writing is an all-or-nothing endeavor. For Konrad, not being able to begin to write equals failure. It does not communicate something *else*; it does not constitute an alternative form of engagement. For him it is quite simply nothing, even if for us, the readers, it is everything. This point is confirmed by the fact that Bernhard's novel takes the form of a twice-mediated report, rather than Konrad's self-narration. Many of Bernhard's novels deal with failure, and many of them are told as first-person narratives, with characters who describe their own failure as scientists, musicians, painters, actors, and so on. But Konrad does not even tell his own story, perhaps because Bernhard wants us to view his failure as complete and unredeemable. If he were to write anything, even an account of his failure to write his study on hearing, we might find some small measure of engagement with his material, as we do in Dyer. Instead, the novel ends with a final statement about the failure to write. The only insight that Konrad has gained, the only development in his thinking, is that he now admits that he was wrong to think that he needed to wait to find the right moment to write. In the novel's closing rant, Konrad finally assumes some of the blame for his failure, but this does nothing to mitigate its definitiveness:

> Zu Fro, mit dem ich heute die Lebensversicherung habe abschließen können, soll Konrad gesagt haben, der Fehler sei gewesen, immer eine noch günstigere, immer die günstigste Ausgangsposition für die Niederschrift der Studie abzuwarten, dadurch, daß er immer wieder geglaubt habe, in wenigstens akzeptabler Zukunft trete auf einmal die ideale oder gar die idealste Konstellation für die Niederschrift der Studie ein, habe er mehr und mehr Zeit, wie er, Konrad, sich ausgedrückt haben soll, die wichtigste Zeit verloren, schließlich müsse er jetzt, tatsächlich am Ende seiner Kräfte (!), einsehen, daß er sage und schreibe zwei oder gar drei Jahrzehnte lang vergeblich auf den idealen Moment, die Studie niederschreiben zu können, gewartet habe, kurz vor dem Unglück (so bezeichnet Fro die Erschießung der Konrad durch ihren Mann) soll Konrad zu Fro gesagt haben, sei er sich der Tatsache bewußt, daß es überhaupt keinen idealen, geschweige denn idealsten Augenblick, die Studie niederschreiben zu können,

gebe, weil es niemals und in keiner Sache und in nichts den idealen, geschweige den den idealsten Moment oder Augenblick oder Zeitpunkt überhaupt geben könne. Wie Tausende vor ihm, sei auch er dem Wahnsinn zum Opfer gefallen, eines Tages, in einem einzigen Augenblick, in dem sogenannten optimalen Zeitpunkt dafür, die Studie durch folgerichtige konzentrierte Niederschrift verwirklichen zu können. Weder in Stein, in der Strafanstalt, noch in Niedernhardt, in der Irrenanstalt, werde er an die Niederschrift gehen können, die Studie Konrads sei, wie Konrad selbst, verloren (Wieser), ein, wie man annehmen müsse, so Fro auf einmal plötzlich umschwenkend, ungeheueres Lebenswerk, vernichtet. Versagen durch ständig hinausgezögerte Realisierung einer als Idee im Grunde gänzlich und das heißt fehlerlos in seinem Kopfe vorhandenen Sache wie seiner Studie, ein vollkommenes phantastisches wissenschaftliches Werk im Gehirn weder durch Mut, noch durch das Mittel der intellektuellen Kühnheit endgültig, und das heißt durch Niederschrift auf dem Papier, auch für die Außenwelt und für die Fach- und für die Nachwelt zu verwirklichen, sei das Deprimierendste. An Rücksichtslosigkeit auch oder gerade gegen sich selber habe es ihm im Hinblick auf die Studie in diesen einerseits, wie er selbst sich ausgedrückt haben soll, demütigend in die Länge gezogen, andererseit erschreckend kurzen Jahrzehnten, nicht gemangelt, aber das Wichtigste habe ihm gefehlt: Furchtlosigkeit vor Realisierung, vor Verwirklichung, Furchtlosigkeit einfach davor, seinen Kopf urplötzlich von einem Augenblick auf den anderen auf das rücksichtsloseste um- und also die Studie auf das Papier zu kippen.[28]

(To Fro, whom I finally managed to sell his policy, Konrad is supposed to have said that his, Konrad's, great mistake was to have kept on waiting for an even more favorable moment, the most favorable moment possible to serve as a point of departure for writing his book, because he had always clung to the belief that the ideal, even the most ideal constellation of circumstances for enabling him to write his book was just around the corner, but in waiting for this moment he had lost more and more time or, as Konrad expressed it, the most valuable time, so that at last he was forced to admit to himself that he had now reached the end of his forces (!), that for two or even three decades he had waited in vain for the ideal moment in which to begin writing his book, and just before the disaster (this is what Fro calls the

---

28 Bernhard, *Das Kalkwerk*, 210–11.

murder of Mrs. Konrad by her husband) Konrad is supposed to have said to Fro that he realized there was no such thing as an ideal, not to mention a most ideal moment in which to write such a work as his, because there simply could be no such ideal moment, or most ideal moment, or point of time whatever for any undertaking or cause of any kind. Like thousands of others before him, Konrad said, he too had fallen victim to a mad dream of one day suddenly bringing his great labor to fruition by writing it all down in one consistent outpouring, all triggered by the optimal point in time, the unique moment for perfect concentration on writing it. And now he would never be able to write it, neither in the prison at Stein nor in the mental institution at Niedernhardt; Konrad's book, like Konrad himself, was a lost cause (Wieser), an immense life work, as one must assume (says Fro, doing a sudden complete about-face) totally wiped out. Here was a failure, owing to a chronic deferment, of the realization of a concept that was basically all there, wholly and flawlessly extant in his own (Konrad's) head, as the book was, a perfect, fantastic, scientific work extant in his brain though unrealized either for lack of courage, of the necessary decisiveness, and finally the failure of intellectual audacity; it was certainly most depressing to think that such a work had remained unrealized on paper where it would have been of great benefit to others, to the world of science, to all posterity. Konrad had certainly not been lacking in the necessary ruthlessness, even or perhaps especially toward himself, for the execution of his tremendous task, during those decades that had dragged on at such humiliating length, as he is supposed to have phrased it himself, though on the other hand they had passed at a terrifying clip, but he had lacked what was perhaps the most important quality of all: fearlessness in the face of realization, of concretization, fearlessness, simply, when it came to turning his head over, suddenly, from one moment to the next, ruthlessly flipping it over to drop everything inside his head onto the paper, all in one motion.)[29]

The passage opens and closes with two simple but crucial statements: first, that the narrator has been talking to Fro and Wieser because he wants to sell them insurance, and second, that all Konrad needed to do all along was tip his head over so that everything inside of it would fall out onto the page. It thus explains both the motive for narration and what Konrad would have needed to do to succeed at writing. The

---

29 Bernhard, *The Lime Works*, 239–41.

image of Konrad's overturned head is remarkable, because it suggests a simple and definitive solution to an intractable problem, as if it were perfectly obvious what it would mean to tip one's head over and shake out its contents. In any event, it can no longer be done. The struggle to write, the subject of the entire book we have just read, gets reduced to one swift motion—"flipping it over to drop everything inside his head onto the paper"—but one that is no longer available to Konrad. Whether we see this as a missed opportunity (Konrad really did find the answer, only he was too late) or just another excuse (given the chance, he would have failed at this too) does not matter: Bernhard's narrative ends with Konrad's complete and utter failure.

This, too, is worth comparing to the end of Dyer's book:

> And there you have it. One way or another we all have to write our studies of D. H. Lawrence. Even if they will never be published, even if we will never complete them, even if all we are left with after years and years of effort is an unfinished, unfinishable record of how we failed to live up to our earlier ambitions, still we all have to try to make some progress with our books about D. H. Lawrence. The world over, from Taos to Taormina, from the places we have visited to countries we will never set foot in, the best we can do is to try to make some progress with our studies of D. H. Lawrence.[30]

Here we see a distinct divergence in attitudes: Dyer ends his book not by conceding failure, but by recognizing the productivity of the struggle. Bernhard's character accepts failure whereas Dyer does not. This is what it means to take inspiration from failure—not in a *schadenfreudig* way ("I will succeed where you failed!"), but in the sense that you truly take the struggles and failures of others seriously, you let them seep into you and affect your creative process; you take inspiration from them, you learn from them, but you also learn how to crawl your way out of them in order to produce *something*—even if this something falls short of the ideal you held in your mind all those years.

Another way to articulate the difference is to say that Bernhard's narrator opportunistically (and perhaps cynically) seizes on the failure of another for his own story, whereas Dyer embraces the dimension of art that is based on failure and its accompanying struggles in good faith. Indeed, Dyer seems to think that one of the great things that writers and artists pass along is their failure: hence he is inspired not only by the spectacular failures that populate Bernhard's novels, but also

---

30 Dyer, *Out of Sheer Rage*, 231–32.

by Lawrence's own failure. The novel opens with this epigraph, from which it also takes its title:

> Out of sheer rage I've begun my book on Thomas Hardy. It will be about anything but Thomas Hardy I am afraid – queer stuff – but not bad.
>
> D. H. Lawrence, 5 September, 1914

In failing to write about Lawrence, Dyer is participating in and extending an illustrious tradition of writers who fail to write about their artistic idols. Lawrence failed to write about Hardy, Dyer failed to write about Lawrence, and maybe someday a future author will fail to write about Dyer. However, all these failures are, as I have suggested, also acts of engagement. They are a way to get closer to your object of study, to find common ground, to discover and posit shared ideas and sensibilities and frustrations. This is the crucial difference from Bernhard: Konrad's failure cannot be configured as anything but a failure; it can only be redeemed on the level of Bernhard's work, via a narrator with self-serving financial interests, not on the level of Konrad's. In Dyer's work, his failure can be redeemed on the level of his own work, as a failed study that still produces a form of writing that engages with the object of the study in an alternative, perhaps more immediate way. Bernhard succeeds because Konrad fails;[31] Dyer succeeds on account of his own failure.

To be sure, some of the differences between Bernhard's and Dyer's approaches to failed writing come down to the fact that one is writing fiction, the other nonfiction. Dyer really is trying to write an essay on D. H. Lawrence, and he does eventually produce one, so it makes sense that some of his knowledge and ideas about this topic will seep

---

31 Patrick O'Neill discusses the idea of failure in *Das Kalkwerk*, arguing that both Konrad and the narrator produce "failed texts": "Bernhard's narrative centres ultimately on the relationship of two complementary and mutually reflective entropic texts: Konrad's unwritten text (on the nature of hearing) remains completely silent, nothing is said; in the narrator's text (made up of accounts *heard* from others) much is said, but what information theorists call the signal-to-noise ratio is heavily weighed towards meaningless noise rather than meaningful signal" (240). O'Neill effectively demonstrates the narrator's unreliability, and his subsequent failure to produce a clear and knowable story (235–39). In the last sentence of his essay O'Neill also calls Bernhard's own novel "a brilliantly successful text about the relationship of two failed texts" (241). Patrick O'Neill, "Endgame Variations: Narrative and Noise in Thomas Bernhard's Das Kalkwerk," in *Hinter dem schwarzen Vorhang: Die Katastrophe und die epische Tradition. Festschrift für Anthony W. Riley*, ed. Friedrich Gaede, Patrick O'Neill, and Ulrich Scheck (Marburg: Francke, 1994).

into his writing. What he lacks is the discipline and focus to actually write the essay, not the insights into Lawrence's life and works that will form its substance. In contrast, Bernhard's fictional protagonist has a fictional writing project—no real knowledge about hearing needs to stand behind that unwritten study. The book on "Das Gehör" is a literary conceit; it is devoid of content.[32]

This point might seem banal, except if one considers the fact that blurring the line between fiction and nonfiction lies at the very heart of Dyer's methodological innovativeness. There is an abundance of evidence to support this claim: the fact that he models his own personal experience of writerly deferral and procrastination on works of fiction; the fact that his own travels that he describes in *Out of Sheer Rage* mirror and call up Lawrence's sojourns abroad; his tendency, exhibited in the essay on Lawrence, to read Lawrence's life into his works;[33] and his tendency to read his own life in terms of Lawrence's life and fiction.[34] *Out of Sheer Rage* is unthinkable without the failures that Bernhard's characters and narrators so dramatically perform, but it also extends and

---

32 Indeed, Bernhard's novel has been read as a satire of the interpretive process. Neumeyer sees the novel's many references to darkness and murkiness as a critique of hermeneutic interpretation and its empty promise of enlightenment. Harald Neumeyer, "'Experimentalsätze' und 'Lebensversicherungen'. Thomas Bernhards Kalkwerk und die Methode des Viktor Urbantschitsch," in *Politik und Medien bei Thomas Bernhard*, ed. Franziska Schößler and Ingeborg Villinger (Würzburg: Königshausen & Neumann, 2002), 4–5. Federmair assumes there is in fact nothing behind the claim to want to write a study on hearing. This is how he reads the novel's final sentences about lacking the strength and resolve to tip his head over and empty out its contents onto the page: "Konrad ist ein Feigling, aber nicht nur das, er ist auch ein Schwindler, und er schwindelt bis zuletzt. [...] Konrad hat überhaupt nichts im Kopf, jedenfalls nichts, was sein Thema, das Gehör, beträfe" (Fedemair, "Als ich *Das Kalkwerk* von Thomas Bernhard las," 56).
33 "Paul Morel is an artist who works 'a great deal from memory, using everybody he knew.' That this is an accurate reflection of his creator's methods of working suggests the extent to which the novel was earthed in Lawrence's own life. The intensely autobiographical nature of the novel should make us extra careful of reading it as autobiography, but Paul's circumstances are almost exactly those of Lawrence himself." Geoff Dyer, "D. H. Lawrence: *Sons and Lovers*," in *Otherwise Known as the Human Condition: Selected Essays and Reviews, 1989–2010* (Minneapolis: Graywolf, 2011), 125.
34 "Like Mrs. Morel in the novel, my parents hoped that, as a result of my university education, I would become part of the secure and respectable middle class. It didn't happen like that. Because of Lawrence. [...] But for working-class boys from England—for *this* working-class boy, at any rate, one who *did* love writers' books—Lawrence was the great role model, because he had come from the same class as me, because his example (leaving England, traveling constantly, living by his pen) made writing a means of—and synonym for—being fully alive: an adventure, in short" (Dyer, "D. H. Lawrence," 127).

modifies the notion of literary failure that Bernhard passes down. Specifically, it makes distraction and deferral into a form of engagement—both with the subject at hand and with the broader history of struggling to write. It is precisely by blending fact and fantasy, autobiography and fiction, that Dyer can find a way out of a purely negative model of writing failure. This is how he manages to make something, rather than nothing, out of "not writing"—since, after all, "the best we can do is to try to make some progress with our studies of D. H. Lawrence."

Three Bernhard, Sebald, and Photography in Holocaust Memory

Agnes Mueller

Susan Sontag famously wrote in 1977, regarding photography, that the person who seeks to record cannot intervene, and that the person who intervenes cannot then faithfully record.[1] The relationship between visual recording and authentic (political) action is therefore a fraught one, and anyone who has lived in the era of digitally altered images and the rise of "fake news" of course knows this all too well. With the onset of photography, a supposedly authentic and authenticating medium, questions of representation and authenticity and how they relate to narrative truth need to be posed anew.

It is a trivial fact that for the most part, we make photographs to keep memories. Yet, this observation, apart from any mundane context, points to the question of what a photograph really does. In any setting, trivial or not, we are asked to ponder what such a direct and visual appeal to the spectator, what a photograph typically is, might have to do with memory, our memory of a particular moment. Does it make the past come alive to stay alive? Or does the visual memory remind us that the past is forever gone, removed from our grasp? Can a particularly artistic photograph, as a quintessentially memorial art form, authenticate emotion and make it always accessible, as common wisdom and the promise of photographic innovation suggest?

W. G. Sebald's novel *Austerlitz* draws attention to this very question by inserting photographs into the core narrative of protagonist Jacques Austerlitz's search for his own concealed past.[2] As readers, we are not

---

[1] Susan Sontag, *On Photography* (New York: Farrar, Straus, and Giroux, 1977).
[2] W. G. Sebald, *Austerlitz* (Munich: Hanser, 2001). And in English: *Austerlitz. Translated by Anthea Bell* (New York: Random House, 2001).

familiar with the photographs. No matter how long or how carefully we study them, we don't know the subjects or landscapes and scenes that have been photographed. Their subjects' identities or the places they reference are also not revealed either in the text or via paratextual clues. So instead of looking at a beloved, familiar face or scene that triggers our remembered emotion, we look at something that is new to us in which we seek to make sense of the unfamiliarity by embedding it into the narrative trajectory of the novel. Or, in J. J. Long's words, in Sebald's texts "the photograph demands narrativisation, making what Sebald terms an 'appeal' to the viewer to provide the image with a narrative context, and thereby to rescue it from its nomadic existence."[3] This particular act on the part of the reader is not so different from exploiting the emotional possibilities of photography in a simple love song. More importantly, however, as J. J. Long also observes—and this is especially the case for *Austerlitz*—Sebald uses the photographs to authenticate the narrative itself. This very technique has several functions. First and foremost, it makes us reflect on who and where the scenes depicted in the photographs might be, and how exactly they may relate to the narrative itself. This reflection, then, accentuates the difficulties of a non-Jewish German telling the story of Jewish Holocaust survivors. As is well known from the extensive literature on the memory of the Shoah, writing any narrative that refers—however loosely—to Holocaust trauma is an undertaking that requires great sensitivity to a narrative of trauma of such magnitude. Yet more importantly, the case of a German writing a narrative of trauma that is conscious of the divergence of the "other" from the "self" poses an even bigger challenge. It also points to the larger question of how to relate memories that are not our own—is it even possible to relate a memory of something that we ourselves haven't experienced?—and thus, to memory in Thomas Bernhard's fiction.

Thomas Bernhard's work found its way into the Anglo-American literary world at a time when the Shoah was rising as a theme of conspicuous significance. What, then, does it mean that Bernhard's work increased in prominence at that particular moment? Sebald's writing, too, belongs to that moment. He did take the Shoah as a theme, asserting new connections between memory and experience, and Bernhard was a major influence on his narrative style. Though neither Thomas Bernhard nor W. G. Sebald are Jewish authors, and their works largely don't address the Shoah directly, they both write fiction that puts the question of Jews and Jewish identity in contemporary Germany

---

3   Jonathan James Long, *W. G. Sebald: Image, Archive, Modernity* (New York: Columbia University Press, 2007), 47.

and Austria front and center. Both are associated even if not entirely with the place of the perpetrator (Sebald lived most of his adult life in England, and Bernhard was an Austrian), then with the language of the perpetrator in that they are both clearly German-language authors. Both, even if not unambiguously German, write for a German-speaking audience in the first place. Most importantly, however, both Bernhard and Sebald grapple with the complex and fraught relationship between fiction, autobiography, and witness testimony in post-Holocaust narrative.[4]

Focusing on *Auslöschung*[5] and on *Austerlitz*, both narratives that are immediately framed by Holocaust memory, this contribution considers the importance of Bernhard's and Sebald's writings within the Anglo-American context of fiction. Narrative structures of an anti-autobiography (Bernhard's term) or of a middle-voiced narrator (Sebald's technique), while embedding imagery into narrative fiction, are original and successful ways to address Holocaust memory. This chapter will show how literary styles that link both writers' works with American (rather than German-language) contemporaries function to establish new modes of writing to address questions of the German-Jewish past. To show how both writers invoke and problematize modes of documentary fiction, it will be important to consider more broadly how narrative experience relates to visual experience, how texts relate to images, and how these relations affect individual reading experience.

Nigerian-American writer Teju Cole has written of the possibility of "memories of things unseen."[6] Of course, this seems like utter nonsense—we can't "unsee" what we have seen, and we can't have a memory of something we have not seen. Yet, what Cole describes is the experience of viewing German artist Thomas Demand's photograph "Clearing," where the clearing in a forest that Demand's photograph shows was not a forest, but a model of a forest. Cole finds it especially compelling that Demand destroyed the model immediately after it was photographed. Hence, the photograph gives us a memory of something

---

4   Cf. on the fraught relationship between Holocaust fiction, documentary fiction, autobiographical styles, and memory, a comprehensive and in-depth analysis on Sebald and other contemporary texts: Richard T. Gray, "Fabulation and Metahistory: W. G. Sebald and Contemporary German Holocaust Fiction," *Literarische Experimente: Medien, Kunst, Texte seit 1950*, ed. Christoph Zeller (Heidelberg: Winter, 2012), 271–302.
5   Thomas Bernhard, *Auslöschung*, in Thomas Bernhard, *Die Romane*, ed. Martin Huber, Wendelin Schmidt-Dengler, et al. (Frankfurt am Main: Suhrkamp, 2008).
6   Teju Cole, "Memories of Things Unseen," *The New York Times* Sunday Magazine (October 18, 2015), MM22. http://www.nytimes.com/2015/10/18/magazine/memories-of-things-unseen.html. Interestingly, Cole makes this observation at the Foto Museum in Antwerp, Belgium, a conspicuous place for *Austerlitz*.

we have never seen. Cole asserts, and I think we can agree, that "when the photograph outlives the body—when people die, scenes change, trees grow or are chopped down—it becomes a memorial"—and this relationship is amplified when it is represented in an artwork, as in Demand's image. Here, the power of the work of art arises from the interplay between the model and the photograph. Of course, Cole gets his ideas for photographs as memorials from the American rather than the German tradition of art photography—even though he uses a German artist as his example.

However, what happens when, as in the case of W. G. Sebald's *Austerlitz*, a novel presents photographs that, as mentioned earlier, are in need of being narrativized by us, the readers? Are they memorials? Or are they counter-memorials to the narrative at hand? They are not strictly or primarily memories or memorials of things unseen—even though they are also that, since the model, the original scene behind the photograph, is as elusive as the model of the forest in Demand. At the same time, the images momentarily stem the flow of the narrative. We stop and look and think. But we can't fully resolve them—the images remain elusive, simultaneously belonging and not belonging to the story. Who was the living child in white costume and tri-corner hat *really*? He is and is not Austerlitz. But what matters in the novel is not so much the absence of the "real," but rather the ways in which we, in our imagination, by filling in the blanks or gaps, are creating a new memory. In our attempts to make sense of the missing link between photographs of scenes and people that are entirely unfamiliar, yet that are at the same time presumed to be of someone, or something, we create a memory, and because of the absence of the real, a memorial for ourselves that arises from the interaction between the photograph and the text. Memories of things unseen thus turn into memorials of things, scenes, or people that we have never known. Memories of the unknown. Even though we non-Jewish Germans, like Sebald—also all other readers—may have never known Jewish victims of the Shoah, this technique of nesting photographs as memorials into the narrative lets us memorialize the victims of the Holocaust as a foil to their possible lives, emphasizing their absence. The nesting of photographs as memorials to people unknown thus evokes an emotion that we transfer onto the characters on display in the novel itself. Hence, the narrative, and the characters that are twice removed via the nesting narrative structure ("Austerlitz said, Elias had told him"), emphasize absence. The past is thus similar to Elias's childhood home—permanently submerged and inaccessible. The photos refer to this absence just as the nesting narrative structure does. The trauma narrative that, via this kind of narrative tact, seems to be merely the trauma of an "other," thus connects with our memories of "self." Instead of being a sentimental journey into someone else's past, our own emotions are kept at a tactful distance vis-à-vis the trauma of the "other."

But what does any of this have to do with Thomas Bernhard? Bernhard's fiction doesn't use photography in the ways that Sebald's does. And the literature on the link between Bernhard's and Sebald's writing is straightforward and clear: as he himself observes in an essay (an essay that incidentally is as much about Kafka as it is about Bernhard), Sebald admired Bernhard, and he might easily have adapted some of his narrative techniques.[7] Specifically, and neither Sebald nor the critical literature explicate this in great detail, both *Austerlitz* and *Auslöschung* display the nested or periscopic narrative structures, where the narrator is removed from the narrative itself via the insert of an additional narrator.[8] The first-person narrator in *Austerlitz* refers to that which Austerlitz tells him as "sagte Austerlitz, habe ihm Elias erzählt": said Austerlitz, Elias had told him. This Bernhardian narrative tactic corresponds exactly with the perspective of Murau in *Auslöschung*, who refers this way to what he had told Gambetti, and what his Uncle Georg had told him. As in other trauma narratives, specifically trauma narratives about the Holocaust, this style can be described, in Dominick LaCapra's terms, as a middle-voiced narrative, where the narrator is

---

7   W. G. Sebald, "Wo die Dunkelheit den Strick zuzieht. Zu Thomas Bernhard." *Die Beschreibung des Unglücks. Zur österreichischen Literatur von Stifter bis Handke* (Salzburg and Vienna: Residenz, 1985), 103–14.
8   There are two recent exceptions in the critical literature: Mireille Tabah, "Gedächtnis und Performanz. W. G. Sebald's *Austerlitz* versus Thomas Bernhard's *Auslöschung*," in *W. G. Sebald: Intertextualität und Topographie*, ed. Irene Heidelberger-Leonhard and Mireille Tabah (Münster: LIT Verlag, 2008), 125–39. Unfortunately, Tabah, while aptly comparing the narrative structure that refers to other third-person narrators, invoking a dialectics of remembering and repressing or forgetting, in both texts seems to want to play off one against the other. In her account, both authors want to break a silence. While Sebald's narrative succeeds, Murau is not capable of empathic engagement, and Bernhard's narrative failed. Bernhard's text, according to Tabah, merely reproduces silence, whereas *Austerlitz* is a resistance against silence. I thus agree with Uwe Schütte's assessment, and this is the second recent engagement with both narrative styles, calling it "periscopic," that Tabah's "Aufrechnung" of *Auslöschung* against *Austerlitz* is misplaced. Schütte is familiar with both Sebald (as his student, he knew him well) and the secondary literature. However, Schütte's account doesn't sufficiently take the texts into consideration—rather, he analyzes what Sebald thought of Bernhard and, in some cases, what Sebald might have thought of Bernhard, which makes his argument not worth considering beyond the level of gossip. Hence, instead of textual analysis, Schütte himself engages in the "Kulturgeschwätz" that Bernhard mocked so poignantly (Uwe Schütte, "Ein Lehrer. Über W. G. Sebald und Thomas Bernhard," in *Thomas Bernhard. Gesellschaftliche und politische Bedeutung der Literatur*, ed. Johann Georg Lughofer [Vienna and Cologne: Böhlau, 2012], 303–19, here 317).

both concealed and made visible as an unreliable entity.[9] It makes us, the readers, keenly aware of the malleability of the narrative, and with that, the unreliability of memory. It is, in a way, a commentary on the absence already on display in the photographs. Not only is memory always unreliable, it is also always to some extent absent.

More importantly, however, pointing to our question of the ways in which the memory of the Holocaust is rooted in both narratives, the *theme* of photography is deeply embedded into Bernhard's narrative. In truly Bernhardian fashion, Franz-Josef Murau, the narrator in *Auslöschung*, turns out to be not only suspicious, but downright angry and scornful toward the very idea of photography:

> Das Fotografieren ist eine niederträchtige Leidenschaft, von welcher alle Erdteile und alle Bevölkerungsschichten erfasst sind, eine Krankheit, von welcher die ganze Menschheit befallen und von welcher sie nie mehr geheilt werden kann. [...] Die Fotografie ist das grösste Unglück des zwanzigsten Jahrhunderts!
>
> (Photography is a base passion that has taken hold of every continent and every section of the population, a sickness that afflicts the whole of humanity and is no longer curable. [...] Photography is the greatest misfortune of the twentieth century!)[10]

(And to think that this was written well before the advent of iPhones with selfie sticks.) The depth of the periscopic narrative in *Auslöschung* is further underscored by the fact that Murau himself is introduced as an embedded narrator both in the beginning and the very end of the text.[11] Bernhard, or rather Murau, divulges his disdain for the falsifying, mendacious, distorting nature of the photographs of his parents and brother. Perhaps not coincidentally, the photographs where Murau considers the "Unmenschlichkeit" (inhumanity) of the portrait of his parents were taken (by him) at Victoria Station—a key and nodal point also in Austerlitz's journey. London as a location outside of Germany or Austria is important to both Murau and Austerlitz. Yet, even while dismissing photography as the greatest misfortune of the twentieth century (!), Murau thinks of the photos that he himself took of his parents as "das absolut Authentische," especially due to their grotesque and perhaps even repulsive representation. Consequently, even in their negativity and their inhumanly distorting authority, the photographs

---

9 Dominick LaCapra, *Writing History, Writing Trauma* (Baltimore: Johns Hopkins University Press, 2001).
10 Bernhard, *Auslöschung*, 1388 and 1389; *Extinction*, 14.
11 Cf. *Auslöschung*, "schreibt Murau" (1375), and in the end, "schreibt Murau (geboren 1954 in Wolfsegg, gestorben 1985 in Rom)" (1766).

do represent a memory, even if that memory is negative. When they function in this way, such as in the case of the image of the decapitated mother, they present a juxtaposition to tactfulness. And since they belong and refer to dead people, parents and brother of the angrily and viciously mourning Murau, these photographs, still, embody memorials, which is why he can't keep from looking at them. In their very pessimism, they are important since they remind both the narrator and us, the readers, of that which we must remember: In this sense, they were victims (of a random accident), and thus here too the photographs serve as memorials. More importantly, the photographs here serve as *memento mori*, even and especially due to Murau's negativity. For it is when Murau puts the photographs on his desk that he realizes "Mit einem Schlag waren alle tot": "All three dead, at one fell swoop."[12] But this time, the photographs represent negative memorials. Rather than memorials (*Denkmale*), they turn into relics of a painful past, ruins (*Mahnmale*). The very notion of the photograph as a ruin is evoked once again, this time even more forcefully, when the snapshots of the dead mother in the newspaper articles become a secret object of tastelessly morbid fascination for Murau.

Both Thomas Bernhard and W. G. Sebald use the art form of photography to emphasize the distance of the narrator (and, implicitly, the reader) from the actual memory of the Holocaust. Both the photographs and the narrative techniques are here used as devices that create aesthetic distance. We commonly expect photographs to illustrate what we are reading and feeling, and we expect a narrative to provide closure and establish meaning in the process of mourning lost lives. We form an emotional response to photographs, and to the lives represented. Yet, both the photographs and the narrative style in Sebald and in Bernhard work the opposite way, shocking us, disturbing us, alienating us from the content. In both cases, photographs are embedded within the distancing narrative structure, just as the narrators are nested in the narrative to create detachment. In both novels, photographs have a crucial function as memorials. Yet, Murau uses images created with language while speaking out angrily about photography (creating a negative foil), whereas Sebald's narrator takes the logic of Bernhard's technique one step further and uses actual photographs. Rather than merely talk about photos, Sebald reproduces the photos themselves in the text. Mercifully, Bernhard spares us newspaper photos of the accident scene. Bernhard's narrator, Murau, seeks to wipe out Wolfsegg and the history of the family so there is no more trace of it—the family members are identified with Nazi perpetrators. The text that erases itself is, in this

---

12 Bernhard, *Auslöschung*, 1403; *Extinction*, 27.

way, the counter-piece to *Austerlitz* where recovery and reconstituting a *Jewish* family, most of whom perished in the Holocaust, is the object of writing. As such, *Austerlitz* provides us, the readers, with Cole's notion of memorials of the things and people unseen. Even though in *Austerlitz* we are exposed mostly to absence, the ultimate aim for us, the readers, is to recall and recover memories—Austerlitz's memories—via the narrative structure of the nested autobiography and via the embedded photographs. We can thus recover our own unseen memory of the Holocaust—though, of course, never fully, as such memories always remain just out of reach, as the past is always just out of reach.

Understood in this context, it becomes clear that Bernhard's writing needs to erase, to obliterate Wolfsegg, which survived Hitler as the living embodiment of Nazi Austria. Its eradication will open a space within which to draw positive attention to the Jews who were, actually, *ausgelöscht*, extinguished. ("Die Auslöscher sind am Werk, die Umbringer" ["the obliteraters are at work—the killers"].[13]) This is what defines the "Antiautobiografie" that Murau's Onkel Georg writes, and that the narrative refers to repeatedly. As Mona Körte aptly observes, the entire project of erasing Wolfsegg that Murau undertakes as a narrator is a substitute for, perhaps even a retracing of Onkel Georg's "Antiautobiographie."[14] Via the vitriolic hatred that Murau launches against his family in the face of their demise, the memory of the dead family is turned into its opposite: anti-memory. Anti-memory is, of course, also memory, much in the way in which a photographic negative is also an image, but one that points to that which is lost rather than writing yet another skewed victory narrative. In this way the act of writing, the act of memorializing via photographs, is also an act of mourning. Murau's anti-memorial of his family reminds us constantly of that which is lost and can't be recovered. It also reminds us, and here the link with Sebald becomes palpable, that Bernhard's approach, while seemingly less imaginatively skilled than Sebald's in his use of photography, is radical and uncompromising in its insistence that memory can only be represented as an anti-memory. In an interview, Sebald both reveals his unbridled admiration for Thomas Bernhard and emphasizes Bernhard's acute sense of linking the "periscopic form of narrative" with memory, especially as it concerns private family memory.[15] The

---

13 Bernhard, *Auslöschung*, 1439; *Extinction*, 27.
14 Cf. Mona Körte, *Essbare Lettern, Brennendes Buch. Schriftvernichtung in der Literatur der Neuzeit* (Munich: Fink, 2012). Körte sees this erasure as a constitutive motif in Bernhard's oeuvre, similar to that of Imre Kertesz.
15 Cf. Michael Silverblatt, "A Poem of an Invisible Subject," interview with W. G. Sebald, in *The Emergence of Memory. Conversations with W. G. Sebald*, edited by Lynne Sharon Schwartz (New York: Seven Stories Press, 2007), 77–86, 83.

effect that Murau's invocations of memories have, says Sebald about Bernhard, is spectral and haunting. This is necessary so that memory can be given a specific weight, and Sebald admires Bernhard for writing against the morally compromised German and Austrian prose fiction of the 1960s and 1970s.

However, the Bernhardian tact or radical form of narrative style invoking memory reaches far beyond comparisons with German language fiction of his time. The international and especially American discourse on writing about the Holocaust has, in the past one and a half decades (i.e., roughly since publication of *Austerlitz*), with the third and fourth generations of writers after the Holocaust, become more wide-ranging concerning aesthetic and interpretative means. What used to be considered taboos of representation (humor, distorting or radically fictionalized "memoirs," etc.) are no longer considered taboos, such as in Jonathan Safran Foer's *Everything Is Illuminated* (2002; incidentally, Foer uses photography in a way that is similar to that of Sebald) or in Jonathan Littell's "memoir" (2006). These changes illustrate the process of an increasing turn away from previously held beliefs as to what represents "appropriate" ways of writing trauma, and writing Holocaust trauma, to purposely expanding the creative means of engaging Holocaust memory. Previously affirmative stances (as explicated to some extent by Marianne Hirsch's concept of *postmemory*)[16] are gradually moving away from witnessing or even invoking the concept of witnessing to writing new forms of fictional and/or creative memory. Traces of transgenerational guilt and shame after the Holocaust, and their prevailing effect on contemporary narrative discourse (anti-Semitic tropes and clichés can still be found in third- and fourth-generation narratives on Germans and Jews), indicate that especially German language writing is still, in spite of these developments, afflicted with aesthetic shortcomings. English-language and especially American discourses have been more successful and, for obvious reasons, more at liberty to engage with the possibilities for writing after Auschwitz. The vast literature on Holocaust memory and the question of trauma memoirs in the American context is just one indicator of this phenomenon, alongside accusations against "Holocaust porn," or the "Holocaust industry."[17] The juxtaposition of Austerlitz's journey into his past with the total obliteration of Wolfsegg indicates a drastic and more radical engagement with Holocaust memory, so to speak *avant la lettre*.

---

16 Marianne Hirsch, *The Generation of Postmemory: Writing and Visual Culture after the Holocaust* (New York: Columbia University Press, 2012).
17 Cf. Norman Finkelstein, *The Holocaust Industry: Reflections on the Exploitation of Jewish Suffering* (London/New York: Verso, 2000).

For, just as Sebald's technique of middle-voiced narrative style and embedded photographs is reconstituting art as lost time and place before the catastrophe, and thus makes it visible and tangible to his readers, Bernhard's writing and use of photography purges memory. In keeping with Bernhardian tact, we as readers decidedly are not to think of photographs as a way to keep memories. Rather, we engage the idea and the art form of photography to work against mass death, to remind ourselves of that which is unseen—and remains unseen. There are no Jewish characters of note in *Auslöschung*, just as they are expunged from Wolfsegg. The only trace of the memory of Jews is when Eisenberg, the Viennese Rabbi, is part of the funeral procession of ex-Nazis. Unlike in *Austerlitz*, there is, ultimately, no place of memory, no location to hold onto, and it is both telling and in keeping with the theme of purging memory that Murau, in the end, gives Wolfsegg as a present to Vienna's Jewish community. In contrast with *Austerlitz*, *Auslöschung* constantly reminds us of that which is lost and can *not* be recovered.

I propose a reading of *Auslöschung* as Holocaust fiction that is both radical and pioneering in ways that Sebald's text, and the international and especially the American discourse on Holocaust memory make discernible for us today, roughly three decades after its first publication. Just as the Jews have been *ausgelöscht*, literally, with the Shoah, and figuratively, from the German and Austrian narrative discourse, so has the possibility to memorialize them in art. Sebald still believes in the promise of art to restore, to save, to make visible and tangible the memories of the unseen. Sebald's novel is a place of memory where the memory of "self" is consciously evoking the question of memory of the "other." For him, narrative has the power to authenticate. Bernhard, roughly a quarter century before, already recognized that all this was no longer possible. Itself an act of mourning, *Auslöschung* narrates the impossibility of art as a form to grasp memory.

Four Radical Style: Bernhard, Sontag, Kertész

Stephen Dowden

In 1986 Susan Sontag published what would turn out to be her best-known story and surely one of her most technically accomplished works of fiction. It takes as its theme the AIDS/HIV crisis. From the perspective of an unnamed narrator it focuses—or rather elaborately refuses to focus—on an absent man dying of an unnamed disease. The news that a close friend had contracted AIDS moved her to write the story, as she reports, but it is crucial that the man in the story remains always absent, because the narrative concerns him and his dying through the lens of what people say and hear about him. We and they are swimming in a sea of words without ever touching bottom.

Entitled "The Way We Live Now," the piece appeared in *The New Yorker* to widespread praise. It captured the death-haunted anxiety of the urban 1980s as the amorphous AIDS crisis was gradually taking shape. What concerns us here, though, is specifically this: her story bears the imprint of Thomas Bernhard's narrative style. Here is a brief sample:

> At first he was just losing weight, he felt only a little ill, Max said to Ellen, and he didn't call for an appointment with his doctor, according to Greg, because he was managing to keep on working at more or less the same rhythm, but he did stop smoking, Tanya pointed out, which suggests he was frightened, but also that he wanted, even more than he knew, to be healthy, or healthier, or maybe just to gain back a few pounds, said Orson, for he told her, Tanya went on, that he expected to be climbing the walls (isn't that what people say?) and found, to his surprise, that he didn't miss cigarettes at all and revelled in the sensation of his lungs' being ache-free for the first time in years. But did he have a good doctor, Stephen wanted to know, since it would have been crazy

not to go for a checkup after the pressure was off and he was back from the conference in Helsinki, even if by then he was feeling better. And he said, to Frank, that he would go, even though he was indeed frightened, as he admitted to Jan ...[1]

The style is that of Bernhard's circuitously reported speech for which the narrator cannot vouch, except to repeat what other people are saying. In particular *Das Kalkwerk* (The Lime Works) comes to mind, the novel in which gossip, rumor, hearsay, and chatter at the local taprooms constitute all we know about Konrad, his so-called great scientific project on the faculty of hearing, and the murder of his wife. Sontag was an acute reader of Bernhard's prose (though it is not clear what, if anything, his plays meant to her). But a look through the holdings of her archive at UCLA show that she read all his prose fiction with care and enthusiasm, often in French translation.

In "The Way We Live Now" Sontag mobilizes Bernhard's style on behalf of a certain mood and ostentatiously narrative view of truth. "Literature," she wrote, "*is* knowledge—albeit, even at its greatest, imperfect knowledge. Like *all* knowledge."[2] Imperfection is a basic Bernhard theme, the imperfection of language, art, and science in particular. Mortality is a grave imperfection. In 1986 there was a great deal of uncertainty concerning the science of AIDS, how or if at all the retrovirus could be cured.

How pervasive would this form of death become? Would it reach far beyond the world of gay men and intravenous drug users or not? What was, is, the nonscientific truth of this radical experience of the world? The view of truth I have in mind is that which is specific to narrative form (preconceptual rather than systematic philosophy or medical science), literary form that communicates the spirit of a moment, a feeling, an emotional reality. It is the organic extension or translation of lived experience, not systematic reflection about experience. Hermann Broch was fond of pointing out that the whole point of literature, its only serious justification, is to illuminate the areas of darkness that are inaccessible to conceptual, philosophical, or scientific thought. Literature itself is for Broch a form of cognition; it *is* knowledge, a way of understanding the world—though at best a modest one. His viewpoint strikes me as germane to understanding Bernhard and Sontag. It bears mentioning, too, that both Bernhard and Sontag were well versed in reading Broch. Though he must

---

[1] Susan Sontag, "The Way We Live Now," http://www.newyorker.com/magazine/1986/11/24/the-way-we-live-now. Accessed November 5, 2015.

[2] Susan Sontag, *At the Same Time: Essays and Speeches*, edited by Paolo Dilonardo and Anne Jump with a foreword by David Rieff (New York: Farrar Straus Giroux, 2007), 212.

have nourished their sensibilities, there is no reason to suppose that Broch exercised any direct influence at work here. Rather, they have presuppositions that Broch's thought helps to clarify.

What drew Sontag to Bernhard? Always she championed the most radical writers, thinkers, and artists in her essays: Antonin Artaud, John Cage, Roland Barthes, Samuel Beckett, Walter Benjamin, William Burroughs, Theodor Adorno, Robert Bresson, Jean-Luc Godard, Robert Walser, E. M. Cioran, Simone Weil, Elias Canetti, Francis Bacon, and many more. Radical style drew her too, the prospect of finding ever more penetrating expressive possibilities for writing, music, and art. What drew her was not "ideas" but instead "the pure untranslated sensuous immediacy" of art.[3] She has in mind especially film because it is so often free of the corrosive influence of cerebral posturing. This view poses the question of what sort of critical practice remains open to the critic if interpretation in the usual sense is ruled out—as she emphatically did in her essay "Against Interpretation." Sontag was drawn to radical art that is not didactic and laden with prefabricated meanings. She wanted an art that did not encode some statement or idea, an art that fashionable techniques of interpretation could not obliterate by resolving it into something else, a message, a statement. She endorsed rigorous thinking in art, art *as* a rigorous form of cognition—literature as knowledge—and consequently she was also a critic of the mechanical techniques that often masquerade as thinking, whether in art or in criticism. The rigor of Bernhard's prose style presents just such a pure, untranslated, sensuous immediacy, a way of writing that was and remains fresh and original, is not complicit in didactics, not a delivery truck for conveying this or that idea. This same aversion sets Bernhard in radical contrast to much postwar German writing, which feels compelled to take positions, traffic in statements, meanings, ideas. Sontag was a political activist herself, but art's main task was illuminating expressivity, not discursive assertion. Her heroes were writers like Bernhard and Nabokov. "I don't know if I learned from Nabokov and Thomas Bernhard," she told an interviewer, "but their incomparable books help me keep my standards for myself as severe as they ought to be."[4]

In "The Way We Live Now" she plainly learned something from Bernhard. A hostile reader might dismiss her as a Bernhard imitator, of course, but that would be wide of the mark. The real question is somewhat different. The success of her story is a matter of record. But what does it mean that she tried on the Bernhard style once, but never again?

---

[3] Susan Sontag, *Against Interpretation* (New York: Farrar, Straus & Giroux, 1966), 9.
[4] Susan Sontag, "The Art of Fiction," *Paris Review* 137 (1995): 175–208, here 197.

By the same token, you could criticize Bernhard as a one-trick pony. Years ago I was invited to write a short book about Bernhard, and even though I had never read any of his fiction, I agreed to do so. The Kafka book I was working on at the time was bogged down and felt all wrong anyway, so I welcomed the opportunity to undertake something new. I bought all of Bernhard's books then available (it must have been about 1987) and began to read them in chronological order in the cramped little Habsburg-era reference room of the main library at the University of Zagreb, where I happened to be staying for a few months. Reading Bernhard out of the blue like that was—*naturgemäss*—a bracing experience. But there was a catch: every book seemed to duplicate the one before it. With so little variation, I wondered how it would ever be possible to write about him at all. It felt like being Josef K. visiting Titorelli for help with his trial. The painter shows K. a landscape and Josef K. buys it. Encouraged, the painter pulls out another painting just like the first one. Josef K. plays along and buys it too. "You seem to like the subject," says the deadpan painter. "Luckily enough I have a similar one right here," and he pulls out a third version of the same picture, identical to the first two.[5] And so on. Reading a lot of Bernhard all at once has much the same effect.

So Bernhard really was a one-trick pony, but it was quite a trick—and one that has made a difference in Germany and abroad. His prose fiction fell over the dead landscape of Gruppe 47 like an illuminating bolt of lightning. What Thomas Bernhard did for postwar fiction-writing in the German language, said W. G. Sebald, "was to bring to it a new radicality which didn't exist before, which wasn't compromised in any sense. Much of German prose fiction, of the fifties certainly, but from the sixties and seventies also, is severely compromised, and because of that aesthetically frequently insufficient."[6] The word "radicality" is key. Sontag was drawn to Sebald's radicality as much as she was to Bernhard's. Our question must be, then, why is this radicality important? Sebald's answer to the question is adumbrated in his view that so much postwar German writing was "aesthetically insufficient." What might constitute "aesthetic sufficiency"? And how does it matter to Sontag?

The staleness of so much postwar German literature is not something that professors of German literature talk about very much, unfortunately. But compared with, say, the American novel since 1945 or South American fiction, European fiction in general and German fiction

---

5   Franz Kafka, *The Trial*, trans. Breon Mitchell (New York: Schocken, 1998), 163.
6   Michael Silverblatt, "A Poem of an Invisible Subject," in *The Emergence of Memory: Conversations with W. G. Sebald*, ed. Sharon Lynn Schwartz (New York: Seven Stories Press, 2007), 77–86, here 83.

in particular, compromised as it is—according to Sebald—leaves one wondering. Certainly the extraordinary force of Bernhard's originality is striking and refreshing, like the windows his protagonists are always hoping to throw open. Murau throws open the windows of the five libraries at Wolfsegg. Bernhard's prose had that effect of letting in fresh air. But what was his style "aesthetically sufficient" *to*? The answer can only be: to the German experience of the Nazi era and its aftermath—the Shoah, the destruction of German and Austrian cities, the squandering of German and Austrian traditions, their severely compromised moral standing in the world of politics and letters. Bernhard's world is one in which the only solution, radical in the extreme, is to obliterate all that is morally compromised. Hochgobernitz, Ungenach, Wolfsegg must be utterly razed, blasted from the face of the earth.

How can such radicality be brought to bear on Susan Sontag and her story? By comparison with Bernhard (and with Sebald too), Sontag's accomplishment in narrative fiction is modest. Her most radical, early experiments never found an audience, and her later two novels are historical fiction written in a more conventional style. And her story "The Way We Live Now" adopts a borrowed style that is radical, but then she drops that style. It was never really Sontag's own voice, and it surely would have been a mistake for her to adopt the Bernhard manner has her own. It might also be reasonable to wonder what the relationship is between a radical style and its formulation of experience.

In the United States, there really was a figure comparable to Bernhard, not because his style is similar but because there exists a correspondence between radical style and historical experience that calls out for an aesthetically sufficient form. That would be William Faulkner. The compromised historical experience of the South cried out for a style aesthetically adequate to its specific mendacity and the suppressed horror of the postslavery South. The aftermath of slavery and a lost war of monstrous destruction are roughly parallel to the aftermath of a genocide and a lost war of monstrous destruction in Europe. Faulkner created a highly individual style to express this collective experience, much as Bernhard created one that was both his own and also gives a radical voice to ongoing experience that was and remains radical. The past, as Faulkner famously said, is never dead; it's not even past. Style makes experience directly intelligible, gives it memorable form, establishes it in collective consciousness as not merely real but also as formidably true and imposing. And as Sontag herself said, it is not so much Bernhard's personal style that she needs as it is the example of his uncompromising artistic rigor. So her experiment in exploiting Bernhard's style on behalf of her own writing did not and could not last. It was too much *his* voice and not enough hers. However, she still has much to offer in aiding and abetting our understanding of Bernhard's afterlife. In this context I want to make two simple points. One is about style and ethics. The other is about the problem of death as it is confronted in Bernhard and in Sontag.

First, the question of style and ethics. Most readers ask of a novel: what is it about? Bernhard's blunt stories are in this regard simple to summarize. They are about the growing darkness all around us; the inevitability of suffering, sickness, cruelty, and death; the failure of politics, science, religion, and even art to redeem us; the wasted, corrupted, betrayed patrimony of Austria and Germany; the ethical imperative of annihilating this historically polluted reality. The real action is in his language, his uncompromised style, its verbal texture and formal achievement. But can style itself exert an ethical force? To concentrate solely on style would seem to be the most self-indulgent kind of aestheticism. Shouldn't subject matter predominate, especially since aesthetic pleasure makes art suspect?

Aesthetic pleasure and moral responsibility are not mutually exclusive. "I find it difficult," says Sontag, "to keep moral feelings out of my desire for pleasure."[7] Moreover, some sensuous pleasures—the pleasure of reading Bernhard's prose, for example—are at the same time intellectual experiences, an education and enlargement of consciousness. So the intellectually, morally, human way to approach art is not as if it were a thesis or a proposition of some sort, but as a kind of experience: "Art is not only about something," she says, "it is something. A work of art is a thing *in* the world, not just a text or commentary *on* the world."[8] To experience a work of art amounts to seeing the world through the lens of its style, the form of its knowing. Consequently, expressivity in art—and radical style ratchets expressivity up to a high torque—should be our preeminent category of artistic value. She puts it this way: "The satisfactions of *Paradise Lost* for us do not lie in its views on God and man, but in the superior kinds of energy, vitality, and expressiveness which are incarnated in the poem."[9]

Similarly, the elation that reading Bernhard excites in readers does not reside in his views, his supposed philosophy or his ideas; for example, the idea that Austria should be erased from the face of the earth, that its past and its future must be annihilated. Rather, we respond primarily to the moral passion that underlies, supports, and informs his vision. That passion finds its most compelling expression not in his hyperbolic statements but in the exhilarating energy, vitality, and

---

7   *Conversations with Susan Sontag*, ed. Leland Poague (Jackson: University of Mississippi Press, 1995), 85.
8   Sontag, "On Style," *Against Interpretation*, 21.
9   Sontag, "On Style," *Against Interpretation*, 22.

radicality of his prose style.[10] It stands as a model that sets the bar of articulate moral feeling very high. In it the sensuous and the moral are indistinguishable.

The most radical experience that belongs democratically to us all is death, and both Bernhard and Sontag were deeply preoccupied with it. They shared powerful experiences of illness. The tuberculosis of Bernhard's late teens furnished him with permanent pulmonary disease, a lifelong threat to his existence. Similarly, Sontag lived with a series of life-threatening cancers for the last thirty years of her life. So it comes as no surprise that illness and death form a fundamental experience that is relevant to their works of fiction. In the end, their diseases killed them, as both knew they would. Sontag published *Death Kit*, a novel, in 1967. She wrote *Illness and Metaphor*, then *AIDS and Its Metaphors* in the 1970s and 1980s, and, of course, the story of a death she called "The Way We Live Now." We live with death and always do, but it comes more to the fore at some times than others, as it did for Bernhard and Sontag because of the way they lived with mortal illness—Sontag from 1975, when she was diagnosed with a usually fatal stage IV metastatic breast cancer, to 2004, when blood cancer killed her; and Bernhard from 1949, when he fell ill with tuberculosis, to 1989, when lifelong pulmonary disease finally killed him. In some sense, all of Bernhard's and Sontag's writings are imbued with the knowledge of death. To be sick, to be mortally ill (as we all ultimately are or will be) means not being in control of one's fate, and this in the most literal sense: language cannot master death. It can only talk around it, as Sontag's stories and Bernhard's *The Lime Works* show.

Still, we all want to have at least a say in what happens to us. We have no say in death (except, as Bernhard likes to harp on about, in our command over the question of suicide—always a Pyrrhic victory). We have little say in illness, which is largely beyond our control. The sphere in which Bernhard and Sontag did exercise supreme control was literature, writing—having a say. Consequently, their ordered art was in effect a blow against ultimate disorder, the chaos of death and the way it dissolves into nothing all that matters to us: life, love, family, friends—everything. It leaves nothing standing. Does this mean that art transcends death? No. That would be the worst kind of kitsch. Even the pyramids will erode and blow away. Do Bernhard and Sontag then

---

10 Bernhard writes his novels and memoirs from the perspective of his rage at Austria. Hence the title of Geoff Dyer's Bernhardian memoir *Out of Sheer Rage*, which concerns his attempts to write a radical book on the radicality of D. H. Lawrence as a writer. See Kata Gellen's chapter in this volume.

hand the last word to fear, despair, and death? How might we then think about the place of death in their writing?

As if in answer to this question, Susan Sontag's son, David Rieff, wrote a memoir about his mother's anguished, painful, horrifying last few years. He entitled it *Swimming in a Sea of Death*. Gloom, fear, and depression were her lifelong companions, as he reports. Talking and writing helped Susan Sontag deal with them, and perhaps Bernhard was much the same way—certainly his protagonists are. Sontag herself appears as a kind of Bernhard protagonist in Rieff's memoir. As soon as she woke in the morning, writes her son, Sontag would begin to talk, as a way of shaking off the darkness, "she would talk, about anything and at breakneck speed," he writes, "as if to overwhelm her mood with a meteor shower of verbiage. And yet," he says, "paradoxical as it may seem, even the ways she parsed her own despair could themselves seem like a subspecies of hope. I only realized this fully," says Rieff, "when I saw on the first page of one of her journals, written in the immediate aftermath of her breast cancer surgery," as he writes, "the sentence 'Despair shall set you free.' At first, I thought she was making a morbid joke, but, reading on," continues her son, "I discovered that she had been entirely in earnest. 'I can't write,' she noted," as Rieff witnesses, "because I don't (won't) give myself permission to voice the despair I feel. Always the *will*," writes Sontag, says Rieff, "My refusal of despair is blocking my energies," she concludes, according to her son.[11]

This was in the mid-1970s, when Sontag underwent a radical mastectomy. Evidently she did learn to open herself to the creative possibilities that despair can release, if you will allow it to liberate them instead of block them. She wrote passionately for another thirty years, all the while with the sword of Damocles dangling above her head. Rieff's memoir helps us to understand the nature of Bernhard's creative energies and their underlying source in despair. To say he wrote out of rage, or outrage, is also to say that illness, death, and despair were for him forces of liberation, which might also help explain why reading Bernhard's dark fables feels so liberating to us.

The world inside Bernhard's fiction is similar. The fact that so many of Bernhard's protagonists are scientists who suffer debilitating anxiety probably has to do with the characteristic limitations of science when it comes to revealing or managing specifically human, unsystematizable, unpredictable truths. Bernhard's protagonists do not narcotize themselves with sedatives or mood enhancers. Neurotic to an extreme, they do not see therapists or psychiatrists, though some are interned

---

11 David Rieff, *Swimming in a Sea of Death: A Son's Memoir* (New York: Simon and Schuster, 2008), 139–40.

in mental institutions such as Vienna's Steinhof. These protagonists do seek transcendence or at least some relief in grand scientific projects, which help them forget but then always fail miserably, as Konrad's study of hearing fails.

The main problem is death, from which there is no escape. I am reminded of Hermann Broch's Richard Hieck, protagonist of *The Unknown Quantity* (1933). It is a minor work, but not one entirely without interest. Hieck is a scientist, an astrophysicist, who learns the limitations of science and reason when faced with the bare incontrovertible and nonquantifiable realities of love and death. Broch is not against science and reason. He is passionately *for* science and reason, which is why he wants to understand their limitations. Bernhard's scientists, artists, and philosophers fail when they crash into this same wall. From this perspective, Bernhard's preoccupation with philosophy remains widely misjudged. Nowhere does Bernhard actually do anything with philosophy. He only talks about what a fine thing it is to be a philosopher and do philosophy, much as his thwarted protagonists talk about the science that always fails them in the end. And when one of his thinkers does succeed, as Roithamer in *Korrektur* (Correction) succeeds in building the perfect house for his sister, it kills her. Thus even the greatest thinker has failed yet again. Philosophy and science do not prevail in Bernhard's world. Even art does not prevail: in *Korrektur* (architecture), *Der Untergeher* (music), and *Alte Meister* (painting) only death prevails.

If futility carries the day, why should Bernhard and Sontag write at all, since art will always fail to conquer death? What art can accomplish is this: to let us see precisely what is in store for us, and to endure this knowledge in good cheer and to wait and see what is going to come of our waiting and seeing. This wording is in part a paraphrase of Hannah Arendt in her essay "On Humanity in Dark Times: Thoughts about Lessing."[12] Arendt's topic is German *Vergangenheitsbewältigung*, mastering the past. It is germane here because Bernhard's topic is also, if only partly, Vergangenheitsbewältigung. But it is also at the same time *Zukunftsbewältigung*, mastering the future. In *Auslöschung* (*Extinction*), Franz Josef Murau, for example, wants at a single stroke to master the Nazi past of Wolfsegg while at the same time mastering its future. Either is predicated on his own death, since he is Wolfsegg's living embodiment, its sole heir. What counts for us, though, is the simple, unhidden truth of the novel that tells his story, which is the story of a stubborn

---

12 Hannah Arendt, "On Humanity in Dark Times: Thoughts about Lessing," in Hannah Arendt, *Men in Dark Times* (New York: Harcourt Brace Jovanovich, 1968), 20.

man's refusal to be reconciled to the past, to the future, and to death. Bernhard's lifelong attraction to death should not be confused as an endorsement of it. Instead, it was a willingness to look at death as it is and see it as it is, sometimes in a tragic mode, sometimes in a comic mode. What is key, though, is style, radical style—or "mind as passion," which is how Sontag describes it in her essay on Elias Canetti. "Mind," wrote Goethe in his old age, "belongs especially to old age or to a senescent epoch."[13] Bernhard's predilection for the thorny speeches of very old men seems to bear this thought out. I am thinking especially of Reger, of Strauch, of Prince Saurau. In his 1947 essay on artistic lateness, "The Style of Old Age," Hermann Broch turns over in his mind the tension between human experience and artistic form, between history and style. The artist who is not at home in the stylistic vocabulary of his age, says Broch, is ripe for the advent of a new expressive means. This thought also underlies what Sebald thinks of as his epoch's "aesthetic insufficiency." Still more famously in a fragment of 1937 entitled "Late Style in Beethoven," Theodor Adorno observes that ripeness in great artists is not like the ripeness of fruit that is round, full, and sweet. The ripeness of great artists' late style is spiny and bitter, furrowed and ravaged. It does not reconcile what is irreconcilable: "Touched by death, the hand of the master sets free the masses of material that he used to form; its tears and fissures, witnesses to the infinite powerlessness of the I confronted with Being, are its final work."[14] Disease and his confrontation with death brought Bernhard to a late style, an *Altersstil*, very early. As of the publication of *Frost* in 1963, when Bernhard was only thirty-two years old, his late style is already in evidence.

It explains why the reception of his works was so invigorating at the outset of his career. The energies that reading Bernhard releases have this strange character of an Altersstil. However, they are not exactly a new departure into a period style. That's why Sontag's imitation of Bernhard is a dead end for her and, I think, for his other imitators, too, no matter how virtuosic. It's the reason there are no serious imitations of Beethoven's late string quartets. Still, we can see and appreciate Sontag's grasp of his importance as we can in the style of other writers whom his style has touched. Bernhard, like Sontag, in the radicality of his style, is writing against death. The circularity of his prose, its verbal and metrical repetitions, its musical force apart from all content

---

13 "Geist gehört vorzüglich dem Alter oder einer alternden Weltepoche," in "Noten und Abhandlungen zur west-östlichen Divan, Allgemeines," *Goethes sämmtliche Werke* (Stuttgart and Tübingen, 1854), 1:357.
14 Theodor Adorno, "Late Style in Beethoven," *Essays on Music*, ed. Richard Leppert, trans. Susan Gillespie (Berkeley: University of California Press, 2002), 564–8, here 566.

paradoxically stand as a passionate endorsement of life and the life of the mind. Reading Bernhard does not offer escape from or reconciliation with death. Still less is it an attempt to give information. Instead it is an illumination: a species of enlightenment, a way of standing up to the truth without being annihilated by it.

The fiction of Imre Kertész bears this out even more radically than that of Sontag does. Sontag turned away from radical style in her final period of writing fiction. Her last two novels, *The Volcano Lover* (1992) and *In America* (1999), are both carried out in the conventional mode of historical fiction. Kertész, by contrast, found that radical style was the only possible way that modern experience could attain to aesthetic sufficiency. His life experience was itself radical: he spent his middle teen years as a Jewish prisoner in Auschwitz and other camps. Once liberated, he returned to his native Hungary, where he lived under the totalitarian rule of its communist dictatorships. The second half of his life felt to him a reprise of the Auschwitz years. Both seemed to him to be an exile from real life, which is to say an existence in which one has been robbed of the fate that one might reasonably expect to live out. Hence the title of his first novel, *Sorstalanság* (1975 and 1985; *Fatelessness*, 2004). It is the story of an adolescent Jew from Budapest who, like Kertész, is sent to Auschwitz and survives to return "home" to Hungary.

However, this return to life is not the typical triumph-over-adversity narrative often associated with Holocaust stories, especially in films such as Spielberg's *Schindler's List*. Kertész's protagonist survives, but "triumph" would not be the right way to describe his failure to die at Auschwitz. Having had his fate obliterated in the death camp, he returns to postwar Hungarian life as a disoriented, somehow posthumous person with no clear way forward in the world. The world of Nazi concentration camps and the world of postwar dictatorships: Kertész sees them as lying beyond the province of conventional understanding, conventional language, and conventional literary form: "Dieses Nicht-Aufgearbeitete, ja, oft Nicht-Aufarbeit*bare* von Erfahrungen: ich glaube, das ist die für dieses Jahrhundert charakteristische und neue Erfahrung" (That which has not been worked up, yes, often un-work-up-able experience: I believe that is what is both characteristic and new in this century).[15]

---

15 Imre Kertész, "Rede über das Jahrhundert," trans. Kristin Schwamm, in Imre Kertész, *Eine gedankenlange Stille, während das Erscheißungskommando neu lädt* (Reinbek bei Hamburg: Rowohlt Taschenbuch Verlag, 1999), 14–40, here 15. Kertész wrote all his fiction in Hungarian, but he also spoke fluent German and checked through the German translations of his work prior to publication. Lacking Hungarian, I am relying in this essay on English and especially on German translations.

Key for understanding Kertész's fiction are two thoughts: first, that the radical experiences of twentieth-century Europe brought with them new and difficult challenges of comprehension; and second, that the received language of narrative fiction would have to be revised accordingly. Nonradical art, he says in his novel *Gályanapló* (1992; Galley Log), is just mediocre art and kitsch: "Der wirkliche Künstler hat keine andere Chance, als die Wahrheit zu sagen und die Wahrheit radikal zu sagen" (The genuine artist has no prospect of success except by telling the truth and telling it radically).[16] In order to convey radical experiences truthfully and in an aesthetically sufficient way, a new and radical style would be required.

Kertész's path to radical style was varied. Kafka's understated, impassive storytelling was important to him, as was Camus's use of the nonlinear journal form in his *Carnets*. Kertész drew significantly on Schoenberg's composing, too, for an analogy to describe his ambition as a writer. He described his literary ideal as "atonal": "Atonale Romankomposition. Es gibt keinen Grundton, zu dem sich die einzelnen Töne der Komposition harmonisch oder disharmonisch verhalten können. Statt den traditionellen (tonalen) Grundton mit einem 'Nicht erlaubt' zu belegen, komponiert sich 'Schicksalslosigkeit' in einer eigengesetzlichen Ton" (Atonal novel composition. There is no tonic note for the other notes to relate to harmonically or otherwise. Instead of marking the traditional tonal center with a "not allowed," "fatelessness" composes itself according to its own nature).[17] He wanted a narrative form that, like Schoenberg's compositional technique, did not have a clear foundation in any tonic key—there is no way for a composition to return to its home key because, so to speak, there is no home.

No home key: Kertész saw himself as a permanent exile. He certainly did not feel at home in postwar Hungary any more than Bernhard had a warm, homey feeling for Austria. Kertész gladly took up residence, after the end of Hungarian communist rule, in cosmopolitan Berlin. It was a comfortable post–Nobel Prize exile, but an exile all the same. Being awarded a Nobel Prize is just as "atonal" or unpredictable an experience as being picked up on the streets of Budapest and sent to a concentration camp. He characteristically referred to his Nobel Prize as a *Glückskatastrophe*, a catastrophe of good fortune.

He wanted his literary work to reflect the modern, post-Auschwitz condition of homelessness not only in theme but also in narrative form.

---

16 Imre Kertész, *Galeerentagebuch: Roman*, trans. Kristin Schwamm (Reinbek bei Hamburg: Rowohlt, 1999), 299. This novel, written in the form of a journal, has not yet been translated into English.
17 Kertész, *Galeerentagebuch*, 189–90.

Bernhard's manic, repetitive, adversarial, and emphatically musical radicality—a radicalism not tied to any specific content—offered one possibility for atonal narrative. "Dem Künstler ist es aufgegeben, der Ideologie die menschliche Sprache entgegenzusetzen, der Vorstellungskraft Raum zu geben und an den Ursprung, die wahre Situation und das Los des Menschen zu erinnern" (The artist's mission is to oppose language to ideology, to make space for the imagination and to recall us to primordiality, the true situation, and the lot of humankind).[18] Historically, exile is a preeminently Jewish form of existence, but Kertész took Jewish exile to be paradigmatic for the modern condition after Auschwitz altogether. Auschwitz itself he took to be not a merely Jewish or German or even European concern, but an event that signaled and embodies a basic change in the character of the world. This knowledge and state of affairs has to be built directly into the form of fiction, into the language itself.

Apart from Kafka and Camus, the writings of Thomas Bernhard strongly appealed to Kertész as a possibility for achieving this aim. In a letter to critic Eva Haldimann, he singles out Bernhard's *Ja* (1978; *Yes*, 1991) and *Ungenach* (1968) to make a point about radical stylization:

> Erinnern Sie sich nicht, daß ich, noch in Wien, ausdrücklich auf Bernhard's *Ja* hingewiesen habe? Es stimmt, diese Erzählung hat mich beim Schreiben von *Kaddisch* stark inspiriert, äußerlich, stilistisch—ich stilisiere schon immmer, entweder weil ich nicht originell genug bin, oder weil die Situation tatsächlich so ist, wie Hermann Broch es beschreibt, daß wir in einer stillosen Epoche leben; es trostet mich, daß es auch andere tun, auch die Besten, auch Thomas Mann zum Beispiel parodiert unablässig. Eine vergleichbar starke Erzählung wie *Ja* habe ich allerdings in Bernhards Werk nicht wieder gefunden (vielleicht noch in *Ungenach*, obwohl es nicht so homogen ist).[19]
>
> (Do you remember that in Vienna I explicitly called attention to Bernhard's *Yes*? It's true, this narrative inspired me powerfully when I was writing *Kaddish for an Unborn Child*—outwardly, stylistically. I am always stylizing, either because I am not original enough or because our situation is in fact as Hermann Broch describes it and we do live in an epoch with no style of its own; it comforts me that others, even the best writers, do it too. Even

---

18 Imre Kertész, "Der überflüssige Intellektuelle," trans. Géza Déreky, in Imre Kertész, *Eine gedankenlange Stille, während das Erscheißungskommando neu lädt* (Reinbek bei Hamburg: Rowohlt Taschenbuch Verlag, 1999), 70–83, here 81.
19 Imre Kertész, *Briefe an Eva Haldimann*, trans. Kristin Schwamm (Reinbek bei Hamburg: Rowohlt, 2009), 35. Letter of September 21, 1992.

Thomas Mann, for example, parodies without respite. But I have not found any other narrative in Bernhard's work that is as strong as *Yes* [except maybe *Ungenach*, though it is not as homogeneous].)

Even the best writers do it: he means taking up, exploring, and developing a borrowed style. This volume of essays attests copiously to the truth of his observation. Kertész found in Bernhard's radical style a mode of poetic thinking—which is to say, a mode of atonal composition—that enables effective novelistic expression of a modern experience that is in essence *unheimlich* in the word's literal sense. In his *Kaddish for an Unborn Child* Kertész imagines a Jewish survivor who marries a Jewish woman later, in his return to post-Auschwitz life. She would like to have a child with him, but when she brings the thought up, he explodes into a sustained, mostly unparagraphed rant of fevered thought and speech. Offering a sample of this prose is like scooping a teacup of water from a torrential river, but a brief illustration will help give the flavor of the book's Bernhardian character. It should also suggest the way in which Kertész seeks to oppose ideology with language itself, to carve out space for the imagination after Auschwitz, and to recall us to primordiality, our true situation, and the human lot:

> … to my way of thinking the explanation for Auschwitz, I most probably must have said, since that was and still is my opinion, is inherent in individual lives, solely in individual lives; Auschwitz, to my way of thinking, is a rational process of individual lives, viewed in terms of a specific organized condition. If mankind were to start dreaming as a whole, that dream would necessarily be Moosbrugger, the good-natured sex-killer, as we can read in Musil's *The Man Without Qualities*, I most probably said. Yes, individual lives, as a whole, and the whole mechanics of carrying them through, that's all there is to the explanation, nothing more, nothing else, all things possible do happen; only what happens is possible, says K. the great, the sad, the wise one, who already knew from individual lives what it would be like when criminal lunatics look upon the world rationally and the world in turn presents a rational aspect to them, that is to say, is obedient to them. And don't tell me, I most probably said, that this explanation is just a tautological way of explaining the facts with facts, because yes, indeed, this explanation, hard as I know it may be for you to accept, that we are governed by commonplace felons—hard even when you already call them commonplace felons and know them as such—nevertheless as soon as a criminal lunatic ends up, not in a madhouse or penal institution, but in chancellery or other government office you immediately begin to search for what is

interesting, original, extraordinary, and (though you don't dare say so, except in secret of course) yes, great in him, so you are not obliged to see yourselves as dwarfs, and history of the world as so absurd, I most probably said, yes, so that you may continue to look upon the world rationally and the *world* in its turn may present a rational aspect to you.[20]

And so forth. K. is, of course, Franz Kafka. Kertész was drawn to Austrian writers, especially Kafka but also Broch, Musil, Canetti, Améry, and of course Thomas Bernhard. Kertész sensed—correctly—that in his late works such as *Heldenplatz* and *Extinction*, Bernhard directly invoked the Jewish characters and Austrian perpetrators who, in his early works, were only indirectly present, conspicuous in their ghostly omission. "Bernhard hat immer mit den Opfern—am Ende seines Lebens mit den Juden—identifiziert," writes Kertész: Bernhard always identified with the victims, and at the end of his life with Jews.[21] But this is not a self-congratulatory insight, precisely because Kertész sees Jews and the Jewish condition as paradigmatic for the modern condition in general. In Bernhard he sees this view confirmed. He sees Bernhard above all as a truth-teller, but the truth resides mainly in the form of Bernhard's fiction. What he drew from these writers, apart from ideas for technical composition, was perhaps above all else the idea, from his own reading experience, that art can transform even the deepest misery into aesthetic pleasure; however, it is a pleasure that is not hedonistic and private, but cognitive and public.

---

20 Imre Kertész, *Kaddish for an Unborn Child*, trans. by Tim Wilkinson (New York: Vintage International, 2004), 37–38.
21 Kertész, *Galeerentagebuch*, 296, 285.

Five The Stains of Cultural Inheritance: Thomas Bernhard and Philip Roth

Byron Spring

In 1986, the publication of Thomas Bernhard's final novel, *Auslöschung*, provoked a variety of critical responses.[1] It was at once Bernhard's most extensive engagement with local cultural history and a work of much broader scope, his "bedingungsloses Geschenk an die Weltliteratur" (unconditional gift to World Literature).[2] The novel formed a timely reflection on national legacy: the protagonist Franz-Josef Murau's sudden inheritance of an estate that once housed his parents' Nazi acquaintances resonated as Kurt Waldheim, whose involvement in the Nazi war effort had recently come to light, successfully campaigned for the Austrian presidency.[3] However, *Auslöschung* has proven transferable far beyond this political moment. Scholars have traced the work's influence on writers in the German-speaking world and beyond;[4] yet an understanding of the consequences of Bernhard's last-published novel need not be limited to its reception. This chapter will reposition

---

1 Hans Höller, "Rekonstruktion des Romans im Spektrum der Zeitungsrezensionen," in *Antiautobiografie. Thomas Bernhards* Auslöschung, eds. Irene Heidelberger-Leonard and Hans Höller (Frankfurt am Main: Suhrkamp, 1995), 53–69.
2 Franz Josef Görtz, "Wer ohne Scham ist, werfe den ersten Stein. Thomas Bernhards bedingungsloses Geschenk an die Weltliteratur: sein Roman *Auslöschung*," *Frankfurter Allgemeine Zeitung*, September 30, 1986.
3 Andreas Gößling, "*Auslöschung*," in *Bernhard-Handbuch, Leben-Werk-Wirkung*, eds. Bernhard Judex and Manfred Mittermayer (Stuttgart: J. B. Metzler, 2018), 88.
4 Manfred Mittermayer, *Thomas Bernhard: Eine Biografie* (Frankfurt am Main: Suhrkamp Taschenbuch Verlag, 2015), 411.

Auslöschung within a wider literary context and consider what it means to say that this novel is Bernhard's gift to World Literature.

This chapter will propose that Bernhard's exploration of how to write the self amid the legacies of history and culture in *Auslöschung* invites a much wider frame of reference. The novel stages a narrative project in which Murau resolves, from his apartment in Rome, to write about the Wolfsegg estate and everything it means to him. He hopes thereby to extinguish this legacy: "das in ihm Beschriebene auszulöschen, alles auszulöschen, das ich unter Wolfsegg verstehe, und alles, das Wolfsegg ist [...]"[5] (to extinguish what it describes, to extinguish everything that Wolfsegg means to me, everything that Wolfsegg is [...]).[6] I will argue that Murau's process of coming to terms via this narrative project relies on his engagement with other people and their stories. His distinctive prose style, which Murau calls his "Übertreibungskunst" (art of exaggeration), has this social understanding at its heart.[7] This assists Bernhard's reflection in *Auslöschung* on literary inheritance alongside Murau's familial and cultural inheritances, and engages with wider concerns regarding the authority of the literary canon in understanding the self. These concerns have consequences far beyond the novel's temporal and geographical setting and, to make this clear, I will construct a new literary relationship for the novel. I will compare *Auslöschung* with a novel by a world-renowned Anglophone author similarly exploring ways of living amid physical and cultural inheritances: Philip Roth's *The Human Stain* (2000).

These writers are yet to be compared in detail, which may be for want of genetic influence.[8] Bernhard featured in an essay by Roth's compatriot John Updike on postwar self-condemnation in Austria and West Germany, yet Roth's writings do not evidence any such engagement with the author.[9] To some extent, this reflects the relatively limited reception of Bernhard's works in the Anglophone world during his lifetime. Donald Daviau's 1988 study of Bernhard's American reception notes the divergence between his scholarly fan base, influenced by an

---

5   Thomas Bernhard, *Auslöschung: Ein Zerfall*, in *Werke 9*, ed. Hans Höller (Frankfurt am Main: Suhrkamp, 2009), 156–57.
6   Thomas Bernhard, *Extinction*, trans. David McLintock (New York: A. Knopf, 1995), 99.
7   Bernhard, *Auslöschung*, 477.
8   See Boyd Tonkin, "The Humbling, by Philip Roth," *The Independent*, October 30, 2009, https://www.independent.co.uk/arts-entertainment/books/reviews/the-humbling-by-philip-roth-5504321.html [accessed May 2020]. Tonkin associates Roth's late fiction with the existential dread of Thomas Bernhard.
9   John Updike, "Studies in Post-Hitlerian Self-Condemnation in Austria and West Germany," in *Odd Jobs* (London: Penguin, 1992), 620–29.

awareness of Bernhard's acclaim in Europe, and a popular readership that was slower to emerge.[10] He attributes this to the limited availability of Bernhard's works in English translation in the 1970s and 1980s, published "in small editions, without any attempt to prepare the public for them."[11] Nor was Bernhard an avid reader of Roth. There is little evidence of Bernhard as a fan of late twentieth-century American metafiction.

Yet this makes their works no less congenial, or their juxtaposition any less fruitful. Roth's writings at this time probe the potential of narrative to remake the experience of readers in history and culture via his authorial alter ego, Nathan Zuckerman. "[W]e are writing fictitious versions of our lives all the time," Roth stated in 1985, "contradictory but mutually entangling stories that, however subtly or grossly falsified, constitute our hold on reality and are the closest thing we have to the truth."[12] *The Counterlife* (1986) explores this theme further, presenting Nathan and his brother Henry variously writing themselves against cultural legacies and the spectre of death.[13] In this chapter, however, I would like to compare *Auslöschung* with Roth's late return to Nathan Zuckerman in *The Human Stain*. Like Bernhard's Murau, Zuckerman in *The Human Stain* is called out of self-imposed exile in a cultural moment dominated by presidential secrets: here, details of the affair between Bill Clinton and Monica Lewinsky and a national "purity binge" playing out against public debates over the claims of the literary canon.[14] Like *Auslöschung*, *The Human Stain* explores ethnic and cultural inheritances alongside literary legacies, similarly examining the potentials of literature for individual processes of coming to terms. Both works reflect on the teaching of literature, shared cultural habits, and modernist intertexts including Kafka, Musil, and Thomas Mann. And, as I will show, they exemplify the significance of both authors as stylists staging unique ways of responding to collective history.

This comparison is intended to have consequences for appreciating the positions of both writers in late twentieth-century literature. I aim to show how, over thirty years after his death, Bernhard's works can be appreciated other than by comparison with the coterie of writers who are conventionally associated with him, and those who profess to admire him. For Roth, this essay seeks to build on recent research into

---

10 Donald G. Daviau, "The Reception of Thomas Bernhard in the United States," *Modern Austrian Literature* 21, no. 3/4 (1988): 243.
11 Daviau, "The Reception of Thomas Bernhard in the United States," 244.
12 Philip Roth, *Reading Myself and Others* (London: Vintage, 2010), 161.
13 Roth, *The Counterlife* (London: Vintage, 2016).
14 Roth, *The Human Stain* (London: Vintage, 2016), 2.

the literary cosmopolitanism of a writer who spent a significant amount of his career in Europe.[15] Yet this juxtaposition also aims to advance appreciation of both writers as stylists. What makes Bernhard such a suitable companion for Roth is the common presence of an authorial mind across his works through his familiar narrators and unmistakeable prose style. Like many of Bernhard's later works, *The Human Stain* also includes exaggerated tirades by an authorial narrator, and a comic flair often underappreciated in scholarship that tends to prioritize Roth's complex treatments of ethnicity and metafiction.

First, therefore, I will analyze how *The Human Stain* presents Nathan Zuckerman's coming to terms with his own position in culture via the story of the disgraced Classics professor Coleman Silk. I will show how the novel explores ethnic inheritance alongside forms of literary inheritance, arguing that processes of reading others in this novel are essential to how his characters feel at home in the world. These elements of *The Human Stain* will help illuminate the ambition of *Auslöschung*, a work variously engaging with literary legacies and responding to contemporary culture via Bernhard's exaggerated tirades. Comparing these works, each emerging in distinct cultural moments, will help me advance an alternative perspective on an issue receiving increasing attention following the thirtieth anniversary of Bernhard's death: his legacy to World Literature.

Both novels present tutors of literature living in exile. In *The Human Stain*, Nathan Zuckerman is called out of his solitude in the Berkshires to participate in the story of Coleman Silk, a black man presenting himself as a white American Jew and living an existence constructed from his study of literature. A classics professor at Athena College, Coleman is disgraced for referring to two absent African American students as "spooks," a term uttered in ignorance of the students' ethnicities and exemplifying his alienation from the multicultural academy of the 1990s.[16] Despite taking place against the distinct backdrop of the American culture wars, *The Human Stain* explores themes of inheritance and authority that are central to *Auslöschung*. Roth, I will argue, mediates the contemporary canon debate to examine, on the one hand, the consequences of literature for living in the world and with others and, on the other, the limits to literary self-definition. However, it is the style of Roth's intervention in the canon debate that most brings Bernhard to mind.

In fact, *The Human Stain* opens with a tirade that would not be out of place in Bernhard. It situates the revelation of Coleman Silk's affair with

---

15 Michael Kimmage, "Philip Roth, Thomas Mann and the Other Other Europe," *Philip Roth Studies* 11, no. 1 (2015): 91–104.
16 Roth, *Human Stain*, 6.

a college janitor less than half his age within a wider political, cultural, and literary moment. Nathan notes that the sexual affair takes place in the same summer as the revelations of Bill Clinton's affair with Monica Lewinsky:

> In the Congress, in the press, in the networks, the righteous grandstanding creeps, crazy to blame, deplore, and punish, were everywhere out moralising to beat the band: all of them in a calculated frenzy with what Hawthorne (who, in the 1860s, lived not many miles from my door) identified in the incipient country of long ago as "the persecuting spirit" [...].[17]

Roth's pun on Congress, the asyndeton of the first three clauses and his alliteration all connote the alignment of state branches in persecuting Coleman—or, as Nathan puts it, in excising "the erection from the executive branch."[18] The order to Roth's syntax suggests that any stoking of the public's persecuting spirit is "calculated." This typifies a wider cultural trend diagnosed by the American literary tradition to which Roth connects this rant: Nathaniel Hawthorne, like Coleman, did not live far from the narrator's door. Coleman Silk's downfall, like that of Bill Clinton, is already written. The style of Nathan's tirade irreverently probes beneath the superficiality of the media frenzy to locate its cultural continuities.

Coleman Silk, too, has written his own identity via "the language of Chaucer, Shakespeare and Dickens" promulgated by his father.[19] He embodies the notion, advanced by neoconservative commentators in the contemporary culture debate, that the shared and transcendental values of literature can improve the individual.[20] His teaching of Homer and Euripides reflects his self-assertion away from the legacies of his family. Even the name of Athena College, alluding to Athena's freedom from maternal inheritance, plays on Coleman's self-construction.[21] However, as Roth shows, there are limits to this literary self-definition. He is, first, unable to communicate in the modern academy. The term "spooks" exemplifies Coleman's inability to control the connotations of his language, as well as the resurfacing of an identity that his study had sought to suppress. When accused of a racist slur, Coleman also lacks

---

17 Roth, *Human Stain*, 2.
18 Roth, *Human Stain*, 2.
19 Roth, *Human Stain*, 92.
20 Patrick Hayes, *Philip Roth: Fiction and Power* (Oxford: Oxford University Press, 2014), 221.
21 Jennifer Glaser, "The Jew in the Canon: Reading Race and Literary History in Philip Roth's *The Human Stain*," *PMLA* 123, no. 5 (2008): 1472.

the authority to defend himself. His attempt to write *Spooks*, an account of his side of the story, turns out to be futile. It is only at his funeral when his colleague Herb Keble, the Chairman of the Political Science Division and the first black man to achieve a custodial position in the university, speaks up for him in a eulogy that Nathan Zuckerman's framing narrative presents directly and in full.[22] Keble speaks with the "authority of the second in power to the sovereign," an authority that Coleman cannot attain.[23]

Keble, however, does not know the full story. At Coleman's funeral, Nathan meets his sister Ernestine and sees a photograph that reveals the professor's true ethnicity. Through a narrative sleight of hand, Roth reveals that Nathan's narrative project forms the text of *The Human Stain*: "I was completely seized by his story, by its end and by its beginning and, then and there, I began this book."[24] Nathan's verb "seized," though, casts him as a reader of Coleman's narrative. His project to write *The Human Stain* is not simply a means of making sense of Coleman's story: Nathan passes the tensions of his own troubled history through this narrative frame.[25] Coleman's negotiation of ethnic inheritance, after all, is of interest to Nathan. As I will show, and what *The Human Stain* will also bring out in *Auslöschung*, is how the protagonist engages with his own burdens through this narrative: his conflicts as an artist; his negotiation of orthodoxies of what a Jewish writer should be; and his own physical decline. Engaging with the story of another facilitates Nathan's engagement with his own.

This becomes clear in Nathan's presentation of his meeting with Coleman in the Berkshires. Nathan fixates on the eroticism of Coleman's body, which reveals a "cunning and wily" competitiveness that Nathan had not appreciated before.[26] "Cunning" is a recurrent term in Roth's Zuckerman novels, used frequently to describe the narratives that his characters imagine for themselves and others, and playing on the term's archaic connotations of magical artfulness. In *The Counterlife*, for example, Nathan's self-determination collides with his wife's attempts "cunningly [to] transform [him] into a pastoralized Jew."[27] Coleman is elsewhere described as a "cunning self-concoction."[28] Coleman's embodied ease in the Berkshires results in part from his new

---

22 Roth, *Human Stain*, 309–11.
23 Roth, *Human Stain*, 309.
24 Roth, *Human Stain*, 337.
25 Andy Connolly, *Philip Roth and the American Liberal Tradition* (Lanham, MD: Lexington Books, 2017), 199.
26 Roth, *Human Stain*, 21.
27 Roth, *Counterlife*, 322.
28 Roth, *Human Stain*, 129.

relationship with Faunia Farley, the janitor at Athena College and a woman who reminds him of a life before his literary self-construction—or, as Nathan puts it in a phrase reminiscent of Bernhard, "all he missed by going in the opposite direction."[29] This relationship, and his completion of the first draft of *Spooks*, appears to take Coleman beyond his previously all-encompassing rage at his dismissal and the death of his wife, his "two-year misanthropic exertion of Swiftian proportions."[30] Coleman's newfound ease inspires the narrator, who is similarly alone, ageing and raging at contemporary culture. Nathan is attracted to the new self-assurance of this figure who has completed his own narrative project. This becomes evident as they dance a fox trot together in a symbol of their narrative relationship: Nathan following the story of Coleman while confronting his own burdens through it.[31]

Coleman's relationship with Faunia Farley becomes the initial focus of Nathan's narrative. Willfully illiterate, Faunia Farley exists outside of art and apart from Coleman's constructed literary ideal. Her vivifying effect on Coleman is apparent as Nathan depicts a pastoral milking scene between the two, "a scene of pathos and hypnosis and sexual subjugation."[32] The conjunctions here reveal how the narrator's gaze transitions from observation to vicarious participation. The scene even reminds him of Thomas Mann's Aschenbach watching the young Tadzio, "his sexual longing brought to a boil by the anguishing fact of mortality."[33] This "anguishing fact," though, is also a central preoccupation for Nathan. His physical decline following prostate cancer treatment is a recurring theme from *The Counterlife* to his final appearance in *Exit Ghost* (2007). Nathan Zuckerman's literary project is an act of writing against this physical decline, of creating a space to consummate his desire, even though he is unable to escape his bodily limitation through art. This treatment of the protagonist's decline will reveal parallels with Murau, a figure who in *Auslöschung* writes against his own death but who, like Nathan, cannot escape his physical limitations.

Faunia Farley, however, expresses the most sensitive understanding of physical and cultural inheritance. On visiting a crow named

---

29 Roth, *Human Stain*, 164. "[E]ntgegengesetzte Richtung" is a common Bernhardian phrase, used frequently in the second volume of his autobiographical pentalogy, *Der Keller. Eine Entziehung* (1976). Thomas Bernhard, *Werke 10*, ed. Martin Huber and Wendelin Schmidt-Dengler (Frankfurt am Main: Suhrkamp, 2004), 113.
30 Roth, *Human Stain*, 20.
31 Roth, *Human Stain*, 25.
32 Roth, *Human Stain*, 51.
33 Roth, *Human Stain*, 51.

Prince unable to reintegrate with the murder for having been raised by humans, Faunia immediately understands the reason for the crow's isolation: "we leave a stain, we leave a trail, we leave an imprint."[34] She recognizes the indelible consequences of the crow's human interaction. Nathan even contemplates whether Faunia's human experience renders her a more accurate reader of Coleman. After learning the secret of Coleman's ethnicity at his funeral, Nathan invents a scenario in which Coleman tells Faunia about his true ethnicity only to learn that she "figured [it] out a long time ago."[35] Coleman's past manifests itself in a physical human stain, a blue tattoo that becomes visible on Coleman's body in the Berkshires, representing Coleman's time in the navy and symbolizing the former identity that Coleman has disavowed. To Nathan, this tattoo prompts reflection on how his literary project, too, is limited in its claims to know another. The tattoo becomes "a tiny symbol to remind me why our understanding of people must always be at best slightly wrong."[36] Nathan casts doubt on the epistemological authority of his own narrative project and thus poses the question of what, in *The Human Stain*, narrative *can* do.

His question plays out in the collision between the humanist Coleman Silk and the Yale-educated French poststructuralist Delphine Roux, a proponent of literary representation and Roth's scathing satire of the hermeneutics of suspicion.[37] Roux's mode of critical reading is apparent in the response of one of Coleman's students that Euripides is degrading to women. Coleman expresses disbelief that this is the result of a week's study of the Classical tragedian, mocking such "mouthwash" via the characteristic locutions of what he considers an intellectually barren generation: "they know, like, *nothing*."[38] Yet Roth aligns with neither side of this debate wholeheartedly. Despite her critical acumen and first-rate education in critical theory, Roth caricatures Delphine as just as self-estranged as Coleman. A "terrible sentimentalist" at the movies, she struggles to experience literature via the theory she espouses and hypocritically expresses the romantic preference only to date white men.[39] Hardly questioning the merits of critical reading, Roth deconstructs the expression of such critique as part of the moralistic and accusatory spirit of the times and of the banality of a phrase that becomes the title of the first chapter: "everyone knows." This phrase, appearing in an anonymous message from Delphine Roux to Coleman

---

34 Roth, *Human Stain*, 242.
35 Roth, *Human Stain*, 341.
36 Roth, *Human Stain*, 22.
37 Hayes, *Philip Roth: Fiction and Power*, 222.
38 Roth, *Human Stain*, 192.
39 Roth, *Human Stain*, 199.

about his sexual affair, is precisely what literature, in *The Human Stain*, seeks to deconstruct: "One's truth is known to no one, and frequently—as in Delphine's own case—to oneself least of all."[40]

The confrontation between Nathan Zuckerman and Faunia Farley's scorned husband, Les, exemplifies the consequences of narrative in *The Human Stain*. Nathan presents Les not only as a threat to Coleman Silk but also to his own identity and narrative authority. Revealing that Coleman died in a car accident, Nathan considers whether Les was responsible for his death, not because of Coleman's sexual affair with Faunia but due to his perceived Jewishness: "killed as a Jew [...] another of the problems of impersonation."[41] At Coleman's funeral, Les Farley arrives adopting the perspective of a rival narrator, who has none of the preoccupations that burden Nathan's writing: "Away from this cemetery he muscled on undisturbed, uncharged with any crime, manufacturing that crude reality all his own, a brute of a being colliding with whomever he liked however he liked for all the inner reasons that justified anything he wanted to do."[42] The active participles "manufacturing" and "colliding" suggest a freedom to Les's actions that Nathan envies, while the syntax of this phrase mimics such collisions against its punctuating commas and the consonants of "liked." The phrase, like Les, continues "undisturbed."

In their final confrontation in an Arcadian New England landscape, Les demands that Nathan send him a copy of the finished novel, threatening him with an augur not to divulge the secret location of his ice fishing and, by extension, his role in the "whodunit" of Coleman's death. Nathan agrees to the demand, realizing that this narrative will force him again into years of hiding. His narrative has consequences beyond anything that either narrator can control, and this becomes apparent in the style of Roth's final portrayal of the Arcadian landscape:

> [T]he icy white of the lake encircling a tiny spot that was a man, the only human marker in all of nature, like the X of an illiterate's signature on a sheet of paper. There it was, if not the whole story, the whole picture. Only rarely, at the end of our century, does life offer up a vision as pure and peaceful as this one.[43]

As I will show, *Auslöschung* also explores the indelible echoes of the past in a similar landscape; yet this final image is crucial for understanding Roth's treatments of Coleman and the canon debate. Neither

---

40 Roth, *Human Stain*, 330.
41 Roth, *Human Stain*, 325.
42 Roth, *Human Stain*, 315.
43 Roth, *Human Stain*, 361.

Coleman Silk nor the narrator Nathan Zuckerman can live outside history or "entanglement with other people."[44] Literature, likewise, cannot create idylls untouched by the stains of cultural inheritance, nor can it presume to tell the "whole story." Yet storytelling leaves an imprint on what it means to live as an individual in culture. The alliterative hendiadys "pure and peaceful" is preceded by the turbulence of the twentieth century, and a literary intervention that has stained such purity. Roth's prose style brings out the consequences of his narrative for living in this world: its ability to probe beneath the surface of images, to deconstruct the authority of what "everyone knows," to elicit continuities and to offer a unique, at times hyperbolic, mode of responding to it. Such claims are pertinent for understanding the last-published novel of an author well known for his own misanthropic exertions of Swiftian proportions, Thomas Bernhard.[45]

Auslöschung, too, reflects on culture at the end of the twentieth century:

> An der Jahrtausendwende wird dieser Menschheit Denken gar nicht mehr möglich sein, Gambetti und der Verdummungsprozeß, der durch die Fotografie in Gang gebracht und durch die beweglichen Bilder zu weltweiter Gewohnheit geworden ist, auf dem Höhepunkt sein.[46]
>
> (Come the millennium, Gambetti, human beings will no longer be capable of thinking, and the process of stultification, inaugurated by the photograph and universalized by motion pictures, will have reached its apogee.)[47]

Murau's forewarning of cultural and intellectual decline sounds not unlike Coleman Silk in Athena College in the 1990s. For Murau, this dwindling faculty to think beyond surface appearances has arisen from an industrialized culture culminating in photography. Yet Murau's condemnation of modern culture is staged in a highly ornate style: the alliterations of voiced consonants and the rhythmically parallel structures of

---

44 David Gooblar, *The Major Phases of Philip Roth* (New York: Continuum, 2011): 137.
45 See W. G. Sebald, "Wo die Dunkelheit den Strick zuzieht: Zu Thomas Bernhard," in *Die Beschreibung des Unglücks: Zur österreichischen Literatur von Stifter bis Handke* (Frankfurt am Main: Fischer, 2012), 113. W. G. Sebald associates Bernhard's worldview with that of Swift.
46 Bernhard, *Auslöschung*, 505. On Bernhard and photography see Agnes Mueller's contribution to this volume.
47 Bernhard, *Extinction*, 324.

his subordinate clauses. His style creates a space for self-expression and artistry outside of such habitual ways of thinking. Moreover, Murau's tirade is performed to a named interlocutor: he does not come to terms with collective history alone. The preceding analysis of *The Human Stain* will frame my interpretation of *Auslöschung*. Bernhard's prose style in *Auslöschung* enables his protagonist to write his social existence with authority amid the collective burdens of history and culture. Engaging with others and their stories is central to Murau's understanding of his collective cultural inheritance. Murau's treatment of this inheritance in *Auslöschung*, I will argue, assists an appreciation of the novel's wider relevance.

Auslöschung even stages its own transmission. Like *The Human Stain*, *Auslöschung* comprises the narrative project of the author's fictional alter ego. Two interjections of the clause "schreibt Murau" (Murau writes) at the text's beginning and end establish that this narrative is framed by an editor, mediating the delivery of Murau's narrative project to Bernhard's reader.[48] This delivery accompanies the novel's climax as Murau, having vacillated between contradictory impulses to destroy his inheritance and to renovate the estate to its former artistic glory, resolves to transfer it as an unconditional gift to his friend Rabbi Eisenberg on behalf of Vienna's *Israelitische Kultusgemeinde*. This is Murau's final act before the extradiegetic editor reveals the death of the narrator in 1983 in Rome:

> Von Rom aus, wo ich jetzt wieder bin und wo ich diese *Auslöschung* geschrieben habe, und wo ich bleiben werde, schreibt Murau (geboren 1934 in Wolfsegg, gestorben 1983 in Rom), dankte ich ihm für die Annahme.[49]
>
> (From Rome, where I now live, where I have written this work entitled *Extinction*, and where I intend to stay, writes Murau [born Wolfsegg 1934, died Rome 1983], I thanked him for accepting it.)[50]

Murau's gift has stimulated various interpretations: as a belated act of atonement for his family's involvement with the Nazi regime;[51] a gesture of Murau's refusal to engage meaningfully with the complexity of national history;[52] and even his impasse before the insurmountable

---

48 Bernhard, *Auslöschung*, 7, 508.
49 Bernhard, *Auslöschung*, 508.
50 Bernhard, *Extinction*, 328.
51 Ulrich Weinzierl, "Bernhard als Erzieher. Thomas Bernhards *Auslöschung*," *The German Quarterly* 63, no. 3/4 (1990): 459.
52 Irene Heidelberger-Leonard, "Auschwitz als Pflichtfach für Schriftsteller," in Heidelberger-Leonard and Höller, *Antiautobiografie*, 191.

task of coming to terms.[53] *Auslöschung* leaves these readings open. Yet it is the final word of the text on which I would like to concentrate. Bernhard's last-published novel ends not on the divestment of *Schloß Wolfsegg*, his metonym for Austrian cultural history, but Eisenberg's acceptance of it and, simultaneously, the acceptance by Bernhard's reader of the text bequeathed to them. This raises a question that aligns *Auslöschung* with the climax to Roth's American Trilogy: what it means to accept the legacies of the cultural and literary past, and how to live with such inheritance.

This is not the only act of textual transmission in the novel. After learning of the deaths of his parents and brother, Murau reacts with remarkable composure, instead recalling five texts that he had recommended to his student Gambetti earlier that day:

> Ich hatte Gambetti fünf Bücher gegeben, von welchen ich überzeugt gewesen bin, daß sie ihm für die nächsten Wochen nützlich und notwendig sein werden, und ihm aufgetragen, diese fünf Bücher auf das aufmerksamste und mit der in seinem Falle gebotenen Langsamkeit zu studieren: *Siebenkäs* von Jean Paul, *Der Prozeß* von Franz Kafka, *Amras* von Thomas Bernhard, *Die Portuguiesin* von Musil, *Esch oder die Anarchie* von Broch […].[54]
>
> (I had given Gambetti five books that I thought would be useful and necessary to him in the next few weeks, telling him to read them slowly and carefully: Jean Paul's *Siebenkäs*, Kafka's *The Trial*, Thomas Bernhard's *Amras*, Musil's *The Portuguese Woman*, and Broch's *Esch or Anarchy* […].)[55]

While various critics have considered the relevance of these works to an understanding of *Auslöschung*, this literary tradition appears to serve further functions here.[56] Following the deaths of Murau's family members, these texts form the basis of the pedagogical relationship between the narrator and Gambetti. Bernhard also questions the authority of the

---

53 Katya Krylova, *Walking Through History: Topography and Identity in the Works of Ingeborg Bachmann and Thomas Bernhard* (Bern and Oxford: Peter Lang, 2013), 240.
54 Bernhard, *Auslöschung*, 7.
55 Bernhard, *Extinction*, 3.
56 See, for example, Georg Jansen, *Prinzip und Prozess Auslöschung: intertextualle Destruktion und Konstitution des Romans bei Bernhard* (Würzburg: Königshausen und Neumann, 2005); Manfred Mittermayer, "Von Montaigne zu Jean-Paul Sartre. Vermutungen zur Intertextualität in Bernhards Auslöschung," in *Thomas Bernhard: Traditionen und Trabanten*, eds. Joachim Hoell and Kai Luehrs-Kaiser (Würzburg: Königshausen und Neumann, 1999), 166.

literary canon in its very transmission. The narrator's assertion that these five works, including Bernhard's own *Amras*, will be "nützlich und notwendig" for Gambetti above all others prompts reflection as to why this is the case. There appears more to Gambetti's education in *Auslöschung* than the solitary study of literary tradition, and this is a theme shared with a number of Bernhard's works written, published, and performed between January 1981 and May 1982, when Bernhard is understood to have composed the majority of *Auslöschung*.[57] It emerges most prominently when Bernhard engages with one canonical figure in particular: Johann Wolfgang von Goethe.

Bernhard repeatedly returns to Goethe's cultural authority at the turn of the 1980s. In *Über allen Gipfeln ist Ruh. Ein deutscher Dichtertag um 1980*, a play first performed in June 1982, Bernhard portrays the literary sensation Moritz Meister, whose insularity, pseudo-intellectualism, and latent anti-Semitism hollows out the contemporary literature industry.[58] In *Goethe schtirbt* (1982), a short text written for the 150th anniversary of Goethe's death, Bernhard depicts Goethe as obsessed by the works of Ludwig Wittgenstein.[59] Goethe's disappointment that Wittgenstein has died before he can accept an invitation to Weimar enables Bernhard to rewrite Goethe's final words on his deathbed as the bleak and eminently Bernhardian phrase: "Mehr nicht."[60] In *Auslöschung*, Murau derides Goethe in a comic tirade:

> [A]uf den Biedermann Goethe, den Insekten und Aphorismensammler mit seinem philosophischen Vogerlsalat, so ich zu Gambetti, der natürlich das Wort *Vogerlsalat* nicht verstand, so hatte ich es ihm erklärt [...] Auf Goethe, den Gesteinsnumerierer, den Sterndeuter, den philosophischen Daumenlutscher der Deutschen, der ihre Seelenmarmelade abgefüllt hat in ihre Haushaltsgläser für alle Fälle und alle Zwecke [...] Er ist nicht der größte Lyriker, er ist nicht der größte Prosaschreiber, habe ich zu Gambetti gesagt, und seine Theaterstücke sind gegen die Stücke Shakespeares beispielsweise so gegeneinander zu stellen, wie ein hochgewachsener Schweizer Sennenhund gegen einen verkümmerten Frankfurter Vorstadtdackel.[61]

---

57 Gößling, "*Auslöschung*," 88.
58 Thomas Bernhard, *Über allen Gipfeln ist Ruh. Ein deutscher Dichtertag um 1980*, in *Werke 18* [*Dramen IV*], ed. Bernhard Judex and Manfred Mittermayer (Frankfurt am Main: Suhrkamp, 2007).
59 Thomas Bernhard, *Goethe schtirbt*, in *Werke 14* [*Erzählungen. Kurzprosa*], ed. Hans Höller, Martin Huber, and Manfred Mittermayer (Frankfurt am Main: Suhrkamp, 2003), 398–413.
60 Bernhard, *Goethe schtirbt*, 413.
61 Bernhard, *Auslöschung*, 450–51.

(Goethe, the honest burgher, the collector of insects and aphorisms, with his philosophical mishmash (Gambetti did not know the meaning of mishmash and I had to explain it to him) [...] Goethe, the classifier of stones, the stargazer, the philosophical thumbsucker of the Germans, who ladled their spiritual jam into household canning jars to be consumed at any time and for any purpose [...] He isn't the greatest lyric poet, he isn't the greatest prose writer, and to compare his plays with Shakespeare's is like comparing a stunted dachshund from the Frankfurt suburbs with a tall Pyrenean mountain dog.)[62]

The voiced consonants of "Sterndeuter" and "Daumenlutscher" chip away at the intellectual achievements of the great German polymath as bathetic, solitary pastimes. The asyndeton of the final sentence dismantles Goethe's worldwide reverence, portraying him as a local "Frankfurter Vorstadtdackel." But the narrator's digressive tirade does more than simply undermine Goethe's authority; it also engages with practices of consuming him. Goethe is portrayed as the poetic pied piper leading the Germans away onto their allotments to read him in isolation. The Germans nourish themselves on Goethe like the "Seelenmarmelade" they keep in their household jars but, as Murau warns his foreign student, Goethe could turn his stomach. J. J. Long has interpreted the references to bottling and pickling in *Auslöschung* to practices of bottling up responses to the cultural past.[63] Reading Goethe, and accepting his canonical authority, is connected with the repression that characterizes Wolfsegg under Murau's parents.

Bernhard stages a response to this malaise within the rant itself. Murau's realization that Gambetti does not understand the word "Vogerlsalat" initially appears a comic aside; yet it signals that this rant is performed to another person. Instead of trailing off into his own self-absorbed monologue, Murau invites Gambetti into understanding him. Whereas reading Goethe is depicted as a solitary pastime, Murau's tirade admits others. Gambetti, furthermore, enables the narrator to express sentiments that he had previously bottled up: "weil ich es ihm gegenüber auch immer als ganz natürlich empfunden habe, ihm meine Empfindungen so zu eröffnen, wie sie sich mir gegeben habe"[64] (because I had always thought it quite natural to reveal my feelings to him).[65]

---

62 Bernhard, *Extinction*, 289–90.
63 J. J. Long, *The Novels of Thomas Bernhard: Form and its Function* (Rochester, NY: Camden House, 2001), 163–64.
64 Bernhard, *Auslöschung*, 135.
65 Bernhard, *Extinction*, 67.

Their relationship is pivotal to the novel. After all, *Auslöschung* does not open with the revelation that Murau's parents and brother have died in a car accident, but instead with Murau's report of his meetings with his student to arrange their future lessons, a meeting that inspires him to take a different route home.[66] If Faunia Farley in *The Human Stain* is the Tadzio to Coleman Silk's desirous Aschenbach, Gambetti can be seen similarly as a source of repressed longing that inspires Murau's artistic confrontation with his own being. The young student's Southern charm reunites the protagonist with an element of his passion preexisting its suffocation in postwar Wolfsegg.

Memories of the estate's past as a center of art have since been overlaid by its involvement in the Nazi war effort. The degeneration of the estate is reflected in the bodies of the family members in Murau's photographs: "Daß der Vater und auch daß Johannes krank geworden seien und daß die Mutter zu ihrer lebenslänglichen Migräne auch noch die Magen- und die Nierenkrankheit bekommen habe"[67] (father and Johannes became ill and Mother started to suffer stomach and kidney disorders in addition to her lifelong migraines). The memory of war is a human stain that stymies any prospect for Murau to renovate the estate to its former glory. Murau reveals to Gambetti that, as a child, he and his sisters would perform plays in the *Kindervilla*, although these plays are now shut away in the attic, "ungelüftet, verstaubt" (shut off from the air and covered with dust).[68] His sister's ominous silence encapsulates the impossibility of restoring the *Kindervilla* now: "Nach und nach soll Wolfsegg wieder ein lebendiges werden, wie ich es mir vorstellte, sagte ich. Caecilia schwieg" (Wolfsegg must gradually become a living place again, as I imagine it. Caecilia said nothing).[69]

The indelible trail of a collective past even continues into Murau's dreams. As in *The Human Stain*, the narrator cannot create a textual idyll separate from the burdens of his identity. Bernhard exemplifies this in a scene reminiscent of the Arcadian climax to Roth's novel. Murau describes to his student a dream in which he meets his friends Eisenberg and Zacchi to discuss Schopenhauer and the work of the poet Maria in a secluded inn named *Zur Klause*, a location that the narrator considers ideal for these investigations. The poet Maria arrives late after attending a performance of *Pelléas and Mélisande* in Paris. Embodying a cosmopolitanism and artistry at odds with the traditional and secluded setting, she kisses both Murau and Eisenberg and runs outside to make

---

66 Bernhard, *Auslöschung*, 7.
67 Bernhard, *Auslöschung*, 54.
68 Bernhard, *Auslöschung*, 314.
69 Bernhard, *Auslöschung*, 314.

new footprints in the snow. Yet the entrance of an innkeeper, angered by Maria's dress and Eisenberg's beard, swiftly destroys this freedom. The innkeeper screams the words "gehört ausgerottet" (should be *exterminated*), encapsulating the Nazism and anti-Semitism that stain this Alpine landscape.[70] Much like Nathan Zuckerman's pastoral scenes in *The Human Stain*, Murau is unable, even in his dreams, to create a narrative space detached from historical legacy.

However, Murau's relationship with the poet Maria also facilitates his confrontation of these burdens. Murau and Maria put the narrator's project of "Auslöschung" into practice in a scene in which Murau writes his past before they burn his papers together: "Ich bin ihr *Auslöscher*, hat sie behauptet. Und das, was ich zu Papier bringe, ist das *Ausgelöschte*"[71] (I was her *extinction expert*, she said: whatever I set down on paper was *extinguished*).[72] The possessive pronoun turns Murau's writing project into a private game in which he tries to contain his historical traumas within the perfect tense, "das Ausgelöschte." The act of writing cannot destroy the collective past, but this relationship renews his impetus to write about it: "*Ich werde die Auslöschung schreiben* und immer wieder mit Gambetti die *Auslöschung* Betreffendes besprechen, und mit Spadolini und Zacchi und natürlich mit Maria" (*I'll write my Extinction* and discuss everything relating to it with Gambetti, Spadolini and Zacchi, and of course with Maria, I thought).[73] As in *The Human Stain*, Bernhard's last-published novel acknowledges that the processes of writing and understanding the self are not performed in isolation from others. The relationship between Murau and Maria reveals a mode of living at odds with the repression and solitude of Schloß Wolfsegg. Their shared narrative practice has consequences for how the protagonist lives with others within and outside art.

Murau's project also continues another familial legacy. Having similarly fled Wolfsegg to Southern Europe, Murau's Onkel Georg opposes the insularity of the Wolfsegg estate. He demands that its libraries be opened and encourages Murau to free himself from the yoke of his parents: "In erster Linie hast du dich von den Deinigen vollkommen freizumachen, hatte mein Onkel Georg gesagt, dich vollkommen selbständig zu machen, zuerst innerlich, dann auch äußerlich" (You must make yourself completely independent, my Uncle Georg had said, first inwardly and then outwardly).[74] Onkel Georg also introduces the protagonist to a love of art, encouraging him to experience artists "wie

---

70 Bernhard, *Auslöschung*, 177–78.
71 Bernhard, *Auslöschung*, 424.
72 Bernhard, *Extinction*, 273.
73 Bernhard, *Auslöschung*, 424.
74 Bernhard, *Auslöschung*, 109.

lebendige Menschen auf einer lebendigen Bühne" (as living actors on a living stage).⁷⁵ The formative role of Onkel Georg in Murau's personal and artistic development is reminiscent of the relationship between the author and his beloved maternal grandfather, the author Johannes Freumbichler, portrayed in detail in Bernhard's autobiographical pentalogy (1975–82). *Ein Kind*, his fifth autobiographical volume, examines the literary career of Freumbichler and acknowledges the texts that he left behind. Onkel Georg, too, left behind a literary estate. Among his notebooks was a two-hundred-page manuscript of an "Antiautobiografie" that Murau suspects to have been destroyed by his mother.⁷⁶ This provides an additional impetus to Murau's project of self-writing, as a means of engaging with and continuing his uncle's literary tradition.

The autobiographical volume *Ein Kind*, furthermore, presents the influence of his maternal grandfather's style of self-expression, both in individual words as well as the long monologues that formed part of their walks. Regarding the word "untätig," for example, Bernhard states: "dieses großväterliche Wort hatte ich immer im Ohr, auch heute noch bestimmt es meinen Tagesablauf" (This was a saying of my grandfather's which I constantly bore in mind; even today it determines the way I live).⁷⁷ His grandfather's use of compound neologisms such as "Artikulierungsdilettantismus" also leaves its imprint on Bernhard's prose style.⁷⁸ *Auslöschung* stages a similar stylistic inheritance, which Murau calls his "Übertreibungskunst":

> Mit diesem Übertreibungsfanatismus habe ich mich schon immer befriedigt, habe ich zu Gambetti gesagt. Er ist manchmal die einzige Möglichkeit, wenn ich diesen Übertreibungsfanatismus nämlich zur Übertreibungskunst gemacht habe, mich aus der Armseligkeit meiner Verfassung zu retten, aus meinem Geistesüberdruß, habe ich zu Gambetti gesagt.⁷⁹
>
> (I've always found gratification in my fanatical faith in exaggeration, I told Gambetti. On occasions I transform this fanatical faith in exaggeration into an art, when it offers the only way out of my mental misery, my spiritual malaise, I told Gambetti.)⁸⁰

---

75 Bernhard, *Auslöschung*, 37.
76 Bernhard, *Auslöschung*, 148–49.
77 Bernhard, *Autobiographie*, 419.
78 Bernhard, *Auslöschung*, 419.
79 Bernhard, *Auslöschung*, 477.
80 Bernhard, *Extinction*, 307.

Even this description of Murau's art of exaggeration is exaggerated. The narrator elevates it to a form of fanaticism he expresses in his art via the compound nouns, parataxis, and appositions in this passage. On the one hand, this style facilitates Murau's individual response to his own burdens. It enables Murau to define himself as engaged in a world with others, constituting the narrative relationship between him and his student Gambetti. At the same time, though, this hyperbole echoes beyond the novel. A reader may perceive the creative mind of Bernhard here from his autobiographical prose, as well as Bernhard's incendiary prize acceptance speeches and *Leserbriefe*. This style exemplifies the trail of Bernhard's linguistic performances beyond the singular literary event. The act of reading may be solitary, but in Bernhard it is not separate from social existence beyond the text. Bernhard stages in Murau a style of responding to the burdens of the past beyond the decline that Murau laments in culture on the verge of the millennium, but also establishing wider continuities across Bernhard's literary project.

This assists an understanding of the final bequest of the novel. Like Onkel Georg, Murau decides to disinherit his family and to pass on his estate via Eisenberg to Vienna's Jewish community. In doing so, Murau exchanges the physical estate for one that he can construct in narrative. The surviving narrative, though, does not simply bear witness to the horrors of the estate. It instead outlives Murau's bodily limitations to attest to the relationships that have enabled his personal and artistic homecoming. Engaging with *Schloß Wolfsegg* in narrative has consequences for how Murau lives with others outside of the text. This may shed light on why Murau transfers the estate to the *Israelitische Kultusgemeinde*, a real organization existing outside of the work, and to a community instead of an individual. The novel acknowledges that the process of coming to terms is not performed alone.

This unites *Auslöschung* with the conclusion to Roth's American Trilogy. Where Nathan Zuckerman negotiates his cultural moment through engaging with Coleman's story, Bernhard stages a prose style that enables Murau to express his self-understanding beyond the pervasive isolation of postwar Wolfsegg. Through the echoes of this style in his nonfiction writings, Bernhard also exemplifies how literature leaves a trail, having consequences beyond the solitary German allotment. As in *The Human Stain*, narrative in *Auslöschung* cannot eradicate the stains of cultural inheritance, but nevertheless intervenes in ways of living with oneself and others in culture. The affinities between Bernhard and Roth's reflections on culture and literature at the end of the twentieth century suggest the ongoing transferability of the Austrian writer beyond his immediate contexts. It prompts reflection on a controversial term often floated in connection with him: *Weltliteratur*.

Many studies of Bernhard's relevance to World Literature focus on his Western reception. In his 1994 study of Bernhard's reception in Europe, Wolfram Bayer states: "die Tendenz [ist] unverkennbar, Bernhard nicht als Bestandteil einer österreichischen Nationalliteratur, sondern umstandslos als Weltliteratur aufzunehmen und zu lesen" (there is an unmistakeable tendency to take up and read Bernhard not as part of Austria's national literature but quite simply as World Literature).[81] The essays in Bayer's volume reveal, among other things, Bernhard's following in France, his assimilation into Spanish realism at the turn of the 1980s, and the wide audiences for his works in Eastern Europe. The Anglophone world is a notable exception to this Western popularity. Della Couling's essay examines the limited success of his dramas in London theatres and his relatively sparse English-speaking readership, attributing this to "die manglende Vertrautheit vieler Leser mit den Erzählweisen nicht-englischer Literatur" (many readers' lack of familiarity with the narrative styles of foreign literature).[82] Bernhard had various prominent admirers in the United States and United Kingdom: the American-Jewish writer Walter Abish heralded the "Age of Bernhard" in American letters in 1986,[83] while George Steiner called Bernhard "the foremost craftsman of German prose after Kafka and Musil."[84] *Holzfällen* is even referenced in Harold Bloom's *The Western Canon* (1994).[85] However, as various studies of Bernhard's reception highlight, his Anglophone fame has predominantly been limited to academic circles.[86]

This chapter has argued that an understanding of *Auslöschung* and its continued relevance to World Literature need not stop at Bernhard's reception. Although *Auslöschung* stages national inheritances in a local setting, the exploration of Murau's burdens via his writerly project for self-understanding resonates far beyond national boundaries. Roth's *The Human Stain* has enabled me to construct a context for appreciating this, situating Bernhard in a literary company that extends beyond his

---

81 Wolfram Bayer, ed., *Kontinent Bernhard: Zur Thomas-Bernhard-Rezeption in Europa* (Vienna: Böhlau, 1995), 11.
82 Della Couling, "Champagner mit einer Prize Strychnin. Bernhards Theaterstücke in England," in *Kontinent Bernhard*, ed. Wolfram Bayer, 429.
83 Walter Abish, "Embraced by Death," in *The New York Times Book Review*, February 16, 1986.
84 George Steiner, "Black Danube," in *George Steiner at the New Yorker*, ed. Robert Boyers (New York: New Directions, 2009), 123.
85 Harold Bloom, *The Western Canon: The Books and School of the Ages* (London: Macmillan, 1994), 556.
86 Sandra Richter, *Eine Weltgeschichte der deutschsprachigen Literatur* (München: C. Bertelsmann, 2017), 428.

usual admirers. While neither Zuckerman nor Murau can live via the authority of literature alone, their narrative undertakings enable them to find ways of living in a shared culture. Bernhard's "Übertreibungskunst" provides a foil to the hyperbole and comedy with which Roth both dismantles claims to define oneself entirely through the canon and exposes the suspicious righteousness of "everyone knows." Together, through metafictional sleights of hand and their treatments of inheritance, both writers explore the claims and stains of their narratives. And together, in the aftermath of global catastrophe and their defining political moments, they assist an understanding of what it means to come to terms with our own cultural burdens, our own *Wolfseggs*.

This essay is part of a doctoral research project cosupported by awards from the Arts and Humanities Research Council in the United Kingdom and All Souls College, University of Oxford.

Six Gaddis before Bernhard before Gaddis

Martin Klebes

Imitation is the sincerest form of flattery, or so they say. There has been no dearth of German-language writers over the past three decades who have shown traces of at least partial sincerity by that criterion in stylistic relation to Thomas Bernhard, from Kurt Drawert to Gert Hofmann and perhaps even Elfriede Jelinek. Imitation (real or imagined) is one thing, but "plagiary" is another. And it is the specter of plagiary that links Bernhard's literary prose work to that of American novelist William Gaddis (1922–98), specifically Gaddis's last novel, *Agapē Agape* (2002).[1]

The unnamed narrator of this text, an old man with a leg "layered with staples"[2] and skin "like parchment"[3] from taking large quantities of the immunosuppressant steroid prednisone, is pondering the shards of his life's work. Confined to a hospital room, he delivers an ongoing—if often halting and repeatedly shape-shifting—monologue as he tries to go through the legal paperwork related to dividing his estate among his three daughters, as well as through heaps of notes on a project accumulated over the years, ostensibly a "secret history" of the mechanical player piano from about 1876 to the moment of its commercial collapse after the Great Depression. The resulting 100-page soliloquy presents him citing either from what remains of his memory or from the notes through which he is riffling, forever interrupting himself when his present train of thought recedes into a blur. The books and notes to which he refers run the gamut of literature (Lord Byron, Melville, Tolstoy, Dostoevsky, Flaubert, Pynchon), philosophy (Pythagoras, Plato, Mill,

---

1   William Gaddis, *Agapē Agape* (New York: Viking, 2002).
2   Gaddis, *Agapē Agape*, 1.
3   Gaddis, *Agapē Agape*, 1.

Nietzsche), and other fields (Johannes Müller, Freud, Barthes, and more than a few others).

The central point of reference in the novel, however, is Thomas Bernhard. Unlike the writers just mentioned, his name is never explicitly invoked in Gaddis's text, but his work makes an unmistakable intertextual appearance, specifically the two prose texts *Beton* (*Concrete*, 1982) and *Der Untergeher* (*The Loser*, 1983).[4] While contemporary German literary texts are not among the most common intertextual points of contact for contemporary American novelists, the repeated reference by Gaddis's narrator to his Austrian counterparts is a well-motivated exception to this rule. Bernhard's narrators, after all, are both involved in the pursuit of projects as elusive as the one Gaddis's narrator is frantically trying to wrap his mind around before he expires, a point in time that the reader is led to surmise may not be far off. Rudolf, the narrator of *Beton*, is introduced in the very first sentence of Bernhard's narrative as being on the verge of writing a book on Mendelssohn-Bartholdy, a project that the reader soon learns has been in a state of perennial postponement for years. In *Der Untergeher* both the unnamed narrator and his friend Wertheimer are, or were, at work on writing projects that do not see completion: Wertheimer accumulates vast piles of notes toward a manuscript of which, after his own cuts and the eventual burning of the notes, nothing remains but the title, "Der Untergeher."[5] The narrator, meanwhile, reports that he has been working on a book to be titled *Über Glenn Gould* (About Glenn Gould), the manuscript of which has been repeatedly destroyed and rewritten and remains unfinished.[6]

In their various states of incompletion, all three projects obviously connect to the magnum opus envisaged by Gaddis's narrator in *Agapē Agape*. As Gaddis's very first print publication, a short essay from 1951,[7] shows, a version of this unrealized project was indeed his own, and one that occupied him for over fifty years—his *Faust*, in a manner of speaking. Goethe's play is repeatedly quoted across Gaddis's work, and also in *Agapē Agape*. But very much unlike Goethe, Gaddis did not develop his accumulated material by sequentially seeing parts of the project into print. Instead, after early outtakes it flashes up as a fictionalized endeavor of would-be writer and physics teacher Jack Gibbs in

---

4 Thomas Bernhard, *Beton* (Frankfurt am Main: Suhrkamp, 1982); translated by David McLintock as *Concrete* (New York: Knopf, 1984). Thomas Bernhard, *Der Untergeher* (Frankfurt am Main: Suhrkamp, 1983); translated by Jack Dawson as *The Loser* (New York: Knopf, 1991).
5 Bernhard, *Der Untergeher*, 78–79; *The Loser*, 54.
6 Bernhard, *Der Untergeher*, 51, 81, 107–9; *The Loser*, 34, 55, 74–75.
7 William Gaddis, "Stop Player. Joke No. 4," in *The Rush for Second Place* (New York: Penguin, 2002), 1–5.

Gaddis's second novel *J R* (1975)[8] before going dormant again, only to be resurrected in *Agapē Agape*, once again in fictional form.

Here, as the narrator attempts to collect and order his notes—and, thereby, he hopes, his thoughts—to finally give an actual shape to this project before time runs out, he faces a fundamental impediment. As he tries to assume authorship of a work that draws on a massive amount of sources and notes, what claim does he really have to be formulating an idea about the significance of the player piano in cultural history that could be said to be *his own*, properly speaking? On its face, we might take this as the entirely unremarkable conundrum of anyone who has ever sat down in front of a blank page, or screen, to write even a single sentence. The situation of Gaddis's narrator, however, is particularly acute insofar as the historical caesura he aims to mark with the appearance of the player piano revolves around the very fragility of an artistic expression of subjectivity. As a would-be writer, Gaddis's narrator is forced to call into question his own role as a creator of a text—a text, that is, which would in turn endeavor to defend the true musical artist as the creative performer of a work who is fundamentally at odds with the preprogrammed playback of rolls on the player piano, or of a piece of computer software. Hence, the would-be subject (or topic) of the fictional work and its enunciating would-be subject (the narrator in his role as writer) are two instantiations of the same problem, with the diegetic and the formal levels mirroring each other throughout Gaddis's text.

In Bernhard's texts we find an analogous superimposition of the thematic and formal levels. In *Beton*, Rudolf is explicitly introduced as a *writing* narrator—"Von März bis Dezember, schreibt Rudolf [...]" (From March to December, writes Rudolf [...])[9]—who turns out to be exceptionally eloquent in describing the circumstances conspiring to prevent him from beginning the work he is actually trying to commit to paper, a book about Mendelssohn-Bartholdy. It is not clear to what extent this potential manuscript would deal with the composer's *biography*, given that Rudolf rejects chronological biography as "die geschmackloseste, gleichzeitig die ungeistigste Methode" (the most tasteless and at the same time the most unintellectual procedure).[10] Meanwhile it is precisely Rudolf's biographical circumstances—his relationship to his sister Elisabeth, as well as his memories of his encounter with Anna Härdtl, culminating in the eventual realization that she has committed suicide—that continue to prevent him from actually writing (or so

---

8 William Gaddis, *J R* (New York: Penguin, 1993), 604–5.
9 Bernhard, *Beton*, 7; *Concrete*, 3.
10 Bernhard, *Beton*, 45; *Concrete*, 31.

he tells himself, at least). In other words, for Rudolf "life" (and life in the face of the deaths of first Peter and then Anna Härdtl) is not just a methodological problem in terms of *how* to deal with his subject matter; it is also what keeps him from beginning that treatment. Appropriately, the concrete slabs surrounding the budget hotel *Zenith* onto which Peter Härdtl falls to his death—alluded to in the book's stark title—find their complement in the manufactured rigidity with which Rudolf aspires to overcome his writer's block. He is ambitiously pursuing a publication that would far surpass "alles bisher von mir die sogenannte Musikwissenschaft betreffende von mir aufgeschriebene Veröffentlichte sowie Nichtveröffentlichte" (everything else, both published and unpublished, which I had previously written in the field of what is called musicology),[11] and yet never manages to write so much as the first sentence of such a work. Instead, the first sentence of the narration before us will be a retroactive telling of the circumstances surrounding that inability to begin.

The particularly striking form of intertextuality to which Gaddis resorts in reference to this text is to set up his narrator as a reader of Bernhard's text:

> reach for a book reach for anything listen, you'll see what I mean, opening page you'll see what I mean, "From March to December" he says, "while I was having to take large quantities of prednisolone," same thing as prednisone, "I assembled every possible book and article written by" you see what I mean? "and visited every possible and impossible library" this whole pile of books and papers here? "preparing myself with the most passionate seriousness for the task, which I had been dreading throughout the preceding winter, of writing" where am I here, yes, "a major work of impeccable scholarship. It had been my intention to devote the most careful study to all these books and articles and only then, having studied them with all the thoroughness the subject deserved, to begin writing my work, which I believed would leave far behind it and far beneath it everything else, both published and unpublished" you see what this is all about? "I had been planning it for ten years and had repeatedly failed to bring it to fruition," but of course you don't know, no that's the whole point of it! It's my opening page, he's plagiarized my work right here in front of me before I've even written it![12]

---

11 Bernhard, *Beton*, 7–8; *Concrete*, 3.
12 Gaddis, *Agapē Agape*, 11–12.

The quoted passages from Bernhard's book are enclosed in quotation marks, although the source is only identified in the paratextual copyright notice that precedes the beginning of the narrative. Rudolf finds himself accused by Gaddis's narrator of what the experimental French writers group Oulipo termed "anticipatory plagiary."[13] In the case of Gaddis's narrator, the invocation of such "plagiary" is prompted by the notion that an idea, though it may be tethered to a form that is external, verbal, and/or in print, need not necessarily take that form in order to be subject to plagiarism.[14] It is not difficult to see why the narrator, having come upon a passage in a work published by someone else that appears to be describing his own experience (with the reference to Mendelssohn-Bartholdy carefully excised), should be hit particularly hard when he is facing such distinct trouble in committing that very idea to writing himself.

What is striking about this passage and the narrator's comments on it, however, is that alongside the claim of detecting anticipatory plagiary in a work authored by someone else, it becomes uncertain what exactly the work that has allegedly been plagiarized would consist in. If indeed the opening page of *Beton* is, for Gaddis's narrator, "my opening page," then any clear distinction between the work that Gaddis's narrator *failed* to write (namely the comprehensive history of the player piano) and the chronicling of that failure becomes difficult to make. For that opening page itself contains writing about *not* writing, detailing preparatory activities that will ultimately not result in the composition and publication of "a major work of impeccable scholarship." If what Rudolf (or Bernhard) had plagiarized in anticipation was a "work" about the interminable preparation of preparing for (another) work, then the work of Gaddis's narrator, too, would

---

13 The group uses the term to designate "writers who, lamentably unaware of the group's existence, could not know that they were creating paleo-Oulipian texts without acknowledgment" (*Oulipo Compendium*, ed. Harry Mathews and Alastair Brotchie [London: Atlas, 1998], 207). These are texts following sets of rules commensurable with the Oulipian practice of generating texts from formal models, though they were composed years or even centuries before some of these rules were ever explicitly formulated. Among them: Lasos of Hermione (author of the first known lipogram), Arnaut Daniel (inventor of the sestina), Lewis Carroll, and Unica Zürn.

14 As the *Oxford English Dictionary* definition specifies, plagiarism is an "action or practice of taking someone else's work, idea, etc., and passing it off as one's own; literary theft" (s.v. "plagiarism"); as a legal standard, the exact scope of the term continues to keep the courts busy, but it is clear that manifest word-for-word identity of two texts, for example, is not a necessary condition for one to be considered a plagiary of another.

have to be of that preparatory kind, rather than about the "subject" of player piano history.[15]

Any attempt at determining the reference(s) of "work" here must take into account the fact that Gaddis's and Bernhard's texts are at bottom not *about* the inability of individual pathological narrator subjects to treat a given subject matter. Much rather, both texts concern themselves with the very nature of writing and the creative process itself, challenging the notion of authorial subjectivity or individual creative genius. Gaddis's and Bernhard's narrators both assert (their claim to) such subjectivity while the textual structure of what they produce denies this claim. Plagiary as the reproduction of something identical to what another has produced (or, in the case of anticipatory plagiary, *will* produce) turns on being able to separate the identical from the nonidentical.

The difficulty of doing so is spread all over the passage cited above, beginning with the means used in both cases to address medical pathology, namely the medication both narrators are taking.[16] Gaddis's narrator claims that the "prednisolone" he is being given in the hospital is the "same thing" as the prednisone that Bernhard's Rudolf is taking to counter the effects of *morbus boeck*. It is, and yet it is not. Tellingly, the *New York Times* book review of the English translation of Bernhard's book chided the translator for rendering the German "*Prednisolon*" as "prednisolone," suggesting that David McLintock should have been using the term "prednisone" instead.[17] In fact, however, the two drugs are distinct, with prednisone acting as a so-called prodrug for prednisolone: the initially inactive prednisone is metabolized in the liver into the

---

15 Gaddis's posthumously published text has its roots in the radio play *Torschlußpanik*, also produced posthumously (though earlier) in 1999 in a cooperation between Deutschlandfunk, Bayerischer Rundfunk, and Westdeutscher Rundfunk. The radio play is not a direct "original" to what would eventually be published as the English text, which explains why the still later German translation of *Agapē Agape* is not entitled *Torschlußpanik* but rather *Das mechanische Klavier* (trans. Marcus Ingenday [Munich: Goldmann, 2003]). In a way, then, we might think of *Torschlußpanik* itself as an anticipatory plagiary that the author Gaddis posthumously committed against himself, proleptically providing one version of the narrator's failed project in spoken German before a different, though related, version would reach English-speaking readers. Incidentally, the copyright page of the first edition of *Agapē Agape* does contain acknowledgments for excerpts from the translations of Bernhard's *Concrete* and *The Loser*, as well as from John Kennedy Toole's *A Confederacy of Dunces*; *Torschlußpanik*, however, is not mentioned.
16 Gaddis and Bernhard not only administered the drug to some of their narrators (with the eponymous narrator of Bernhard's *Wittgensteins Neffe* [Wittgenstein's Nephew] (1982) among them, who takes it in the aftermath of respiratory surgery), but also took it themselves to counter the symptoms of lung emphysema.
17 John Simon, "The Sun Never Rises on Rudolf" (*New York Times*, July 1, 1984).

prednisolone compound, which then unfolds its glucocorticoid effects.[18] Prednisolone may also be taken directly, though the prodrug prednisone was developed to improve its bioavailability, and thus its effectiveness for many patients. If prednisone (taken by Gaddis's narrator) therefore structurally *precedes* prednisolone (taken by Rudolf), at the same time it *is* prednisolone, at least with respect to its active compound, which is the ultimate reason for most people to take any medication at all. Speaking in terms of narrative, the structural priority of prednisone may buy it increased effectness if compared to prednisolone, but the "pro" in "prodrug" will not support an ultimate claim to "originality."

To consider the "work" supposedly plagiarized by Rudolf his own, to consider the first page of *Beton* to be *his* "opening page," Gaddis's narrator would need to establish the self-identity of both parts in question—the book, and himself. With the first of these already in doubt to some degree, let us proceed to the second, namely the "I." Feeling his body disintegrating and losing motor control over it as he writes, Gaddis's narrator finds his own identity repeatedly beginning to merge with figures in the texts he has read and excerpted, and which are piled up next to his bed. One of these sources is the seminal 1938 book *Homo Ludens* by the Dutch cultural anthropologist and historian Johan Huizinga[19] in which he argues for the fundamental basis of all of human culture in the *spel* [play]:

> Getting old your only refuge is your work, can't see the bone can't see the needle in the vein drip drip God knows what hour after hour new treatment down below to strip the romantic veil off the naked animal's only function to perpetuate the species the race the tribe the, down in the recovery room leg jumps up by itself not mine no, don't dare stand up like horses the legs go first and darlin yer dancin days are done like the, book right here a minute ago like Huizinga's kangaroo just reading it wasn't I? Can't see across the room everything's a blur that's the prednisone so they're testing the eyes but I can read can't I, up close read ten point eight point but the, the, standing up just standing up take the two steps I can't I can't, I, I can't, it's the, not my leg jumping up it's the kangaroo, it's the savage doing the magic ritual kangaroo dance he is the kangaroo, one of them has become the other, he doesn't

---

18 Yana Puckett and Abdullah A. Bokhari, "Prednisone," StatPearls [Internet] (Treasure Island, FL: StatPearls Publishing, 2019).
19 Johan Huizinga, *Homo Ludens. Proeve eener Bepaling van het Spel-Element der Cultuur* (Haarlem: H. D. Tjeenk Willink & Zoon, 1938). English translation: *Homo Ludens. A Study of the Play-Element in Culture* (London: Routledge and Kegan Paul, 1955).

know words, doesn't know image and symbol, doesn't know belief from make-believe Huizinga says, he has become the other and the other is the, the other has taken him over when I stand up and I I, I am the other, take two steps I can't breathe can't stand can't sp, speak can't walk across the the, I can't I can't I can't! Got to stop it's got to end right here can't breathe the other can't speak can't cross the room can't breathe can't, can't go on and I'm, I am the other. I am the other.[20]

In the book to which Gaddis's narrator makes direct reference in this passage, Huizinga points to the particular repetitive character of the German phrase "ein Spiel spielen" (which neither the Dutch phrase "een speeletje doen" nor the English translation "to play a game" can quite render), which he takes to signify that the activity of *spelen* (playing) is more than just one among many, and "*geen doen in den gewonen zin*" (no doing in the ordinary sense).[21] Huizinga identifies three formal properties of play:

- it is characterized by "*vrijheid*" (freedom)
- it is separate from the "eigenlijke leven" (ordinary life), a "tijdelijke handeling, die in sich zelf afloopt, en verricht wordt om de bevrediging, die in die verrichting zelf gelegen is" (a temporary activity satisfying in itself and ending there)[22]
- it is separated from regular life by being played out within certain limits of time and place.[23]

Huizinga's subsequent discussion of archaic rites as important instantiations of those formal properties actually complicates them to some degree. Huizinga rejects the notion that participants in an archaic ritual were simply subject to a complete and utter rapture and illusion, and holds that they in fact retain "[e]en achtergrondbewustzijn van het 'niet echt zijn'" (an underlying consciousness of things "not being real").[24] Such consciousness would seem to necessitate the retention of an ability to still distinguish between the real and the illusory. But at least during a ritual such as the Kangaroo Dance itself, as Huizinga writes three pages later, the falling away of the corresponding distinction between "being" and "playing" turns out to constitute the very essence of the ritualistic dance; Huizinga here calls this a "magic" rather than a

---

20 Gaddis, *Agapē Agape*, 19–20.
21 Huizinga, *Homo Ludens*, 54–55; English transl., 37.
22 Huizinga, *Homo Ludens*, 11–13; English transl., 8–9.
23 Huizinga, *Homo Ludens*, 14; English transl., 9–10.
24 Huizinga, *Homo Ludens*, 32–33; English transl., 22.

"symbolic" unity of individuals belonging to different orders, such as the animal and the human.

> De wilde, in zijn tooverdans, *is* kangaroe. [...] Hij heeft het wezen van den kangaroe aangenomen. Hij speelt den kangaroe, zeggen wij. Maar de wilde zelf weet van geen begripsonderscheidingen zijn en spelen, weet van geen identiteit, beeld of symbool. En derhalve blijft het de vraag, of men niet den geestesstaat van den wilde bij zijn sacrale handeling het best benadert, door aan dien primairen term spelen vest te houden. In onze notie spel gaat de onderscheiding van het geloofde en het geveinsde te loor. Dit begrip spel verbindt zich zonder gedwongenheid aan het begrip van wijding en heiligheid. Ieder praeludium van Bach, iedere regel der tragedie bewijst het.
>
> (In his magic dance the savage *is* a kangaroo. [...] He has taken on the "essence" of the kangaroo, says the savage; he is playing the kangaroo, say we. The savage, however, knows nothing of the conceptual distinctions between "being" and "playing"; he knows nothing of "identity," "image" or "symbol." Hence it remains an open question whether we do not come nearest to the mental attitude of the savage performing a ritual act, by adhering to this primary, universally understandable term "play." In play as we conceive it the distinction between belief and make-believe breaks down. The concept of play merges quite naturally with that of holiness. Any Prelude of Bach, any line of tragedy proves it.)[25]

The lack of knowledge of the *"wilde"* [savage] (Huizinga's choice of terms from over eighty years ago is obviously problematic) about identity clearly corresponds to the uncertainty of Gaddis's narrator confined in his hospital room amidst his stacks of notes about who he "is"—and it inspires doubt as to whether this state, while ongoing, can be reliably distinguished from what is "real."

Huizinga's contention that *spel* is at bottom more fundamental than a clear sense of subjectivity or identity is echoed by Hans-Georg Gadamer.[26] Like Huizinga, Gadamer holds that on the one hand the *Spieler* (player) "knows" the difference between the "seriousness" of the real

---

25 Huizinga, *Homo Ludens*, 37; English transl., 25.
26 Gadamer repeatedly quotes Huizinga in Part II, Chapter 1 of *Wahrheit und Methode* ("Spiel als Leitfaden der ontologischen Explikation"). See *Wahrheit und Methode. Grundzüge einer philosophischen Hermeneutik*, Vol. 1 of *Gesammelte Werke* (Tübingen: J. C. B. Mohr [Paul Siebeck], 1990), 107–39. English translation: *Truth and Method*, 2nd revised ed., trans. by Joel Weinsheimer and Donald G. Marshall (New York: Continuum, 1995), 101–34.

world and the nonserious *Spiel* (play), but that taking the *Spiel* seriously, in turn, requires a forgetting of the character of the *Spiel* as *Spiel*. It means to forget what Huizinga called the "Nichtechtsein," the illusory character of the *Spiel*. Only such taking seriously would presumably unlock the *Spiel* as "Seinsweise des Kunstwerks selbst" (mode of being of the work of art itself)[27] rather than as a manifestation of subjective freedom (which is at the heart of Schiller's notion of *Spielen* in his *Briefe über die ästhetische Erziehung des Menschen* [Letters on the Aesthetic Education of Man] to which Gadamer takes exception).

The unrealized work presented in, and ultimately making up, Gaddis's narrative does not seem to command such an essential mode of being—an authenticity first accessed through the artwork as *Spiel*— that could serve as a hermeneutic guidepost. If the *Spiel* were taken *seriously*, Gadamer suggests, it would be possible to lift the artwork into the absolute presence of a fully remembered *Wirkungsgeschichte* (effective history), and thus to mediate its meaning without residue. There could be no more effective repudiation of this view of the artwork than Gaddis's narrator's ensuing comical pseudodialogue on the waning authenticity of the artwork that has him alternately taking the sides of Huizinga and Walter Benjamin in turn. He claims that Benjamin "picked up" his ideas from Huizinga, although Huizinga published his book two years after Benjamin had written "Der Ursprung des Kunstwerks im Zeitalter seiner technischen Reproduzierbarkeit" (The Origin of the Artwork in the Age of its Mechanical Reproduction), which might make this another case of anticipatory plagiary.[28] Toward the end of this ventriloquized exchange of corresponding arguments, both converge on the view that authenticity is inevitably replaced by a pervasive nonauthenticity:

> Authenticity's wiped out when the uniqueness of every reality is overcome by the acceptance of its reproduction, so art is designed for its reproducibility. Give them the choice, Mr. Benjamin, and the mass will always choose the fake. Choose the fake, Mr. Huizinga! Authenticity's wiped out, it's wiped out, Mr. Benjamin. Wiped

---

27 Gadamer, *Wahrheit und Methode*, 107; *Truth and Method*, 101.
28 In a letter to Gregory Comnes, Gaddis revealed that he only became aware of Benjamin's famous essay long after he had been accumulating material for his player piano project: "I hadn't known of him, & certainly would have been pilloried for plagiary had I ever completed [m]y own *Agapē Agape: The Secret History of the Player Piano* […] in my ignorance Benjamin had already clearly, concisely, brilliantly & briefly covered the ground." *The Letters of William Gaddis*, ed. Steven Moore (Champaign, IL, London, and Dublin: Dalkey Archive, 2013), 477 (Letter of October 15, 1992). A few years later, Gaddis would skillfully turn this potential plagiary accusation on its head in *Agapē Agape*, which keeps the title but drops the subtitle of the earlier project.

out, Mr. Huizinga. Choose the fake, Mr. Benjamin. Absolutely, Mr. Huizinga! Positively, Mr. Benjamowww! Good God! a way to find a sharp pencil just sit still avoid stress stop singing what, anybody heard me they'd think I was losing my, that I'd lost it yes maybe I have [...].[29]

Rather than taking Huizinga's and Benjamin's respective theses on the destruction of authenticity seriously, Gaddis's text stages a satirical simulacrum of a Gadamerian conversation that ends in a tautologically indistinct mutual affirmation ("Authenticity's wiped out, it's wiped out, Mr. Benjamin. Wiped out, Mr. Huizinga"), properly punctuated by the narrator sitting on his apparently sharpened pencil (with Derrida's well-known comments on Nietzsche in mind, we could say: he is sitting on his own *stilus*, his *éperon stylé*). The *Spiel* is thus transferred onto the metalevel of narration itself: the *Spieler*, playfully assuming the voices of thinkers who argue discursively for the loss of authenticity, unmasks those discursive texts as themselves subject to the plague of plagiarism. The dispute concerning originality and copy has at this point been moved beyond any *serious* consideration of whether it could possibly avoid becoming itself ensnared in the mechanism of textual reproduction.

While Benjamin's and Huizinga's texts deal primarily with examples from the visual arts when addressing the thoroughly ambivalent legacy of modernist reproducibility of the artwork, the key metaphor and manifestation of the same process in Gaddis's text is given in the subject of the narrator's elusive project: the player piano, and the both relatively brief and thoroughly instructive history of that medium. Here it is the reproducibility of *sound*, the imitation by mechanical means, which holds out the questionable promise that the competent performance of the canon of classical piano music is accessible to anyone. Glenn Gould, the central figure of the second of Bernhard's intertexts that Gaddis weaves into the fabric of his novel, would seem to be the perfect counterexample to this particular milestone of constitutively inauthentic art on the march in the twentieth century. After all, as Bernhard's narrator says of the (fictionalized) Canadian pianist in *Der Untergeher*: "bei Glenn war es von vorneherein klar, daß der ein Genie ist" (with Glenn it was clear from the very start that he was a genius).[30] So overpowering are the effects of Gould's palpable genius that both the narrator and his and Gould's mutual friend, Wertheimer, are prompted to give up their careers as pianists not long after being exposed to Gould's rendition of Bach's *Goldberg Variations* in a practice room at the Salzburg Mozarteum (Gould's presence in Salzburg as a student of Vladimir Horowitz is part

---

29 Gaddis, *Agapē Agape*, 35.
30 Bernhard, *Der Untergeher*, 46; *The Loser*, 31.

of Bernhard's fictional ruse): "Weil wir nicht bis zum Äußersten und über das Äußerste hinausgegangen sind, dachte ich, aufgegeben haben im Hinblick auf ein Genie in unserem Fach" (Because we didn't reach the absolute limit and go beyond that limit, I thought, because we gave up in the face of a genius in our field).[31] They give up in different ways: "Wertheimer war, so er selbst immer wieder, in die Geisteswissenschaft hineingegangen" (Wertheimer had gone, as he always said, into the human sciences)[32] and ultimately commits suicide, while the narrator decides to devote himself to "philosophical matters," "wenn ich naturgemäß auch nicht die geringste Ahnung haben konnte, was dieses Philosophische sei. Ich bin absolut kein Klaviervirtuose, sagte ich mir, ich bin kein Interpret, ich bin kein reproduzierender Künstler. Überhaupt kein Künstler" (even though of course I didn't have the faintest idea what these philosophical matters might be. I am absolutely not a piano virtuoso, I said to myself. I am not an interpreter, I am not a reproducing artist. No artist at all).[33] For all their differences, however, both the narrator and Wertheimer become—like Rudolf and like Gaddis's narrator—writers engaged in projects that do not see completion. They transition from piano performance to writing performance, but rather than offering a refuge from their perceived shortcomings as artists when compared to Gould, writing as a practice only serves to demonstrate that the very notion of art on which their prior "failure" was predicated does not have a conceptual leg to stand on. Wertheimer accumulates notes toward his work "Der Untergeher" without ever integrating these into a work with that title (with the enveloping diegetic level carrying the same title only *documenting* his failure rather than remedying it), while the narrator repeatedly rewrites his own manuscript "Über Glenn Gould," ever in pursuit of a more faithful study of its subject, "eine noch konzentriertere, eine noch authentischere, dachte ich. Denn immer glauben wir, wir sind authentisch und sind es in Wirklichkeit nicht" (an even more intense, even more authentic one, I thought. For we always think we are authentic and in truth are not).[34]

If the encounter with Gould prompts his two friends to give up, each in his own way, what exactly would have constituted the opposite? What would going to the "absolute limit" and beyond be, which Gould presumably did and therefore became, unlike the narrator, a true "reproducing artist"? On this point of Glenn Gould's presumable singularity Gaddis's narrator works Bernhard's text into a pastiche, claiming that Gould:

---

31 Bernhard, *Der Untergeher*, 22; *The Loser*, 14.
32 Bernhard, *Der Untergeher*, 11; *The Loser*, 6.
33 Bernhard, *Der Untergeher*, 14–15; *The Loser*, 8.
34 Bernhard, *Der Untergeher*, 108; *The Loser*, 75.

wanted to be the Steinway because he hated the idea of being between Bach and the Steinway because if he could be the Steinway he wouldn't need Glenn Gould he'd be the other! He'd be the Steinway and Glenn in one like the kangaroo he'd be the other! He'd be in control, he'd be in total control with his splicing and editing and altering pitch what he called creative cheating for a perfect performance with an arching melodic line that couldn't be mechanically imitated but it could be it was that's what all this is to, damn.[35]

Conflating Otto Friedrich's 1989 Glenn Gould biography[36] and Bernhard's text, Gaddis's narrator ends up citing as ultimate evidence of Gould's genialistic perfectionism his desire to "be the Steinway" when engaged in his *Klavierspiel* (piano playing),[37] analogous to the way in which, according to Huizinga, the "savage" *is* the kangaroo in the context of the ritualistic *Spiel*. While the desire to erase the medium in order to become the message does indeed ring all requisite romantic bells, the way in which Gould sets out to realize this goal ends up glossing the meaning of what Bernhard's narrator calls being a "reproducing artist" somewhat differently. Only by means of another, presumably more perfect medium—the sound recording—is Gould able to achieve the identity transformation, thus becoming the Steinway by means of carefully edited studio work. The sonic aftertreatment of the recorded performance, in other words, carries the potential to heighten the perceived perfection of that performance and help remove auditory traces of any limiting contingencies. Structurally equivalent to anticipatory plagiary, postprocessing will let us evaluate the anterior in a different way. Perfected thus, piano playing itself always constitutes a "cheating" of the medium by which it must be carried out.[38] In addition, the music played by means of that medium, the *Goldberg Variations*, actually does not conform to the ideal of peerless aesthetic perfection "without interest" (as Kant would say). It was composed, according to a Bernhard passage that Gaddis's narrator does not fail to note,[39] "die Schlaflosigkeit eines

---

35 Gaddis, *Agapē Agape*, 39.
36 Otto Friedrich, *Glenn Gould: A Life and Variations* (New York: Random House, 1989).
37 Bernhard's narrator explicitly notes that Gould consistently preferred to use the term "*Klavierspieler*" (piano player) over that of "Pianist" (*Untergeher*, 118; *Loser*, 82).
38 In his essay "Music and Technology" Glenn Gould himself reports that by adjusting the sonic properties of the acetate of his first radio recording in 1950 to make the studio piano sound better than it actually did, he had essentially "learned the first lesson of technology; I had learned to be creatively dishonest" (*The Glenn Gould Reader*, ed. Tim Page [New York: Knopf, 1984], 354).
39 Gaddis, *Agapē Agape*, 38.

lebenslang an Schlaflosigkeit Leidenden erträglich zu machen" (for the sole purpose of helping an insomniac put up with the insomnia he had suffered from all his life).[40] In other words, even a cultural pinnacle of the sort represented by Bach's famous composition—likened by Huizinga "quite naturally" to holiness, as cited above—cannot be fully separated from the contingencies related to its external manifestation.

Such dependence of the artwork on the external world to which it is connected in performance and reception suggested to Glenn Gould that manipulation is the solution, not the problem. In an essay written in defense of his optimistic view of recording technology, Gould coined the phrase of the "van Meegeren syndrome." To him, the story of the infamous Dutch forger Han van Meegeren stands as a comment on art in the contemporary world rather than a cautionary tale of criminal activity.[41] Forgery is not rejected as a legal transgression but is much rather identified as part of the condition under which modern art may come into being:

> As the performer's once-sacrosanct privileges are merged with the responsibilities of the tape editor and the composer, the van Meegeren syndrome can no longer be cited as an indictment but becomes rather an entirely appropriate description of the aesthetic condition in our time. The role of the forger, of the unknown maker of unauthenticated goods, is emblematic of electronic culture. And when the forger is done honor for his craft and no longer reviled for his acquisitiveness, the arts will have become a truly integral part of our civilization."[42]

The craft of the auditory forger in his creation of "unauthenticated goods" would be to *retroactively* alter the conditions under which the

---

40 Bernhard, *Der Untergeher*, 222; *The Loser*, 155.
41 Van Meegeren had successfully fooled the art world by producing a series of masterfully forged paintings falsely attributed to famous Flemish masters and was exposed only in the context of having sold his forgeries to the Nazis. Fascinatingly, none other than Johan Huizinga (who was neither art historian nor art critic) had voiced early skepticism about the Vermeer painting *Christ at Emmaus* that was van Meegeren's first "discovery"/forgery in 1938. Huizinga commented that Vermeer, "a painter of every-day life," "fails precisely when he depicts holy scenes, for instance Christ at Emmaus" (Johan Huizinga, *Dutch Civilisation in the Seventeenth Century and Other Essays*, trans. Arnold J. Pomerans [New York: Ungar, 1968], 84–85) several years before van Meegeren himself exposed this alleged "failure" of composition as his own handiwork. Gaddis's debut novel *The Recognitions* (1955) and its forger protagonist Wyatt Gwyon are partially modeled on the van Meegeren case.
42 Glenn Gould, "The Prospects of Recording," in *The Glenn Gould Reader*, 343.

recorded performance was committed to tape to remove its contingent failings. In paradoxical fashion, this can only mean to confirm that artistic production always amounts to failure of some sort, but in Gould's assessment, for art to become "truly integral" to life would mean to remove the auratic character of the artwork, to celebrate rather than to conceal its failure to be authentic, its groundlessness in relation to both precedent and afterlife.

The venom that Gaddis's narrator directs at the object of his study and its descendants—player piano, television, computer—could without much difficulty be read in the mode of a critique of ideology. Many passages in the novel, taken in isolation, might lead the casual reader to believe that what Gaddis's text is primarily concerned with is to expose the increasingly commercialized, prepackaged state of the arts in the course of the twentieth century. Not dissimilar to much of the reception of Bernhard's work, here, too, the referents of the narrator's verbal invective might invite the reader to take them at face value, leaving aside the consideration of the literary form into which these are inscribed.[43] The history of the player piano that Gaddis did *not* write might indeed have taken this tack. What we have instead, however, is the literary rendering of the realization that the player piano is, in the end, only a variation of the piano player Glenn Gould.

This 1925 ad (Fig. 6.1) for the Gulbransen "Registering Piano," several passages of which are quoted by Gaddis's narrator without direct acknowledgment, not only admits to the auditory deception involved in using the device as pictured, it actually celebrates it. Whereas the eye can spot the passivity of the player's hands in the mirror, the listener relying only on her ears will become the victim, the ad triumphantly announces, of a peerless act of plagiarism. The plagiarist aspect (in contrast to the phonograph and the radio that would begin to displace the player piano in the late 1920s, leading to the near total collapse of the industry in the wake of the Depression) is the creation of an illusion of artistic activity to prop up the self. "The Biggest Thrill in Music is playing it *Yourself*"—where "*Yourself*," of course, is liberated from using his fingers, free to perhaps develop his footwork in hopes of turning into a Horowitz of the bellows. As the famous "Gulbransen Baby" at the foot

---

43 In this vein, the preeminent Gaddis scholar Steven Moore compares Gaddis and Bernhard by pointing out that both "share an elitist outlook and an adversarial relationship with their countries: Bernhard despised Austrian culture as much as Gaddis did American culture, maybe more, and both used their novels to express their contempt in the harshest, most insulting terms" (Steven Moore, *William Gaddis*, expanded ed. (New York and London: Bloomsbury, 2015), 197). Although Moore also writes that Gaddis's text "formally […] closely resembles the Austrian's relentless novels" (ibid.), he foregrounds referential content at the expense of form.

132 Thomas Bernhard's Afterlives

Figure 6.1 Gulbransen Co. Advertisement for the Registering Piano, 1925.

pedals in the lower right-hand corner of the ad assures us: "Easy to Play." Playing "itself" in this fashion, the self that thus merges with the machine in pursuit of the "thrill of personal creation" becomes one with the machine—at least to ears coupled with undiscerning eyes—to parallel Gould's desire to merge with the Steinway, effected through careful selection and editing of recordings. "You could not do more if you played by hand"—this maxim applies not just to the popular device of which about 200,000 were sold in the United States at its commercial peak in 1923, but just as much to the "singular" artist who would go, in Bernhard's words, "to the absolute limit" and perhaps beyond. In both cases, the limit of the self is crossed, and once it has been crossed, the very notion of "personal creation" finds itself crossed out.

When Bernhard's narrator calls Gould's recording studio a "Verzweiflungsmaschine" (desperation machine)[44] and Gould himself a self-made "Kunstmaschine" (art machine)[45] that only marginally resembles a human being, he is both echoing Gould's affirmation of forgery and artifice (even though Bernhard's fictional Glenn Gould, it should be noted, is explicitly described as *not* aspiring to writing, unlike Wertheimer and the narrator) and anticipating Gaddis's extension of the argument to mechanical and computational forms of reproduction. The artist's attempt at avoiding the trappings of identification may also be discerned in (the nonfictional) Glenn Gould's penchant for assuming pseudonymous alter egos in his writings and audio broadcasts, among them the fictive personality of Herbert von Hochmeister, a figure vaguely resembling the conductor Herbert von Karajan but residing in the Northern Canadian territories.

Gaddis's reinscription of Bernhard's subversive portrait of Glenn Gould brings it full circle and in agreement with Gould's own championing of the counterfeiter as the true artist. Diegetically, both Bernhard's and Gaddis's narrations of this paradox must result in failed projects. The manuscripts "Über Glenn Gould" and "Der Untergeher" (ostensibly *about* the individuals Gould and Wertheimer, but present in the text only as empty referents) cannot be completed, just like the player piano history (*about* the corrosive influence of technology), not least because any manuscripts about the former two would *also* have to be about the technological conditions under which "genius" can alone manifest itself, whether to the effect of aesthetic pleasure or personal destruction. Wertheimer's *Nachlaß*, which the narrator had hoped to find in Wertheimer's house in Traich, in fact no longer exists, the mountains of notes having been purposely incinerated.[46] Bernhard's text fittingly ends with the narrator listening to Gould's recording of the *Goldberg Variations* in Wertheimer's room,[47] the turntable left open just as the reader's questions are left unresolved as to whether this scene

---

44 Bernhard, *Der Untergeher*, 57; *The Loser*, 38.
45 Bernhard, *Der Untergeher*, 132; *The Loser*, 92.
46 Bernhard here returns to the idea of a quasi-Wittgensteinian form of a *Nachlaß* in the form of *Zettel* that he had already used for Roithamer's writings in *Korrektur* (Correction) (1975). Unlike Wertheimer, Gaddis's narrator, of course, hangs on to his heaps of notes rather than destroying them.
47 Bernhard, *Der Untergeher*, 243; *The Loser*, 170.

promises a moment of integration of art with other dimensions of life, as Gould would have it,[48] or simply functions as a marker of Wertheimer's death. It remains open, just as the love feast of mutual, brotherly understanding that *agapē* denotes remains unachieved, agape, in the world of Gaddis's narrator.

In an early imitative approximation of Bernhardian prose, Gaddis faxed a missive to Muriel Oxenberg Murphy, simply entitled "In the Style of Thomas Bernhard," in which he glosses the end of their romantic relationship in the manner of Bernhard's *Das Kalkwerk* (*The Lime Works*).[49] In stylistic terms he is here largely doing what the fax title promises, namely constructing extended paratactic cadences that report the speech either of others (Konrad or Fro) or of the narrator himself. In the years preceding this letter, Gaddis had discovered Bernhard's texts in English translation, and he was sufficiently taken by them to remark to the literary scholar Gregory Comnes that in Bernhard he had found his "Cicero for all further engagements."[50] It is all the more noteworthy, therefore, that the way in which Bernhard's prose is invoked in *Agapē Agape* very much steers clear of the quasi-Ciceronian eloquence of Bernhard's recognizable style. Rather than imitating Bernhard's obsessive deployment of "grammatical structures meant to yoke two entities in a relationship of contrast or identity"[51] and the scrupulous attention to punctuation that goes with it, Gaddis instead transforms his own style—familiar from his previous four novels—which is a quasi-dramatic form of prose writing with frequently unattributed dialogue or speech fragments that the reader must piece together in context. He retains the ceaselessly interrupted cadence of the spoken word in his last text, but there is no clearly identifiable dialogue partner present in the entire novel. Instead, the frequent referential ruptures in the flow of the narrator's prose—as he stops himself, changes direction, or second-guesses himself—stem from an unmarked sliding between speaking and quoting/reading from the stacks of notes by his bedside. The "other" that the narrator is addressing, therefore, is not any determinate figure on the diegetic level but repeatedly nothing but *the other text*. If anticipatory plagiary and forgery are phenomena that

---

48 Glenn Gould, "Forgery and Imitation in the Creative Process," in *The Art of Glenn Gould*, ed. John P. L. Roberts (Toronto: Malcolm Lester Books, 1999), 221.
49 *The Letters of William Gaddis*, 511–13 (Letter of February 17, 1995).
50 Gregory Comnes, "'Unswerving Punctualities of Chance': The Aporetics of Dialogue in William Gaddis," in *Reading William Gaddis*, ed. Brigitte Félix (Orléans: Presses Universitaires d'Orléans, 2007), 56.
51 Douglas Glover, "A Scrupulous Fidelity: Thomas Bernhard's *The Loser*," in *Attack of the Copula Spiders and Other Essays on Writing* (Windsor, ON: Biblioasis, 2012), 147.

undermine the very idea of authorial agency, it seems only appropriate that the decisive *rapprochement* between William Gaddis and his Austrian Cicero Thomas Bernhard should occur not on the level of individual style, but rather on the formal plane. The reinscription of the projects of Bernhard's narrators reveals to Gaddis's reader that wherever and whenever we find ourselves under the influence of a prodrug, hastened by *Torschlußpanik*, hoping to create our own order by imposing meaning on disintegrating forms of experience, we are confronted with the fact that such orders precede us in writing, and have always done so.

Seven   Thomas Bernhard, a Writer for Spain

Heike Scharm

Thomas Bernhard's influence in Spain has been noted by some of the best writers Spain has had to offer, among them the philosopher María Zambrano, who in the 1980s called Bernhard one of the new epic poets of literature, and the cosmopolitan writer Javier Marías, who on several occasions admitted that the Austrian writer shaped the formative stages of his career. Indeed, when we read Marías's first novels we can clearly recognize Thomas Bernhard's presence, as I have shown elsewhere.[1]

But there is more to Thomas Bernhard's presence in Spain in the post-Franco years than a few sporadic admirers. In Wolfram Krömer's study on literary contacts between Spain and Austria in the twentieth century, there is mention of Bernhard's immense popularity in the 1980s.[2] Félix de Azúa, a well-known novelist of the *Transición*, places him among the best writers of Spanish realism. One of the often-cited reasons for Bernhard's popularity among readers and writers of those years is Bernhard's strong criticism of the lack of dealing with the historical past in Austria, something clearly reflected in his work, and which would resonate in the generation of the Spanish *Desencanto*, the years following the transition to democracy.

Despite the noted importance of Bernhard for the post-Franco literary scene, there is a lack of studies detailing his presence in the Spanish literary tradition, beyond the impact he had on the formative years of

---

1   Heike Scharm, "Rostros y trastornos: Marías, Bernhard y el género de la confesión," *Ínsula* 785–86 (May 2012), 20–23.
2   Patricia Cifre Wibrow, "Warum fand Thomas Bernhard im Spanien der achtziger Jahre so viele Leser?" *Spanien und Österreich im 20. Jahrhundert. Direkte und indirekte Kontakte,* ed. Wolfgang Krömer (Salzburg: Verlag Mueller-Speiser, 2002), 149–66.

the Spanish writers (the "Nuevos narradores"). Therefore, in this chapter I not only will focus on Thomas Bernhard's actual presence in Spanish literature from the 1980s on, but also would like to propose that there is a certain "Spanishness" to Bernhard's work itself, which invites us, at least hypothetically, to place him into a Spanish literary tradition. Whereas Stephen Dowden, in his *Understanding Thomas Bernhard*, aims to "sketch out for the American audience a picture of Thomas Bernhard and his works from the perspective of his Austrian context,"[3] my aim here is to sketch out a picture of Thomas Bernhard, albeit in a much reduced and simplified manner, as painted by his Spanish readership "through the lens of [Austrian Spanish] history and cultural assumptions," tying him first and foremost to the particularities of Spanish realism, and especially to the generation of '98.

In 1978, thanks to Javier Marías's insistence—and against professional evaluators of the publishing press Alfaguara—Bernhard's *Verstörung*, or *Gargoyles*, translated in Spain as *Trastorno*, hit the Spanish market in 1978. Marías's generation of new writers, who desperately were looking outside of Spain for models to renovate what they, the "Novísimos" or *Nuevos narradores*, considered an outdated, stale, inward-looking literature, promoted Bernhard's writing against all odds, despite his first sluggish sales on the mainstream market. As I have explained elsewhere,[4] one of Marías's first novels, *El siglo* (1983), considered a foundational work of his own successful writing career, was heavily inspired by Bernhard's *Gargoyles*.

Indeed, echoes of Bernhard's musical style and idiosyncrasies, as well as overt synchronicities of both writers, accompany all of Marías's novels in different degrees. Despite the popularity of Bernhard's works among the generation of the Novísimos, however, the Austrian novelist could not connect with the general Spanish readership until the mid-1980s. Patricia Cifre Wibrow explains Bernhard's delayed success in Spain with the later publication of Bernhard's autobiographically inspired works in the mid-1980s. Not only were works such as *Der Keller* or *Das Kalkwerk* shorter and much less difficult to read than his previously published novels in Spain, they also happened to appear on the Spanish market at the height of the *Desencanto*, the disenchantment with democracy. Less than a decade after Franco's death, a national sentiment of depression was widespread and growing, as the promises and hopes of a new Spain gave way to a reality that, to many, did not seem all that different from the Franco years. Readers were able to identify with Bernhard's narrators,

---

3   Stephen D. Dowden, *Understanding Thomas Bernhard* (Columbia: University of South Carolina Press, 1991), xii.
4   Scharm, "Rostros y trastornos," 20–23.

their criticism of institutions, of national politics, patriotism, and so on, as well as with the deep-rooted Bernhardian skepticism bordering on nihilism, and with some of his characters' complete loss of faith in the project of modernity, all of which began to set the tone in the cultural and sociopolitical areas of Spanish life. Cifre Wibrow writes that:

> Das zunehmende Interesse, das sich sowohl aus den ansteigenden Verkaufszahlen also auch aus der sich stets vermehrenden Anzahl der Pressereaktionen entnehmen lässt, könnte ein Hinweiss darauf sein, dass das Spanische Publikum damals began, die Anschuldigungen, die Bernhard in seinen Texten gegen Österreich richtete, auf die Spanische Situation zu beziehen. Vor allem Bernhard's Angriffe auf die Demokratie, auf die Parteien im allgemeinen und die Verworfenheit der politischen und kulturellen Elite insbesondere dürften die spanische Leserschaft von 1984 nicht mehr so unbeteiligt lassen wie sechs jahre zuvor.[5]

> (The rising interest [in Bernhard] that became noticeable thanks to the increase in sales and commentaries in the press, could have been an indication that the Spanish readership began to appropriate the accusations against Austria from Bernhard's works and applied them to the situation in Spain. Especially Bernhard's attacks on democracy, on the political parties in general, and on the corruption of the political and cultural elite would not have left the Spanish readership of 1984 as indifferent as it did six years earlier.)[6]

It is not my intention here to "prove" that Thomas Bernhard was a Spanish writer. Besides being an absurd and pointless proposal, my contributions to literary criticism have consistently aimed to reach beyond conceptual boundaries of the national imaginary. Rather, my intention here is to show why and how a Spanish reader of the post-Franco years would have felt such an attraction for Thomas Bernhard's writing, not necessarily because he was different from Spanish writers, but rather because his voice rang all too familiar. Nevertheless, I certainly do agree with the arguments presented by his critics in Spain. In the 1980s, Bernhard's translated works published in Spain would have attracted the generation of new writers such as the Novísimos or *nuevos narradores*, including Marías, Azúa, and Foix, among others, who were searching for literary models outside Spain in a conscious effort to break with

---

5 Wibrow, "Warum fand Thomas Bernhard im Spanien der achtziger Jahre so viele Leser?", 149–66, here 153.
6 Unless otherwise indicated, all translations in this chapter are my own.

tradition and to escape what they conceived to be the cultural and political provincialism dominating Spanish literary production well into and beyond the later Franco years. Second, it is also likely that Bernhard's autobiographically inspired works translated into Spanish in the mid-1980s would have attracted a broader readership, as they were shorter and more accessible to the public. And, finally, it is also accurate to assume that Bernhard's overall tone and critical attitude toward Austrian institutions—in his mind eternally tied to Nazism—echoed the distrust and disillusionment that shaped the Spanish *Transición*. Thus, Patricia Cifre Wibrow answers her question as to "why Thomas Bernhard found so many readers at the beginning of the 1980s in Spain" by pointing to parallels between Spanish and Austrian political and cultural circumstances, in particular the fact that, according to Bernhard, Austria never experienced a break with—or healthy transition from—Nazism. Indeed, this lack of transition from dictatorship to democracy—and the consequent national and cultural disenchantment—would have been quite familiar to the Spanish readership of the 1980s, as Miguel Sáenz and others also have pointed out.[7] Nevertheless, we can add to this empirical familiarity a perceivable Spanishness very much present in Bernhard's writing.

Taking a closer look at the similarities and parallelisms between Thomas Bernhard's narrative voices, characters, themes, and attitudes, and those of other well-known Spanish novelists, including those who do not admit to or could not have had a direct Bernhardian influence in their works, we may understand the "Bernhard Fieber" in Spain. Spanish readers are drawn to Bernhard's tone, his dark humor, his obsession with death and suicide, his nihilism, his anarchistic tendencies, his complete distrust of authority, and his love-hate relationship with his country; apart from otherness, in all those aspects mentioned, Bernhard is all too familiar to them. Thanks to Miguel Sáenz, his main translator, the prosody, intonation, and overall syntax of his particular style of writing—long and short strings of intercalated chains of phrases—only gain in musicality when transported into a syllable-timed language such as Spanish, while also providing the market with a much needed literary innovation.

As I have mentioned, Spanish novels such as those by Javier Marías, for example, owe much to Thomas Bernhard's writing, in content as well as form. But in addition to Bernhard's Spanish contemporaries, readers of *Frost* could certainly recognize similarities with works from earlier generations of Spanish writers, such as Baroja's *Tree of Knowledge* (1911). Or, readers of Valle-Inclán's *Bohemian Lights* would be especially

---

7   Miguel Sáenz, *Thomas Bernhard: una biografía* (Madrid: Siruela, 1996), 184.

receptive to Bernhard's particular grotesque humor, so akin to Valle's *esperpento*. Thomas Bernhard's literary voices resonate in Spanish literature, and vice versa, in his contemporaries as much as in prior generations. At the same time, of course, there are noted differences. Thomas Bernhard is not a Spanish writer. However, readers tend to assimilate what they read to their own contexts and, less familiar with Austrian or German idiosyncrasies, would not necessarily detect those differences as otherness. Rather, they accept Bernhard as one of their own, based on their ability to recognize and at times even identify with what they deem familiar situations, characters, observations, and reflections presented in his works.

Félix de Azúa—a contemporary of Javier Marías and also one of the *nuevos narradores*—calls Bernhard's literature the most realist he has read. Azúa proposes that Bernhard writes for those who are damaged, "para lesionados, para inválidos, para quienes sufrieron la amputación de una sección interesante del espíritu" (for the wounded, for the handicapped, for those who suffered an amputation of a special part of their spirit).[8] The spiritual or mental damage, in Bernhard's case, would refer, of course, to the consequences of Nazism and Catholicism; for the non-Francoist, nonreligious Spaniard, the same could be said after decades under the rule of Catholic fascism. Azúa appreciates Bernhard, because (among other qualities) he is one of the writers who best describes the situation in Spain in the mid-1980s, a time of transition that began to look a lot more like a continuation of—rather than a break with—the totalitarian dynamics of the Franco years. He writes this commentary in 1986 after reading a series of recently published works by Bernhard in Spain, among them *Frost*.[9] Azúa goes as far as to propose that Miguel Sáenz, rather than being the Spanish translator of Thomas Bernhard's works, must be the original author, and Bernhard his Austrian translator (137).

Miguel Sáenz is not only the main translator of Bernhard in Spain, he also wrote an excellent biography of the author who would provide him with his life's work. Perhaps there is no better way to understand how Bernhard was assimilated into Spanish letters than through an account of his life as seen through the eyes—and the filter—of the Spaniard most familiar with his work. Every chapter of the biography features the epigraph of a Spanish writer before addressing a particular theme in Bernhard's life. Sáenz includes authors ranging from the Middle Ages to the Baroque, from the *Ilustración* to romanticism, to the generation of 1927 (cosmopolitan and avantgarde) whose verses resonate

---

8   Félix de Azúa, *Lecturas compulsivas* (Barcelona: Anagrama, 1998), 132.
9   de Azúa, *Lecturas compulsivas*, 134.

in Bernhard's life and frame his work—visually, conceptually, and artistically—with a Spanish literary context. Sáenz also agrees with other critics who stipulate that Bernhard's success in the 1980s in Spain is the result of the similarities between Austrian and Spanish history, such as the never-ending presence of fascism and fervent Catholicism, even in times of democracy. However, Sáenz adds his own interpretation, which is worth citing in its entirety:

> Para mí (dejando aparte las fuerzas imprevisibles y caóticas que mueven el mundo editorial, las reacciones del lector), la razón principal puede ser que Bernhard, como ha dicho Maria Fialik, fue un "anarquista conservador" (no un "artista aristocrático," como pretendía Hilde Spiel) …, lo que quizá definiría muy bien al español de los últimos decenios. A ello hay que añadir, sin lugar a dudas, que Bernhard es un escritor con un mundo y un estilo absolutamente únicos. ¿Qué más se puede pedir? Bernhard en España … Una feliz historia de amor correspondido.[10]
>
> (For me [aside the unforeseeable and chaotic forces that move the editorial market, meaning, the reactions of the reader], the main reason could be that Bernhard, as Maria Fialik said, was a "conservative anarchist" [not an "aristocratic artist," as Hilde Spiel proposed] …, which perhaps could define very well the Spaniard of the last decades. To this we must add, without a doubt, that Bernhard is a writer with a completely unique world and style. What else could one ask for? Bernhard in Spain … A happy and requited love story.)

And a happy and requited love story it was indeed. While Bernhard's love-hate relationship with Austria motivated much of his writing, Spain offered him a haven where he felt physically better and was able to write undisturbed. His biographer writes that his favorite hotel was the Ritz in Madrid, and his favorite city was Palma de Mallorca. His last trip, two months before his death, was to Gibraltar. When Krista Fleischmann asked him in one of his interviews about Mallorca, Bernhard replies that "Wenn's mir in Österreich den Hals zuschnürt, dann fahr' ich halt da herunter, und das ist ideal" (When I feel like I can't breathe in Austria, then I come down here, and it is ideal).[11] He later explains his attraction to Spanish culture through music, his first passion: "Italien ist wie eine leichte Rossini-Oper, und Spanien ist wie

---

10 Sáenz, *Thomas Bernhard: una biografía*, 184.
11 Krista Fleischmann, *Thomas Bernhard, eine Begegnung: Gespräche mit Krista Fleischmann* (Vienna: Edition S. Verlag der Österreichischen Staatsdruckerei, 1991), 12.

ein Händel'sches Oratorium. Ich habe Oratorien immer lieber gehabt als spritzige Opern. Die waren mir immer zu blöd" (Italy is like a light opera by Rossini, and Spain is like an oratorio by Händel. I have always preferred oratorios to fizzy operas. To me, they were always too silly).[12]

But interviews aside, what better declaration of his love for Spain than his fiction? The main character of *Der Untergeher* (translated into Spanish as *El malogrado, The Ill-Fated*, in my opinion a more fitting translation than the English, *The Loser*) lives in the center of Madrid, close to the Prado museum, the museum of Bernhard's favorite painters, Goya and Velázquez. Throughout the novel, the narrator includes comparisons between his home country and his chosen home, Spain. He calls Austria "stumpfsinniges Land" and Vienna a "stumpfsinnige Stadt" (a land and a city that dull the senses and destroy the soul), adding that without the opportunity to emigrate to Spain, a decision he never once regretted, he wouldn't have survived long.[13] One of his former friends, Wertheimer (his last name, ironically, is a compound of "worth" and "home"), commits suicide in his native country. According to the narrator, had Wertheimer also moved to Spain instead of staying in Austria, he might not have taken his own life:

> Daß es meine Rettung gewesen ist, aus Wien sozusagen auch engültig wegzugehen und gerade nach Madrid, das mir zum idealen Existenzmittelpunkt geworden ist, nicht erst mit der Zeit, sondern vom ersten Augenblick an, dachte ich. In Wien wäre ich nach und nach aufgefressen worden, wie Wertheimer immer gesagt hat, von den Wienern erstickt und von den Österreichern überhaupt vernichtet worden. Alles in mir ist so, daß es in Wien ersticken und in Österreich vernichtet werden muß, dachte ich, wie auch Wertheimer dachte [...] Aber Wertheimer war nicht der Mensch, über Nacht nach Madrid zu gehen [...].[14]

> (That it was my salvation, to leave Vienna for good and to go to Madrid, which became the center of my existence, right from the first moment on and not just with time, I thought. In Vienna I would have been slowly devoured, as Wertheimer also always said, suffocated by the people of Vienna and destroyed by the Austrians. Everything in me is such that it would have to suffocate in Vienna and be destroyed in Austria, I thought, and that is also what Wertheimer thought [...] But Wertheimer was not the type of person who would just take off overnight to Madrid [...].)

---

12 Fleischmann, *Thomas Bernhard, eine Begegnung*, 264.
13 Thomas Bernhard, *Der Untergeher* (Frankfurt: Suhrkamp Verlag, 1983), 114.
14 Bernhard, *Der Untergeher*, 59–60.

Whereas he presents Spain as salvation, Austria's dullness and unhealthy climate, as he repeats again later during a visit to his home country, drives one insane or to commit suicide. Here, Desselbrunn serves as a microcosm of the nation:

> Aber die Hälfte aller Leute bringen sich hier um, früher oder später, geht nicht von selbst zugrunde, wie gesagt wird. Hat nichts anderes als ihren Katholizismus oder die socialistische Partei, beides die widerlichsten Einrichtungen unserer Zeit. In Madrid gehe ich wenigstens einmal im Tag aus dem Haus, um zu essen, dachte ich, hier wäre ich nie aus dem Haus gegangen in meinem fortschreitenden rettungslosen Verwahrlosungsprozess.[15]
>
> (But half of the people here kill themselves, sooner or later, they don't perish on their own, like they say. They don't have anything but their Catholicism or the socialist party, both the most disgusting institutions of our time. In Madrid I go out at least once a day to eat, I thought, here I would never leave the house in my continuing hopeless state of deterioration.)

It goes without saying that passages like these have earned Bernhard a terrible reputation among many of his fellow Austrians. Some refer to him as the most choleric writer of the twentieth century.[16] Others describe his narrators as "narcissistic, and hopelessly self-absorbed individuals preoccupied with their 'fatal' illnesses, their futile intellectual projects, or their own suicide."[17] However, neither the tone, nor the pessimism, nor the severe criticism of his home country would be shocking or off-putting to a Spanish readership.

Dowden summarizes Bernhard's approach to literature in a way that comes close to the Spanish literary tradition, especially to the generation of '98 or even of the Spanish realists of the mid-twentieth century. Thomas Bernhard, he writes, "takes malicious delight in unmasking the weaknesses and self-deceptions of his countrymen. But in revealing the 'truth' about Austria, what he really makes visible is the moral grounding of his pessimism about human nature, about history, and even about art itself."[18] In what follows in his *Understanding Thomas Bernhard*, Dowden explains the philosophical undertones in Bernhard's works in a way that can also be applied to the Spanish tradition of

---

15 Bernhard, *Der Untergeher*, 122.
16 Carlos Fortea, *Dos cambios de siglo: ensayos sobre literatura alemana traducida* (Bern/New York: Peter Lang, 2009), 105.
17 Joseph Federico, "Heimat, Death, and the Other in Thomas Bernhard's *Frost* and Verstörung," *Modern Austrian Literature* 29, 3/4 (1996), 223–42, here 225.
18 Dowden, *Understanding Thomas Bernhard*, xii.

philosophical writing: not through a system of philosophy but through creative, imaginative writing; not subjected to maintaining consistency or coherence, but welcoming contradictions and incongruities. Indeed, Spanish "philosophical" writers equally refrain from "impartial detachment, systematic analysis, reasoned critique, a unified and coherent message," as Dowden describes Bernhard's works; instead, Bernhard's themes are impassioned. "He deals with them imaginatively, even musically, but never analytically. Indeed, he sets them in a fictional context and explores them unsystematically, if not baldly *anti*systematically."[19]

The particular characteristics of Bernhard's voice, public or as manifest in his fictional or autobiographical works, are very much present among prior generations of Spanish writers, not just the *Novísimos* of the Spanish Transition. When reading Bernhard's prose in Spanish translation, one cannot shake off the feeling that he must be a contemporary of Pío Baroja or Ramón María Valle-Inclán, members of the generation of '98, who reacted to another low in national sentiment in Spain in the first decades of the twentieth century. Following the loss of the last colonies, Spain's self-image turned from national empire to national disaster. Despite their differences in style, the Spanish writers of that generation shared many of the defining characteristics of Bernhard's writing: a permeating abulia, a kind of national *Verstörung* of spirit and mind leading to apathy. The origins of abulia in literature, as Donald Shaw reminds us, can be found in Europe in the postromantic era, before it is fully incorporated into fiction in Spain. Philippe Chardin describes abulia in a way that we can clearly recognize in works such as *Gargoyles* or *Frost*, just to mention two examples of Bernhard's novels: "la tentation du nihilisme sur le plan psychologique (schoppenhauérienne) de l'inertie, de l'aboulie, de l'abolition du vouloir-vivre, voire du suicide, qui guette à un moment ou à un autre" (the temptation to nihilism in a psychological [Schopenhauerian] way of inertia, of abulia, of the loss of will to live, even suicide, which comes up at any moment), or "une sorte de mort dans la vie" (a kind of death in life).[20] Rather than an individualistic, romantic *spleen* or *Weltschmerz*, however, abulia indicates a cultural and spiritual crisis deeply and closely tied to the disenchantment with fatherland and, as such, a particular Spanish way of writing, which seems even closer to Bernhard's writing than to his Spanish contemporaries of the 1980s. This appears especially true in the case of Pío Baroja, with whom he shares an affinity for anarchistic ideologies and characters who impersonate the sentiment of abulia.

---

19 Dowden, *Understanding Thomas Bernhard*, xiii.
20 Donald L. Shaw, "More about abulia," *Anales de la literatura española contemporánea* 23, 1/2 (1998), 451–64, here 457–58. He quotes Philippe Chardin, *Le roman de la conscience malheureuse* (Geneva: Droz, 1982), 41.

When we go back to the beginning of the twentieth century, the years of the generation of '98, we notice striking similarities between the cultural and sociopolitical climates that shape both Vienna and Madrid. Helga Stipa Madland relates the *Untergangsstimmung* (a widespread presentiment of apocalypse) in Vienna with the "discouragement and despair masked as frivolity and the pursuit of pleasure" in Madrid at the time. She also notes that "the Habsburgs ruled both Austria and Spain for some two hundred years," and that "the Spanish and Austrian nobility were closely inter-related."[21] Furthermore, even though Baroja wrote more than half a century before Bernhard's novels entered the Spanish market, he was long praised as a precursor, and, many generations later, he would still be valued as a modern writer due to his capacity to address Spain's national maladies. José Ortega y Gasset, perhaps the most important philosopher and intellectual of the 1920s, for example, predicted correctly that "dentro de cincuenta años, los libros de Baroja tendrán principalmente valor de síntomas nacionales" (fifty years from now, Baroja's novels will foremost have value as national symptoms).[22]

The close cultural ties and historical similarities between the two former empires could explain the affinity between Baroja and Bernhard, and also why the Spanish readership would read Bernhard as one of their own, as a "Spanish" writer. In addition, both writers are fervently "anti-system" and express a strikingly conflicted attitude toward their home countries. Their main characters display a deep-rooted mistrust in institutions, revere Nietzsche and Schopenhauer, and exhibit clear misanthropic tendencies. Even their renowned pessimism and particular humor appear to be cut from the same cloth. A case in point may be José María Calles's brief description of Baroja's work, equally applicable to Bernhard's writing: "Tras la visión de Baroja aflora la nada existencial, el nihilismo que apunta hacia una vida sin objeto […]. La modernidad de Baroja radica, entre otros aspectos, en la singular pregunta sobre el sentido de la vida que trasluce la sospecha, como en los últimos realistas europeos, de un mundo absurdo" (In Baroja's vision an existential nothingness shines through, a nihilism that points to a life without objective […]. Baroja's modernity is shaped by, among other aspects, the singular question of the meaning of life, all the while suspecting, just like the last European realists did, the absurdity of existence).[23]

---

21 Helga Stipa Madland, "Baroja's 'Camino de perfectión' and Schnitzler's 'Leutnant Gustl': Fin de Siècle Madrid and Vienna Author(s)," *Comparative Literature Studies* 21, 3 (Fall 1984), 306–22, here 307.
22 Cited in Juan María Calles, "Hablando de libros: foros de literatura," *Biblioteca valenciana* (2003), 10–11, here 11.
23 Calles, "Hablando de libros," 11.

Given Bernhard's affinity with Spanish writers in areas such as thought, attitude, politics, even humor, the differences in their literary style—Baroja prefers shorter sentences and a more sober syntax, although he has also compared the act of writing with making music—would only satisfy the Spanish market's need for innovation without compromising the sense of familiarity. Whereas Bernhard had the reputation of being the most choleric writer of his century, Pío Baroja was well known as el *cascarrabias vasco*, the Basque grouch, who shocked his contemporaries with Bernhardian-sounding misanthropic beliefs, such as his proclamation that friendships were merely a measure of stupidity. In his *Hojas sueltas*, Baroja wrote that "Sólo los tontos tienen muchas amistades. El mayor número de amigos marca el grado máximo en el dinamómetro de la estupidez" (Only stupid people have a lot of friendships. The biggest number of friends indicates the highest level on the stupidity meter).[24] Similarly, when Bernhard talks about his stays in Spain, he admits not knowing the language. Instead of suffering from linguistic isolation, he valued not being able to communicate as one of the perks of living in Spain. He enjoyed watching TV *because* he could not understand what was said, and he enjoyed listening to the Spaniards in the streets, in bars, because he could then imagine that every show would be intellectual, and every conversation deeply philosophical.[25]

In order to illustrate Bernhard's affinity with Spanish realism and in particular the Spanish realism of the generation of '98, let us now look at some specific passages from his fictional works and compare them with Baroja's well-known novel *El árbol de la ciencia* (*The Tree of Knowledge*, 1911). I am hoping to show to what extent Bernhardian reflections and observations are echoed in Spanish realism. *Helada*, Miguel Sáenz's impressive translation of *Frost*, is still among Bernhard's most mentioned novels in Spain. In one of the first obituaries published in Spain, *Frost*, *Gargoyles*, and *The Cellar* were listed as the most recognizable of Bernhard's works.[26] *Frost* was published in the mid 1980s in Spain, six years after *Gargoyles* and around the same time as his autobiographical works entered the Spanish market. As mentioned earlier, these were the years when the Bernhard fever began to spread.

Frost is written as a medical student's diary, comprising twenty-seven days, during which the narrator documents his walks through the Austrian countryside with the ageing painter Strauch, mostly taking on the role of the listener. Strauch's voice dominates the men's conversations

---

24 Pío Baroja, *Hojas sueltas* (Madrid: Editorial Caro Raggio, 1973), 283.
25 Fleischmann, *Thomas Bernhard, eine Begegnung*, 33.
26 https://elpais.com/diario/1989/02/17/cultura/603673201_850215.html

and, as such, forms the main part of the novel, which is only sparingly interrupted or complemented by the student's comments and observations. Baroja would have approved of Bernhard's choice to frame several of his novels as a series of one-sided conversations among walking companions. As a matter of fact, Baroja defines the novel, freely citing from Stendhal's *Le rouge et le noir*, as a mirror someone takes along on a walk, even adding that "No es otra cosa cuando vale algo" (it is nothing else when it merits something).[27] Baroja frames some chapters of *Tree of Knowledge* as conversations among the main characters, which allows him to bring in different viewpoints and to contrast opposing ideas on politics, philosophy, thought, art, or life.

Whereas Bernhard focuses on Strauch, Baroja places the younger Andrés Hurtado in the center of his novel. The similarities between both characters are indeed striking, although not as much as equals, but rather as a hypothetical continuation of one and the same character who would mature over the years. The last line of the novel, when Andrés' body is discovered, reads "había en él algo de precursor" (there was something of a predecessor in him).[28] This, of course, brings to mind again Ortega y Gasset's verdict of Baroja as a writer for a future time in Spain (which essentially is Bernhard's time). However, from a literary perspective, one could indeed imagine a younger Strauch in Andrés, as much as an older version of Andrés in Strauch, had the latter not committed suicide when he was young. At least hypothetically, this would allow us to read *The Tree of Knowledge* as an unwritten, imagined bildungsroman of Bernhard's older, disillusioned, and misanthropic characters.

The settings of both novels could not be any more different than the wintery scenery of the Austrian valley Weng and the hot, dry, desolate Southern region of La Mancha, the same area that was home to Don Quixote. However, both writers use the description of their setting as an amplifier of concepts, rather than crafting a realist and region-specific portrait. As Bernhard himself explained, he avoids all realist description of landscapes in his novels, but rather creates them as reflections of ideas and attitudes toward the home country:

> Ich schreibe immer nur über innere Landschaften, und die sehen die meisten Leut' nicht, weil sie innen fast nix sehen. […] Ich glaub' ich hab' überhaupt noch in keinem Buch eine

---

27 Quoted in Domingo Ynduráin, "Teoría de la novela en Baroja," *Biblioteca virtual Miguel de Cervantes*. http://www.cervantesvirtual.com/obra-visor/teoria-de-la-novela-en-baroja/html/f86dccec-a101-11e1-b1fb-00163ebf5e63_5.html#I_0_
28 Pío Baroja, *El árbol de la ciencia* (Madrid: Alianza editorial, Biblioteca Baroja, 2008), 255.

Landschaft beschrieben. Das gibt's nämlich gar net. Ich schreib' immer nur Begriffe, und da heißt's immer Berge oder eine Stadt oder Strassen, aber wie die ausschauen—ich hab nie eine Landschaftsbeschreibung gemacht. Das hat mich nie interessiert.[29]

(I always only write about inner landscapes, the ones most people don't see, because they tend to see hardly anything on the inside. [...] I think I've never described a landscape in any of my books. They don't exist. I only write concepts, and it might say mountain or a town or streets, but how they look—I've never described landscapes. That never interested me.)

This lack of regional specificity and the use of scenery as a reflection of ideas is typical for Spanish realism. Especially the generation of '98 applied a technique called "paisajismo," perhaps freely translatable as literary landscaping. It expresses the idea that these writers do not observe and document the physical reality of their surroundings, but rather they invent and construct it in a way that they believe best reflects an inner, rather than outer state of reality. In *The Tree of Knowledge*, when Andrés spends time in the rural areas, the descriptions of the place and people serve the purpose of amplifying the political and sociocultural maladies of the nation (the village becomes the microcosm of the nation), but also to show how nature destroys the body and corrupts the mind. Nature, and especially the rural landscapes of La Mancha, becomes, for Baroja's generation, a critical representation and almost grotesque manifestation of the ills of the nation. Spanish realism at the time, as Rafael Núñez Florencio so fittingly puts it, "veía el medio físico en general y muy especialmente el español como la imagen especular de un estado de cosas francamente negativo: una tierra pobre, mísera, árida y despoblada venía a ser así la resultante inevitable en el terreno físico de un país decadente, atrasado, fanático y exangüe" (considered the physical environment in general, and especially the Spanish landscape as a mirror image of the negative state of the country: the poor, miserable, dry and depopulated land became the inevitable result, in the physical terrain, of a backwards, fanatical and bloodless decadent nation).[30]

One of the premises of Baroja's novel, as the title implies, is to show the incompatibility between the tree of life and the tree of knowledge, meaning, between science and nature, or better yet, reason and life. Before Andrés Hurtado, now a medical doctor, continues his road to disillusionment during his stay in the countryside, he still believes

---

29 Fleischmann, *Thomas Bernhard, eine Begegnung*, 15
30 Rafael Núñez Florencio, "Naturaleza y ética en Baroja: Mala hierba: el paisaje físico, espejo del paisaje moral," *Pasajes* 37 (Winter 2011–12), 29–39, here 32.

in science and knowledge as an antidote to nature. Surroundings, such as the countryside, represent the destructive, malignant force of nature; brutal and strong, but incompatible with knowledge or culture. In *El caballero de Erláiz* (*The Knight of Erlaíz*, 1943), one of Baroja's later works, he calls life an infectious disease that only sustains itself through the proliferation of germs. The only cure is death or stupidity: "Todo cambia, todo se agota, siempre hay una decadencia en el sentido de la energía, y quizá lo más agotador es la inteligencia; por eso los pueblos más estacionarios son los más fuertes y los más brutos, y los hombres menos inteligentes son los que tienen más seguridad en sí mismos" (Everything changes, everything exhausts itself, there is always decadence, a loss in energy, and perhaps what exhausts itself most is intelligence; therefore, the most stagnant villages are the strongest and the most brutish, and the least intelligent men are the ones most sure of themselves).[31] This resonates in both the description of Alcolea del Campo, the village that appears in *The Tree of Knowledge*, as well as the Austrian valley of Weng that provides the backdrop of *Frost*; both are illustrations of their creators' vision concerning the state of the nation, its backwardness, political divisions, corruption, greed, and stupidity, all represented in the corrupt and dying landscape and its inhospitable climate. The dry air is sickening, "todo el campo parecía quemado, calcinado (all fields seemed burned, calcinated)," to the point where "todo este pueblo, grande, desierto, silencioso, bañado por la sueva claridad de la luna, parecía un inmenso sepulcro" (the entire village, so big, desert-like, quiet, bathed in soft moonlight, seemed an immense tomb).[32] It should be noted that "pueblo," in Spanish, also has the meaning of *Volk* or people, in the sense of nation. Similarly, in *Frost*, Strauch points to "[r]ivers stinking of corruption," "mountains like ridged brains," "emboliefördernde Witterungseinflüsse" (a climate that engenders embolisms), "die Hunde [...] fallen Menschen an" (dogs [...] attacking people), and concludes that "alles ist gänzlich ausgestorben. Keine Bodenschätze, kein Getreide, nichts. [...] Eine verfallene Kirche. Skelette. Spuren von eingedrungendem Wild" (everything has died. No minerals, no crops, nothing. [...] A ruined church. Skeletons. Traces of wild animals).[33] It does not make a difference that the climate in one novel is suffocating and in the other bitter cold; Weng and Alcolea are dead zones that can only perpetuate physical and moral degeneration.

---

31 Quoted in Ynduráin, "Teoría de la novela en Baroja," n.p.
32 Baroja, *El árbol de la ciencia*, 157–58.
33 Thomas Bernhard, *Frost* (Frankfurt am Main: Suhrkamp, 1972), 14–15, followed by English quotes from Michael Hofmann's translation of *Frost* (New York: Alfred A. Knopf, 2006), 11–13.

In both novels the outlandish descriptions of the villagers fall into the grotesque to the point of eliciting laughter. In *The Tree of Knowledge*, Andrés Hurtado compares the men of Alcolea to troglodytes. He observes faces that look like a butcher's, "de aire poco inteligente" (of a less than intelligent appearance), or like a "degenerado, cara juanetuda, las orejas muy separadas de la cabeza y el labio colgante" (degenerate, with protruding facial bones, ears standing far from the head and with a sagging lip).[34] Their cavemen-like appearances are the result of nature: stifling heat, sickly air, lack of hygiene, a diet exclusively made up of meat and alcohol with the occasional toad mistaken as seafood. Since the land is dry, the people abstain from washing, adding stench to their brutishness. The villagers fill Andrés with a hatred, "uno de esos odios profundos, que llegan a dar serenidad al que lo siente; un desprecio épico y altivo" (one of those profound hatreds that end up providing serenity to those who experience it; an arrogant contempt of epic proportions).[35]

In Bernhard's *Frost*, the same arrogant contempt of epic proportions shines through the descriptions of the villagers, who are not any less grotesque. Strauch decries their "hemdsärmelige Stumpsinn" (morons in short sleeves),[36] children are "verschlagen, O-beinig, mit Ansätzen zum Wasserkopf [...] mit großen Händen, flachen Stirnknochen" (cunning, bandy-legged, with a tendency to hydrocephalus [...], with shovel hands, flat low foreheads,"[37] women are promiscuous and STD riddled, infants are dosed with brandy to keep them quiet, and the body parts and blood of slaughtered animals fill the valley. But rather than drifting into the melodramatic tone of Naturalism, the descriptions become an invitation to laughter, as Bernhard's Strauch reminds us: "Und ich bin beim Anblick der auf so grauenhaften Weise zerstückelnden Tiere in Gelächter ausgebrochen, in ungeheures Gelächter. Wissen Sie, was das heißt? Das Fürchterliche muß sein Gelächter haben" (And when I saw the grisly chopped-up animals, I had to burst out laughing. I burst out into extraordinary laughter. Do you know what that means? It means horror demands laughter).[38] Spanish readers would indeed respond well to Bernhard's dark humor, since laughter tied to horror is deeply ingrained in the Spanish literary tradition. Bernhard has often been compared to Kafka, but I would argue that the grotesqueness of his humor far surpasses *The Castle* or *The Metamorphosis*. Bernhard's humor is the result of what he calls his philosophical *Lachprogramm*, a deeply tragic

---

34 Baroja, *El árbol de la ciencia*, 162.
35 Baroja, *El árbol de la ciencia*, 185–86.
36 Bernhard, *Frost*, 153, transl., 165.
37 Bernhard, *Frost*, 69, transl., 73.
38 Bernhard, *Frost*, 278, transl., 302.

and nihilistic view of life as an absurd state, grounded in pessimistic philosophical thought and made bearable only through an aesthetics of laughter. For that reason, Bernhard values Kant and Schopenhauer as "die großen Spaßmacher in der Geschichte [...] Also die Allerernsten im Grund" (the great comedians of history [...] Meaning, the most serious after all).[39] And commenting directly on his own novel, he adds that "Wenn man *Frost* ließt zum Beispiel, ich hab ja immer schon Material zum Lachen geliefert. Das ist eigentlich alle Augenblick' hellauf zum Lachen. Aber ich weiß nicht, haben die Leut' keinen Humor oder was? Ich weiß es nicht. Mich hat's immer zum Lachen gebracht, bringt mich auch heut' noch" (When you read *Frost*, for example, I've always provided comical material. That [novel] constantly makes one laugh out loud. But I don't know, don't people have a sense of humor anymore, or what? I don't know. It always made me laugh, still makes me laugh today).[40] It is this particular grotesque humor that vacillates between repulsion and laughter, that defines the Spanish realism of the twentieth century, from Pío Baroja and his contemporary Valle Inclán to Camilo José Cela some generations later. Just like Bernhard's, Baroja's humor is tied to a deep-rooted pessimism, as Edith Rogers well explains, which comes to the surface in his writing when his characters realize that life is tragic, "pero la tragedia no debe tomarse completamente en serio" (but one should not take tragedy all too seriously).[41] Or, as Shaw puts it, Baroja's humor "is the expression, in artistic terms, of [his] need for relief from the frustration and misery of an existence dominated by metaphysical despair."[42] Other Spanish writers made use of the same literary device. Valle Inclán called it *esperpento*, an aesthetics that places reality in front of a carnival mirror and distorts its reflection in order to reveal a truer reality than what the eye could perceive. Camilo José Cela called it *tremendismo*, the tendency to push horror and violence into the grotesquely comical. Bernhard's humor, thus, would be quite familiar to the Spanish readership, and would be well received, as Javier Marías and Félix de Azúa have shown.

Besides the penchant for the grotesque, the particular humor and the pessimistic view of life and nature, it is perhaps Bernhard's *antisystematic* attitude that most closely associates him with Spanish realism and also Spanish thought in general. From the outset, both *Frost* and *The Tree of Knowledge* criticize institutions such as universities, the medical

---

39 Fleischmann, *Thomas Bernhard, eine Begegnung*, 44.
40 Fleischmann, *Thomas Bernhard, eine Begegnung*, 43.
41 Edith R. Rogers, "Sobre el Pesimismo de Baroja," *Hispania* 45, 4 (Dec., 1962), 671–74, here 672.
42 D. L. Shaw, "A Reply to Deshumanización, Baroja on the Art of the Novel," *Hispanic Review* 25, 2 (Apr., 1957), 105–11, here 110.

profession, education, family, and politics. Both main characters are medical students, and their negative medical experiences inform their philosophy. In both cases, the writers' personal life feeds into their characters' critical observations and attitudes. Pío Baroja studied medicine and worked as a country doctor while writing some of his novels, while the young Thomas Bernhard spent a considerable time in hospitals and sanatoriums due to chronic illnesses. Both novels share their bleak view of the medical profession, especially regarding the dysfunctional administrative and dehumanizing aspects. The first paragraph of *Frost*, Day 1 of the medical student's diary, provides a grotesque summary of what a medical internship does *not just* consist:

> Eine Famulatur besteht ja nicht nur aus dem Zuschauen bei komplizierten Darmoperationen, aus Bauchfellaufschneiden, Lungenflügelzuklammern und Fußabsägen, sie besteht wirklich nicht nur aus Totenaugenzudrücken und aus Kinderherausziehen in die Welt. Eine Famulatur ist nicht nur das: abgesägten ganze und halbe Beine und Arme über die Schulter in den Emailkübel werfen. Auch besteht sie nicht aus dem ständig hinter dem Primarius und dem Assistenten und dem Assistenten des Assistenten Dahertrotteln, aus dem Schwanzdasein der Visite. Aus dem Vorspiegeln falscher Tatsachen allein kann eine Famulatur auch nicht bestehen, nicht aus dem, daß ich sage: »Der Eiter wird sich ganz einfach in Ihrem Blut auflösen, und Sie sind wieder gesund.« Und aus hunderterlei anderen Lügen. Nicht nur daraus, daß ich sage: »Es wird schon!« – wo nichts mehr wird. Eine Famulatur ist ja nicht nur eine Lehrstelle für Aufschneiden und Zunähen, für Abbinden und Aushalten.
>
> (A medical internship consists of more than spectating at complicated bowel operations, cutting open stomach linings, bracketing off lungs, and sawing off feet; and it doesn't just consist of thumbing closed the eyes of the dead, and hauling babies out into the world either. An internship is not just tossing limbs over your shoulder into an enamel bucket. Nor does it just consist of trotting along behind the registrar and the assistant and the assistant's assistant, a sort of tail-end Charlie. Nor can an internship be only the putting out of false information; it isn't just saying: "The pus will dissolve in your bloodstream, and you'll soon be restored to perfect health." Or a hundred other such lies. Not just: "It'll get better"—when nothing will. An internship isn't just an academy of scissors and thread, of tying off and pulling through.)[43]

---

43 Bernhard, *Frost*, 7, transl., 3.

The blatant irony and meticulous descriptions of all "flesh-related" medical procedures, of course, only subvert the negated into the solely affirmed, as the medical student denounces the dehumanization of the sick and dying, hints to the futility of medical science, as well as to the hypocrisy and corruption of medicine as an institution.

Equally, as a student, Andrés describes the dehumanizing and grotesque treatment of patients and those who had died. He observes his fellow students desecrating cadavers or playing pranks with their severed body parts. He sees workers dragging the dead to and then away from the dissecting tables, describing in detail the banging of their heads against the staircases or the rattling of their mummified bodies.[44] He remembers "cómo metían todos los pedazos sobrantes en unas calderas cilíndricas pintadas de rojo, en donde aparecía una mano entre un hígado, y un trozo de masa encefálica, y un ojo opaco y turbio en medio del tejido pulmonar" (how all the leftovers were dumped into some red-painted cylindrical boilers, where one could spot a hand between a liver and a chunk of encephalic matter, or a cloudy opaque eye woven into a piece of lung).[45] Reminiscent of the poorhouse described in *Frost*, the dehumanizing treatment of patients continues at the women's hospital, which Andrés calls an "estercolero humano,"[46] a pile of human manure, kept in "un edificio inmundo, sucio, mal oliente" (a filthy, dirty, reeking building), with barred up windows where "no entraba [...] el sol ni el aire" (no sun, no air could enter).[47] These descriptions would resonate in Strauch's memories of "Zimmer mit der Luft von Gestorbenen [...] Betten, die, aufgeschlagen, den Geruch der Toten ausatmen" (rooms full of air of dead people. Beds that, turned back, reek of death)[48] when he was hospitalized as a child. In both literary worlds, doctors are sadistic, cruel, and incompetent, professors are stagnant, arrogant, and greedy, and all are tied to the shortcomings of the nation. Andrés's uncle explains to him the dreadful state of education as something "natural," because "[e]l español todavía no sabe enseñar; es demasiado fanático, demasiado vago y casi siempre demasiado farsante" (the Spaniards still don't know how to teach; they are too fanatical, too lazy, and too much of a fraud).[49]

The misery Andrés witnesses opens him up to Schopenhauer. He accepts the German philosopher as "una verdad casí matemática" (an almost mathematical truth) and begins to understand the world as "una mezcla de manicomio y de hospital" (a mix of insane asylum and

---

44 Baroja, *El árbol de la ciencia*, 27.
45 Baroja, *El árbol de la ciencia*, 27.
46 Baroja, *El árbol de la ciencia*, 49
47 Baroja, *El árbol de la ciencia*, 50.
48 Bernhard, *Frost*, 69, transl., 73.
49 Baroja, *El árbol de la ciencia*, 126.

hospital).⁵⁰ The consequences of his experiences, the death of his little brother from tuberculosis, the death of his wife and child during childbirth, the disillusionment with knowledge and science, the absence of all hope due to a stagnant and deeply corrupt country, all push him further and further into nihilism and toward suicide. In Baroja's novelistic world, nature is bloody and infectious. Science and knowledge are powerless. Families are abusive and divided. The nation, human nature, are corrupt. Physical love leads to venereal diseases, spiritual love leads to abandonment and suffering. The only means to happiness are stupidity and egotism; the only response to horror, laughter.

When Strauch suggests that "Die Natur ist grausam" (nature is bloody) or that "das Primitive ist Allgemeingut" (the primitive is everywhere), that "das Geschlechtliche ist es, das alle umbringt. Das Geschlechtliche, die Krankheit, die von Natura us abtötet" (sex is what does it for them all, Sex, the disease that kills by its nature),⁵¹ he echoes Spanish realism. Strauch is an older version of Andrés, had he decided to continue his life after realizing that knowledge—which he first thought could be the solution to a life devoid of meaning—is as much as a farce as morals, religion, or love. Just like Strauch, Andrés would have told his companion that "dieser Kopf, müssen Sie wissen, ist unfähig. In seiner Mitte glüht ein noch unbeholfener Erdball, und alles ist voller zerissener Harmonien!" (this head, you see, is useless. At the center of it there is a crude glowing planet, and everything else is full of fractured harmonies!).⁵² And Andrés could have just as easily pronounced Strauch's words just before taking his life, had he been in the company of somebody willing to listen:

> [...] sehen Sie, wie aus den Religionen und aus den A-Religionen und aus den in die Länge gezogenen Lächerlichkeiten aller Gottesanschauungen nichts geworden ist, gar nichts, sehen Sie, wie der Glaube, sowie der Unglaube nicht mehr da sind, wie die Wissenschaft, die heutige Wissenschaft, wie der Stein des Anstoßes, das jahrtausendealte Vorgericht, alles hinausgeworfen und hinauskomplimentiert und hinausgeblasen hat in die Luft, wie alles jetzt Luft ist ... Hören Sie: alles ist nur mehr Luft, alle Begriffe sind Luft, alle Anhaltspunkte sind Luft, alles ist nur mehr Luft ...
>
> ([...] all the religions and the irreligions and the protracted absurdities of all forms of worship have turned into nothing, nothing at all, you see, how belief and unbelief no longer exist,

---

50 Baroja, *El árbol de la ciencia*, 49.
51 Bernhard, *Frost*, 17, transl., 15–16.
52 Bernhard, *Frost*, 43, transl., 43.

how science, modern science, how the stumbling blocks, the millennial courts, have all been thrown out and ushered out and blown out into the air, how all of it is now just so much air ... Listen, it's all air, all points of reference are air, everything is just air.)[53]

Strauch ends his life on his own terms, just as Andrés did, only decades later. Alone, removed from society, he realizes that "das Leben ist reine, klarste, dunkelste, kristallinische Hoffnungslosigkeit" (life is the purest, clearest, darkest, most crystalline form of hopelessness), and that "dahinein führt nur ein Weg durch Schnee und Eis in Menschenverzweiflung, dahineine, wo man hineingehen muß; über den Ehebruch des Verstandes" (there is only one way to go, through the snow and ice into despair; past the adultery of reason).[54] Strauch continued living, although, as he admits, it is an empty life, since

> meine Zeit ist vergangen, so wie eine Zeit vergeht, die man nicht haben will. Ja, ich habe meine Zeit nie haben wollen [... Ich] sah langsam alles Erdachte falsch werden, wertlos werden, alles wurde nacheinander, folgerichtig, wissen Sie, sinn- und zwecklos ... Und ich entdeckte, daß die Umgebung nicht haben will, daß man sie aufklärt" (my time has passed as if I didn't want it. I didn't want it. [...] I saw all thought become impossible, worthless, everything successively, logically, became pointless and meaningless ... And I discovered that my surroundings didn't want to be explained by me).[55]

Thomas Bernhard's universe, his characters and observations, would ring all too familiar to a Spanish readership. At the same time, the content and distinct literary style of his novels would appeal to a readership not only deeply critical of their nation, but also yearning for artistic innovation. It is not without irony that Bernhard saw Spain as a counterpart to Austria, almost like an idealized utopian haven made up of fresh ocean breezes, palm trees, and good coffee,[56] while the Spanish readers he attracted valued his novels in part *because* they were able to superimpose the Spanish reality onto his fervent criticism of Austria. Thomas Bernhard was not a Spanish writer. However, meshed deeply into the Spanish literary tradition and mindset, he was—and continues to be—a writer *for* Spain.

---

53 Bernhard, *Frost*, 152–53, transl., 164–65.
54 Bernhard, *Frost*, 295, transl., 320.
55 Bernhard, *Frost*, 28, transl., 27.
56 Fleischmann, *Thomas Bernhard, eine Begegnung*, 37.

Eight   Immersions into Bernhard's Works in Recent Francophone Literature

Olaf Berwald

How do contemporary Francophone writers emulate, incorporate, and temporarily disappear into Bernhard's oeuvre? What narrative approaches, from agonistic appropriations to rehearsals of sympoetic communion through porous textual boundaries, are at play?[1] A brief etymological glance at the term "reception" reminds us of its fertile ambiguity: a *receptor, receptrix* is a dealer in stolen goods or "fence"; *receptio* denotes admission, inclusion, or absorption; *receptus* refers to *a* retreat or recourse; and *recipere* means to save, liberate, expose oneself, to suffer, to offer shelter.

While Tim Parks points out in his book-length essay, *The Novel: A Survival Skill* (2015), that "many writers have succumbed for years to Bernhard's influence to the point of offering stories of their own that feel like mechanical reproductions of Bernhard's rhetoric and vision,"[2] none of the texts that I will briefly discuss in this essay are reducible to being mere vessels of Bernhardian topoi and rhetorical techniques. They are not mere stylistic variations on Bernhard or self-perpetuating exercises in intertextual cloning. They rather perform the permeability of textual boundaries that can be experienced by the reader as moments in Freudian "Fort-Da" games, coping with, and perpetuating, the palinodic trauma of proximity to another writer and irrevocable "interauctorial" disorientation. Committed to performing creative continuations of, and at the same time conducting escape attempts from, Bernhard's

---

1 This chapter has benefited immensely from conversations with Alessandra M. Pires.
2 Tim Parks, *The Novel: A Survival Skill* (New York: Oxford University Press, 2015), 32.

texts, these authors are engaged in what could be called *Von-Bernhard-Fort-und-Wieder-Da-Hineinschreibungen* in evocative strands of artistic repetition compulsion, or *Wiederholungszwangshandlungssträngen*.

This chapter discusses how Francophone writers Hervé Guibert, Gemma Salem, Israel Eliraz (in collaboration with Jacques Dupin), Linda Lê, and Cyril Huot have responded to the irresistible ethical challenge and rhetorical pull of Bernhard's works. Their narrative approaches range from agonistic and highly intertextual emulative appropriations of Bernhard's style and topoi to vertiginous fantasies of coinhabiting palimpsests. Working through Bernhardian voices, they offer oscillations between reflective distancing from and immersive performances of Bernhard's style, and they sometimes even stage Bernhard as a fictional addressee and poetic voice.

In his notebooks from 1976 to 1991 published as *Le Mausolée des Amants* (The mausoleum of lovers, 2001), and in his novel *À l'ami qui ne m'a pas sauvé la vie* (To the friend who didn't save my life, 1990), Hervé Guibert employs violent allegories of reading, evoking scenes of cutting, poisoning, and lethal contagion to describe his protagonist's experience of being exposed to Bernhard's works. In contrast, Gemma Salem offers accounts of a liberating effect of reading Bernhard in her introduction to the essay volume, *Thomas Bernhard et les siens* (1993), as well as in her epistolary novel, *Lettre à l'ermite autrichien* (Letter to the Austrian hermit, 1989), which is an extended apostrophe to Bernhard, and in her novel, *L'Artiste* (The artist, 1991). In his genre-bending poetry volume and theater play *Chez Thomas Bernhard à Steinhof* (With Thomas Bernhard in Steinhof, 2006), Israel Eliraz presents Bernhard and Bachmann as haunted lyrical protagonists. In her essay volume *Par Ailleurs (Exils)* (Elsewhere (exiles), 2014), and in her novels *les dits d'un idiot* (Utterances of an idiot, 1995), *Voix: Une crise* (Voice: a crisis, 1998), and *Les Aubes* (Daybreaks, 2000), Linda Lê provides a nuanced interplay of ethics and aesthetics that is sustained by her ongoing creative dialogue with Bernhard's works. Cyril Huot's essay volume *Le rire triomphant des perdants (Journal de guerre)* (The triumphant laughter of the losers, 2016) discusses and enacts what he calls Bernhard's "poetics of citations." In his novel *Le spectre de Thomas Bernhard* (The specter of Thomas Bernhard, 2016), a bold metanarrative experiment that fuses hyperreflexivity and evocative urgency, Huot emulates Bernhard's prose style while he insists on the importance of a "naked" approach to understanding Bernhard, unprotected by academic jargon, and reveling in merging one's voice with those of Bernhard's characters.

Readers might be familiar with a true anecdotal case of mistaken auctorial identity. The publisher Maurice Nadeau felt certain that when Nicolas Stakhovitch sent him the manuscript of his novel, *Les Aphorismes de Gralph*, in the late 1980s, Stakhovitch must have been a pseudonym, and the text must have been authored by the recently deceased Bernhard. It is indicative of Nadeau's professional integrity that he accepted the manuscript, which was published in 1991 even after he learned that Bernhard did not pen the novel. What had triggered Nadeau's erroneous attribution of the novel to Bernhard were the work's spiraling prose style, and its topoi and points of constant return: The narrator learns that his best friend has committed suicide, and the whole novel is interlaced with streams of polemical consciousness weaving together repeated meditations on dying, loss, and friendship, spiraling reflections that the narrator repeatedly calls "vertigineuses," as well as a steady supply of invectives against society.

In his journal *Le Mausolée des Amants*, Guibert offers a gnomic parenthetical definition of Bernhard's work: "(L'oeuvre, c'est le découpage: Thomas Bernhard)." The semantic field denoted by "découpage" is incisively crafty and violent and can be translated as "cutting," "chopping," "excision," "slitting," "carving," "dissecting," "shredding," and "encrypting."[3] In his narrative, *À l'ami qui ne m'a pas sauvé la vie*, Guibert describes his experience of reading Bernhard as a poisoning and contagion. He even likens exposing oneself to Bernhard's works to contracting HIV (Guibert died at the age of thirty-six of complications related to AIDS):

> Un diable s'est glissé dans mes soutes: T.B. Je me suis arrêté de le lire pour stopper l'empoisonnement. On dit que chaque réinjection du virus du sida par fluides, le sang, le sperme ou les larmes, réattaque le malade déjà contaminé, on pretend peut-être [...] pour limiter les dégâts.[4]
>
> (A devil has slipped inside me: T.B. I've stopped reading him in order to stop the poisoning. They say that every reinjection of the AIDS virus through fluids, blood, sperm or tears, results in a new attack on the already contaminated sick person. They probably make this up to limit the damage.)[5]

Guibert's recourse to violent biological metaphors to express rage against, and ingestion of, Bernhard's streams-of-grief-and-anger-stricken consciousness is countered by Gemma Salem, who was born in Turkey in 1943 and has lived in Paris, Geneva, and Vienna. In the introduction to her edited essay volume, *Thomas Bernhard et les siens* (1993), Salem resolutely contradicts Guibert's aggressive metaphors

---

3 Hervé Guibert, *Le Mausolée des Amants: Journal 1976–1991* (Paris: Gallimard, 2001), 378.
4 Hervé Guibert, *À l'ami qui ne m'a pas sauvé la vie* (Paris: Gallimard, 1990), 12.
5 All translations are mine.

and admits to a more salutary, if equally obsessive, addiction to Bernhard's oeuvre:

> On a ces dernières années souvent comparé Thomas Bernhard à un virus [...] qu'il se grefferait à nous comme un maladie. [...] je ne me suis jamais sentie "malade" de l'avoir lu, au contraire, je me portais de mieux en mieux pour l'essentiel, c'est-à-dire dans mon Coeur et ma tête, ce qui s'y passait s'accordait de mieux en mieux à mes actes et mes paroles, je m'acceptais enfin comme j'étais.[6]
>
> (In recent years Thomas Bernhard has often been compared to a virus [...] that is grafting itself on us like an illness. [...] I have never felt "ill" from reading him. On the contrary, it made me more and more aware of that which really matters, living according to my Heart and my head, aligning my words with my actions, accepting myself the way I've been.)

For Salem, who barely knew Bernhard in person but who absorbs his texts with an unparalleled intimate approach, his death triggered a suicidal crisis: "Depuis qu'il était mort, je voulais mourir aussi et parler de lui était le moyen de supporter la vie [...]"[7] (After he died, I also wanted to die, and I stayed alive by talking about him).

Salem considers Bernhard an exemplary role model for intellectual honesty and courage, reconciling ethics and poetics: "La première chose qui m'ait frappé chez Thomas Bernhard c'est son amour de la vérité, sa volonté d'honnêteté en toutes choses. Je crois qu'aucun artiste n'a fait autant pour la vérité [...]"[8] (The first thing that struck me about Thomas Bernhard is his love of the truth, his commitment to honesty in all things. I believe that no artist has done as much for the truth [...]). One of the essays in Salem's volume *Bernhard et les siens* is written by the Swiss jazz pianist and composer, René Bottlang. In his essay, "À Glenn Gould à cent pour cent," Bottlang highlights his indebtedness to Bernhard's works because, as Bottlang asserts, Bernhard exposes our individual and collective "stupidity" and "hypocrisy" ("Il a mis le doigt sur la bêtise, l'hypocrisie [...]"):[9] "Thomas Bernhard m'a éclairé dans ce sens qu'il ne faut pas tricher, ni avec les autres ni avec soi. Il m'a fait prendre conscience qu'il ne fallait craindre personne [...] Et qu'il fallait suivre son instinct, se battre, oser dire les choses, jusqu'au bout."[10]

---

6 Gemma Salem, *Thomas Bernhard et les siens* (Paris: La Table Ronde, 1993), 8.
7 Salem, *Thomas Bernhard et les siens*, 7.
8 Salem, *Thomas Bernhard et les siens*, 9.
9 René Bottlang, "À Glenn Gould à cent pour cent," in Salem, *Thomas Bernhard et les siens*, 196.
10 Bottlang, "À Glenn Gould à cent pour cent," 201.

(Thomas Bernhard helped me comprehend clearly that we shouldn't lie, neither to others nor to ourselves. He made me aware that one doesn't need to fear anyone [...] And that we need to follow our instinct fighting, daring to articulate everything, right to the end.)

In her partially autobiographical apostrophic novel, *Lettre à l'ermite autrichien* (1989), written not long before Bernhard's death, Salem's narrator addresses a silent Bernhard who never responds. The novel starts with a disarming epistolary gesture, "Mon cher Thomas Bernhard"[11] (My dear Thomas Bernhard), and ends with an intimate declaration of a maturation process in the course of which the narrator appears to have reconciled deep affection for her beloved writer and a regained sense of autonomy: "Aujourd'hui je retrouve mon autonomie, même si vous êtes là, dans ma vie [...] car je reste à l'écoute de vous, mais libre, comme vous."[12] (Today I have reclaimed my autonomy, even though you are present in my life [...] I continue to listen to you but at the same time I am free, like you.)

Salem dedicated her novel *L'Artiste* (The Artist, 1991) "aux amoureux de la musique, de Thomas Bernhard"[13] (to the lovers of music, of Thomas Bernhard). Huntemann has lamented the blurred boundaries between "work and author" in Salem's interweavings of Bernhard into her texts, but his dismissive reading of Salem might in turn exemplify the one-dimensionality of which he accuses her work.[14] Future explorations of Salem's apparently naïve and yet subversively sophisticated narrative approaches to Bernhard will benefit from comparative glances at Bettina von Arnim's blending of (auto)biography and fiction in her works featuring Günderrode and Goethe.

The Vietnamese-French novelist and essayist Linda Lê provides a sustained creative and critical dialogue with Bernhard's voices throughout her works. Her novel, *les dits d'un idiot* (1995), starts with an epigraph that is a Bernhard quotation.[15] The narrator in Lê's novel,

---

11 Gemma Salem, *Lettre à l'ermite autrichien* (Paris: La Table Ronde, 1989), 7.
12 Salem, *Lettre à l'ermite autrichien*, 173.
13 Gemma Salem, *L'Artiste* (Paris: La Table Ronde, 1991), n.p. Salem mentions the role of Bernhard for her life and her writing in her autobiography, *La Rhumba à Beethoven* (Paris: Roux, 2014), 154–65.
14 Willi Huntemann, "Fan-Post ins Jenseits. Anmerkungen zur posthumen Bernhard(iner)-Literatur," in Wolfram Bayer, ed., *Kontinent Bernhard: Zur Thomas-Bernhard-Rezeption in Europa* (Vienna/Cologne/Weimar: Böhlau, 1995), 154: "Eine geradezu schwärmerische Bernhard-Idolisierung [...]" 155: "[...] Werk und sein Autor in dieser Auseinandersetzung nicht auseinandergehalten [...]" See also Claude Porcell, "Die Verklärung des heiligen Bernhard. Zur Rezeption der Erzählprosa in Frankreich," in Bayer, ed., *Kontinent Bernhard*, 241–68.
15 Linda Lê, *les dits d'un idiot* (Paris: Bourgois, 1995), 7: "*Cela avait voulu être un monde grandiose, il en est resté un detail dérisoire.* Thomas Bernhard."

Voix: Une crise (1998), declares, not unlike Bernhard's protagonists: "La seule vérité, c'est la solitude de l'homme sur terre, et la souffrance, et l'ennui, et la mort [...]"[16] (The only truth is man's loneliness on earth, and the suffering, and boredom, and death [...]). The final passage of Lê's novel, *Les Aubes* (2000), offers an existentialist interplay of ethics and poetics that can be read in fruitful dialogue with Bernhard's (and Salem's) voices: "Je rêve d'un livre de deuil et de renaissance, de mort et de sensualité, un livre qui me sauverait de moi, que la pensée du suicide a toujours accompagné"[17] (I dream of a book of mourning and rebirth, of death and of sensuality, a book that might save me from myself, since the thought of suicide has always accompanied me).

In Lê's novel, *Oeuvres Vives* (Living works, 2014), a young journalist becomes obsessed with the life of a writer who took his own life and who wrote a book, *Naufrages*, whose title is reminiscent of Bernhard's *Der Untergeher*. In her essay volume, *Par Ailleurs (Exils)* (Someplace else (exiles), 2014), Lê offers an incisive essay on Bernhard, using anaphorical parallelisms, a stylistic device also often employed by Bernhard:

> Il est difficile de lire Thomas Bernhard [...] sans resentir un certain malaise et une intense jubilation tout à la fois, car il met à mal ce qui nous tient lieu de garde-fous. Il est difficile de le lire sans reviser les croyances qui ont toujours été les nôtres, à tel point que les preserver relevait de l'instinct de conversation. Il est difficile de le lire sans mettre sur la sellette notre ancient moi [...] Il est difficile de le lire sans éprouver un effondrement intérieur, parce que le monde qu'il décrit est un monde enténébré.[18]
>
> (It's hard to read Thomas Bernhard [...] without reliving at the same time a certain discontent and an intense kind of euphoria, because he deprives us of what we used to cling to as our handrails (or guard railings). It's hard to read him without revising all the beliefs that we used to hold on to [...]. It's hard to read him without bringing charges against our old self [...] It's hard to read him without plowing through ourselves and launching an inner disintegration.)

Lê then shifts her focus to the impact that our reading of Bernhard can have on the way in which we approach society:

> Il est difficile de le lire sans vouloir nous retrencher de la société, dont il dit en substance qu'elle est au mieux une école

---

16 Lê, *Voix: Une crise* (Paris: Bourgois, 1998), 17.
17 Lê, *Les Aubes* (Paris: Bourgois, 2000), 192.
18 Lê, *Par Ailleurs* (Paris: Bourgois, 2014), 149.

du conformisme, au pire une association de malfaiteurs. Il est difficile de le lire sans avoir la certitude que vivre pleinement, c'est souvent savoir *aller contre*, ne pas consentir [...] Il est difficile de le lire sans redresser la tête quant nous nous sommes longtemps soumis aux oukases des pharisiens. [...] Il est difficile de le lire sans dire non aux usurpateurs, si nombreux en politique, qui se font passer pour des sauveurs, alors qu'ils ne sont que des profiteurs tirant parti de notre crédulité.[19]

(It's hard to read him without wanting to retreat from society, of which he basically says that it's at best a school of conformism, and at worst an association of criminals. It's hard to read him without becoming convinced that in order to live to the fullest, we have to know how to go against the grain, and not to consent anymore [...] It's hard to read him without lifting our head that we kept down for so long to the decrees of the pharisees [...] It's hard to read him without saying no to the usurpers and profiteers in politics who want to pass as saviors.)

In the same essay, Lê describes the act and process of reading Bernhard as a potentially dangerous and liberating experience, both emotionally and physically:

Il est difficile de le lire sans nous préparer à subir une secousse, aussi foudroyante que salutaire. Il est difficile aussi de le lire sans nous sentir heureux et stimulés en trouvant dans sa prose concise, obsédante, virulente, la rage et l'aggressivité dont nous avons besoin pour lutter contre le monde.[20]

(It's hard to read him without preparing us to undergo a shock that will be at once overwhelming and salutary. [...] It's hard to read him without feeling happy and stimulated finding in his concise, insistent, virulent prose the rage and aggressiveness that we need in order to fight the world.)

Cyril Huot, a theater and film director and writer, has put his creative metanarrative focus on Bernhard in his recent works. Huot's essay volume, *Le rire triomphant des perdants (Journal de guerre)* (2016), operates with an abundance of quotations from Bernhard's novels *Verstörung*

---

19 Lê, *Par Ailleurs*, 151.
20 Lê, *Par Ailleurs*, 151–52. See also Nancy Huston's biographical essay on Bernhard, and her essay on Lê, in "Femmes teintées de noir: Sarah Kane, Christine Angot, Linda Lê," in Nancy Huston, *Professeurs de Désespoir* (Arles: Actes Sud, 2004), 305–33.

and *Auslöschung*, and from his play *Minetti*.[21] Quoting a passage from Bernhard's *Verstörung* in which the protagonist expresses his horror at the realization that we are all trapped inside a world consisting of quotations, Huot refers to Bernhard as a writer who celebrated the art of quotation more than any other author and who turned it into the very heart of the art of writing.[22]

Huot's novel and performative theory-experiment, *Le spectre de Thomas Bernhard* (2016), begins with the promise not to be yet another choir singing to the glory of T.B. ("[…] un nouveau cantique à la gloire de T.B.").[23] Insisting on a radical readiness for existential experiments in immersing into realms of madness in order to comprehend Bernhard's narrative and dramatic voices, Huot issues never-ending, punctuation-free prose spirals while mentioning that Bernhard uses similar stylistic devices of cascading prose rhythms:

> Quand il nous […] n'entrons pas dans la folie de T.B., nous ne pouvons pas entrer dans l'oeuvre de T.B. […] nous nous refusons à entrer dans la folie, aussi bien dans la sienne que dans la nôtre, tant que nous nous refusons à faire nôtre sa folie qui aussi bien est la nôtre […] nous nous condamnons à ne rien comprendre à T.B., quand la folie est la clef de l'oeuvre de T.B. comme elle est la clef de l'oeuvre de tout auteur digne de ce nom.[24]
>
> (If we don't immerse into T.B.'s madness, we won't be able to enter T.B.'s work […] if we refuse to immerse into madness, his as well as our own, to the extent to which we refuse to make his madness, which is also our very own madness, our own, we

---

21 Cyril Huot, *Le rire triomphant des perdants (Journal de guerre)* (Paris: Tinbad, 2016a), 25–26: "Mais si nous n'avions pas l'orgueil, nous serions perdus,/ce n'est d'ailleurs rien d'autre qu'un moyen d'agir contre un monde qui, sans cela, c'est-à-dire sans cet orgueil, nour avalerait tout crus." (*Extinction*) 45–46: "Tête baissée dans l'oeuvre d'art,/Madame […]" (*Minetti*) 184: "Chaque tête d'homme, dit le prince, contenait la catastrophe humaine en rapport avec cette tête. […] L'homme aimait sa détresse [misery/helplessness] […] la recherche de leur détresse. Il n'y a pas d'homme sans la détresse humaine [*Perturbation*], faisait dire à l'un de ses porte-parole ce Thomas Bernhard qui, mieux que quiconque, aura su nous peindre, sans aucune concession, la catastrophe humaine et la rage d'autodestruction […]"
22 Huot, *Le rire triomphant des perdants*, 102: "Les citations me tapent sur les nerfs. Mais nous sommes enfermés dans un monde qui cite en permanence tout ce qu'il est possible de citer, dans une citation permanente qui est le monde même, docteur," [*Perturbation*] fait dire à l'un de ses personnages Thomas Bernhard, celui qui, mieux que quiconque, a su jouer de la citation, allant jusqu'à la mise en abyme de la citation, pour en faire le coeur même de l'art littéraire."
23 Huot, *Le spectre de Thomas Bernhard*, 12.
24 Huot, *Le spectre de Thomas Bernhard*, 12.

condemn ourselves to not understanding T.B.'s work because madness is the key to his work, as it is the key to any author's work who is worthy of this name.)

Huot also offers sustained poetological metareflections in which he performatively argues against our addiction to the preposterous preposition "about" and to possessive pronouns in the context of reading.[25] Referring to Bernhard's refusal to write an article "about" Wittgenstein, Huot's narrator outlines that his desire to write is encapsulated in a conflicted bundle of desires (and, of course, this passage is written in a style that is reminiscent of Bernhard's spiraling streams of consciousness):

> [...] écrire, non pas *sur* T.B., comme se croire autorisés à écrire *sur* un écrivain, *sur* un philosophe, *sur* un artiste [...] mais puis-je écrire *mon* T.B., sans ainsi l'anéantir, lui, et sans m'anéantir moi-même dans l'opération?[26]
>
> (To write, but not *about* T.B., as if we were authorized to write *about* a writer, *about* a philosopher, *about* an artist [...] but perhaps I can write *my* T.B. without annihilating him, and without obliterating myself in the course of the operation?)

Huot's narrator further poses the question of

> Quand personne ne saurait écrire *son* T.B. sans détruire le T.B. qui lui seul fut T.B. pour lui substituer un spectre de T.B. et sans se laisser entièrement dévorer par ce spectre, sans phagocyter T.B. et sans être soi-même phagocyté par T.B. dans l'opération, sans l'anéantir et sans s'anéantir en lui [...][27]
>
> (Whether anyone can write his or her T.B. without destroying the T.B. who alone was T.B. in order to substitute him with a specter, a ghost of T.B. and without letting oneself being completely devoured by that ghost, without swallowing T.B. and without being swallowed whole by T.B. in the course of the procedure, without annihilating him and without being obliterated oneself by or inside him [...])

---

25 For a gentle attack on the lazy mindset of "aboutness" in different literary contexts, see Olaf Berwald, "Against Aboutness: The Corpse That Almost Got Away," in *The Scofield* 1.4 (Spring 2016): Special Issue: Max Frisch & Identity, 196–7.
26 Huot, *Le spectre de Thomas Bernhard* (Paris: Tinbad, 2016b), 31.
27 Huot, *Le spectre*, 31.

At the very end of this passage, Huot's narrator leaves it open whether anyone is capable of "ever letting T.B. emerge except in the form of a fantasy, a merely hallucinatory vision" ("[...] pour n'en laisser jamais émerger qu'une vision fantasmée à caractère purement hallucinatoire").[28] Huot's narrator evokes, in capital letters, the "HORROR or TERROR" of emptiness, leaving it open whether "our T.B." and "his Montaigne" or "his Pascal" are just so many manifestations of a traumatic void, or also at the same time therapeutic devices to make it a bit more bearable. ("HORREUR du vide [...] *notre* T.B., etc. [...] *son* Montaigne [...] *son* Pascal, etc.")[29]

Le spectre de Thomas Bernhard ends with a passage that offers a performative dialectics of hyperreflexive and, one might add, exhilarating, self-denial through intertextual self-inscriptions:

> Mais rassure-toi, je lui [his dying friend Herman] dit, je n'écrirais jamais mon livre sur T.B., je n'en écrirais même jamais la première phrase, comme tu sais, j'ai accumulé de tonnes de note au sujet de T.B. et je continuerai probablement à en accumuler jusqu'à la fin de ma vie, c'est une activité absurde obsessionelle [...] mais je n'écrirais bien entendu jamais mon livre sur T.B., de ce côté-là tu peux mourir tranquille, j'avais dit à Herman.[30]
>
> (But rest assured, I tell him (his dying friend Herman), I will never write my book about T.B., I won't even ever compose the first sentence; as you know, I've accumulated tons of notes on the subject matter of T.B. and I'll probably continue to accumulate more until the end of my life, this is an absurd and obsessive activity, but I will definitely never write my book about T.B., in this regard you can die peacefully, I told Herman.)

One last example of recent Francophone creative receptions of Bernhard is a book-length poem in three parts or "movements" by Israeli poet Israel Eliraz, *Chez Thomas Bernhard à Steinhof* (2006). In a note at the end of the book, Eliraz mentions that during the writing process of the poem, he constantly read Bernhard's plays *Vor dem Ruhestand*, *Ritter Dene Voss*, and *Heldenplatz*.[31] Eliraz first wrote this work in Hebrew, and he cotranslated its first "movement" together with the poet Jacques Dupin, who also translated, and was translated by, Paul Celan, and who together with Celan, Dupin, Bonnefoy, Bataille, Klossowski, and others

---

28 Huot, *Le rire triomphant des perdants*.
29 Huot, *Le spectre*, 32.
30 Huot, *Le spectre*, 217.
31 Israel Eliraz, *Chez Thomas Bernhard à Steinhof* (Paris: José Corti, 2006), 137.

coedited the short-lived but influential literary magazine *L'Éphémère* with Bonnefoy, Bataille, Celan, Klossowski, and others in the early 1960s.

Each poem in Éliraz's lyrical volume of hauntingly sparse musicality and slow commemorative ellipses offers its own textual world while at the same time being interwoven into a continuous, if fragmented, evocative narrative. Many lines mark preceding verses as (fictional or "real") quotations from Bernhard and also from Ingeborg Bachmann ("Thomas said" ... "Ingeborg said ..."). According to Éliraz's poem, patients of the Steinhof hospital that plays a central role in Bernhard's life and textual worlds are experts in recognizing a "musical lucidity" in "the monotony" that is Steinhof ("Une lucidité musicale dans/la monotonie, expertise/de Steinhof").[32]

Éliraz has "Thomas" declare that "Stupidity and exploitation are limitless" and call himself a "chronicler of consternation" in the face of "the great slaughtering and the *essential thing* that nestle up against us and penetrate us" ("Elles ne connaissent pas de limites/la bêtise, l'exploitation//[...] dit/Thomas,//je suis chroniqueur de la stupeur/du grand massacre et/de l'objet *essentiel*//qui nous épousent et nous/pénètrent").[33] Evoking an irreconcilable conflict triggered by an unfulfilled mutual longing of Bernhard the adult and Bernhard the child for each other ("Thomas cherche l'enfant qui/cherche Thomas"),[34] Éliraz presents Bernhard's eventual silence as a "scream that is getting louder amidst the nakedness of things" ("[...] un cri qui s'accentue dans la nudité des choses").[35]

To end, and to end up with, a small but open wound and question: Do current, and will future creative receptions of Bernhard's oeuvre consist in experiments of recovering, and recovering from, what Éliraz's "With Thomas Bernhard in Steinhof" cantata calls "the terror of writing," "La terreur d'écrire"?[36] An uncharted, vulnerable, and "naked" kind of Bernhard reception is possible every time anybody risks and revels in reading and merging their voice with Bernhard's characters' lines. Are we sturdy and courageous enough to transform the trauma of, and our addiction to, "receiving" Bernhard through dangerous, unpredictable, and ecstatic reading immersions possibly disappearing into unmappable points of no return from radical joys of reading?

---

32 Éliraz, *Chez Thomas Bernhard à Steinhof*, 15.
33 Éliraz, *Chez Thomas Bernhard à Steinhof*, 64.
34 Éliraz, *Chez Thomas Bernhard à Steinhof*, 131.
35 Éliraz, *Chez Thomas Bernhard à Steinhof*, 135.
36 Éliraz, *Chez Thomas Bernhard à Steinhof*, 120.

Nine Thomas Bernhard's Influence on Gabriel Josipovici's Monologue Novels

Gregor Thuswaldner

When Gabriel Josipovici's novel *Moo Pak* (1994) appeared in German translation in 2010, the publisher, Suhrkamp, went the extra mile in marketing the novel. The book came with a detachable sleeve that announced in big letters that this was the work of "the English Thomas Bernhard." This was not a coincidence, as Suhrkamp also publishes Thomas Bernhard's oeuvre. To be sure, in *Moo Pak* Josipovici pays tribute to Bernhard, but to reduce the author to a mere copycat proved to be a marketing disaster. Why would German readers unfamiliar with Josipovici's works buy a novel that tries to imitate Bernhard? Why read the German translation of a wannabe Bernhard, if you can read the Austrian author in the original? Probably also due to the questionable marketing campaign, "the English Thomas Bernhard" has not found a large reading audience in the German-speaking world, and today the translation of *Moo Pak* is no longer available. In his review, Willi Huntemann bemoans this unnecessary label, as Bernhard's influence on the novel does not deserve extra mentioning. Drawing too much attention to Bernhard, Huntemann fears, may distort Josipovici's reception in the German-speaking world.[1]

Suhrkamp's unfortunate marketing strategy may have also put off reviewers. The cultural online magazine, *Perlentaucher*, which provides summaries as well as links to book reviews in all major German-speaking news outlets, only lists Renate Wiggershaus' review essay in *Neue*

---

1 Cf. Willi Huntemann, "Ein Monolog-Roman im Gehen," literaturkritik.de, December 22, 2010. https://literaturkritik.de/id/15111, 2010.

Zürcher Zeitung.[2] Wiggershaus does not even mention Bernhard in her review; instead she refers to Josipovici's fascination with Proust, Kafka, and Beckett, which are also quite noticeable.[3]

To call Josipovici Bernhard's British doppelganger is utterly misleading: neither his life nor most of his works stand in close connections with the Austrian writer. Josipovici's parents were of Jewish descent. Born in Nice, France in 1940, Josipovici grew up in Cairo, Egypt before his family settled in England in 1956. At Oxford he studied literature and became a professor at the University of Sussex where he taught from 1963 until his retirement in 1998. Josipovici has written novels, short stories, dramas, radio plays, as well as literary and scholarly essays. As a literary scholar and writer, Josipovici admires several modernist authors, including Thomas Bernhard, whom he calls "Austria's greatest post-war writer"[4] and "the most truthful, the funniest and the most musical of writers since Marcel Proust."[5]

Bernhard, on the other hand, was neither of Jewish decent, nor was he trained as an academic. Bernhard studied singing, directing, and acting in Salzburg with mixed results; the conductor, Josef Knirps, suggested he should consider becoming a butcher instead of a singer.[6] It was Bernhard's grandfather, the rather unsuccessful author Johannes Freumbichler, who had a lasting impact on Bernhard's thought and writing. Bernhard's main characters, who competently compensate

---

2 Josipovici recently bemoaned the fact that his work has not been successful in the German-speaking world: "My work was first translated into German and was well received, but sales were lukewarm, even though my publisher was keen on my writing. We had a happy five or six years together and then he went bankrupt. Other publishers followed, including Suhrkamp, who tried to market my book like a new Thomas Bernhard which was a big mistake. My agent still tries to find new publishers for me, but to no avail" (Georgia DC, "Interview: Gabriel Josipovici, author & critic." https://bookblast.com/blog/interview-gabriel-josipovici-author-critic/).
3 Renate Wiggershaus, "Adorno in Shorts," *Neue Zürcher Zeitung*, October 30, 2010. https://www.nzz.ch/adorno_in_shorts-1.8195591.2010.
4 Gabriel Josipovici, "Thomas Bernhard and His Prizes: An Essay Review by Gabriel Josipovici," n.d. https://www.thomasbernhard.org/essays/gjmyprizesns.shtml. A modified version of the essay was published in New Statesman, in which Josipovici describes Bernhard as "Austria's finest postwar writer" (Gabriel Josipovici, "Wittgenstein's Awkward Nephew," *New Statesmen America*, January 13, 2011. https://www.newstatesman.com/books/2011/01/bernhard-austria-prize-comic).
5 Josipovici, "Thomas Bernhard and His Prizes," https://www.newstatesman.com/books/2011/01/bernhard-austria-prize-comic
6 Hans Höller, *Thomas Bernhard* (Reinbek: Rowohlt, 1993), 54.

their incompetence[7] to complete their intellectual or artistic work by constantly talking about it, are modeled on Freumbichler.[8]

Josipovici, who appreciates the satirical and quite subversive Austrian literary project spanning from Nestroy all the way to Nobel Laureate, Elfriede Jelinek, finds Bernhard "much more unsettling [than Jelinek] because it is impossible to tell where he stands."[9] In interviews and in his essays, Josipovici refers to Bernhard and the sophisticated nature of his novels. In an essay in which he, among other things, touches on Marcel Duchamp's work, Josipovici writes:

> [Duchamp's last work, *Etant Donnés*] is extremely beautiful and meticulously made, Duchamp spending eight years transferring its elements—the Bride above and the 'Bachelor machine' below—from sketches and preliminary works onto the two glass panels. The Large Glass, as has come to be known, is also accompanied by boxes of detailed notes on physics, alchemy, metaphysics and much else, which—Duchamp being Duchamp—it is difficult to know whether to take seriously or as a spoof. They have of course, like the novels of Thomas Bernhard, to be taken both ways.[10]

Bernhard's oeuvre is used as a touchpoint, an object of comparison, that encapsulates the same modernist idea present in Duchamp's work. However, Josipovici does not elaborate on how Bernhard's novels have to be taken "seriously and as a spoof" at the same time.

In another essay, Josipovici points out a similarity he discovers in the theatrical works of Pinter and Bernhard:

> Pinter and Bernhard […] seem able to put on stage characters who are at least recognizable, even if they strain them in every turn. In fact seeing how far these artistic conventions (which mesh of course with the conventions by which bourgeois society lives) can be strained, becomes part of what drives their dramaturgy.[11]

---

7 The phrase is borrowed from the philosopher Odo Marquard (cf. Odo Marquard, "Inkompetenzkompensationskompetenz? Über Kompetenz und Inkompetenz der Philsophie," *Abschied vom Prinzipiellen: Philsophische Studien* [Stuttgart: Reclam, 1981]).
8 Cf. Höller, *Thomas Bernhard*, 34–48.
9 Josipovici, "Thomas Bernhard and His Prizes," https://www.newstatesman.com/books/2011/01/bernhard-austria-prize-comic.
10 Josipovici, *What Ever Happened to Modernism?* (New Haven: Yale University Press, 2010), 134.
11 Josipovici, *What Ever Happened to Modernism?* 2010, 139.

But as in the passage about Duchamp, the reader is left in the dark about the true nature of Pinter's and Bernhard's stage figures. Josipovici's descriptions are as evocative as they are enigmatic; he touches on what he sees as closely related poetological or artistic strategies without fleshing them out. When Josipovici presents his view of modernism, he sides with Georges Perec and Bernhard against Updike, Roth, and James Joyce's *Finnegans Wake*:

> My own 'story', as I have tried to present it here, discovering what it was as I went along, is that only an art which recognizes the pitfalls inherent in both realism and abstraction will be really alive. That is why I warm to the novels of Perec and Bernhard more than to *Finnegans Wake* or the novels of Updike and Roth [...].[12]

As in the previous examples, Josipovici does not elaborate on what makes the works of Perec and Bernhard superior in his eyes. How Perec and Bernhard "recognize [...] the pitfalls inherent in both realism and abstraction" is not mentioned.

Although non sequiturs like the ones cited above can be found throughout his dense essay-length book, *What Ever Happened to Modernism?*, they are interspersed in longer, more thought-out passages. Clearly, in this regard one may say his essay on modernism is also a manifestation of modernism. Thus, as one critic suggests, "[i]f you're looking for a solution to the current debate over modernism in Gabriel Josipovici's book, look elsewhere."[13]

In an interview in 2012, Jason Rotstein asked Josipovici, "Do you think it's possible to learn from writers as different as say Thomas Bernhard and Henry James? Can two writers as different exist in the same man? Perhaps, they are not so different?" Josipovici answered, "I'm not sure one learns anything from other writers, except the confidence to go at things in one's own way."[14] Josipovici seems to imply that learning from other authors would mean using the same methods and mechanics. Instead, an author needs to be courageous enough to create and not imitate.

Then why was Josipovici labeled as "the English Thomas Bernhard?" Did he fail to be courageous, and did he just mimic the work of another

---

12 Josipovici, *What Ever Happened to Modernism?* (New Haven: Yale University Press, 2010), 187.
13 James Purdon, "What Ever Happened to Modernism? by Gabriel Josipovici," *The Guardian*, October 2, 2010. https://www.theguardian.com/books/2010/oct/03/whatever-happened-to-modernism-gabriel-josipovici.Purdon.
14 James Rotstein, "Q&A Re Infinity and Other Matters," April 2012. http://www.gabrieljosipovici.org/interviewjrotstein.shtml.

author he admires? After all, there are obvious similarities between *Moo Pak* and some of Thomas Bernhard's novels.[15] In fact, there are two other novels by Josipovici, *The Big Glass* (1991) and *Infinity: The Story of a Moment* (2012), that are monological in nature and show intertextual affinities with Bernhard's works.[16] According to Monika Fludernik, Josipovici's monologue novels

> [...] feature one or more protagonists whose tirades occupy the bulk of the text. Despite the monotony of such a deluge of words issuing from the monologist, these texts mitigate the seemingly uncheckable tide of monomania by cleverly framing it with another discourse. They therefore expose the tirade to a humorous, even ironic viewpoint. The monologue, then, reveals itself to be a failed dialogue, and the reasons for that failure are so obvious that, whatever pathos, or bathos, is involved in the subject matter (the human predicament in its seedier aspects), the monologist himself cannot but appear a little pathetic and laughable, and therefore quite likable.[17]

What Fludernik is describing is Josipovici's attempt to write novels that should be simultaneously taken "seriously and as a spoof,"[18] which, of course, as previously mentioned, he sees as a quality of Bernhard's novels. To achieve this goal, Josipovici uses several poetological strategies that are present in Bernhard's works. Take, for example, the narrator in *Moo Pak*, Damian Anderson, who is mentioned only three times by name, once in the beginning and twice at the end of the novel. Anderson records Jack Toledano's monologues as the two friends walk through London's heaths and parks from 1977 until 1990. The first sentence reads, "On Tuesday I received a note from Jack Toledano asking me to meet him today at the Star and Garter in Putney at the usual time,

---

15 Huntemann, "Ein Monolog-Roman im Gehen," https://literaturkritik.de/id/15111.
16 Monika Fludernik also points out that Josipovici's *Contre-Jour* (1986) has monological tendencies. However, unlike *The Big Glass*, *Moo Pak*, and *Infinity: The Story of a Moment*, *Contre-Jour* features several dialogues and is much more episodic than the three other truly monological novels (cf. Monika Fudernik, *Echoes and Mirrorings: Gabriel Josipovici's Creative Oeuvre* [Frankfurt: Lang, 2000], 81).
17 Fludernik, *Echoes and Mirrorings*, 81. Apart from that, Bernhard's influence on Josipovici's oeuvre is less visible. His dramas are usually seen in the context of contemporary British avantgarde theater. Monika Fludernik describes Josiovici's works in general "as a late Modernist venture with a moderate tendency towards postmodernist techniques" (Fludernik, *Echoes and Mirrorings*, 7).
18 Josipovici, *What Ever Happened to Modernism?*, 134.

wrote Damien Anderson."[19] This reminds one of Bernhard's last novel, *Extinction* (1986), which begins as follows:

> Nach der Unterredung mit meinem Schüler Gambetti, mit welchem ich mich am Neunundzwanzigsten auf dem Pincio getroffen habe, schreibt Murau, Franz Josef, um die Mai-Termine für den Unterricht zu vereinbaren und von dessen hoher Intelligenz ich auch jetzt nach meiner Rückkehr aus Wolfsegg überrascht, ja in einer derart erfrischenden Weise begeistert gewesen bin, dass ich ganz gegen meine Gewohnheit, gleich durch die Via Condotti auf die Piazza Minerva zu gehen, auch in dem Gedanken, tatsächlich schon lange in Rom und nicht mehr in Österreich zuhause zu sein, in eine zunehmend heitere Stimmung versetzt, über die Flaminia und die Piazza die Popolo, den ganzen Corso entlang in meine Wohnung gegangen bin, erhielt ich gegen zwei Uhr mittag das Telegramm, in welchem mir der Tod meiner Eltern und meines Bruders Johannes mitgeteilt wurde.[20]

> (On the twenty-ninth, having returned from Wolfsegg, I met my pupil Gambetti on the Pincio to discuss arrangements for the lessons he was to receive in May, writes Franz Josef Murnau, and unimpressed once again by his high intelligence, I was refreshed and exhilarated, so glad to be living in Rome and not in Austria, that instead of walking home along the Via Condotti, as I usually do, I crossed the Flaminia and the Piazzo del Popolo and walked the whole length Corso before returning to my apartment in the Piazza Minerva, where at about two o'clock I received the telegram informing me that my parents and my brother, Johannes, had died.)[21]

Even though the first sentences of *Moo Pak* and *Extinction* differ significantly in length, they both mention the narrators by name as well as an individual that they engage with throughout the novels. While Gambetti is Murnau's pupil in *Extinction*, Anderson appears as Toledano's student in *Moo Pak*, who uncritically records Toledano's monologue. The last sentence in *Extinction* provides the dates of the narrator's birth and death: "geboren 1934 in Wolfsegg, gestorben 1983 in Rom"[22] (born Wolfsegg 1934, died Rome 1983).[23] Josipovici also mentions the name of

---

19 Gabriel Josipovici, *Moo Pak* (Manchester: Carcanet, 1994), 9.
20 Thomas Bernhard, *Auslöschung* (Frankfurt: Suhrkamp: 1986), 7.
21 Thomas Bernhard, *Extinction*, trans. David McLintock (New York: Alfred A. Knopf, 1995), 3.
22 Bernhard, *Auslöschung*, 651.
23 Bernhard, *Extinction*, 326.

the narrator again at the end of *Moo Pak*.²⁴ But unlike *Extinction*, *Moo Pak* concludes with the narrator and Toledano parting ways.

The first sentence of *The Big Glass* is also reminiscent of Bernhard's style and motifs: "I began work on the big glass on 27 July 1967, wrote Harsnet."²⁵ This corresponds with the first line of Bernhard's *Wittgenstein Nephew: A Friendship* that also begins in the year 1967.²⁶ The big glass is an artwork the artist Harsnet created, and the novel chronicles the creation of the art work and presents a conglomerate of Harsnet's philosophy of art, as well as quite mundane thoughts, "breathless jottings,"²⁷ vulgarities, profanities, and personal rants.²⁸ As in Bernhard's novels, the artist's account is mediated by someone else. In the case of *The Big Glass*, it is Goldberg's task to type Harsnet's handwritten notes on his typewriter. The recurring phrase, often in parentheses, "typed Goldberg," reminds the reader that they are reading a typed account and not necessarily Harsnet's *ipsissima verba*. Some words and phrases appear underlined; it remains unclear if Harsnet highlighted them himself or if Goldberg felt the need to emphasize them. Bernhard also uses variations of this technique in several of his prose works, including *Frost*, *The Lime Works*, and *Extinction*. But unlike Bernhard, Josipovici gives the mouthpiece of the monological artist a distinguished voice. Goldberg, a friend of Harsnet's, openly questions the artist's assertions and his memory. He often interrupts typing Harsnet's, notes, writes marginalia if he finds questionable or remarkable words and phrases. At times Goldberg scribbles his own notes on his notepad to record his commentary, which contradicts Harsnet's account. At one point, Goldberg considers adding an appendix to Harsnet's book to present "the real facts (sic!)"²⁹ Even though Goldberg admires his artist friend and takes on the laborious task of transcribing Harsnet's notes, he does not simply and passively accept the artist's account at face value.

Harsnet's account is laced with repetitious structures and phrases, which reminds one of Bernhard's use of syntactical and lexical repetitions, as the following passage shows:

> There was the revulsion at the <u>fluidity</u> of life and the first tube of paint, the revulsion at the <u>meticulousness</u> of painting with a brush and the first pot of paint, the revulsion at the <u>viciousness</u>

---

24 Josipovici, *Moo Pak*, 150–51.
25 Gabriel Josipovici, *The Big Glass* (Manchester: Carcanet, 1991), 9.
26 Thomas Bernhard, *Wittgensteins Neffe* (Frankfurt: Suhrkamp, 1982), 7.
27 Fludernik, *Echoes and Mirrorings*, 83.
28 The inspiration for the book was Duchamp's "Large Glass." Cf. Gabriel Josipovici, "The Big Glass: A Note," *Salmagundi* 88/89: 333–38.
29 Josipovici, *The Big Glass*, 43.

of paint and the first readymade, the revulsion at the <u>arbitrariness</u> of the readymades and the first use of glass. Perhaps, he wrote, that is enough for a lifetime. Four real beginnings, wrote Harsnet, and four real rejections; the rejection of a life without art, the rejection of art, the rejection of any form of making, and the final rejection of all absolutes and the acceptance of compromise. Four beginnings, he wrote, each prompted by a sense of revulsion. *Four beginnings*, scribbled Goldberg in the margin of his typescript, *four revulsions*.[30]

Toledano, a former university lecturer and the main character in *Moo Pak*, reminds one of Bernhard's *Geistesmensch*, a term that does not have an equivalent in English. In English translations, the word *Geistesmensch* is translated as "intellectual," which is misleading. Although a *Geistesmensch* pursues intellectual studies to a certain degree, he clearly lacks some of the main characteristics of an intellectual. According to the definition found in one dictionary, an intellectual is "an extremely rational person; a person who relies on intellect rather than on emotions or feelings."[31] Bernhard's *Geistesmenschen*, however, such as Rudolf, the narrator in Bernhard's narrative work *Concrete*,[32] are not guided by intellect but rather by their own extreme feelings and irrational thoughts. Rudolf shows other features that are typical for the *Geistesmenschen* in Bernhard's works as he struggles with sarcoidosis, a lung disease from which Bernhard himself suffered.[33] Throughout the narrative, it becomes obvious that Rudolf's physical condition resembles his troubled mental state, a characteristic also shared by other *Geistesmenschen*.[34]

Toledano can be seen as a variation of Bernhard's *Geistesmensch*. Even though Toledano is rather idiosyncratic and his impetus to completely dominate conversations is similar to *Geistesmenschen*, he also differs

---

30 Josipovici, *The Big Glass* (Manchester: Carcanet, 1991), 13.
31 *Webster's New Universal Unabridged Dictionary. Fully revised and updated* (New York: Barnes & Noble Books, 1996), 990.
32 Thomas Bernhard, *Concrete*, trans. David McLintock (New York: Alfred A. Knopf, 1984).
33 See Charles W. Martin, *The Nihilism of Thomas Bernhard: The Portrayal of Existential and Social Problems in His Prose Works* (Amsterdam: Rodopi, 1995), 163.
34 See the figure of Paul Wittgenstein in Thomas Bernhard, *Wittgenstein's Nephew: A Friendship* (Alfred A. Knopf: New York, 1989). For a detailed discusion of the Geistesmensch, see Hajo Eickhoff, "Die Stufen der Disziplinierung: Thomas Bernhards Geistesmensch," in *Thomas Bernhard: Die Zurichtung des Menschen*, eds. Alexander Honold and Markus Joch (Würzburg: Königshausen & Neumann, 1999), 155–62.

from Bernhard's characters. Toledano does not suffer from any physical and/or mental illness, and his monologue is free from any tirades.

In the case of *Frost*, Bernhard's first novel of 1963, a nameless medical student narrates his encounters with the artist Strauch, a questionable artist and compulsive talker, in an Alpine village. It seems impossible to engage the artist in a true dialogue, as he seems to lack any social skills in conducting conversations. Instead, the narrator, who has to record Strauch's ongoing monologue for Strauch's brother, who happens to be the narrator's professor, does not seek to engage the artist in a dialogue. Instead, the medical student follows his object of study wherever Strauch may lead them.

Walking and talking go hand in hand in Bernhard's works. His novella, *Walking* (1971), makes this interrelatedness explicit:

> Außerdem gehe ich zweifellos und naturgemäß mit Ihnen anders als mit Karrer, sagt Öhler, weil es sich bei Karrer um einen ganz anderen Menschen als bei Ihnen und also bei Karrers gehen (und also Denken) um ein ganz anderes Gehen (und also Denken) handelt, sagt Öhler.[35]

> (Besides which, I doubtless, and in the nature of things, walk differently with you than I did with Karrer, says Öhler, because with Karrer it was a question of a quite different person from you and therefore with Karrer it was a question of quite different walking (and thinking) says Öhler.)[36]

The interplay of walking and talking is also an important theme in *Moo Pak*: "[T]here is nothing better than going for a walk with Jack Toledano. London is a walkers' paradise, he says, but you have to know where you go. Paris is for the flâneur, he says, but London is for the walker."[37] Walking and thinking, however, do not coincide for Toledano:

> The only way to think is, he says, is at a desk, the only way to make something which will cause others to think is at a desk with a typewriter in front of you. I am quite incapable of thought, he says, but with a typewriter in front of me and a nice think wad of A4 at my right hand I can, if all goes well, stimulate thought.[38]

---

35 Thomas Bernhard, *Gehen* (Frankfurt: Suhrkamp 1971), 8.
36 Thomas Bernhard, "Walking," in Thomas Bernhard, *Three Novellas*, trans. Kenneth J. Northcott (Chicago: University of Chicago Press, 2003), 114.
37 Josipovici, *Moo Pak*, 9.
38 Josipovici, *Moo Pak*, 9.

Toledano's thoughts are often illuminating and reveal that he is widely read and broadly educated. He touches on V. S. Naipaul's autobiographical novel *The Enigma of Arrival*, a book about a migrant settling down in a foreign country, a subject Toledano can relate too as he, like Josipovici himself, is a Jew from Egypt who settled in England.[39] Like Bernhard's protagonists, Toledano evokes Wittgenstein, whom he juxtaposes with Shakespeare. Milton, Fielding, Richardson, Kleist, Adorno, Kierkegaard, Lichtenberg, Thomas Mann, and many other thinkers and authors are referred to throughout the novel. Toledano's musings include critiques of psychoanalysis,[40] British Jewry,[41] as well as television and radio,[42] to name but a few topics he tackles.

But Toledano's thoughts are never fully developed. This, of course, makes sense, as his monologue is not a well-thought-out lecture but more of a conglomeration of unrelated thoughts, "a fluid entity in which one topic merges unfettered into another."[43] As Fuldernik astutely points out, "the significance of philosophical themes [in both *Moo Pak* and *The Big Glass*] is displaced by the harangues of the main protagonists, Harsnet and Toledano, and is thereby relativized and framed."[44]

Bernhard's main characters, on the other hand, often utter sentences that are highly questionable. The medical student, who has to record the artist's Strauch's monologues in *Frost*, has great difficulty in deciphering the seemingly undecipherable, unless one accepts Strauch's distorted perspectives as epistemologically valid:

> Was für eine Sprache, die Sprache Strauchs? Was fange ich mit seinen Gedankenfetzen an? Was mir zuerst zerrissen, zusammenhanglos schien, hat seine "wirklich ungeheuren Zusammenhänge": das ganze ist eine alles erschreckende Worttransfusion in die Welt, in die Menschen hinein, "ein rücksichtsloser Vorgang gegen den Schwachsinn," um mit ihm selber zu reden, "ein regenerationswürdiger ununterbrochener Tonnfallgrund."[45]
>
> (What sort of language is Strauch's language? What can I make of his scraps of thought? Things that initially struck me as disjointed and incoherent, actually possess "truly immense

---

39 Josipovici, *Moo Pak*, 46.
40 Josipovici, *Moo Pak*, 79.
41 Josipovici, *Moo Pak*, 66–67.
42 Josipovici, *Moo Pak*, 71.
43 Lucasta Miller, "Walk on the Word Side," https://www.independent.co.uk/arts-entertainment/books/book-review-walk-on-the-word-side-moo-pak-gabriel-josipovici-carcanet-1499-1441650.html
44 Fludernik, *Echoes and Mirrorings*, 88.
45 Thomas Bernhard, *Frost* (Frankfurt: Suhrkamp, 1963), 137.

connections": the whole thing is in the nature of an enormous transfusion of words into the world, into humans, "a pitiless processing against stupidity," as he would say, "an uninterrupted, regeneration-worthy backdrop of sound.")[46]

Bernhard's *Geistesmenschen* are always working on a *Geistesarbeit*, an intellectual work, usually a book, that they find impossible to complete. Toledano fits the *Geistesmensch* category in this regard, as he too is working on a book that he never finishes. But unlike Bernhard's *Geistesmenschen*, however, he comes to the realization that his book will never see the light of day:

> [...] I cannot quite accept that I was wrong to spend so long trying vainly to write [the book], and I cannot quite accept that I will never write it again. It is a bleak prospect though, [Toledano] said, when something that has lived with you all your conscious life and to which you have given the best of your life and to which you have given the best of yourself eventually lets you down.[47]

Bernhard's prose has often been praised for its musicality, which can be seen in its often exuberantly long sentences and repetitious structures and phrases. Josipovici uses repetition not only in *The Big Glass* as it was pointed out, but also in *Infinity: The Story of a Moment*, a book about the eccentric Sicilian composer Tancredo Pavone from the perspective of Massimo, Pavone's former butler.

> The piano is not an instrument for young ladies, Massimo, [Pavone] said, it is an instrument for gorillas. Only a gorilla has the strength to attack a piano as it should be attacked, he said, only a gorilla has the uninhibited energy to challenge the piano as it should be challenged. It was when I realised this, he said, that I made a point of going to Africa to study the gorilla. When you see the chest and the brow of a gorilla, he said, you realise what a puny being man is. Liszt was a gorilla of the piano, he said. Scriabin was a gorilla of the piano. Rachmaninov was a gorilla of the piano. But the first and greatest gorilla of the piano was Beethoven, he said.[48]

---

46 Thomas Bernhard, *Frost*, trans. Michael Hofmann (New York: Knopf, 2006), 148.
47 Josipovici, *Moo Pak*, 150.
48 Gabriel Josipovici, *Infinity: The Story of a Moment* (Manchester: Carcanet, 2012), 36f.

Bernhard's main characters are pessimists through and through. Living in Vienna leads to schizophrenia,[49] Austrians are 100 percent national socialists and 100 percent Catholic,[50] and progress is usually seen as decay, as the artist Strauch says: "Nichts ist fortschrittlich, aber nichts ist weniger fortschrittlich als die Philosophie. Fortschritt ist Unsinn. Unmöglich."[51] (Nothing is progressive, but nothing is less progressive than philosophy. Progress is tripe. Impossible.)[52]

Unlike Bernhard's protagonists, Josipovici's main characters are not mere pessimists. At times the composer Pavone appears as a misanthrope, who confesses that "I am a man who is drawn to extremes."[53] Thus, Pavone has some extreme views when it comes to cultures and civilizations:

> The English were once the most civilised people in the world, but they are now among the most barbaric. The French are the only civilised people left, he said. They are resisting the barbarism of America, the barbarism of the New World, but they will not be able to resist forever. Soon nobody will know what the world civilisation means. We must turn away from the world, as the Hindu sages have long known, he said, because the world will never be able to live up to our idea of what the world should be.[54]

Bernhard's characters hold similar extreme views, but unlike Pavone, they see no alternatives. Even though Pavone never attempts to overcome the materialism of this world by following Hindu spirituality, as he is indicating in this passage, he recognizes that cultural pessimism cannot be the answer to the problems modernity has caused. Toledano in *Moo Pak* recognizes the benefits of technological advances and sees positive value in democracy and cultural institutions. He rejects the thought of the mythical Golden Age: "Who would wish to return to the 1750s or 1850 or even the 1950s?"[55] He even calls himself an optimist at times, which he sees as grounded in his Jewish heritage: "[D]espite all evidence to the contrary, I never really feel we are done for. That may be my Jewish optimism, he says, what distinguishes me from Beckett and Bernhard."[56] His optimism is also steeped in the love he experienced as a child:

---

49 Thomas Bernhard, *Heldenplatz* (Frankfurt: Suhrkamp, 1988), 44.
50 Bernhard, *Heldenplatz*, 64.
51 Bernhard, *Frost* [1963], 81.
52 Bernhard, *Frost* [2006], 86.
53 Josipovici, *Infinity: The Story of a Moment*, 27.
54 Josipovici, *Infinity: The Story of a Moment*, 6.
55 Josipovici, *Moo Pak*, 62.
56 Josipovici, *Moo Pak*, 146.

We cannot achieve very much unless we love ourselves, he said, and we cannot love ourselves unless our parents have loved us. That is why, he said, in spite of everything, I am an optimist. If, like Bacon, I have an optimistic nervous system, I must owe that to the unstinting love my mother gave me and the trust I had in her. I am helped of course by the authors I treasure, he said. Proust, Dante and Wallace Stevens and the rest.[57]

Despite his claim that he is an optimist, Toledano shares the cultural pessimism of Bernhard's characters and the author himself. He explicitly mentions Bernhard and praises him for not giving in to the temptation to become a media sensation:

Perhaps Dante and Swift and Kafka were lucky, he said as we entered the deserted cathedral, they never had to endure the temptation of what is called media attention. Perhaps if they had been subjected to it they too would have succumbed, but somehow I doubt it. After all, Beckett did not succumb, Bernhard did not succumb, Pinget has not succumbed.[58]

Toledano's view is not correct, however. Bernhard craved media attention. He knew how to draw attention to himself and his works. Bernhard realized early on that public scandals would positively impact his popularity and book sales. From 1955 until his posthumously published testament, Bernhard caused a number of scandals.[59] Josipovici's works, on the other hand, are not associated with any scandals, as his characters are not as extreme in their views as Bernhard's. Even though they express their frustration with modern-day culture, they never attack their homeland, politicians, or cultural institutions with the intensity Bernhard was known for. Neither does Josipovici have a reputation as a fierce critic of Britain and British politics.

It is quite clear that Josipovici did not aim to mimic Bernhard's books, nor did he intend to cause any public scandals with his monologue novels. His appropriation of some of Bernhard's poetological strategies has different effects. Bernhard's consistent pessimism and nihilism are absent from Josipovici's monologue novels. The use of repetitions in *Infinity: The Story of a Moment* adds a level of musicality that corresponds with the topic of the novel. The staccato tone of *The*

---

57 Josipovici, *Moo Pak*, 70.
58 Josipovici, *Moo Pak*, 47.
59 Cf. Gregor Thuswaldner, "Skandale und Erregungen," in *Bernhard Handbuch: Leben – Werk – Wirkung*, eds. Martin Huber and Mandred Mittermayer (Stuttgart: Metzler, 2018).

Big Glass is caused by the short and often incomplete sentences. And Toledano's stream of consciousness in *Moo Pak* offers a glimpse into a curious and learned mind and not into the abyss of a soul. Josipovici takes his inspiration from several sources, which he makes quite explicit in *The Big Glass* and *Infinity: The Story of a Moment*. While the former points out in a note at the beginning of the novel that the book was inspired by Marcel Duchamp's work *Large Glass*, the artist's writings, as well as Octavio Paz's *Marcel Duchamp or the Castle of Purity*, the latter mentions that the book was based on the life and work of the Italian composer Giacinto Scelsi. In the note at the end of *Infinity*, Josipovici thanks the Fondazione Isabella Scelsi in Rome "for permission to incorporate fragments from Scelsi's own writings into the narrative."[60] While Bernhard's oeuvre also incorporates (auto)biographical material, he never explicitly revealed his sources. In the case of *Woodcutters* (1984), he even tried to deny the autobiographical nature of the work.[61] As this essay demonstrated, his three monologue novels can be read as Josipovici's sophisticated and very original homage to Thomas Bernhard. But labeling Josipovici as the "English Thomas Bernhard," as Suhrkamp did, would be, as the author himself says, "a big mistake."[62]

---

60 Josipovici, *Infinity: The Story of a Moment*, 122.
61 Cf. Karl Wagner, "Holzfällen. Eine Erregung," in *Bernhard Handbuch: Leben – Werk – Wirkung*, eds. Martin Huber and Manfred Mittermayer (Stuttgart: Metzler, 2018), 74–79.
62 Georgia DC, "Interview: Gabriel Josipovici, author & critic." https://bookblast.com/blog/interview-gabriel-josipovici-author-critic/

Ten Thomas Bernhard, Italo Calvino, Elena Ferrante, and Claudio Magris: From Postmodernism to Anti-Semitism

Saskia Elizabeth Ziolkowski

La penna è una vanga, scopre fosse, scava e stana scheletri e segreti oppure li copre con palate di parole più pesanti della terra. Affonda nel letame e, a seconda, sistema le spoglie a buio o in piena luce, fra gli applausi generali.

The pen is a spade, it exposes graves, digs and reveals skeletons and secrets, or it covers them up with shovelfuls of words heavier than earth. It bores into the dirt and, depending, lays out the remains in darkness or in broad daylight, to general applause.
    —Claudio Magris, Non luogo a procedere (Blameless)

In 1967, Italo Calvino wrote a letter about the "molto interessante e strano" (very interesting and strange) writings of Thomas Bernhard, recommending that the important publishing house Einaudi translate his works (*Frost, Verstörung, Amras,* and *Prosa*).[1] In 1977, Claudio Magris held one of the first international conferences for the Austrian writer in Trieste.[2] In 2014, the conference "Il più grande scrittore europeo? Omaggio a Thomas Bernhard" (The Greatest European Author? Homage to

---

1 Italo Calvino, *Lettere: 1940–1985* (Milan: Mondadori, 2001), 1051.
2 See Luigi Quattrocchi, "Thomas Bernhard in Italia," *Cultura e scuola* 26, no. 103 (1987): 48; and Eugenio Bernardi, "Bernhard in Italien," in *Literarisches Kolloquium Linz 1984: Thomas Bernhard*, ed. Alfred Pitterschatscher and Johann Lachinger (Linz: Adalbert Stifter-Institut, 1985), 175–80. Both Quattrocchi and Bernardi describe the conference in their discussions of Bernhard's early Italian reception.

Thomas Bernhard), whose title reveals the author's significant presence in contemporary Italy, included contributions by Micaela Latini, Michele Sisto, and Anita Raja, who some claim is the person behind the pen name Elena Ferrante.[3]

Building on these three moments of Bernhard's remarkable Italian appreciation, I examine how Bernhard can shed light on the works of Italo Calvino (1923–85), Claudio Magris (born 1939), and Elena Ferrante (birthdate unknown, but after Magris). First I outline Calvino's discovery of Bernhard, before moving to a comparison of Ferrante's and Bernhard's critiques of institutional structures and societies. The potential identification of Raja as Ferrante would add an extratextual link between Ferrante and Bernhard, but their works themselves manifest intriguing similarities, including their harsh critiques of society through a character's intense (and at times disturbing) reflections.[4] I end with Magris and what his relationship with Bernhard reveals about Austro-Italian connections, as well as about Magris's own work. Although Magris was born in the 1930s, like Bernhard, his novel *Non luogo a procedere* (*Blameless*, 2015) is the most recent work discussed in this chapter.[5] While these three authors reveal diverse aspects of Bernhard in Italy, including his significance for postmodernism, for critiquing society, and for reevaluating Austrian history, they all suggest Bernhard's significance for considering the role of the author after the Shoah.

Although Italian translations of *Frost*, *Verstörung*, and *Amras* that Calvino recommended to Einaudi in 1967 were not published until the eighties, Calvino continued to promote Bernhard. In 1977 he commented that the Austrian author should be better known and listed him

---

3   The conference is available online: https://www.youtube.com/watch?v=NaKp-TYOcOkQ. At the conference, Luigi Reitani states that when Bernhard talks about Austria, he is discussing all of Europe, and cites Bernhard's admiration of Cesare Pavese as a sign of Bernhard's European nature. His reference to Pavese reveals how Italian critics have also been interested in Bernhard because of how Italian authors inspired the Austrian author.
4   For an overview of why Ferrante as been identified as Raja, as well as the numerous problems with the identification, see Alexandra Schwartz, "The 'Unmasking' of Elena Ferrante," *The New Yorker*, October 3, 2016, https://www.newyorker.com/culture/cultural-comment/the-unmasking-of-elena-ferrante.
5   At the 2014 conference Raja examined the metaphorical functions of Bernhard's title in a discussion of the difficulties of translating Bernhard into Italian. The title of Magris's novel also functions on multiple levels, with the English translation obscuring some of the elements of the Italian. "Non luogo a procedere" is a legal term that means there is not enough evidence to proceed to trial, "no indictment" or "acquittal," rather than "blameless." The title is also reflected in the last words of the novel.

as someone who deserved the Nobel Prize.⁶ In 1978 Calvino declared Bernhard the best living author in the world.⁷ As the critic Luigi Quattrocchi explains, although it is surprising that Bernhard's Italian translations came so late (relatively), equally impressive is how quickly many of the Austrian's works were then published in Italian.⁸ Calvino's vocal admiration of Bernhard helped give the author a standing in Italian culture, before most of his works had been published in Italian.⁹

Adelphi ultimately became the Italian press that published the largest number of Bernhard's works. Revealing the publishing house's dedication to Bernhard, Adelphi has issued eighteen of Bernhard's works, from "È una commedia? È una tragedia" (originally "Ist es eine Komödie? Ist es eine Tragödie?" and in English "Is it a comedy? Is it a tragedy?") in 1971 to *Camminare* (originally *Gehen* and in English *Walking*) in 2018.¹⁰ Bernhard's "Is it a Tragedy? Is it a Comedy?" immediately precedes Calvino's "Dall'opaco" ("On the opaque") in the *Adelphiana 1971* collection, which is organized into sections. Both works narrate a walk, during which the ambulators contemplate the relationship between literary art and life. The two pieces offer musings on perception that have been read as significant for understanding the authors' points of view throughout their oeuvres. In Bernhard's story, a man considers going to the theater, but then instead takes a walk with a stranger, who offers his thoughts on the theater. It turns out the stranger

---

6 Calvino, *Lettere*, 1339.
7 Italo Alighiero Chiusano, *Literatur: Scrittori e libri tedeschi* (Milan: Rusconi, 1984), 616. Calvino read Bernhard in French and English translations.
8 Quattrocchi, "Thomas Bernhard in Italia," 46.
9 Two other significant contributors to Bernhard's pretranslation presence in Italy are Claudio Magris, discussed in this chapter, and Isabella Berthier Verondini, "Trilogia dell'intellettuale: *Frost, Verstörung, das Kalkwerk* di Thomas Bernhard," *Studi Germanici* 12, no. 1 (February 1974): 69–97.
10 Adelphi has published the following translations of Bernhard (with the Italian publication title and date following the German): "Ist es eine Komödie? Ist es eine Tragödie?" ("È una commedia? È una tragedia?") in *Adelphiana* (1971), *Verstörung* (*Perturbamento*, 1981), *Die Ursache* (*L'origine*, 1982), *Der Keller* (*La cantina*, 1984), *Der Untergeher* (*Il soccombente*, 1985), *Der Stimmenimitator* (*L'imitatore di voci*, 1987), *Der Atem* (*Il respiro*, 1989), *Wittgensteins Neffe* (*Il nipote di Wittgenstein*, 1989), *Holzfällen. Eine Erregung* (*Il colpo d'ascia. Una irritazione*, 1990), *Die Kälte* (*Il freddo*, 1991), *Alte Meister* (*Antichi Maestri*, 1992; rereleased in a new edition 2019), *Ein Kind* (*Un bambino*, 1994), *Auslöschung: ein Zerfall* (*Estinzione: uno sfacelo*, 1996), *Billigesser* (*I mangia a poco*, 2000), *Meine Preise* (*I miei premi*, 2009), collection of five autobiographical works (*Autobiografia*, 2011), *Goethe schtirbt* (*Goethe muore*, 2013), and *Gehen* (*Camminare*, 2018). Haas discusses the special place Bernhard, as a living Austrian author, has in Adelphi's publications; see Franz Haas, "In Italien," in *Blick von Aussen: Österreichische Literatur im internationalen Kontext*, eds. Franz Haas, Hermann Schlösser, and Klaus Zeyringer (Innsbruck: Haymon, 2003), 147.

killed his wife and is wearing her clothes. The ties between these clothes and the theater potentially reveal speech as script, "emblematic of the more general process of performative identity production in Bernhard's writing."[11] Ultimately, in answer to the questions, "Is it a comedy? Is it a tragedy?" the murderer suggests nothing in the theater can be as tragic as life and that therefore all art can be considered comedic.

Calvino was also aware of the disenchanted position of the modern writer. His "On the opaque" ends:

> dal fondo dell'opaco io scrivo, ricostruendo la mappa d'un aprico che è solo un inverificabile assioma per i calcoli della memoria, il luogo geometrico dell'io, di un me stesso di cui il me stesso ha bisogno per sapersi me stesso, l'io che serve solo perché il mondo riceva continuamente notizie dell'esistenza del mondo, un congegno di cui il mondo dispone per sapere se c'è.[12]
>
> (From the opaque, from the depths of the opaque I write, reconstructing the map of a sunniness that is only an unverifiable postulate for the computations of the memory, the geometrical location of the ego, of a self which the self needs to know that it is itself, the ego whose only function is that the world may continually receive news of the existence of the world, a contrivance at the service of the world for knowing if it exists.)[13]]

Calvino dwells on the important relationship between writing and life, suggesting that to promote this relationship as a positive one requires a mendacious leap of faith that is impossible in modern times. In this piece, Calvino experiments with an abstract, fluid narrative style that attempts to reflect the difficulty of writing after the discovery of the breakdown between the world and representing the world.

Similar to Bernhard's narrator, Calvino's observer dwells on the world as theater and human beings' role as interpreters. "On the Opaque" begins:

> Se allora mi avessero domandato che forma ha il mondo avrei detto che è in pendenza, con dislivelli irregolari, con sporgenze e rientranze, per cui mi trovo sempre in qualche modo come su

---

11 Andrew Webber, "Costume Drama: Performance and Identity in Bernhard," in *A Companion to the Works of Thomas Bernhard*, ed. Matthias Konzett (Rochester: Camden House, 2002), 156.
12 Italo Calvino, *La strada di San Giovanni*, ed. Cesare Garboli (Milan: Oscar Mondadori, 2011), 91.
13 Italo Calvino, *The Road to San Giovanni*, trans. Tim Parks (Toronto: Vintage Canada, 1995), 150.

un balcone, affacciato a un balaustra, e vedo ciò che il mondo contiene disporsi alla desta e alla sinistra a diverse distanze, su altri balconi o palchi di teatro soprastanti e sottostanti, d'un teatro il cui proscenio s'apre sul vuoto, sulla striscia di mare alta contro il cielo attraversato dai venti e dalle nuvole.[14]

(If they had asked then what shape the world is, I would have said it is a slope, with irregular shifts in height, with protrusions and hollows, so that somehow it's as if I were always on a balcony, looking out over the balustrade, whence I see the contents of the world ranged to the right and to the left at various distances, on other balconies or theatre boxes above or below, a theatre whose stage opens on the void, on the high strip of sea against the sky crossed by winds and clouds.)[15]

Although the world as a stage is an old trope, Bernhard and Calvino engage the idea as it functions in a modern, insecure, and violent world. Not only this, but both authors write from a place where this insecurity and violence are accepted. There is no hope of returning, or turning, to a time when art played, or could play, a more idealistic role in society. Calvino's opening sentence positions the narrator not on stage, but from a peripheral position of observation. The stage and void are describable, but not alterable. While Calvino and Bernhard's pessimistic outlooks are often read as based on autobiographical experiences, Calvino's war experiences and Bernhard's childhood, the two authors formulate their negative views as inherently part of contemporary society.

In 1981, when asked about his feelings on novels, as expressed in *Se una notte d'inverno un viaggiatore* (*If on a winter's night a traveler*, 1979), Calvino replied that it was difficult to believe in them anymore:

Vivo sempre nella speranza d'incontrare un romanziere che sia semplice, naïf, e che dica qualcosa di veramente nuovo. Ma non ne incontro fra i contemporanei. Anche nel caso di un autore che è autentico e magnifico narratore come l'austriaco Thomas Bernhard ci si accorge che i suoi testi narrativi sono molto costruiti e intellettuali.[16]

(I live with the hope of encountering a novelist who is simple, naïve, and says something really new. But I do not see this among my contemporaries. Even in the case of an authentic and magnificent author, like the Austrian Thomas Bernhard,

---

14 Calvino, *La strada*, 79.
15 Calvino, *The Road*, 129.
16 Italo Calvino, *Sono nato in America: Interviste 1951–1985*, eds. Luca Baranelli and Mario Barenghi (Milan: Mondadori, 2012), 436–37.

one realizes that his narrative texts are very fabricated and intellectual.)

For Calvino, all contemporary authors are too self-conscious and their literature expresses this abstraction from life. The sentences he had been asked about from *If on a winter's night a traveler* reflect on Calvino's own artistry and make clear that Calvino includes himself in this category of contemporary authors: "proprio ora che cominciavi a interessarti davvero, ecco che l'autore si crede in dovere di sfoggiare uno dei soliti virtuosismi letterari moderni, ripetere un capoverso tal quale. Un capoverso, dici? Ma è una pagina intera, puoi fare il confronto, non cambia nemmeno una virgola"[17] (just when you were beginning to grow truly interested, at this very point the author feels called upon to display one of those virtuoso tricks so customary in modern writing, repeating a paragraph word for word. Did you say paragraph? Why, it's a whole page; you make the comparison, he hasn't changed even a comma).[18] While Calvino is in part commenting on reading practices, book production, and his own writing in *If on a winter's night a traveler*, this description also suggests why Calvino viewed Bernhard as an author whose artifice was often apparent. Bernhard's repetition identifies his unique, powerful style, but for Calvino this quality also marks it as constructed, modern writing.

Calvino's view of artifice of course did not mean he believed contemporary literature was meaningless. In his posthumously published *Lezioni americane* (*Six Memos for the Next Millennium*) Calvino states: "My confidence in the future of literature consists in the knowledge that there are things that only literature can give us, by means specific to it."[19] Bernhard and Calvino were both prolific writers, for whom literature potentially did bear a significant relationship to the world and how the world is shaped. Calvino's *Six Memos for the Next Millennium* makes clear how with his experimental works, he did not mean to divide literature from the world. As Alan Tinkler has summarized, "Calvino realized that in order for literature to probe epistemological as well as ontological concerns, literary experimentation was necessary."[20]

---

17 Italo Calvino, *Se una notte d'inverno un viaggiatore* (Milan: Mondadori, 2002), 24.
18 Italo Calvino, *If on a winter's night a traveler*, trans. William Weaver (New York: Harcourt Brace & Company, 1981), 25.
19 Italo Calvino, *Six Memos for the Next Millennium*, trans. Patrick Creagh (New York: Vintage Books, 1993), 1. These essays were originally prepared for the Charles Eliot Norton lectures Calvino was supposed to give at Harvard, but he died before being able to deliver them. When criticism by Italian authors has been published in English, I have provided just that.
20 Alan Tinkler, "Italo Calvino," *The Review of Contemporary Fiction* 22, no. 1 (Spring 2002): 59.

In a 1977 interview, William H. Gass identified Calvino and Bernhard as especially significant living authors: "Lots of European writers are overblown, especially some of the French experimentalists, but Italo Calvino is wonderful. Thomas Bernhard's *The Lime Works* is impressive."[21] Calvino and Bernhard were doing more than just providing examples of a new style of writing.

Within the Italian context, Calvino's later works, including *If on a winter's night a traveler*, have been critiqued for moving away from his neorealism of the past, for moving away from committed literature.[22] While Bernhard and Calvino both employ repetition in their fiction and could be considered postmodernist writers in part because of their geometric and self-referential writing styles, Bernhard's work also clearly critiques society. Although postmodernism, like modernism, remains a debated term, that it expresses the problems of being without values comes to the fore in Italian considerations of the category. The term points to authors who explore what it means to live in the world without ideology. Whereas "modernism" had a negligible role in the Italian intellectual landscape of the twentieth century, "postmodernism" had a larger presence. Bernhard was attractive to Italians in part because of his critique of society, a critique that often suggests that the desire for an alternative to the existing social order will remain unrealized.[23]

Stefano Tani divides Italian postmodern or "young narrative" works of the 1980s into the "watchers," narrators who both describe the world from a somewhat alien, emotionally detached point of view and thematize the act of looking (Calvino, De Carlo, Del Giudice), and the "storytellers," narrators who describe history as "weighing down" the present and returning (Eco, Manfredi, Elkann).[24] Bernhard fits both

---

21 William H. Gass, "The Art of Fiction 16," interviewed by Thomas LeClair, *Paris Review* 70 (Summer 1977): 92.
22 See, for instance, Alessia Ricciardi's critique of Calvino, Alessia Ricciardi, *After La Dolce Vita: A Cultural Prehistory of Berlusconi's Italy* (Stanford, CA: Stanford University Press, 2012) and the response by Lucia Re, "Pasolini vs. Calvino, One More Time: The Debate on the Role of Intellectuals and Postmodernism in Italy Today," *MLN* 129, no. 1 (2014): 99–117.
23 "[T]he search for authenticity, truth and subjectivity, so crucial in the modernist novel, is abandoned in postmodern literature. To authors like Alain Robbe-Grillet, Umberto Eco, Thomas Pynchon or Thomas Bernhard, the entire problem of values seems meaningless because the longing for an alternative to the existing social order appears to them as utopian in the original sense of the word: as aiming at a reality that does not exist (and cannot exist)" (Peter V. Zima, *Modern/Postmodern: Society, Philosophy, Literature* [London; New York: Continuum, 2010] 194).
24 Stefano Tani, "*La Giovane Narrativa*: Emerging Italian Novelists in the Eighties," in *Postmodern Fiction in Europe and the Americas*, eds. Theo D'Haen and Hans Bertens (Amsterdam: Rodopi, 1988), 162–72.

descriptions. Bernhard's lookers are often concerned with the past and how it intersects and problematizes the very act of looking. In *Alte Meister* (*Old Masters*), the past, personal and historical, disrupt Reger's gaze. Partially because of the fluidity with which Bernhard's narrators, like the observer of Reger, the man in the museum, move from the personal to social to national critiques and back, Bernhard is often characterized as an intensely critical and candid author.

The adjectives candid, intense, blunt, cruel, searing, angry, honest, and merciless, have all been used to describe not only Bernhard's work but also Ferrante's novels. Although it may seem unusual to compare an author at times described as a misogynist to one frequently considered to be engaged in a feminist critique, critics and journalists have characterized the two authors using similar terms for several reasons, including their portrayals of communities and institutional structures. Both represent families unsentimentally, with an emphasis on how the family unit oppresses its individual members. For instance, in *Old Masters*, parents prevent Reger from living: "Die Eltern mußten tot sein, damit ich leben konnte, als die Eltern starben, lebte ich auf"[25] (My parents had to be dead for me to be able to live, when my parents died I revived).[26] The works of Ferrante, from her first novel *L'amore molesto* (*Troubling Love*, 1992) to her Neapolitan tetralogy (2011–2014), reveal how families oppress individuals, especially women, often making it nearly impossible for them to establish their own identities and live life freely.

In *Troubling Love*, Delia describes the imposition of her mother's visits. Delia lives in Rome, and her mother comes up from Naples, invading her space: "Si svegliava all'alba e, secondo le sue abitudini, lustrava da cima a fondo la cucina e il soggiorno. Cercavo di riaddormentarmi ma non ci riuscivo: irrigidita tra le lenzuola, avevo l'impressione che sfaccendando mi trasformasse il corpo in quello di una bambina con le rughe"[27] (She woke at dawn and, as was her habit, cleaned the kitchen and the living room from top to bottom. I tried to get back to sleep, but couldn't: rigid between the sheets, I had the impression that as she bustled about she transformed my body into that of a wizened child).[28] The presence of her mother forces Delia back into childhood, framed as a negative space of imprisonment. She feels oppressed in her own home. After her mother leaves, Delia rearranges the items her mother touched.

---

25 Thomas Bernhard, *Alte Meister: Komödie*, eds. Martin Huber and Wendelin Schmidt-Dengler (Frankfurt am Main: Suhrkamp, 2008), 67.
26 Thomas Bernhard, *Old Masters: A Comedy*, trans. by Ewald Osers (Chicago: The University of Chicago Press, 1992), 52.
27 Elena Ferrante, *L'amore molesto* (Rome: Edizioni e/o, 1992), 7–8.
28 Elena Ferrante, *Troubling Love*, trans. Ann Goldstein (New York: Europa Editions, 2006), 11.

Even her mother's smell leaves a disturbing trace: "Anche l'odore della sua presenza—un profumo che lasciava in casa un senso d'inquietudine—dopo un po' passava come d'estate l'odore d'una pioggia di breve durata"[29] (And in a little while the odor of her presence—a scent that left in the house a sense of restlessness—faded, like the smell of a passing shower in the summer).[30] This scent, however slight, affects Delia's psychological state, and she needs time to recover from it.

In Bernhard's *Concrete* the narrator feels an even stronger oppression when his sister visits. As in Delia's case, he has no control over when his family member will appear, and her disruptive presence keeps him from committing to his writing. In *Concrete* and *Troubling Love*, the solidity of the family members irritates the narrators. The intrusive habits of Delia's mother and Rudolf's sister reflect their seemingly stable identities, which unsettle the narrators. Similar to Delia's experience of her mother, the sister's different life view destroys Rudolf's concentration. As with Delia's mother, the smell of family continues to bother the narrator after his sister is gone: "Und obwohl ich schon, wie gesagt, dreimal gelüftet hatte, war noch immer der Geruch meiner Schwester im Zimmer, tatsächlich war ihr Geruch noch immer im ganzen Haus, mich ekelte vor diesem Geruch"[31] (And although I'd opened all the windows, as I've already said, my sister's smell was still in the room. In fact it permeated the house and made me feel sick).[32] The German emphasizes even more than the English how the repeated attempts to air out the house cannot remove the sister's smell. Even the lingering, invisible trace of a relation is disturbing, because it reflects the memory of the family member.

At the end of *Troubling Love*, Delia alters her identity papers to make her photo look more like her mother's image. This moment has been read both positively and negatively in terms of Delia's development, but in both cases it is not triumphant or restorative. Neither Ferrante nor Bernhard offers the hope of transcendence, which contributes to why both authors are described as brutal. Ferrante reflected on how uncomfortable this move away from transcendence makes some readers: "I'm always surprised when someone points out as a flaw the fact that my stories contain no possibility of transcendence."[33] Both authors portray

---

29 Ferrante, *L'amore molesto*, 8.
30 Ferrante, *Troubling*, 12.
31 Thomas Bernhard, *Beton*, eds. Martin Huber and Wendelin Schmidt-Dengler (Frankfurt am Main: Suhrkamp, 2006), 12.
32 Thomas Bernhard, *Concrete*, trans. David McLintock (New York: Vintage, 2010), 11.
33 Elena Ferrante, *Frantumaglia: A Writer's Journey*, translated by Ann Goldstein (New York: Europa Editions, 2016), 373.

the significance of art that does not offer transcendence. Many of Bernhard's works critique even the hope for transcendence. Stephen Dowden examines this in *Old Masters*: "Tintoretto's *Man with a White Beard* embodies for Reger all that is false and treacherous in great art: the utopian promise of transcendence, of human nobility, of perfection."[34] Ferrante says she clings to stories that "arise from a profound crisis of all our illusions."[35] Bernhard's works fit this description well.

Bernhard and Ferrante may be as famous for their publication choices as for their literature. Bernhard's will forbade his work's publication, performances, and sale in Austria. Ferrante continues to conceal her identity. Since the publication of *Troubling Love*, Ferrante has rejected banquets, awards, lectures, and other events that would require her appearance to promote her works. Bernhard's uncomfortable, critical descriptions of these experiences seem to validate Ferrante's decision. Their choices have been held up as critiques of how their contemporary societies function. At the same time, Bernhard and Ferrante's authorial decisions have both been called ploys, ostensible self-erasures that ultimately call more attention to the author's presence.

In their own writing, Ferrante and Bernhard's characters often operate around an absence, one that reveals the characters' inability to forget. In *Troubling Love*, Delia creates a dialogue with her dead mother. The work centers around the obsessive process of remembering in part due to an inability to fully function. In *L'amica geniale* (*My Brilliant Friend*, 2011), the missing friend prompts a four-volume work that insists on remembering and recreating the presence of someone who would like to disappear. This work, like many of Bernhard's, reveals how another person's phrases become part of oneself. Many of the authors' works raise questions about the problems of speaking for others, but also how others become part of oneself, often against one's desires. They also suggest the power of literature to recreate what has been forgotten or to suggest what people have tried to forget.

Bernhard and Ferrante examine the suffering of an individual in society and offer detailed descriptions of a specific society (Austrian, often Vienna; Italian, often Naples), that then leads to a reconsideration of European and Western society more generally. The international recognition of Bernhard's work helped to counterbalance the *The Sound of Music* idea of Austria; Ferrante's fame has offered a sharp counterpoint

---

34 Stephen Dowden, *Understanding Thomas Bernhard* (Columbia, SC: University of South Carolina Press, 1991), 63.
35 Ferrante, *Frantumaglia*, 373.

to the common *Room without a View* idea of Italy.[36] The local and specific nature of both authors' works is part of their appeal for reconsidering global issues. The precision of the authors' descriptions of their Austrian and Italian societies, especially in terms of the emotions these societies produce, have often caused readers not only to have intense reactions to their works, but to have viewed them as reflections of the authors' own lives as well.

Despite Ferrante's anonymity, her novels are frequently framed as autobiographical, with the assumption that such a detailed, honest portrayal of Neapolitan female experience must correspond to the author's own reality. Mark M. Anderson's description of Bernhard's work as "deeply personal" can help resituate Ferrante, in order to avoid the autobiographical-fictional bind: "Whether 'autobiographical' or 'fictional,' however, these texts are deeply personal and deeply performative."[37] Ferrante herself sees the need to firmly divide literary fiction from nonfiction as problematic and uses Virginia Woolf to clarify her position: "Because writing is innately artificial, its every use involves some form of fiction. The dividing line is rather, as Virginia Woolf said, how much truth the fiction inherent in writing is able to capture."[38] While Bernhard mocks the idea of an Austrian Woolf in *Holzfällen* (*Woodcutters*), the English author is an important figure in both his and Ferrante's literary genealogies. She contributes not only stylistically, in terms of their extensive portrayals of thought, but also in terms of suggesting how literature can capture truth through fiction.

Critics often situate Bernhard's reflections on crisis and truth in a longer Austrian tradition, especially the "Sprachkrise" (language crisis). Hermann Bahr's "das unrettbare Ich," Ernst Mach's "Das Ich ist unrettbar," Hugo von Hofmannsthal's Lord Chandos who declared, "Est ist mir völlig die Fähigkeit abhanden gekommen, über irgend

---

36 The works *Under the Tuscan Sun* and *Eat, Pray, Love* also frequently come up in considerations of Italy, a place where foreigners discover themselves and their passion. As significant as these three literary works for this sense of Italy are their film adaptations.
37 Mark M. Anderson, "Fragments of a Deluge: The Theater of Thomas Bernhard's Prose," in *A Companion to the Works of Thomas Bernhard*, edited by Matthias Konzett (Rochester: Camden House, 2002), 120.
38 Elena Ferrante, "I'm tired of fiction, I no longer see a reason to go hunting for anecdotes," in *The Guardian*, trans. by Ann Goldstein (February 17, 2018), https://www.theguardian.com/lifeandstyle/2018/feb/17/elena-ferrante-im-tired-of-fiction-i-no-longer-see-a-reason-to-go-hunting-for-anecdotes. Numerous opinion pieces by Ferrante were first published in *The Guardian* in English, but have now been collected and published in the original; see Elena Ferrante, *L'invenzione occasionale* (Rome: Edizioni e/o, 2019), 18. The Woolf reference has been removed.

etwas zusammenhängend zu denken oder zu sprechen" (I have completely lost the ability to think or speak coherently about anything at all),[39] and Ludwig Wittgenstein's lion suggest the complex richness of this Austrian heritage. The inability to express oneself raises the question of the instability of one's place in the world, a significant element of fin de siècle Austrian modernism. The Sprachkrise and crises of identity, which are both especially prominent in Austrian literature and thought, are inseparable.

Ferrante's work also interrogates language's ability to adequately express reality. Her much discussed term "smarginatura," which has become a defining term through which to understand her recent work, is understood as the blurring of boundaries.[40] While discussions of smarginatura often focus on the term's significance for understanding the female experience, of being at the margins, the term can also be understood as developing from and related to the language crisis, since it offers another way to discuss an experience that seems to lie beyond language. In *My Brilliant Friend,* Lila experiences her first episode of smarginatura: "Diceva che in quelle occasioni si dissolvevano all'improvviso i margini delle persone e delle cose. Quando quella notte, in cima al terrazzo dove stavamo festeggiando l'arrivo del 1959, fu investita bruscamente da un sensazione di quel tipo, si spaventò e si tenne la cosa per sé, ancora incapace di nominarla."[41] (She said that on those occasions the outlines of people and things suddenly dissolved, disappeared. That night, on the terrace where we were celebrating the arrival of 1959, when she was abruptly struck by that sensation, she was frightened and kept it to herself, still unable to name it.[42]) Lila's sense of not being firmly rooted in the world relates both to her position as a poor woman in Naples and to the inability to label or name her feeling of blurred boundaries. She faces an unavoidable disintegration that causes her to feel outside of society and without identity. In Bernhard the inability to truly express oneself is associated with the inability to truly live, a common feeling for many of his characters.

---

39   Hugo von Hofmannsthal, *The Lord Chandos Letter and Other Writings,* trans. Joel Rotenberg (New York: New York Review of Books, 2005), 121.
40   For a discussion of this term that examines it especially in terms of gender, see "*Smarginatura*: Motherhood and Female Friendship" (Part III), in *The Works of Elena Ferrante: Reconfiguring the Margins,* eds. Grace Russo Bullaro and Stephanie V. Love (New York: Palgrave Macmillan, 2016). Tiziana de Rogatis provides a clear examination of the term and its significance in Tiziana De Rogatis, *Elena Ferrante. Parole Chiave* (Rome: Edizioni e/o, 2018), 87–91.
41   Elena Ferrante, *L'amica geniale* (Rome: Edizioni e/o, 2011), 85.
42   Elena Ferrante, *My Brilliant Friend,* trans. Ann Goldstein (New York: Europa Editions, 2012), 89.

In a discussion of how Bernhard's works relates to those of Musil, Wittgenstein, Kafka, and Bachmann, the Italian intellectual Aldo Giorgio Gargani places Bernhard's relationship to language and reality in this aforementioned Austrian heritage: "Bernhard starts off writing that the main fact of our existence is not an existence which we describe and which is always a lie, rather the impossibility of saying what it is like. There is no truth to be hooked onto in spite of our will to tell the truth."[43] Calling attention to a connection between two of the reasons for Bernhard's Italian reception, Gargani's work bridges Italy's focus on Austrian culture and its attention to Bernhard's postmodernism. He was responsible both for a number of important works on Bernhard that placed him in an Austrian context, including *La frase infinita: Thomas Bernhard e la cultura austriaca* (*The Infinite Phrase: Thomas Bernhard and Austrian Culture*, 1990), and for the earlier edited volume *La crisi della ragione* (*The Crisis of Reason*, 1979), which contributed to the appreciation of postmodernism in Italy.[44] During the period in which postmodern literature was developed, there was a "boom" of Mitteleuropean works in Italy.[45] Franz Haas has described how in the sixties and seventies Arthur Schnitzler, Joseph Roth, and Alexander Lernet-Holenia were more popular in Italy than they were in their homeland.[46] As revealed in the previous case of Calvino, Austrian literature, including Bernhard's, played a role in shaping the Italian development of postmodernism.

Austrian literature has continued to have a notable presence in Italian critical writing and publishing. In 1992 the journal *Studi austriaci* (*Austrian Studies*) was founded and has featured numerous articles on Bernhard. The Italian author Roberto Calasso describes the continued significance of Austrian, as opposed to German, literature as follows: "Today is a difficult moment for that culture: the Frankfurt School, after the death of Adorno, survives only as a parody of itself, and the rare recent surprises in narrative have come from Austrian writers such as Thomas Bernhard, heirs of a tradition that is in many respects incompatible with Germany."[47] There are numerous attestations to Bernhard's

---

43 Aldo Giorgio Gargani, "'Thomas Bernhard's Infinite Phrase': A Summary," *Argumentation* 6 (1993): 447.
44 For a reading of Bernhard's postmodernism in terms of his Austrian heritage, see Elrud Ibsch, "From Hypothesis to *Korrektur*: Refutation as a Component of Postmodernist Discourse," in *Approaching Postmodernism*, eds. Douwe Fokkema and Hans Bertens (Amsterdam: John Benjamins Publishing Company, 1986), 119–34.
45 "überraschenden Boom von allen möglichen 'mitteleuropäischen' Werken in den sechziger und siebziger Jahren" (Haas, "In Italien," 146).
46 Haas, "In Italien," 147.
47 Roberto Calasso, *The Art of the Publisher*, trans. Richard Dixon (New York: Farrar, Straus and Giroux, 2013), 110.

enduring significance in Italy. From new editions, to performances of his plays, to conferences, Bernhard continues to be a subject of attention.[48] In May 2019 Franz Haas moderated a conference about Thomas Bernhard, "Tributo a Thomas Bernhard: Dialoghi 1989–2019" (Tribute to Thomas Bernhard: Dialogues 1989–2019), that brought together translators (Samir Thabet), directors (Monica Giovinazzi), and scholars (Micaela Latini, Stefano Apostolo, and Paolo Massari) to discuss Bernhard's role in the arts and Italy.

The reasons for the Austrian-Italian connections are multiple, including historical and cultural connections, travel between the two places, and political formations. The Catholic Austro-Hungarian Empire's control of large portions of now Italian territory and the Italian Marxist readings of many Austro-Hungarian authors (thanks in part to Lukács) are important contributing elements. Bernhard's depictions of Italy can be situated in this complex and rich tradition of Austro-Italian cross-pollinations. For instance, Bernhard's "Wahre Liebe" ("True Love") follows Kafka's "Der Jäger Gracchus" ("The Hunter Gracchus"), which was inspired by Kafka's Italian travels.[49] The Italian of "True Love" owns a villa on Riva on Lake Garda, where Kafka's "The Hunter Gracchus" is set. While "The Hunter Gracchus" describes a living corpse on a boat, in "True Love" the Italian rides the lake with his love, a mannequin, which draws on and parodies the uncanny of Kafka's story.[50] Bernhard's piece describes how a letter about the odd relationship appears in the newspaper of Desencano (Desenzano), another Italian location Kafka visited. With "True Love," Bernhard builds on an Austrian tradition of portraying Italy.

Italian people, places, and works appear repeatedly in Thomas Bernhard's oeuvre. Bernhard's "Pisa und Venedig" ("Pisa and Venice") offers a funny commentary on tourism, politics, and sanity. In the one-paragraph story, the mayors of the Italian cities are institutionalized, because they planned to put the leaning tower of Pisa in place of the Venetian campanile, and vice versa.[51] In *Beton* (*Concrete*), Rudolf speaks of having "viel gesehen" (seen a great deal of the world), listing Italy first and naming Taormina, Palermo, Agrigento, Calabria, Rome,

---

48 Ubulibri published a four-volume collection of Bernhard's plays, recently reissued by Einaudi. The publisher SE has published several of his works. In 1992 and again in 2007, the Eliseo theater in Rome staged Patrick Guinand's adaptation of *Wittgenstein's Nephew*.
49 Kafka and Bernhard have often been connected.
50 Thomas Bernhard, *Erzählungen: Kurzprosa*, eds. Hans Höller, Martin Huber, and Manfred Mittermayer (Salzburg: Suhrkamp, 2003), 307. Thomas Bernhard, *The Voice Imitator*, trans. Kenneth J. Northcott (Chicago: The University of Chicago Press, 1997), 67.
51 Bernhard, *Erzählungen: Kurzprosa*, 240. Bernhard, *The Voice Imitator*, 6.

Naples, Trieste, and Abbazia, a longer list than he provides for any of the other countries he mentions.[52] In *Auslöschung* (*Extinction*), Rome at times seems the positive counterbalance to the narrator's Austrian home of Wolfsegg.

Like London, Italy in Bernhard's work is often ultimately revealed as positive only in its distance from Austria, representing not an escape, but a place where Bernhard's characters can consider the idea of escape.[53] In "Der Italiener" ("The Italian"), a precursor to *Extinction*, the eponymous title character intimates that his country may be a place where one could flee the "darkness" and historical violence the Austrian narrator describes: "als der Italiener, der mich, nach kurzer Zeit schon, zu sich nach Florenz eingeladen hatte, nachdem wir über der Brücke waren, sagte: 'Die Finsternis, die hier herrscht …', und dann schwieg"[54] (the Italian had invited me to visit him in Florence; after we were over the bridge, he said 'The darkness which prevails here …, ' and then trailed off into silence).[55] Although the Italian suggests Florence may be a happier place, he concludes that there is "kein Mittel, sich selbst zu entfliehen"[56] (no means of escaping oneself).[57] Bernhard's "In Rom" ("In Rome"), which draws on Ingeborg Bachmann's life, states even more clearly how inescapable "Austria" is.[58] In this short piece, the narrator reflects on his friend's death by fire:

> Die an den Selbstmord der Dichterin glauben, sagen immer wieder, sie sei an sich selbst zerbrochen, während sie in Wirklichkeit naturgemäß nur an ihrer Umwelt und im Grunde an der Gemeinheit ihrer Heimat zerbrochen ist, von welcher sie auch im Ausland auf Schritt und Tritt verfolgt worden war wie so viele.[59]
>
> (Those who believe in the poet's suicide keep saying that she was broken by herself, whereas in reality and in the nature of things she was broken by her environment and, at bottom, by the

---

52 Bernhard, *Beton*, 51. Bernhard, *Concrete*, 57.
53 Ferry Radax adapted "The Italian" from Bernhard's screenplay of the same name. Suhrkamp has published it and the story "Der Italiener" together in a collection called *Der Italiener* (which is different from *An der Baumgrenze*).
54 Thomas Bernhard, *Erzählungen*, eds. Martin Huber and Wendelin Schmidt-Dengler (Frankfurt am Main: Suhrkamp, 2004), 1:258.
55 Thomas Bernhard, "The Italian," in *Relationships: An Anthology of Contemporary Austrian Prose*, ed. Donald G. Daviau and trans. Eric Williams (Riverside, CA: Ariadne Press, 1991), 75.
56 Bernhard, *Erzählungen*, 1:258.
57 Bernhard, "The Italian," 75.
58 One of the Italian's previous statements had already revealed that Italy does not in fact provide a refuge from the problems of Europe or of the world.
59 Bernhard, *Erzählungen: Kurzprosa*, 341.

meanness of her homeland, which persecuted her at every turn even when she was abroad, just as it does so many others.)[60]

The significant Italian presence in Bernhard's work is partially due to the author's travels in the peninsula, including ones with Bachmann, who had moved to Rome in 1953. While Bernhard mostly describes his contempt for the Ministry of Culture and Art in "The Austrian State Prize for Literature," he mentions being grateful for the grants from the Ministry that covered a couple of his trips to Italy.

Bernhard's visits contributed to his notable role in the Italian intellectual landscape, since Italians were then invested in Bernhard's depictions of their country and several of the Italians he met circulated his work.[61] The earliest Italian publications of Bernhard are testaments to these two elements of his reception. In 1981 the first freestanding Italian editions of Bernhard's works were published: Guanda's *L'italiano* (*An der Baumgrenze*) and Adelphi's *Perturbamento* (*Verstörung*). The change from the German's title of "On the tree-line" to "The Italian" in Guanda's edition stressed the stories' connections with Italy.[62] Bernhard's personal interactions with the author and editor Roberto Calasso helped cement the significant relationship between Adelphi and the Austrian author.

Calasso first met Bernhard in Rome in the 1970s, along with Bachmann, whose role in Bernhard's Italian fortunes has been noted.[63] Bernhard memorably talked all night about "The Irish, cemeteries, sleeping pills, farmers."[64] Calasso later saw him in Vienna: "Several years later, in Vienna, I delivered to him a volume of his autobiography that had just been published. He leafed through it, looked carefully at the print, and seemed pleased. Then he said the paper was good."[65] Calasso recounts how Bernhard's admiration for this Italian edition of his work then altered the format of the German edition of *In der Höhe*, with paper and a cover more similar to Adelphi editions than previous Residenz

---

60 Bernhard, *The Voice Imitator*, 90.
61 For instance, the author and artist Monica Sarsini met Bernhard, whom she later described as "her hero," "in 1982, when he came to Florence to accept the Premio Prato"; see Minna Zallman Proctor, *Landslide: True Stories* (New York: Catapult, 2017), 42.
62 This emphasis on Bernhard's Italian connections can also be seen with the inclusion of photos of Bernhard in Italy in Italian discussions of the Austrian author. For instance, the information from the Trent conference "Homage to Thomas Bernhard" ("Omaggio a Thomas Bernhard," 2000) reproduces several photographs, including one of Bernhard in Sicily from 1977.
63 Chiusano, *Literatur*, 616.
64 Calasso, *The Art of the Publisher*, 30.
65 Calasso, *The Art of the Publisher*, 30.

editions. Bernhard's Italian experiences and reception influenced Bernhard's German-language legacy.

In 1977 the Austrian author traveled to Trieste for the conference Magris organized on him.[66] Magris, an author and Germanist from the formerly Austro-Hungarian city of Trieste, is a key figure for the Austrian presence in Italy. His fictional and scholarly examinations of culture, history, and literature both shaped the international concept of Austrian literature and drew Italian attention to the historical connections between their country and Austria. Bernhard's first novel *Frost* and Magris's *Il mito absburgico nella letteratura austriaca moderna* (*The Habsburg Myth in Modern Austrian Literature*), based on his dissertation, both came out in 1963.[67] Magris's monograph, translated into German in 1966 (and still not translated into English), is often credited with exploding the idea of Austro-Hungarian nostalgia. Magris later commented that his *Il mito absburgico* may have even contributed to the myth itself, a myth much of Bernhard's work aimed to deconstruct. Magris's characterization of his first monograph illustrates how personal the question of Austria-Hungary is to the Triestine author:

> E per questo credo che il mio libro *Il mito asburgico* esprima un giudizio negative su quel mondo, ma attraverso il quale passa anche una fortissimo corrente di fascinazione. E alla fine sì, anche senza volerlo, è un libro autobiografico, poiché quello che ho riconosciuto nell'Impero asburgico in qualche misura è un processo, un tentativo di tenere insieme unità e frammentazione. Un problema che riguarda anche la mia stessa esistenza.[68]
>
> (And because of this I think that my book *Il mito asburgico* (*The Habsburg Myth*) expresses a negative judgment on that world, but through it there also flows an incredibly strong sense of fascination. And in the end, yes, even without wanting it, it is also an autobiographical book, since what I identified in the Habsburg Empire is in some ways a process, an attempt to keep together unity and fragmentation. A problem that also concerns my own existence.)

---

66 Bernhard's editor Siegfried Unseld and the critic Wendelin Schmidt-Dengler also attended the conference.
67 The title of Magris's book spells Habsburg "absburgico," but in referencing the work publishers sometimes alter the title to their preferred spelling of "asburgico." I have kept it as is in all the texts, which leads to some variety.
68 Magris, *Se non siamo innocenti: Marco Alloni dialoga con Claudio Magris* (Rome: Aliberti editore, 2011), 47.

Both born in the thirties, Magris and Bernhard grappled with many of the same issues in their works, including how Austria itself reflects and relates to personal struggles to navigate between deceptive unity and destructive fragmentation.

In 1972, Magris published an essay on Bernhard entitled, "Beckett su Danubio" ("Beckett on the Danube").[69] The following year, in a volume dedicated to the prominent Germanist Ladislao Mittner, Magris and other scholars wrote essays on the best German novels of the century, starting with Thomas Mann's *Buddenbrooks*. In the penultimate entry, which is dedicated to Bernhard's *Verstörung* (*Perturbazione*, later translated as *Perturbamento*, published in English as *Gargoyles*), Magris examines how Bernhard's obsessive prose of decomposition reveals the author's attraction to inescapable, horrible order, not chaos.

Magris mentions Bernhard in his esteemed literary work *Danubio* (*Danube*, 1986): "Debitrice della nuova estraniante letteratura di villaggio fiorita in Austria con Bernhard, Handke o Innerhofer, Herta Müller ne prosegue originalmente la sensitiva e cupa radicalità"[70] (Owing much to the new, alienating, "village literature" flourishing in Austria with Bernhard, Handke or Innerhofer, Herta Müller explores its dark, sensitive roots in an original manner).[71] This concept of "village literature," and even of "national literature," contributes to why critics do not often put Magris and Bernhard in conversation with each other, even though much of Magris's work resists these divisions and indicates some of the problems with them. Although the authors are invested in and investigated what being Austrian means, they are divided in terms of their linguistic and national identities. One English subtitle of *Danube, A Sentimental Journey from the Source to the Black Sea*, reveals another reason why Magris, despite his numerous connections with Bernhard, is rarely paired with the Austrian author.[72] While Magris's works are, like Bernhard's, often obsessive and focus on the return of the past, they are frequently described as nostalgic, sentimental,

---

69 Originally printed in *Il mondo*, August 10, 1972, the article was renamed and reprinted; see Claudio Magris, "Tenebra e geometria," in *Dietro le parole* (Milan: Garzanti, 2002), 285–90. *Danubio* (*Danube*) would later provide the title for Magris's famous literary work about the culture and history along the river.
70 Claudio Magris, *Danubio* (Milan: Garzanti, 2003), 361.
71 Claudio Magris, *Danube*, trans. Patrick Creagh (New York: Farrar, Straus and Giroux, 1990), 306.
72 For a notable exception, see Elena Morachielli, "Il triangolo dell'assoluto nei romanzi *Un altro mare* di Claudio Magris e *Il soccombente* di Thomas Bernhard," *Nuova antologia* 572 (January–March 1994): 480–500. Morachielli notes two elements that are also significant in my discussion (although examining different works by both authors): their presentation of history and the construction of a triangular narrative pattern.

or even romantic, not searing like those of Bernhard. Magris's more recent work, however, explores more directly the violent legacies of history, especially in Trieste.

The last part of this chapter puts *Blameless* in conversation with Bernhard's work in order to discuss the novel's formal experimentation, how it reveals Italian ties to Austrian culture, its indictment of society after the Second World War, and issues of suppressed memory.[73] Magris was inspired to write *Blameless* in part because of how Italian collective memory often ignores the death camp, Risiera San Sabba, located in Trieste. Bernhard's *Heldenplatz* provides one of the most powerful examples of how art can prompt a nation to revisit its relationship to its past. Bernhard's depictions of Austria, its Nazi past, and its anti-Semitism offer a productive model for Magris's depiction of Italy, its Fascist past, and its anti-Semitism. Both authors produce works that in part ask if art—plays, paintings, novels, and museums—can change a nation's relationship to its historical past. Their works contribute to a revisiting of their nation's identities and understandings of themselves. Both works suggest that silence can be a form of violence.

Like several of Bernhard's works, *Blameless* operates around a gap, a death, and missing papers. While the narrative covers a vast swath of history and numerous characters, it is primarily organized around two figures, a Triestine proponent of a museum dedicated to showcasing objects of war and a Triestine woman named Luisa. After the death of the proponent of the museum (henceforth referred to as "the man"), Luisa, who had worked with the man, is charged with organizing the remaining objects and papers in preparation for the museum's construction. While the man remains unnamed in the novel, in the note following the work Magris mentions the name of the historical figure that helped inspire the story, Diego de Henriquez. The "Museo della guerra per la pace Diego de Henriquez" (Museum of War for Peace Diego de Henriquez) now exists in Trieste. Much of *Blameless* revolves around real mysteries and ambiguities, like the mysterious death of Diego de Henriquez, who died in a fire. The novel suggests that in addition to this human loss, the fire consumed important papers that included information about Nazi perpetrators and the Triestine contribution to the deaths at Risiera San Sabba. Through their burning, the novel links the disappearance of the man, the victims of the Risiera death camp,

---

73 For a great analysis of the novel, see Sandra Parmegiani, "Remembering War: Memory and History in Claudio Magris's *Blameless*," in *Transmissions of Memory: Echoes, Traumas, and Nostalgia in Post-World War II Italian Culture*, ed. Patrizia Sambuco (Vancouver/Madison: Fairleigh Dickinson University Press, 2018), 91–107. She places the novel in the context of Magris's other works and analyzes how history and memory function in the work.

and the papers on which the man recorded the victims' names. The absence of these papers indicates that Triestines, years after the events, are invested in hiding the traces of their roles in the Shoah.[74] Magris's work is part of a current move in Italy to discuss how Italians contributed to the tragedies of the Second World War.

Fascist Italy has often been contrasted with Nazi Germany, putting Fascist rule in a comparatively positive light and at times framing Mussolini as having been merely misled by Hitler. The myth of "Italiani brava gente," the idea that Italians are fundamentally good people and therefore did not really contribute to the violence of the Second World War, has been hard to disrupt.[75] More recent works, like Simon Levis Sullam's *The Italian Executioners*, concentrate on the role of Italian perpetrators. Literature like Magris's contributes to this slow process of reshaping national self-awareness. *Heldenplatz* dwells on how Austria has not properly dealt with its relationship to the Holocaust. Bernhard's famous critiques of Austria, given many names, such as "Osterreichbeschimpfung," "Beleidigung des österreichischen Volkes," and "Nestbeschmutzung," present a picture of an Austria that numerous Austrians resisted. Part of the picture certain Austrian citizens held onto was possible because they were not Germans. As Rebecca S. Thomas has argued, authors like Bernhard "see the official denial of Austrian complicity in the machinations of the Third Reich as the primary repression upon which an entire edifice of false national self-consciousness rests."[76] Italy has similarly faced a difficult process in terms of its national self-consciousness, with many refusing to acknowledge its country's role in the Shoah.

While Bernhard repeatedly indicated that neither Austria nor Europe can distance itself from the atrocities of the Second World War, Magris suggests more overtly that violence connects people and that no society is innocent. Weapons and perpetrators travel. The man thinks that perhaps exhibiting all weapons will put an end to war, but one problem is perhaps nothing would then remain outside of the museum, since

---

74 Parmegiani has discussed how the novel raises "questions of local Triestine personalities as supporters or informers of the Germans, people instrumental to the efficient daily running of the concentration camp and of its load of human suffering" (Parmegiani, "Remembering War," 92).
75 In the last two decades, an increasing amount of work has been done to deconstruct the myth of "Italiani brava gente." For one article that clearly relates the myth to persecution of the Jews, see Davide Rodogni, "*Italiani brava gente*? Fascist Italy's Policy toward the Jews in the Balkans, April 1941–July 1943," *European History Quarterly* 35, no. 2 (2005): 213–40.
76 Rebecca S. Thomas, "Elfriede Jelinek's *Die Liebhaberinnen*: On the (Re)-Production Line," in *Modern Austrian Prose: Interpretations and Insights*, ed. Paul F. Dvorak (Riverside, CA: Ariadne, 2001), 76.

even a scarf can be a weapon. Another problem is no one wanted to listen to the man when he was alive. No one wanted the museum. Luisa's preparation of the papers and museum objects potentially suggest that Trieste, and the world more broadly, may be ready to consider the museum's existence. Works like Bernhard's are one reason for this shift. Bernhard's angry, shocking prose and theater made it less possible to ignore Austria's, and other European countries', role in the Shoah.

Bernhard's work often suggests that history not discussed will repeat, that the anti-Semitism of Austria is in part due to the country's failure to recognize its role in the Shoah: "Bernhard demands that spectators understand how the tenets of National Socialism remain indigenous to Germany and Austria."[77] *Blameless* similarly draws attention to how Italy has not dealt with its role in the Shoah, and therefore, anti-Semitism continues to be an issue. In the 2010s *Stolpersteine* (stumbling stones) have been dug up in the streets of Rome and swastikas have appeared on buildings. While Bernhard's works often argue that Nazi Germany was not an aberration, *Blameless* makes even clearer how embedded destructive prejudice is in human societies by referencing a larger geographical area and historical period. Italy's belated discussions of its anti-Semitism coincide with its belated discussions of its colonialism and racism. Magris's novel connects anti-Semitism and racism in order to draw attention to the tangles of hatred in society and the importance of dwelling on both of these issues, in Italy and beyond.

While the man and Luisa are located in Trieste and the sections are steeped in Trieste's specific history, the novel also includes discussions of the Chamacoco (indigenous people who dwelled primarily in what is now Paraguay), the slave trade, Otto Schimek (an Austrian buried in Poland who may or may not have refused to participate in a firing squad), and Su Tzu (a fifth-century BCE Chinese military strategist), among other figures and places. Luisa's background itself connects disparate histories of oppression and pain. Her father was an African American soldier stationed in Trieste, and her mother a Triestine Jew who had hidden in order to survive the Second World War. In part through her attempts to understand her parents, the issues of contemporary racism and anti-Semitism are interwoven and made personal. Certain images, like exodus, are used to consider both the slave trade and Jewish persecution. The pain of those who have survived oppression connects them: "Non che avesse importanza; tutta la terra è un cimitero e questo vale per tutti, ma ancora di più per noi, per i figli

---

77 Gene A. Plunka, *Holocaust Drama: The Theater of Atrocity* (Cambridge: Cambridge University Press, 2009), 49.

del Galuth e della Tratta"[78] (Not that it mattered; the whole world is a cemetery and that goes for everyone, but even more so for us, for the children of Galuth and Slavery).[79] At the same time, the novel details the very different experiences Luisa's black father had from her Jewish Italian mother. Her father's reticence to talk about his past is framed in terms of her mother's having survived the Shoah: "Doveva aver avuto imbarazzo a parlare di oltraggi razziali a chi era passato attraverso la Shoah"[80] (He must have been embarrassed to talk about racial insults to someone who had endured the Holocaust).[81] Magris's novel, unlike the man's ideas for a museum that it describes, does not offer potential resolutions to the tangle of violence and hate we have created. Sometimes all that we can do is write and read, knowing, as Bernhard often argued, that neither will necessarily change anything but may lead to awareness.

Like *Heldenplatz*, *Blameless* makes clear how personal and disturbing the unacknowledged legacies of violence and anti-Semitism can be. Luisa is the granddaughter of Deborah, who was killed in the Risiera. Luisa considers not only the Risiera from an analytical point of view, as she reads the man's papers that describe it, but also from personal perspective, in terms of how it has shaped her family. The reader of *Blameless* discovers only after having encountered Deborah as Luisa's grandmother and a victim of Risiera, that she most likely gave up the names of other Jewish family and friends, leading to their deaths. As in Bernhard, the divide between victim and perpetrator is blurred: "*Heldenplatz* ultimately undermines stark oppositions of victims and perpetrators and instead reveals a problematic relationship between the two."[82] Both focus on complicated victims, undercutting the idea of "pure" victimhood. In *Heldenplatz*, the Jewish professor is painted as cruel to many of the people around him and especially dismissive of women.

Bernhard and Magris reveal how numerous personal interactions, before and after the Second World War, prevent a clear separation of victim and victimizer. In *Troubling Love* and *Concrete* the smell of family disturbed the narrators by highlighting their inescapable proximity. In *Blameless*, odors suggest the discomfort of remembering victims and the disturbing closeness of victims to their perpetrators: "Nelle celle della Risiera ristagna la puzza delle vittime, e non degli aguzzini. Lerch, in quelle belle serate in Carso, non puzzava; forse in quel momento era più sgradevole l'odore di sua madre, che a vederlo cominciava a

---

78 Claudio Magris, *Non luogo a procedere* (Milan: Garzanti, 2015), 267.
79 Claudio Magris, *Blameless*, trans. Anne Milano Appel (New Haven: Yale University Press, 2017), 249.
80 Magris, *Non luogo a procedere*, 235.
81 Magris, *Blameless*, 219.
82 Fatima Naqvi, "Dialectic at a Standstill: The Discourse of Victimhood in Thomas Bernhard's *Heldenplatz*," *The German Quarterly* 77, no. 4 (Autumn 2002): 408.

sudare"[83] (In the cells of the Risiera the stink of the victims, not the perpetrators, hangs heavy. Lerch, on those lovely evenings in the Karst, did not stink; perhaps more unpleasant at the time was her mother's odor, since she would start sweating when she saw him).[84] Lerch, the former Nazi, attends social gatherings with Luisa's mother Sara, who survived the Shoah. Sara's reaction to the encounter, not Lerch's, recalls the tragedy they were part of, with Sara as persecuted and Lerch as persecutor. *Blameless* reflects on the disturbing fact that hate and prejudice are often felt for one's neighbor: "Non si pesta lo straniero, ma l'indigeno, chi è figlio della tua terra come te ma tu non credi che lo sia come te e lui pensa la stessa cosa di te"[85] (You don't tread on the foreigner, but on the local, on the one who is a native son of your country just as you are, but you don't think he's like you, and he feels the same about you).[86] Even the "tread upon" is not absolved from feeling distanced from his or her neighbors. Bernhard similarly draws attention to the disturbing ugliness of how anti-Semitism occurs despite how integrated Jews were and continue to be in Austrian society.

The confusion of perpetrator and victim function on a stylistic level as well as a thematic one. In Bernhard's work, a reader is often unsure of the original source of a quote until the end of a sentence. In *Heldenplatz*, for instance, characters share a thought that ends with "the professor said": "Ich komme mir vor wie in einem Museum/hat der Professor immer gesagt"[87] (I seem to myself to be in a museum/the Professor always said).[88] Thomas Cousineau has examined the "triadic patterns" in Bernhard's work that help blur the lines between different characters: "he introduces a first-person narrator who appears to be speaking directly to us, only to shift a moment later to a detail that points, rather, to a triangular narrative situation."[89] The narratives in *Blameless* are also embedded and in conversation with each other. *Blameless* alternates between chapters taken from the man's remaining notes, Luisa's thoughts about the museum, reflections on Luisa's own story, and other stories related to materials that will potentially be in the museum. At times the reader does not know who narrates a section until partway through the passage. While some of the chapters appear distinct with labels such as "Luisa's Story," the

---

83 Magris, *Non luogo a procedere*, 267.
84 Magris, *Blameless*, 250.
85 Magris, *Non luogo a procedere*, 236.
86 Magris, *Blameless*, 220.
87 Thomas Bernhard, *Dramen*, eds. Martin Huber and Bernhard Judex (Berlin: Suhrkamp Verlag, 2012), 6:251.
88 Thomas Bernhard, *Heldenplatz*, trans. by Meredith Oakes and Andrea Tierny (London: Oberon, 2010), 47.
89 Thomas J. Cousineau, *Three-Part Inventions: The Novels of Thomas Bernhard* (Newark: University of Delaware Press, 2008), 144.

themes and ideas are recurring and interwoven. Voices of victims are woven together with others.

In *Heldenplatz*, as in many other of Bernhard's works, thoughts of one character become part of the perspective of another. Interaction is a form of contamination. In *Blameless*, Luisa spends so much time reading the man's notebooks, trying to organize the museum project he left behind, that his mode of thinking becomes part of hers:

> Un bacio, un morso—sto diventando anch'io come lui; furia di leggere le sue carte sino a confondermi con lui e di occuparmi delle sue mitragliatrici e delle sue spade, adesso poi che ho preso l'abitudine di portarmi anche a casa, la era, un po' di quelle carte e di quelle fotografie per studiare come sistemarle finché mi viene sonno, finirò per credere anch'io che tutto sia solo guerra e ogni segno una cicatrice.[90]
>
> (A kiss, a bite—I'm becoming just like him; as a result of reading his papers, of identifying with him and dealing with his machine guns and swords, now that I've gotten into the habit of taking some of those papers and photographs home in the evening so I can ponder how to display them until I fall asleep, I'll end up believing, like him, that everything is war and every mark a scar.)[91]

The works reveal the power of whom you spend time with or read. At the same time, neither Magris nor Bernhard propose culture and literature will solve their country's or the world's problems.[92] Bernhard's works often shed light on the culture and education of the Nazis. *Blameless* reveals the madness of believing a museum can bring about peace. As discussed in terms of Calvino and Bernhard, they write from a more pessimistic place. As discussed in terms of Ferrante and Bernhard, the idea of transcendence is presented as naïve and dangerous. Bernhard's works and Magris's *Blameless* embed doubts about how or if culture can really change anything in works that nevertheless aim to change culture and memory. Bernhard and Magris remind us of the potential significance of writing and reading, even as the world seems to be going up in flames and even if writing and reading will not change this.

---

90 Magris, *Non luogo a procedere*, 12.
91 Magris, *Blameless*, 6.
92 See, for instance, Plunka's discussion of the *Eve of Retirement*: "Vera and Rudolf appear to be good citizens, albeit Nazis. They appreciate art and music, share a love of nature, are well respected in the community, take care of their handicapped sister, and successfully fight against a poison gas factory being built in their neighborhood" (Plunka, *Holocaust Drama*, 47).

Eleven Thomas Bernhard's *Extinction*: Variations/Variazioni/ Variaciones

Juliane Werner

Since the early days of his international reception, Thomas Bernhard has been a "writer's writer": an author whose works hold creative stimuli for kindred spirits. Many of his high-profile readers—ranging from Imre Kertész to Gabriel Josipovici, and from Jon Fosse to William Gaddis—find the encounter with Austria's foremost literary agitator inspiring enough to introduce his idiosyncrasies into their own writing, often to the extent of producing whole books à la Bernhard. While some of these take the form of parodies at the expense of the original text, most of them prove to be appreciative pastiches. However, not all authors concerned create homages willingly; *exercices de style* can be responses to an influence described by some as nothing less than a curse that can only be overcome by imitation.

After a brief overview of the various shapes these adaptations take, this paper explores three "variations" of Bernhard's last published novel *Extinction* (1996; *Auslöschung. Ein Zerfall*, 1986): Tim Parks's *Destiny* (1999), Horacio Castellanos Moya's *El asco: Thomas Bernhard en San Salvador* (1997), and Vitaliano Trevisan's *Il ponte: Un crollo* (2007). Through a comparative analysis of these adaptations in three different languages and cultural contexts I provide insights into the transposability of his narrative techniques, the universality of his topics, and ultimately into where the fascination of Bernhard's "formula" lies.

The Author as a Virus, the Author as a Curse

In a letter to his publisher Siegfried Unseld written in 1970, seven years after his literary breakthrough with his novel *Frost*, Thomas Bernhard cannot help but notice how many of his colleagues seem to have read his work: "Bei etlichen jungen Leuten, deren Schreibweise sehr stark an die meinige erinnert, weiss ich nicht, soll ich mich freuen, oder das ganze schreibende Gesindel verfluchen!"[1] (With very many young people, whose writing style is very reminiscent of mine, I don't know if I should be happy or curse the whole writing rabble!) Three years later, joy is no longer an option. With regard to the similarities between *Frost* and the novel *In Trubschachen* (1973) by the Swiss author E. Y. Meyer, Bernhard feels plagiarized and tells Unseld that Meyer should be forbidden to write this way and not be published at all: "[…] soviele Bücher, die ich aufmache, beweisen mir, wieviele Schriftsteller meine Prosa gelesen haben. Andauernd kommen [mir] lauter Enkel und mit diesen Enkeln verwandte Enkel meiner Figuren auf mich zu. Wirkung ist letztenendes etwas Furchtbares"[2] ([…] so many books that I open prove to me just how many writers have read my prose. I am constantly confronted with grandchildren and related grandchildren of my characters. Impact is something terrible after all). This aversion does not include the "unproductive" receiving audience, given Bernhard's belief that "[…] ein Wert entsteht nur dadurch, wie etwas aufgenommen wird. Im Echo. Wenn's keines hat, hat's auch keinen Wert"[3] ([…] worth only comes from how something is received. From the echo. If it has none, it is of no worth either). In other words: "Wenn Sie glauben, Sie schreiben ein Buch, Sie schreiben's nur für sich, und das liest die Omi und der Opa und irgendein blöder Germanist, na das wäre zu wenig"[4] (If you think you're writing a book, you're writing it just for yourself, and grandma and grandpa and some stupid German philologist will read it, well that wouldn't be enough). It's precisely those philologists and their reviews, essays, and teaching that he can rely on when it comes to attaining his admitted aim, "weltweit ausstrahlen"[5] (to resonate worldwide). Among those, whose "pure" reception becomes productive—that is, whose reading of Bernhard's work inspires the production of new literature—there are many writers with a background in German Studies, such as the aforementioned E. Y. Meyer (1946–) from Switzerland, Jörg Uwe Sauer (1963–) from Germany, Alexander Schimmelbusch (1975–) from Austria, Barbi Marković (1980–) from Serbia, and Gordon

---

1   Thomas Bernhard, Letter to Unseld, April 28, 1970, *Thomas Bernhard und Siegfried Unseld. Der Briefwechsel*, ed. Raimund Fellinger, Martin Huber, and Julia Ketterer (Frankfurt am Main: Suhrkamp, 2009), 171–72.
2   Bernhard, Letter to Unseld, March 21, 1973, *Thomas Bernhard und Siegfried Unseld*, 352.
3   Thomas Bernhard, Interview with Kurt Hofmann, in *Aus Gesprächen mit Thomas Bernhard* (Vienna: Löcker, 1988), 19–20.
4   Thomas Bernhard, "Die Ursache bin ich selbst. Madrid 1986," Interview with Krista Fleischmann, in *Thomas Bernhard. Eine Begegnung. Gespräche mit Krista Fleischmann* (Frankfurt am Main: Suhrkamp, 2007), 142–43.
5   Bernhard, "Die Ursache bin ich selbst. Madrid 1986," 115.

Lish (1934–) from the United States. Scholars of other disciplines, such as British scholar Gabriel Josipovici (1940–) or Argentinian novelist Ricardo Piglia (1941–2017), also add to this list. This striking presence of creative admirers of Bernhard in academia hints at the symbolic capital at stake, as one of multiple reasons—personal, economic, and political—that may play a role in the adaptation of another author's text.[6]

The majority of books à la Bernhard appropriate both the author's content and style, with the latter being more clearly recognizable, since topics such as mania, sickness, or solitude as well as recurring motives such as writing a study that will never be finished, insulting cities and countries along with the people that live in them, questioning truths and the means of expressing them, or sudden deaths of relatives combined with unwanted inheritances could well be found in other works of fiction, albeit less compressed. As for language, the situation is unambiguous, says Andreas Schäfer in the German weekly *Die Zeit*: "Bernhard hat bestimmte Stilmittel so exzessiv benutzt, dass er sie zu seinem Eigentum gemacht hat"[7] (Bernhard has used certain stylistic devices so excessively that he has made them his property). This property, however, can hardly be kept to himself, since he apparently voices what like-minded spirits think and feel but have not yet had the time to write down. This is the case when the fatally ill hero of William Gaddis's last novel *Agapē Agape* (2002)—unable to finish his major study on player pianos—reads the beginning of *Concrete* and is left aghast: "It's my opening page, he's plagiarized my work right here in front of me before I've even written it!"[8] Gaddis's is not the only example: the protagonist of Jörg Uwe Sauer's novel *Uniklinik* is stunned in a similar way: "Ich war damals unglaublich entsetzt, als ich Bernhards Buch aufschlug, um dortselbst meine eigenen Aussagen, teilweise sogar wörtlich, lesen zu müssen"[9] (I was incredibly shocked back then, when I opened Bernhard's book, to have to read my own utterances there, some of them even literally). In an absurd take on the idea that significant literary works develop a kind of maelstrom and invite imitation, here the "mighty dead" of literary history are resurrected "through the quasi-willing mediumship" of later authors, as Harold Bloom notes in *The Anxiety of Influence*: "[…]

---

6   For further discussion see the chapter "Why Adapt?" in Linda Hutcheon, *A Theory of Adaptation* (New York: Routledge, 2006).
7   Andreas Schäfer, "Sein Schreibstil war ein Virus," *Die Zeit*, June 2, 2014.
8   William Gaddis, *Agapē Agape* (London: Penguin, 2003), 12. Gaddis, who in the early 1990s after reading *The Lime Works* finds in Bernhard "my Cicero for all future engagements" (Letter to Gregory Comnes, http://www.williamgaddis.org/agape/wordsruin.shtml), herewith writes "an homage to Bernhard and, particularly, to that work [*Concrete*]," says Sven Birkerts in his introduction to *Agapē Agape*, xii.
9   Jörg Uwe Sauer, *Uniklinik* (Reinbek: Rowohlt, 1999), 151.

the triumph of having so stationed the precursor, in one's own work, that particular passages in *his* work seem to be not presages of one's own advent, but rather to be indebted to one's own achievement, and even (necessarily) to be lessened by one's greater splendor."[10] As if suspecting such postmodern experiments, Bernhard's narrators frequently elaborate on the thought that every text belongs to "a tissue of quotations"[11] by stating: "alles, was gesagt wird, zitiert"[12] ("everything that is said is a quotation").[13]

Related to Bernhard's obtaining advantage over fellow authors with similar intentions is the notion that his style is infectious and can only be conquered (and gotten rid of) by imitation. The French author and photographer Hervé Guibert (1955–1991) in his novel *To the Friend Who Did Not Save My Life* (*A l'ami qui ne m'a pas sauvé la vie*) describes, for example, how parallel to the HIV infection in his body, the "métastase bernhardienne"[14] ("Bernhardian metastasis")[15] with its devastating dominance spreads in his writing. Bernhard's tone, Schäfer concludes, is simply "zu markant" (too distinctive) to not let the author appear like "ein Fluch" (a curse), and his style like "ein Virus"[16] (a virus).

The degree of proximity of the—voluntary or imposed—appropriations to Bernhard's work varies. There are texts that adapt a single hypotext: Barbi Marković's *Izlaženje* (2006), a rejuvenating "remix" of Bernhard's novella *Walking* (*Gehen*), for example, sticks close to the original sentence structure and word order when catapulting the 1971 story about a group of *flâneurs* strolling through the ninth district of Vienna into the world of young clubbers in Belgrade. Other texts adapt a variety of identifiable hypotexts, such as *Kaddish for a Child Not Born* (*Kaddis a meg nem született gyermekért*, 1990) or *Liquidation* (*Felszámolás*, 2003) by Hungarian Nobel Laureate Imre Kertész.[17] A further group of imitative texts cannot be linked

---

10 Harold Bloom, *The Anxiety of Influence: A Theory of Poetry*, 2nd ed. (New York, Oxford: Oxford University Press, 1997), 140, 141. For the notion of anticipatory plagiarism (a term coined by Oulipo co-founder François Le Lionnais), cf. Pierre Bayard, *Le Plagiat par anticipation* (Paris: Éditions de Minuit, 2009).
11 Roland Barthes, "The Death of the Author," *Image. Music. Text*, trans. Stephen Heath (London: Fontana, 1977), 146.
12 Thomas Bernhard, *Gehen* (Frankfurt am Main: Suhrkamp, 1971), 22.
13 Thomas Bernhard, *Walking: A Novella*, trans. Kenneth Northcott (Chicago, London: The University of Chicago Press, 2015), 17.
14 Hervé Guibert, *A l'ami qui ne m'a pas sauvé la vie* (Paris: Gallimard, 1990), 232.
15 Hervé Guibert, *To the Friend Who Did Not Save My Life*, trans. Linda Coverdale (New York: Atheneum, 1991), 198.
16 Schäfer, "Sein Schreibstil war ein Virus."
17 Cf. Gudrun Kuhn, "Eingedenken. Imre Kertész im Dialog mit Thomas Bernhard," in *Thomas Bernhard Jahrbuch 2007/2008*, eds. Martin Huber, Bernhard Judex, Manfred Mittermayer, and Wendelin Schmidt-Dengler (Vienna, Cologne, Weimar: Böhlau, 2009), 37–51.

to specific works of Bernhard's, but in general imitates style, topics, and motifs, such as Jon Fosse's novel *Melancholy* (*Melancholia I*, 1995), which plunges its protagonist into a crisis bordering on hallucination and manifesting itself on the syntactic level by overextended sentences and the abandonment of paragraphs. As one of Bernhard's translators into Norwegian (in 1997 the play *Ritter, Dene, Voss*, in 1999 the play *Destination* [*Am Ziel*]), Fosse is highly familiar with the author's idiosyncrasies, obviously allowing him to keep his stylistic independence. This seems to hold true for all translators of Bernhard's works, whose number is disproportionately high among those who also write books in the style of Bernhard. If Bernhard's style has been called the most influential in German-speaking literature after World War II, his catching "fix und fertige Schreibweise"[18] (ready-made diction) can only be partly preserved in other languages. What is lost in translation, due to structural differences and a lack of interlingual equivalents, are, for instance, the compounds that make up for so many of Bernhard's typical neologisms (e.g., turning the "Weinflaschenstöpselfabrikanten"[19] into "the wine cork manufacturer.")[20] The three texts on which this chapter focuses—written in English, Italian, and Spanish[21]—all do without the word-clusters that Bernhard uses so generously in the underlying hypotext *Extinction*. This is the price one has to pay, says British author, scholar, and translator Tim Parks (1954–), who, living in Verona, got to know Bernhard's work in Italian. In his book *Translating Style* he comments on the gains and losses of reading translations:

> No one wants to suggest that a dumbing down is involved in reading Dostoevsky or Bernhard or Calvino in English. Many of my own most important reading experiences have been of authors read in translation. All the same, that absolute congruity between language and subject, typical of the work read in the original, is inevitably lacking in the translation, and with it goes a certain intensity of cohesion and the corresponding mental engagement it stimulates.

---

18 Schäfer, "Sein Schreibstil war ein Virus."
19 Thomas Bernhard, *Auslöschung. Ein Zerfall* [= Werke 9], ed. Hans Höller (Frankfurt am Main: Suhrkamp, 2018), 10.
20 Thomas Bernhard, *Extinction*, trans. David McLintock (New York: Vintage, 2011), 5. Cf. Erstes internationales Bernhard-Übersetzer-Symposium, eds., *"Ein übersetztes Buch ist wie eine Leiche." Übersetzer antworten Thomas Bernhard* (Mattighofen: Korrektur Verlag, 2017).
21 The novel *Auslöschung. Ein Zerfall* (1986) was translated into Italian (*Estinzione. Uno sfacelo*, trans. Andreina Lavagetto [Milan: Adelphi, 1996]) the same year as into English (*Extinction*, trans. David McLintock [New York: Knopf, 1996]). The Spanish version, *Extinción: un desmoronamiento* (Madrid: Alfaguara, 1992), was published four years earlier, translated by Miguel Sáenz, who, unlike the varied translators for the English and Italian versions, is responsible for most of Bernhard's body of work.

This, however, should not be a cause for concern:

> In general it is foolish, as a reader, to be anxious that you might not be getting the original author as heard in his own language. You are not. But if one thinks of this as no more than a confirmation of the real and unbridgeable difference between one culture and another, the demonstration that languages cannot be reduced to an underlying code, then this distance from the original can become cause for rejoicing. So long as we have different languages, different cultures, the world cannot become the monolithic thing globalization otherwise threatens to make it. Also, as long as there are different languages we will be free to shake off our individual identities, often more a burden than a boast, and reconstruct ourselves in otherness.[22]

The experience of cultural otherness constitutes the core of Parks's novel *Destiny* (1999), revolving around a middle-aged British expatriate reflecting on his life in Italy, just as Bernhard's Austrian hero Franz-Josef Murau does in his adopted home Rome.

Variations

For *Destiny*, Parks was "after something radically new in terms of plot, structure, rhythm and voice,"[23] and succeeded in that attempt, insofar as critics who weren't familiar with Thomas Bernhard underlined the singularity of Parks's language, whereas others recognized its likeness to the Austrian predecessor. Regarding similarities with Bernhard's last published novel *Extinction*, *Destiny* is the most subtle of the three books in question. While the other two incorporate Bernhard by naming their protagonists "Thomas" (Vitaliano Trevisan) or even "Thomas Bernhard" (Horacio Castellanos Moya, who also involves Bernhard's name on a peritextual level with the title *El asco: Thomas Bernhard en San Salvador*), Parks's novel includes neither quotations nor explicit

---

22 Tim Parks, *Translating Style. A Literary Approach to Translation. A Translation Approach to Literature* (London, New York: Routledge, 2014 [2007]), 247. Parks didn't translate Thomas Bernhard, but Alberto Moravia and Italo Calvino, the latter of which famously praised Bernhard in 1977: "[…] il Nobel dovrebbe cercare scrittori non ancora abbastanza conosciuti, come l'austriaco Thomas Bernhard che ha già ora la statura da 'Nobel'." Italo Calvino, *Lettere. 1940–1985*, ed. Luca Baranelli (Milan: Mondadori, 2000), 1339. ("[…] the Nobel ought to seek out writers who are not well enough known, like the Austrian Thomas Bernhard who already has the stature of a Nobel writer." Italo Calvino, *Letters, 1941–1985*, trans. Martin McLaughlin [Princeton and Oxford: Princeton University Press, 2013], 476).
23 Tim Parks, "Novels," http://tim-parks.com/novels/.

references. The plot outline, however, points to an obvious comparison with *Extinction*: all three novels present rather self-centered intellectuals torn between their native and their adopted countries after being faced with the news of a family member's death. In *Extinction*, a telegram informs protagonist Franz-Josef Murau that his brother and parents met an untimely death in a car accident, forcing him to return to the Upper Austrian family estate, where he is confronted with his family's past. The first sentence reads:

> Nach der Unterredung mit meinem Schüler Gambetti, mit welchem ich mich am Neunundzwanzigsten auf dem Pincio getroffen habe, schreibt Murau, Franz-Josef, um die Mai-Termine für den Unterricht zu vereinbaren und von dessen hoher Intelligenz ich auch jetzt nach meiner Rückkehr aus Wolfsegg überrascht, ja in einer derart erfrischenden Weise begeistert gewesen bin, daß ich ganz gegen meine Gewohnheit, gleich durch die Via Condotti auf die Piazza Minerva zu gehen, auch in dem Gedanken, tatsächlich schon lange in Rom und nicht mehr in Österreich zuhause zu sein, in eine zunehmend heitere Stimmung versetzt, über die Flaminia und die Piazza del Popolo, den ganzen Corso entlang in meine Wohnung gegangen bin, erhielt ich gegen zwei Uhr mittag das Telegramm, in welchem mir der Tod meiner Eltern und meines Bruders Johannes mitgeteilt wurde.[24]

> (On the twenty-ninth, having returned from Wolfsegg, I met my pupil Gambetti on the Pincio to discuss arrangements for the lessons he was to receive in May, writes Franz-Josef Murau, and impressed once again by his high intelligence, I was so refreshed and exhilarated, so glad to be living in Rome and not in Austria, that instead of walking home along the Via Condotti, as I usually do, I crossed the Flaminia and the Piazza del Popolo and walked the whole length of the Corso before returning to my apartment in the Piazza Minerva, where at about two o'clock I received the telegram informing me that my parents and my brother, Johannes, had died.)[25]

The first sentence of *Destiny* contains the whole situation *in nuce* as well, also ending with a death notice that sets the plot in motion:

> Some three months after returning to England, and having at last completed—with the galling exception of the Andreotti

---

24 Bernhard, *Auslöschung*, 7.
25 Bernhard, *Extinction*, 3.

interview—that collection of material that, once assembled in a book, must serve to transform a respectable career into a monument—something so comprehensive and final, this was my plan, as to be utterly irrefutable – I received, while standing as chance would have it at the reception desk of the Rembrandt Hotel, Knightsbridge, a place emblematic, if you will, both of my success in one field and my failure in another, the phone call that informed me of my son's suicide.[26]

After their son took his life in a psychiatric facility, parents Chris and Mara Burton return to Italy, which they had initially left in the hope of creating a sense of distance and helping their son get better. Like Murau in *Extinction*, who upon learning the tragic news immediately proceeds to talk about his pupil Gambetti and his favorite works of fiction, Burton directly starts to contemplate the possibility of a divorce.[27] Fully absorbed by his thoughts, he ignores how his organs cease to work, after his medication is misplaced during a flight change. His increasingly delusional stream of consciousness covers various aspects of demise: the suicide of his son, the end of his marriage, and a corpse-like politician he is supposed to interview. All the while, mentions of the here and now are tightly woven into the plot: "Your wife was remembering your son's birth, it occurs to me now in my granddaughter's room, still trying to understand into what situation exactly I have awakened."[28] Elements such as "I remember," "I reflect," or "I remark"[29] correspond to Bernhard's typical insertions "I thought" or "I said" that connect layers of current and past reflections and memories; they can also be found on

---

26 Tim Parks, *Destiny* (London: Secker and Warburg, 1999). The mention of Knightsbridge can be considered as one of several references to Bernhard's prose *Concrete (Beton*, 1982), whose hero decides to bequeath his inheritance to a stranger living in London's Knightsbridge, a woman he selects at random from the telephone book. *Concrete*, composed around the same time as *Extinction* in the early 1980s, is close enough regarding content and style to be published together with it as one book in Spain; cf. Thomas Bernhard, *Hormigón. Extinción*, trans. Miguel Sáenz (Madrid: Alfaguara, 2012). In Vitaliano Trevisan's *Il ponte: Un crollo* (Turin: Einaudi, 2007) the hero Thomas lives in a street called "Am Steingrab 21/b," which also hints at the Palma-episode in Bernhard's *Concrete*, as do the compulsive travel preparations of both heroes.
27 Parks, *Destiny*, 207, 208: Unlike Castellanos Moya and Trevisan—and unlike Bernhard in the majority of his books—who choose heroes without marital bonds, *Destiny* features a marriage that, portrayed as a "drama" and a "farce," at least confirms the standard impression that love is "ein Absurdum." Thomas Bernhard, *Verstörung* [= Werke 2], ed. Martin Huber and Wendelin Schmidt-Dengler (Frankfurt am Main: Suhrkamp, 2018), 162 ("an absurdity." Thomas Bernhard, *Gargoyles*, trans. Richard and Clara Winston [New York: Vintage, 2006], 161).
28 Parks, *Destiny*, 78.
29 Parks, *Destiny*, 70, 123, 79.

almost every page of Trevisan's novella, such as "pensavo sfogliando il giornale" (I thought flipping through the paper) or "pensai bevendo il caffè"[30] (I thought drinking the coffee).

Chris Burton is not only preoccupied with the status of his marriage after the loss of his son, but also with his scholarly work: *Destiny* introduces Bernhard's "Motiv der Motive"[31] (motif of motifs) early on. Burton's "monumental book"—already ten years in the making—is to become "[a]n extraordinary achievement," and "a fitting monument to my career"; its subject fits well into the areas of interest of many Bernhardian heroes: "national character and the essential predictability of human behaviour."[32] Dedicated to exploring questions of causality, chance, and determination, Burton associates the sudden death of his son with the fact that he had felt torn between two cultures, and furthermore with "particularly Italian forms of schizophrenia"[33] running in the family, analogous to the various manifestations of alpine insanity that Bernhard's narrators report.

The death of a family member serves as a driving force in Parks's *Destiny*, in Trevisan's text (the car accident of the hero's cousin) and in Castellano Moya's novel (the death of the hero's mother). In an overwhelming number of Bernhard's works (*Extinction, The Lime Works, Correction, The Loser, Woodcutters, Old Masters, Playing Watten, Concrete, Yes,* etc.) an impulse to write is sparked by the death of a more-or-less close and more-or-less loved one. In the novella *Yes*, for instance, the main character wants to put down his feelings in writing to find relief after the loss of his friend, "the Persian woman," but also hopes to thereby

---

30 Trevisan, *Il ponte*, 5, 7.
31 Christoph Bartmann, "Vom Scheitern der Studien. Das Schriftmotiv in Bernhards Romanen," *Text + Kritik* 43, 1991, 24. The way Burton's study is announced as a piece of impeccable scholarship is especially reminiscent of Bernhard's *Concrete* and the (potentially) unequalled book on Felix Mendelssohn-Bartholdy described therein.
32 Parks, *Destiny*, 5, 60, 209, 134. In Trevisan's *Il ponte*, the hero Thomas wonders about how character and destiny are one (99–100): "Il [...] carattere, pensavo, ha molto a che fare col destino, tanto che a volte si dice destino e si intende carattere, si parla di un carattere, si tenta di descriverlo, e si finisce per tracciare un destino." ([...] character, I was thinking, has a lot to do with destiny, so much so that sometimes you say destiny and you mean character, you talk about a character, you try to describe it, and you end up tracing a destiny.) The topic is brought up in *Auslöschung* (158) to the effect that character and destiny are mainly a consequence of origin, leading to formidable *Herkunftskomplexe* concerning that "woraus wir schließlich entstanden und gemacht und von welchem wir die ganze Zeit unserer Existenz *geprägt* sind" ("what we emerged from, what we are made of, and what has *determined our being* for as long as we've lived." Bernhard, *Extinction*, 100).
33 Parks, *Destiny*, 140.

open up an approach to his studies once again.[34] He is not the only scholar who ends up not composing his long-planned *magnum opus*, but his considerations on the impossibility of writing it instead.[35]

Staying with his daughter and grandchildren, wishing that that would enable him to start working on his book, Burton, too, only writes *about* his "monumental contribution" to the field of imagology; by doing so, however, he elaborates on his views on Italy—the "city of tombs and monuments, moths and candlelight and balmy evenings"—and its atmosphere of living death, revealed for instance in his parents-in-law's residence, a "gloomy house with its coffin-inspired furniture and its photographs of the dead."[36] If there's anything working in Italy, Trevisan's Italian hero (living in Northern Germany) explains, it's funeral services, one of several observations he makes that mirror those made by Parks's protagonist. Others are corruption and all kinds of misconduct by a government in which laws and regulations are applied arbitrarily, with the chances of being punished varying as the weather changes. While Trevisan's hero can hardly endure these shortcomings, Parks's Chris Burton, quasi-Italian by choice, has a rather favorable view:

> I find Italy with all its old traditions, its superficial idealism, its gauche bad taste, its puffed up national pride and Catholic

---

34 Cf. Thomas Bernhard, *Ja* (Frankfurt am Main: Suhrkamp, 2006), 122. (Thomas Bernhard, *Yes*, trans. Ewald Osers [London: Quartet Books, 1991], 115). Thomas from *Il ponte* similarly uses his walking companion to remain sane, to keep "mia malattia" (105) [my illness] at bay. In Bernhard's *Concrete*, the hero Rudolf is not shy to call the consequences of exploiting others by name: "Der sogenannte Geistesmensch geht ja immer wieder über einen Menschen, den er *dafür* getötet und also zur Leiche gemacht hat für seinen Geisteszweck." Thomas Bernhard, *Beton* [= Werke 5] ed. Wendelin Schmidt-Dengler (Frankfurt am Main: Suhrkamp, 2018), 25. ("The so-called man of the intellect constantly walks all over others, killing them and making corpses of them for his intellectual purposes." Thomas Bernhard, *Concrete*, trans. David McLintock [New York: Vintage, 2010], 25.)

35 Elfriede Jelinek's theater monologue *Das Schweigen* [Silence] comments on how the obsessive mentioning of a project makes the thing itself superfluous in the end: "Die Schrift. Sie entsteht, indem sie nie entsteht, indem aber unaufhörlich von ihr die Rede ist. Die Schrift übernimmt nun die Vormacht über mein Sprechen, indem sie, als Schrift, nur noch schweigt und schweigt […]. Doch indem ich spreche, merke ich, was ich vorher schon ahnte: sie ist ja gar nicht mehr nötig, die Schrift!" (The writing. It comes into being by never coming into being, but by being constantly talked about. The writing now assumes supremacy over my speaking, in that it, as writing, only remains silent and silent […]. But when I speak, I notice what I suspected before: it is no longer necessary at all, the writing!) Elfriede Jelinek, *Das Lebewohl: 3 kl. Dramen* (Berlin: Berlin Verlag, 2000), 44–45.

36 Parks, *Destiny*, 60, 234, 236.

paranoia ridiculous – Italy is quite ridiculous, I am telling my dead son, the way people here believe in the evil eye and are always convinced there are conspiracies against them – but I would not swap it for anything I have to offer. For an Englishman's empty and pragmatic eclecticism.[37]

An Anglo-Saxon "seduced by Latin enigma,"[38] he condemns his own background only moderately compared to Bernhard's, Moya's, and Trevisan's main characters, the latter seeing in Italy a place where the present is deliberately and continuously confused with the past.[39] While this is something Bernhard's protagonists would likely say about Vienna, Franz-Josef Murau in *Extinction* denies these assertions with regard to Rome; for him, it is not "das uralte Zentrum der abgelaufenen Weltgeschichte" ("the ancient center of a superannuated history"), but "*das heutige Zentrum der Welt*"[40] ("*the modern center of the world*").[41] If Trevisan's hero is asked, Rome is nothing less than "la capitale delle esistenze intellettuali fallite"[42] (the capital of intellectual failures), the general state of mind and especially that of intellectuals being petty bourgeois and thoroughly Catholic: "Non per niente in Italia non ci sono filosofi degni di questo nome"[43] (It is no coincidence that in Italy there are no philosophers worthy of the name). Italy's culture is based on "una rovina di falsi valori" (a ruin of false values) consisting of "la chiesa, la patria, la famiglia, l'obbedienza, la disciplina, l'ordine eccetera"[44] (church, country, family, obedience, discipline, order, etc.). Murau, to whom the situation in Italy seems much better, because according

---

37 Parks, *Destiny*, 159. Cf. Trevisan, *Il ponte*, 62.
38 Parks, *Destiny*, 34.
39 Trevisan, *Il ponte*, 94.
40 Bernhard, *Auslöschung*, 158.
41 Bernhard, *Extinction*, 101. In San Salvador, the setting of Castellanos Moya's novel, the opposite is the case; the city has a culture "sin ninguna vocación de registro o memoria histórica, sin ninguna percepción de pasado" ("without any vocation of record or historical memory, without any perception of the past"), which is why the historical center has been converted "en una porquería" ("into a garbage dump") by people whose "única preocupación es destruir cualquier arquitectura que mínimamente recuerde el pasado para construir gasolineras Esso y hamburgueserías y pizzerías" ("only preoccupation is to destroy whatever architecture minimally suggests the past in order to construct Esso gas stations and hamburger joints and pizzerias"). Horacio Castellanos Moya, *El asco: Thomas Bernhard en San Salvador* (San Salvador: Arcoiris, 1997), 78–79, 46 (Horacio Castellanos Moya, *Revulsion: Thomas Bernhard in San Salvador*, trans. Lee Klein [New York: New Direction Books, 2016], 52, 28).
42 Trevisan, *Il ponte*, 52.
43 Trevisan, *Il ponte*, 52.
44 Trevisan, *Il ponte*, 49, 48.

to him the Italians have not been entirely swallowed up by Fascism and Catholicism,[45] says the same thing about the intellectual life in Austria: "Der Katholizismus ist daran schuld, daß es in Österreich so viele Jahrhunderte keine Philosophen und also überhaupt kein philosophisches Denken und dadurch auch keine Philosophie gegeben hat. Die katholische Kirche hat das Denken in diesem Jahrtausend, kann ruhig gesagt werden, brutal und vollkommen unterdrückt."[46] ("Catholicism is to blame for the fact that for so many centuries Austria had no philosophers, no philosophical thought, no philosophy. It's fair to say that in the last thousand years all thought has been ruthlessly suppressed by the Catholic Church.")[47] While Bernhard places Murau, coming from a Roman Catholic background, merely in a gradually different environment, Parks and Trevisan (and to a lesser extent Castellanos Moya)[48] locate their main characters in contrasting surroundings, allowing them to reflect on the differences between Protestant and Catholic spheres.[49]

Variazioni

Like Franz-Josef Murau, meandering on the Austrian and Italian soul, Chris Burton, preparing a "comparative study of national characters,"[50] and Castellano Moya's protagonist Edgardo Vega, whose "especialidad consiste en estudiar las culturas"[51] ("specialty consists of studying cultures"),[52] the hero of *Il ponte: Un crollo* by Italian novelist, playwright, and stage director Vitaliano Trevisan (1960–) is preoccupied with stereotypes

---

45 Cf. Bernhard, *Auslöschung*, 347; and Bernhard, *Extinction*, 223.
46 Bernhard, *Auslöschung*, 114.
47 Bernhard, *Extinction*, 72–73.
48 Although El Salvador is predominantly Roman Catholic (however, more heterogenous concerning religion than other Latin American countries), the church plays a relatively minor role in the plot, which makes sense, given that the main character doesn't go into detail about his place of residence, Montréal, in the narrative.
49 While the non-Catholic background, a lack of similar conditions, and a difference in mentality were long made responsible for the "woeful stature" (Dale Peck, "Thomas Bernhard, the Alienator," *The New York Times*, December 24, 2010) Bernhard had in the English-speaking world, at odds with the narrative preferences and literary expectations of the recipients, there has been an inverse trend over the years. Among the famous proponents in the United Kingdom and the United States are the "English Thomas Bernhard" Gabriel Josipovici, William Gaddis, Paul Auster, Louis Begley, George Steiner, Jonathan Lethem, and Jonathan Franzen. For the reception of Bernhard's oeuvre in the English- and Spanish-speaking world as well as in Italy, see the relevant chapters by J. J. Long, Miguel Sáenz, and Luigi Reitani in *Bernhard Handbuch. Leben – Werk – Wirkung*, ed. Martin Huber and Manfred Mittermayer (Stuttgart: Metzler, 2018).
50 Parks, *Destiny*, 137.
51 Castellanos Moya, *El asco*, 84.
52 Castellanos Moya, *Revulsion*, 56.

and intercultural differences. The thirty-five-year-old Italian Thomas, a journalist and language teacher at the University of Bremen in the North of Germany, discusses these issues with his neighbor Karl Ignaz Hennetmair, a real estate agent named exactly like the real-life neighbor of Bernhard in the Upper Austrian village of Ohlsdorf. The fictitious Hennetmair, a parallel character to Murau's student of German Gambetti, takes Italian lessons in the form of long walks and talks in the woods. He and Thomas, too, find that the "momentum of national character"[53] is in language after seeing how its weight corresponds with the essence of its speakers with the help of *Extinction* by Bernhard, "autore che, sia io che Hennetmair, conoscevamo molto bene" (an author whom both I and Hennetmair knew very well):

> [...] per il suo e mio divertimento, citai diverse frasi di Pasolini, prima in italiano, poi in tedesco [...]. Anch'io, come Murau, posi idealmente le parole sulla bilancia delle mie mani, evidenziando cosí come il piatto tedesco della bilancia, rappresentato dalla mia mano sinistra, scendesse, mentre il destro, che rappresentava l'italiano, salisse. È vero, dissi a Hennetmair, non c'è dubbio: le parole tedesche sono decisamente piú pesanti.[54]
>
> ([...] for his and my amusement, I quoted several phrases from Pasolini, first in Italian, then in German [...] Like Murau, I, too, mentally placed the words on the balance of my hands, thus highlighting how the German scale of the balance, represented by my left hand, went down, while the right one, representing Italian, went up. It is true, I told Hennetmair, there is no doubt: the German words are much heavier.)

In *Extinction*, Schopenhauer's *The World as Will and Representation* (*Die Welt als Wille und Vorstellung*) is taken as an example to convey the gravity of the German language,[55] but the philosophical milestone, once essential for Murau, is of no help anymore:

---

53 Parks, *Destiny*, 68.
54 Trevisan, *Il ponte*, 50.
55 The part in question in the Italian translation, *Estinzione*, closely resembles the abovementioned quote: "D'improvviso ho recitato a Gambetti, prima in tedesco e poi in italiano, una frase di Schopenhauer tratta dal *Mondo come volontà e rappresentazione*, e ho cercato di dimostrare a lui, Gambetti, quanto pesantemente scendesse il piatto tedesco della bilancia simulato dalla mia mano sinistra, mentre quello italiano, per così dire, balzava in alto con la mia mano destra." Thomas Bernhard, *Estinzione. Uno sfacelo*, trans. Andreina Lavagetto (Milan: Adelphi, 1996), 13. ("Using my hands to simulate a balance, the left representing the German scale and the right the Italian, I quoted a sentence from Schopenhauer's *The World as Will and Idea*, first in German and then in Italian, and showed Gambetti how the German scale sank and the Italian sprang up." Bernhard, *Extinction*, 4.)

> Montaigne, sagen Sie, Gambetti, und ich weiß im Augenblick gar nicht, was das ist, hatte ich zu Gambetti gesagt. Descartes? ich weiß es nicht. Schopenhauer? ich weiß es nicht. Ebenso könnten Sie *Butterblume* sagen und ich wüßte nicht, was es ist, hatte ich zu Gambetti gesagt. [...] Nietzsche, hatte ich zu Gambetti gesagt, ich klopfe mir an den Kopf und er ist leer, vollkommen leer. Schopenhauer sage ich mir und ich klopfe an meinen Kopf und er ist leer. Ich klopfe an meinen Kopf und sage Kant und ich habe einen vollkommen leeren Kopf. Das deprimiert fürchterlich, hatte ich zu Gambetti gesagt.[56]
>
> (You say Montaigne, Gambetti, but right now I don't know what that means. Descartes? I don't know what that means, any more than I know what Schopenhauer means. You might just as well say *buttercup*: I wouldn't know what that meant either. [...] Nietzsche, I say, then I tap my head and find that it's empty, quite empty. Schopenhauer, I say to myself, and tap my head— and again it's empty. I tap my head and say Kant, only to find a complete void. It's unutterably depressing, Gambetti.)[57]

The great minds and grand names that pervade Bernhard's entire body of work now turn into mere cues representing inaccessible intellectual concepts. Trevisan's hero Thomas experiences how his own literary inspirations (all fitting into the realm of Bernhard's role models, except for Hamann and Walser) deny him the peace once granted:

> Che altro fare se non cercare rifugio nei cosiddetti classici? Ma la questione evidentemente era un'altra, perché neanche cosí trovavo pace, non tra le pagine di Melville, non tra quelle di James, e non Kafka, non Walser, non Stifter, non Bernhard né Beckett. Allora tornavo nel reparto filosofia, cercavo in un Kierkegaard, ma Kierkegaard non mi calmava, e neanche Wittgenstein, né Pascal, né Montaigne, né Hamann, addirittura Schopenhauer, tra i pensieri del quale avevo sempre trovato un po' di conforto, mi appariva vuoto et privo di senso.[58]
>
> (What else can we do but seek refuge in the so-called classics? But the question was obviously different, because even in this way I didn't find peace: not between the pages of Melville, not between those of James, nor Kafka, nor Walser, nor Stifter, nor Bernhard, nor Beckett. Then I went back to the philosophy section, I had

---

56 Bernhard, *Auslöschung*, 125.
57 Bernhard, *Extinction*, 79–80.
58 Trevisan, *Il ponte*, 86.

a look at Kierkegaard, but Kierkegaard did not calm me down, and neither did Wittgenstein, nor Pascal, nor Montaigne, nor Hamann; even Schopenhauer, in whose thoughts I had always found some comfort, seemed empty and meaningless to me.)

Thomas refers to his bookshelf as a cemetery, no longer containing living authors, only "[u]omini morti, pensieri morti, parole morte" (dead men, dead thoughts, dead words)—appropriate, as Bernhard has almost exclusively made allusions to deceased authors—even Thomas's first book by Bernhard himself, *Il nipote di Wittgenstein* (*Wittgenstein's Nephew*), was purchased the morning after the author died:

> E io avevo comprato, e poi letto, il mio primo Bernhard, nello stesso anno della sua morte, pensai, e andai subito a cercare la data della morte di Thomas Bernhard, ma nell'edizione che tenevo in mano era scritta solo la data di nascita. [....] Trovai quello che cercavo in una raccolta di testi brevi, che recava in appendice una esauriente scheda bio-bibliografica. Lessi:
>
> Il 12 febbraio 1989 Thomas Bernhard muore nella sua abitazione di Gmunden, assistito dal fratello Peter Fabjan, per le conseguenze della cardiomegalia. La notizia della morte viene comunicata per volontà dello scrittore solo il 16 febbraio, a funerali avvenuti. Nel testamento Bernhard dispone che ...[59]
>
> (And I had bought and then read my first Bernhard in the very year of his death, I thought, and went immediately to look for the date of Thomas Bernhard's death. But only his date of birth was written in the edition I held in my hand. I found what I was looking for in a collection of short texts, which contained in the appendix an exhaustive bio-bibliographical entry. I read:
>
> On the 12th of February 1989 Thomas Bernhard died in his home in Gmunden, assisted by his brother Peter Fabjan, of cardiomegaly. The news of his death was communicated through the writer's will on the 16th of February, only after the funeral had taken place. In his will, Bernhard states that ...)

Carrying the explicit intertextual reference further, Thomas mentions that he has put a picture of his father in a book by Thomas Bernhard but does not remember which one it was, either *L'origine* (*An Indication of the Cause*) or *La cantina* (*The Cellar*). The certainty with which he

---

59 Trevisan, *Il ponte*, 91, 89–90.

claims to have inserted a picture of his unbeloved mother into a book by Beckett, on the other hand, hints at the absurdity of their relationship, which seems even more likely, when Albert Camus's *L'étranger* (*The Stranger*)—a narrative famously including a mother's death and a son's seeming lack of grief—emerges as the only alternative. It is noteworthy that the hero of *Il ponte*—a text that clearly exhibits the impact of Bernhard's *Extinction*—categorically rejects any underlying meaning to the intertextual reference. Where he put the pictures

> [...] non ha niente a che fare col contenuto di quei libri, non ha niente a che fare con gli scrittori che li hanno scritti, o col rapporto di detti scrittori con le rispettive madri, che comunque, almeno nel caso di Beckett e di Bernhard, era stato un rapporto spaventoso, e soprattutto non ha niente a che fare col rapporto spaventoso che ho sempre avuto con mia madre, e in definitiva non ha niente a che fare con niente e con nessuno.[60]
>
> ([...] has nothing to do with the content of those books, has nothing to do with the writers who wrote them, or with the relationship of those writers with their mothers, which at any rate, at least in the case of Beckett and Bernhard, had been a dreadful relationship, and above all has nothing to do with the dreadful relationship that I have always had with my mother, and ultimately has nothing to do with anything and with anyone.)

His family relations are indeed very much like those in *Extinction*: Thomas's two sisters are subjugated by their mother, as is the father, who has settled into his office. Thomas for his part has studied literature to the disappointment of his mother, who had brought him into the world for the sole purpose of taking over the family business. Feeling like a perfect stranger, he reluctantly returns to this "perversa trappola famigliare"[61] (perverse family trap) for his cousin's funeral, entering a totally hostile environment, akin to the situation Murau finds himself in. Haunted by the mindlessness and the gruesome past of his family, which Murau plans "zu zersetzen, sie zu vernichten, auszulöschen"[62] ("dissecting, annihilating, and extinguishing"),[63] as he deliberately proclaims in problematic terms, he writes his anti-autobiography *Extinction*. Like him, Trevisan's Thomas doesn't survive the process: he leaves behind his notes—so far written as a first-person account—in the last

---

60 Trevisan, *Il ponte*, 99.
61 Trevisan, *Il ponte*, 126.
62 Bernhard, *Auslöschung*, 232.
63 Bernhard, *Extinction*, 147.

sentence of which the insertion "scrive Thomas"[64] (writes Thomas) insinuates his suicide.

The similarity of *Il ponte: Un crollo* to Thomas Bernhard's writings is already suggested by the form of the title (consisting of a specific article and a subject) and the subtitle (an indefinite article and a subject). In addition, "crollo" means "disintegration," "decay," "collapse," and is synonymous with "sfacelo," the Italian subtitle of Bernhard's *Auslöschung: Ein Zerfall*; *Estinzione: Uno sfacelo*. Strikingly, the French translator of Trevisan's *Il ponte: Un crollo* translates "crollo" as "effondrement" and thus copies the subtitle of the French version of Bernhard's *Extinction* (*Extinction: Un effondrement*, 1990). As are *Destiny* and *El asco*, *Il ponte* is based primarily on *Extinction*, but stresses certain set pieces, such as the motif of writer's block, that are more pronounced in works like *Concrete* or *The Lime Works*. Like all Bernhardian *Geistesmenschen* equipped with "a mind that never stays still,"[65] Thomas, "[c]ome tutte le persone che pensano di continuo" (like all people who think all the time), continuously gets caught up in a "spirale di pensieri"[66] (spiral of thoughts). He does not succeed in tilting the contents of his head onto the paper, the declared goal of the main character in *The Lime Works*, who lacks the "Furchtlosigkeit einfach davor, seinen Kopf urplötzlich von einem Augenblick auf den andern auf das rücksichtsloseste um- und also die Studie auf das Papier zu kippen"[67] ("fearlessness, simply, when it came to turning his head over, suddenly, from one moment to the next, ruthlessly flipping it over to drop everything inside his head onto the paper, all in one motion").[68] Trevisan's hero wishes he could only "scaricare sulla carta il contenuto della mia testa" (unload on paper the contents of my head), but by the time his thoughts reach his writing hand it is "già tutta un'altra storia"[69] (already a whole other story). It is common knowledge among Bernhard's *Geistesmenschen* that

---

64 Trevisan, *Il ponte*, 147. The decisive moment is when Thomas finds the bike of his late cousin's deceased son, for whose accident he feels responsible, since he had shown him the bridge where the accident occurred. The child went on a bicycle excursion on his own, evoking the trip in Bernhard's *Ein Kind*, which nearly ended fatally. For a discussion of the motif of the bike ride in Bernhard's autobiography as primal scene, "una scena primaria, una *Urszene*," see Raoul Kirchmayr, "La via di fuga. Immagini dell'infanzia nell'autobiografia di Thomas Bernhard," *Cultura Tedesca* 32, January–June (2007): 116.
65 Parks, *Destiny*, 79.
66 Trevisan, *Il ponte*, 102, 103.
67 Thomas Bernhard, *Das Kalkwerk* [= Werke 3], ed. Renate Langer (Frankfurt am Main: Suhrkamp, 2018), 231.
68 Thomas Bernhard, *The Lime Works*, trans. Sophie Wilkins (New York: Vintage, 2010), 241.
69 Trevisan, *Il ponte*, 113.

the written word is a falsification of the truth. The situation is as bad, if not worse, when it comes to the spoken word, as Chris Burton suspects in *Destiny*: "It has often occurred to me how ridiculous I make myself when I move from thought to speech."[70]

More so than in the stream of consciousness in *Destiny*, there is a dialogical dimension to the inner monologues in *Il ponte* and in *El asco*, whose main characters constantly address their silent listeners in the style of "Gambetti, habe ich zu Gambetti gesagt"[71] or "I had said to Gambetti, You know, Gambetti."[72] Insertions like "Hennetmair, dissi a Hennetmair"[73] (Hennetmair, I said to Hennetmair) identify it as spoken language, more precisely its representation, narrated speech, which for Elfriede Jelinek explains "die große Suggestivität der Bernhardschen Texte"[74] (the great suggestiveness of Bernhard's texts). While the escalating monologues pretend to be dialogues through the heavy use of *inquit* formulas, the addressees Gambetti, Hennetmair, and Moya never get to enter the flow of speech: there aren't even cautious attempts at communication. As usual, everything said is misunderstood, as the character of the father in *Gargoyles* has aptly summarized: "'Es ist alles ganz anders. Es ist immer alles ganz anders. Sich verständlich machen ist unmöglich.'"[75] ("It's very different from what you think. Everything is always very different. Communication is impossible.")[76] Accordingly, words aren't worth much in *Il ponte*: "Non mi faccio illusioni, tutto verrà frainteso, come sempre, tutto comunque frainteso."[77] (I have no illusions, everything will be misunderstood, as always, everything will be misunderstood.) All the more reason to constantly conjure up the truth, with phrases such as "la verità è questa"[78] (that is the truth), or "ésa es la verdad"[79] ("this is the truth").[80] In contrast to this, commonly accepted truths are presented as mere assertions by way of the signature expressions "per cosí dire" (so to speak), "come si dice" (as they say), or "cosiddetto" (so-called), as in "le cosiddette scienze dello spirito"[81] ("the so-called humanities") or, in Castellanos Moya's

---

70 Parks, *Destiny*, 63.
71 Bernhard, *Auslöschung*, 506.
72 Bernhard, *Extinction*, 324.
73 Trevisan, *Il ponte*, 133.
74 Elfriede Jelinek, quoted in *Thomas Bernhard – eine Einschärfung*, eds. Alexander Honold and Kai Luehrs-Kaiser (Berlin: Verlag Vorwerk 8, 1998), 98.
75 Bernhard, *Verstörung*, 29.
76 Bernhard, *Gargoyles*, 25.
77 Trevisan, *Il ponte*, 152.
78 Trevisan, *Il ponte*, 71.
79 Castellanos Moya, *El asco*, 25.
80 Castellanos Moya, *Revulsion*, 12.
81 Trevisan, *Il ponte*, 86.

novel, "los llamados 'espectáculos artísticos'"[82] ("the so-called 'artistic events'"),[83] emphasizing the arbitrariness of the connection between signified and signifier, indicating that language is an agreed-upon convention, an approximation to what is really meant.

The gap between idea and materialization, between reality and its depiction becomes particularly evident in the subject of photography, at first sight much in line with Walter Benjamin's understanding: "Der gesamte Bereich der Echtheit entzieht sich der technischen—und natürlich nicht nur der technischen—Reproduzierbarkeit."[84] ("The whole sphere of authenticity eludes technological—and of course not only technological—reproduction.")[85] Not only have the pictures of Thomas's young parents little or nothing to do with the people they represent, the whole worldwide "febbre della fotografia" (photography fever) is dangerous for pretending to be objective, while falsifying and having "effetti perversi"[86] (perverse effects) on the truth. This passage is practically a paraphrase of Murau's rant about humanity's "gemeine Sucht" ("vulgar addiction") to this distorting medium that is nothing but "eine heimtückische perverse Fälschung"[87] ("a perverse and treacherous falsification"),[88] after looking at a photograph of his parents and brother.

The newspaper pictures go well with the distasteful coverage of the car accident, from which sensation-seeking Murau repeatedly quotes, not sparing, like Thomas, any of the gruesome details described. Working or having worked in journalism, all protagonists comment on their need to read "die Tageszeitungen, mit welchen ich mich tagtäglich nur zu dem einen und einzigen Zweck vollgefressen hatte, mit ihrem unerträglichen Dreck, um mich nicht tödlich zu langweilen" ("the daily press with its unbearable garbage, on which I'd gorged myself daily in order to escape from my deadly boredom"), even though feeling perturbed by the "Gemeinheit und Niedrigkeit"[89] ("crudeness and vulgarity")[90] of

---

82 Castellanos Moya, El asco, 75.
83 Castellanos Moya, Revulsion, 49.
84 Walter Benjamin, "Das Kunstwerk im Zeitalter seiner technischen Reproduzierbarkeit," Gesammelte Schriften I.2, ed. Rolf Tiedemann and Hermann Schwepphäuser (Frankfurt am Main: Suhrkamp, 1991), 437.
85 Walter Benjamin, "The Work of Art in the Age of Its Technological Reproducibility," [Second Version], The Work of Art in the Age of Its Technological Reproducibility, and Other Writings on Media, ed. Michael W. Jennings, Brigid Doherty, and Thomas Y. Levin, trans. Edmund Jephcott, Rodney Livingstone, Howard Filand, and others (Cambridge, MA; London: The Belknap Press of Harvard University Press, 2008), 21.
86 Trevisan, Il ponte, 100.
87 Bernhard, Auslöschung, 24, 22.
88 Bernhard, Extinction, 14, 13.
89 Bernhard, Auslöschung, 160, 316.
90 Bernhard, Extinction, 101, 203.

the provincial press. Thomas has subscribed to the *Giornale di Vicenza* to stay up to date, but gets agitated about the journalists who produce that "insulso quotidiano" (daily insult) in the "stupido foglio di provincia" (stupid provincial paper), muckraking like no others in the world; due to the lowest level of their "sciocchezze economico-politico-culturali" (economic-political-cultural nonsense), all Italian papers are only usable as "carta igienica"[91] (toilet paper). Castellanos Moya's hero for his part would presumably be glad to read economic-political-cultural nonsense of that kind: the papers in San Salvador are not even newspapers in the true sense of the word, but nauseating "catálogos de ofertas" ("collections of special offers") and ads, and therefore "la mejor muestra de la miseria intelectual y espiritual de este pueblo"[92] ("the best evidence of the intellectual and spiritual misery of the people in this country").[93] The subject of newspapers provides the opportunity to practice the art of exaggeration: Italian papers are "i peggiori giornali d'Europa, e sicuramente tra i peggiori del mondo" (the worst newspapers in Europe, and certainly among the worst in the world), just as the whole economic-political-cultural situation in Italy—a "regime fascista democratico-cristiano"[94] (Christian Democratic fascist regime)—is the worst in Europe and in the world.

Variaciones

Trevisan's hero knows that insulting his country as "[u]n disastro totale" (a total disaster) will have him accused of being a *"Nestbeschmutzer,"* a word he cites in German and thereby links to Thomas Bernhard's reputation, explaining it as "letteralmente uno che insozza il proprio nido, ovvero uno che sputa del piatto dove mangia"[95] (literally one who fouls his own nest, or one who spits on the plate he eats from). Like his creator Thomas Bernhard, in whose life the conflict between the author and his country of origin culminates a few years after the publication of *Extinction* in the scandal sparked by the play *Heldenplatz*, Franz-Josef Murau has been threatened with

> [...] unter anderem meine Verfolgung und Tötung [...]. Ich ziehe Österreich andauernd in den Schmutz, sagen diese Leute, die Heimat mache ich auf die unverschämteste Weise herunter, ich unterstellte den Österreichern eine gemeine und niederträchtige katholisch-nationalsozialistische Gesinnung wann und wo ich

---

91 Trevisan, *Il ponte*, 55, 45, 47, 45.
92 Castellanos Moya, *El asco*, 58.
93 Castellanos Moya, *Revulsion*, 37.
94 Trevisan, *Il ponte*, 46, 48.
95 Trevisan, *Il ponte*, 49, 45.

nur könne, wo es in Wahrheit diese gemeine und niederträchtige katholisch-nationalsozialistische Gesinnung in Österreich gar nicht gäbe, wie diese Leute schreiben. Österreich sei nicht gemein und es sei nicht niederträchtig, es sei *immer nur schön* gewesen, schreiben diese Leute, und das österreichische Volk sei ein ehrbares.[96]

([...] among other things, prosecution and death. I am always dragging Austria in the dirt, they say, denigrating my own country in the most outrageous fashion and crediting the Austrians with base and despicable Catholic and National Socialist opinions whenever and wherever I can, whereas according to the writers, no such base and despicable opinions exist in Austria. Austria is not base and despicable, they say; it has *never been anything but beautiful*, and the Austrians are decent people.)[97]

The writer and journalist Horacio Castellanos Moya (1957–) has been confronted with death threats after the publication of his novel *El asco: Thomas Bernhard en San Salvador* (1997), causing him to once again leave his native San Salvador. In *El asco*, he expresses his disgust at the situation in El Salvador after the war,[98] taking *Nestbeschmutzung* to the next level. His main character, Vega, a thirty-eight-year-old, physically frail art history professor at McGill University, returns to San Salvador after the death of his mother. To him, his country is "el peor de todos" (the worst of all), "el más estúpido" ("the stupidest"), and "el más criminal" ("the most criminal"), as he tells his old friend and silent listener Moya in a bar, starting many of his sentences with exclamations such as "Horrendo, Moya" ("Horrendous, Moya"), "Horrible, Moya" ("Horrible, Moya"), or "Tremendo, Moya"[99] ("Tremendous, Moya").[100] Castellanos Moya surpasses the radicality of Bernhard's statements in their totalizing and exclusionary quality, signaled by words like "whole," "always," "everything," "everywhere," "absolute," and "perpetual," to evoke the impression of a state of exception, of an extreme situation.[101] Bernhard's strategy to generalize and catastrophize phenomena has been perceived as preventing differentiation, reducing complexity, and consequently as

---

96 Bernhard, *Auslöschung*, 17.
97 Bernhard, *Extinction*, 9–10.
98 For further discussion of the political implications, see Megan Thornton, "A Postwar Perversion of Testimonio in Horacio Castellanos Moya's *El asco*," *Hispania* 97, no. 2 (2014): 207–19.
99 Castellanos Moya, *El asco*, 17, 112, 50, 46.
100 Castellanos Moya, *Revulsion*, 5, 79, 16, 28.
101 Cf. Wendelin Schmidt-Dengler, "Der Tod als Naturwissenschaft neben dem Leben, Leben," ed. Anneliese Botond, *Über Thomas Bernhard* (Frankfurt am Main: Suhrkamp, 1970), 34–36.

being either highly manipulative or arbitrary and therefore futile. The superlatives Castellanos Moya uses for the sake of exaggeration—"la cosa más repulsiva, te lo juro" ("the most repulsive thing, I swear"), "nada tan abominable como" ("nothing so abominable"), "nada tan repulsivo como"[102] ("nothing more repugnant than")[103]—seem to question their own validity through their frequency alone. Many examples concerning rather unimportant aspects of life appear out of proportion: "Lo peor que me podía suceder era venir de Montreal a San Salvador para escuchar esa detestable música interpretada por tipos que se disfrazan de latinoamericanos […]."[104] ("The worst thing that could ever happen to me would be to come from Montreal to San Salvador to hear that detestable music interpreted by guys disguising themselves as Latin Americans […].")[105] That he was born in San Salvador of all places is what he calls "la cosa más cruel e inhumana" (the cruelest and most inhuman thing), to return to "esta podredumbre" ("this rottenness") would be "la peor pesadilla" ("the worst nightmare"): "este país es una alucinación, Moya"[106] ("this country is a hallucination, Moya").[107]

Concrete objects of criticism range from local beer to climate—as is the case with almost all Bernhardian heroes, Vega's well-being depends on the weather conditions and the "infierno achicharrante y embrutecedor de la costa tropical"[108] ("blistering, brutal hell of the tropical coast")[109] couldn't be worse—or sports, as represented in the following passage, which also illustrates how Castellanos Moya's prose, slightly more than Parks's and Trevisan's, is based on repetitions and on parallel syntactical structures:

> No hay nada que me resulte más detestable que los deportes, Moya, nada me parece más aburrido y estupidizante que los deportes, pero sobre todo el fútbol nacional, Moya, no entiendo cómo mi hermano puede dar la vida por veintidós subalimentados con sus facultades mentales restringidas que corren detrás de una pelota, sólo un tipo como mi hermano puede emocionarse hasta el infarto con los trompicones de

---

102 Castellanos Moya, *El asco*, 22, 41, 76–77.
103 Castellanos Moya, *Revulsion*, 9, 24, 44.
104 Castellanos Moya, *El asco*, 77.
105 Castellanos Moya, *Revulsion*, 51.
106 Castellanos Moya, *El asco*, 17, 41, 18, 20.
107 Castellanos Moya, *Revulsion*, 5, 24, 6, 7.
108 Castellanos Moya, *El asco*, 93.
109 Castellanos Moya, *El asco*, 63.

veintidós subalimentados que corren tras una pelota haciendo gala de sus restringidas facultades mentales [...].[110]

(There's nothing more detestable to me than sports, Moya, nothing seems more boring and stupid than sports, most of all the National Soccer League, I don't understand how my brother could give a damn about twenty-two undernourished morons running after a ball, only someone like my brother could almost have a heart attack about the stumbling of twenty-two undernourished men running after a ball and making a show of their mental deficiency [...].)[111]

While the subject of this example appears rather banal, compulsive reiterations concerning things that are otherwise not talked about can act as counterparts to concealment, taboos, and a nation's distinctive "conspiracy of silence."[112] This applies mostly to the war enthusiasts that are his fellow countrymen, criminal and militaristic "personas realmente siniestras"[113] ("truly sinister people").[114] Vega also despises his family, which, not in possession of a single book, represents "una cultura ágrafa"[115] ("an illiterate culture")[116] in a country where the few who *could* read never do, where there are no students of literature, since everyone is after a degree in business administration. While certain groups of people wouldn't be particularly prone to fall victim to verbal attacks in Bernhard's fiction, such as the bus drivers who are here considered to be pathological criminals, former torturers who participated in massacres during the civil war, others seem reprehensible on a supranational level, such as corrupt physicians, "los tipos más amorales que puedan existir" ("the most immoral people that exist"), and politicians that are "evidentemente analfabetos" ("obviously illiterate") and "tipos tenebrosos"[117] ("dismal types").[118] As regards the latter, different political tendencies cannot be distinguished from one another in *El asco* and *Il ponte*: the Bernhardian *leitmotiv* of the interchangeability of political

---

110 Castellanos Moya, *El asco*, 39–40. In Parks's *Destiny*, variations and repetitions often span several pages: "There is a terrible simultaneity to our marriage." (223) "There is a terrible simultaneity about the kaleidoscope of our marriage." (227) "There is a terrible simultaneity, I thought, about the back-and-forth of our marriage." (228)
111 Castellanos Moya, *Revulsion*, 23.
112 Parks, *Destiny*, 118.
113 Castellanos Moya, *El asco*, 22.
114 Castellanos Moya, *Revulsion*, 9.
115 Castellanos Moya, *El asco*, 78.
116 Castellanos Moya, *Revulsion*, 52.
117 Castellanos Moya, *El asco*, 53, 26, 27–28.
118 Castellanos Moya, *Revulsion*, 33, 13, 14.

parties (according to Trevisan's hero, veritable "maestri nell'arte del trasformismo" (masters in the art of transformation), arises especially in the context of the fact that "un sicópata criminal que mandó a asesinar a miles de personas en su cruzada anticomunista se haya convertido en el político más popular"[119] ("a psychopathic criminal who assassinated thousands in an anticommunist crusade transformed himself into the most popular politician").[120] Murau, who is appalled that an acquaintance of his—the miner Schermaier who ended up in a concentration camp for listening to the wrong radio station during World War II—has not been paid noteworthy reparations, while former SS members receive an impressive pension from the Austrian state, sees it as his duty to write about the injustice Schermaier suffered, representing so many others, "die das nationalsozialistische Denken und Handeln auf dem Gewissen hat, das nationalsozialistische Verbrechertum, das heute nur totgeschwiegen wird, nachdem es so viele Jahrzehnte gründlich verdrängt worden ist"[121] ("whom the National Socialists have on their conscience, the National Socialist criminals whose crimes are never mentioned today, having been hushed up for so many years").[122]

Murau's literary commitment, his willingness to fight against a specific injustice have earned *Extinction* a reputation of being Bernhard's "einziges dezidiert politisches Buch"[123] (only decidedly political book), contrary to the many narratives that were perceived to dissolve in vague accusations. Here, a precise diagnosis is offered amid the exaggerations, which in Bernhard's opinion are understatements anyway: in reality things are even worse. In this sense, a warning precedes Castellanos Moya's text, explaining that the original views of the real Vega had been relayed more emphatically, but were softened, so that certain readers wouldn't be offended.[124] The reactions to *El asco* (similarly, to *Heldenplatz*) are the most impressive confirmation that the exaggerated insults do not disarm them or diminish their provocative power, considering that the artificiality of Bernhardian prose has often been understood as ruling out all political weight, underpinned by an author who

---

119 Castellanos Moya, *El asco*, 31.
120 Castellanos Moya, *Revulsión*, 16.
121 Bernhard, *Auslöschung*, 358.
122 Bernhard, *Extinction*, 230.
123 Ulrich Weinzierl, "Bernhard als Erzieher. Thomas Bernhards *Auslöschung*," in *Spätmoderne und Postmoderne. Beiträge zur deutschsprachigen Gegenwartsliteratur*, ed. Paul Michael Lützeler (Frankfurt am Main: Fischer, 1991), 192.
124 Cf. Castellanos Moya, *El asco*, [9]: "Quise suavizar aquellos puntos de vista que hubieran escandalizado a ciertos lectores."

stressed on several occasions that it is more important how, not what, you write.[125]

Of all three works in the style of Thomas Bernhard, Castellanos Moya's "little imitation novel" is the only one that went far beyond the original text, and the one that had the most far-reaching consequences, posing a threat to the personal safety of the author, who started it as "an exercise in style," but then chose to "demolish the culture and politics of San Salvador, same as Bernhard had done with Salzburg, with the pleasure of diatribe and mimicry."[126] What aggravated the situation is that the author involved his own name, even if it was only for the character of the quiet addressee Moya, who then reports Vega's diatribe— as in "así se lo dije a Tolín, me dijo Vega"[127] ("which is what I said to Tolín, said Vega").[128] *El asco* is a report by hearsay, a narrative technique that isn't particularly prevalent in Bernhard's 1980s prose *Extinction* or *Concrete*, but dominates his earlier writings, with the effect of releasing the concerned narrator from all responsibility since they can't be held accountable for the accuracy of the related incidents. The main character Vega himself also chose the name of an existing person for his Canadian passport: "Mi nombre es Thomas Bernhard, me dijo Vega, un nombre que tomé de un escritor austriaco al que admiro y que seguramente ni vos ni los demás simuladores de esta infame provincia conocen."[129] ("My name is Thomas Bernhard, Moya, said Vega, it's a name I took from an Austrian writer I admire and who surely neither you nor the other simulators in this infamous place would recognize.")[130]

When Thomas Bernhard insists on writing world literature and on being "kein Heimatdichter"[131] (not a regional writer), he (rightly) implies that when portraying individuals such as a butcher's daughter from Eferding (*Correction*), this local color wouldn't pose a problem for readers in France or Korea. It certainly doesn't diminish the enthusiasm of the authors of bernhardesque tales, who translate such specific cultural elements into equivalent phenomena, as the three examples discussed in this paper have illustrated. On the other hand, adapting the Austrian atmosphere to the circumstances of San Salvador, Rome, and Vicenza shows that there is—for instance, in the depiction of

---

125 Thomas Bernhard, "Austriacus infelix," interview with Rita Cirio, in *Von einer Katastrophe in die andere. 13 Gespräche mit Thomas Bernhard*, ed. Sepp Dreissinger (Weitra: Bibliothek der Provinz, 1992), 101: "'Wichtiger ist, wie man schreibt, nicht was.'"
126 Castellanos Moya, "Author's Note," *El asco*, 88, 86.
127 Castellanos Moya, *El asco*, 77.
128 Castellanos Moya, *Revulsion*, 51.
129 Castellanos Moya, *El asco*, 118–19.
130 Castellanos Moya, *Revulsion*, 83.
131 Bernhard, "Die Ursache bin ich selbst. Madrid 1986," 115.

injustices—always "etwas Allgemeingültiges"[132] (something universal) in Bernhard's works. The three texts, to differing degrees, not only mimic Bernhard's prose in rhythm and diction—remaining clearly discernible in English, Spanish, and Italian—but also explore the experience of living between two cultures following the general outline of the plot of *Extinction*, appropriating a range of characteristic motifs and themes, and adding novel impulses to a persistently encouraging basis.

---

[132] Wendelin Schmidt-Dengler, "Den ganzen Erdball überstrahlend. Thomas Bernhard, Österreich und Europa," in *Wenn Ränder Mitte werden. Zivilisation, Literatur und Sprache im interkulturellen Kontext*, ed. Chantal Adobati, Maria Aldouri-Lauber, Manuela Hager, and Reinhart Hosch (Vienna: Facultas, 2001), 706.

Bibliography

Adorno, Theodor. "Late Style in Beethoven." In *Essays on Music*, edited by Richard Leppert and translated by Susan Gillespie, 564–68. Berkeley: University of California Press, 2002.
Améry, Jean. "Morbus Austriacus." *Merkur* 30.1 (1976): 91–94.
Anderson, Mark M. "Fragments of a Deluge: The Theater of Thomas Bernhard's Prose." In *A Companion to the Works of Thomas Bernhard*, edited by Matthias Konzett, 119–35. Rochester, NY: Camden House, 2002.
Anon. "Liebeserklärung an das Innergebirg." *meinbezirk.at*, September 18, 2017, https://www.meinbezirk.at/pongau/c-lokales/liebeserklaerung-an-das-innergebirg_a2250475.
Anon. "Nachruf: Helmut Qualtinger." *Der Spiegel*, October 6, 1986.
Arendt, Hannah. *Men in Dark Times*. New York: Harcourt Brace Jovanovich, 1968.
Barthes, Roland. "The Death of the Author." *Image. Music. Text*. Essays selected and translated by Stephen Heath, 142–48. London: Fontana, 1977.
Bartmann, Christoph. "Vom Scheitern der Studien. Das Schriftmotiv in Bernhards Romanen." *Text und Kritik* 43 (1991): 22–29.
Bayard, Pierre. *Le Plagiat par anticipation*. Paris: Les Éditions de Minuit, 2009.
Bayer, Wolfram. *Kontinent Bernhard. Zur Thomas-Bernhard-Rezeption in Europa*. Vienna: Böhlau, 1995.
Benjamin, Walter. *Gesammelte Schriften*. Edited by Rolf Tiedemann and Hermann Schwepphäuser. Frankfurt am Main: Suhrkamp, 1972.
Benjamin, Walter. *Illuminations: Essays and Reflections*. Edited by Hannah Arendt and translated by Harry Zohn. New York: Harcourt Brace Jovanovich, 1968.
Benjamin, Walter. *The Work of Art in the Age of Its Technological Reproducibility, and Other Writings on Media*. Edited by Michael W. Jennings, Brigid Doherty, and Thomas Y. Levin. Cambridge, MA: Belknap Press, 2008.
Bernardi, Eugenio. "Bernhard in Italien." In *Literarisches Kolloquium Linz 1984: Thomas Bernhard*, edited by Alfred Pittertschatscher and Johann Lachinger, 175–86. Linz: Adalbert Stifter-Institut, 1985.
Bernhard, Thomas. *An der Baumgrenze*. Munich: Deutscher Taschenbuch-Verlag, 1971.
Bernhard, Thomas. *Argumente eines Winterspaziergängers*. Berlin: Suhrkamp, 2013.
Bernhard, Thomas. *Bernhard für Boshafte*. Berlin: Insel, 2014.
Bernhard, Thomas. *Beton*. Frankfurt am Main: Suhrkamp, 1982.
Bernhard, Thomas. *Camminare*. Translated by Giovanna Agabio. Milan: Adelphi, 2018.
Bernhard, Thomas. *Concrete*. Translated by David McLintock. New York: Knopf, 1984.
Bernhard, Thomas. *Concrete*. Translated by David McLintock. New York: Vintage, 2010.

Bibliography

Bernhard, Thomas. *Correction*. New York: Vintage, 2010.
Bernhard, Thomas. *Das Kalkwerk*. Frankfurt: Suhrkamp, 2015.
Bernhard, Thomas. *Die Ehehölle: Acht Szenen*. Edited by Raimund Fellinger. Frankfurt am Main: Suhrkamp, 2008.
Bernhard, Thomas. *Der Untergeher*. Frankfurt am Main: Suhrkamp, 1983.
Bernhard, Thomas. *Eine Begegnung: Gespräche mit Krista Fleischmann*. Frankfurt am Main: Suhrkamp, [1991] 2006.
Bernhard, Thomas. *Erzählungen: Kurzprosa*. Edited by Hans Höller, Martin Huber, and Manfred Mittermayer. Salzburg: Suhrkamp, 2003.
Bernhard, Thomas. "È una commedia? È una tragedia?" In *Adelphiana 1971*. Translated by Vittoria Rovelli Ruberl, 291–98. Milan: Adelphi, 1971.
Bernhard, Thomas. *Estinzione. Uno sfacelo*. Translated by Andreina Lavagetto. Milan: Adelphi, 1996.
Bernhard, Thomas. *Extinción. Un desmoronamiento*. Translated by Miguel Sáenz. Madrid: Alfaguara, 1992.
Bernhard, Thomas. *Extinction*. Translated by David McLintock. New York: Vintage, 2011.
Bernhard, Thomas. *Gargoyles*. Translated by Richard and Clara Winston. New York: Vintage, 2006.
Bernhard, Thomas. *Gathering Evidence: A Memoir*. Translated by David McClintock. New York: Knopf, 1985.
Bernhard, Thomas. *Gehen*. Frankfurt am Main: Suhrkamp, 1971.
Bernhard, Thomas. *Ja*. Frankfurt am Main: Suhrkamp, 2006.
Bernhard, Thomas. *Heldenplatz*. Frankfurt am Main: Suhrkamp, 1988.
Bernhard, Thomas. *Heldenplatz*. Translated by Meredith Oakes and Andrea Tierny. London: Oberon, 2010.
Bernhard, Thomas. *Hormigón. Extinción*. Translated by Miguel Sáenz. Madrid: Alfaguara, 2012.
Bernhard, Thomas. *In der Höhe*. Salzburg: Residenz, 1989.
Bernhard, Thomas. "The Italian." In *Relationships: An Anthology of Contemporary Austrian Prose*, edited by Donald G. Daviau and translated by Eric Williams, 67–75. Riverside, CA: Ariadne Press, 1991.
Bernhard, Thomas. *Der Italiener*. Salzburg: Suhrkamp, 1989.
Bernhard, Thomas. *L'italiano*. Translated by Enza Gini. Parma: Ugo Guanda Editore, 1981.
Bernhard, Thomas. *Meine Preise*. Frankfurt am Main: Suhrkamp, 2009.
Bernhard, Thomas. *The Lime Works*. Translated by Sophie Wilkins. New York: Vintage, 2010.
Bernhard, Thomas. *The Loser*. Translated by Jack Dawson. New York: Vintage, 2006.
Bernhard, Thomas. *My Prizes: An Accounting*. Translated by Carol Janeway. New York: Knopf, 2010.
Bernhard, Thomas. *Old Masters: A Comedy*. Translated by Ewald Osers. Chicago: University of Chicago Press, 1992.
Bernhard, Thomas. *Perturbamento*. Edited by Eugenio Bernardi. Milan: Adelphi, 1981.
Bernhard, Thomas. *Städtebeschimpfungen: Düsseldorf oder München oder Hamburg: Lauter Provinzen*. Berlin: Suhrkamp, 2016.
Bernhard, Thomas. *The Loser*. Translated by Jack Dawson. New York: Knopf, 1991.
Bernhard, Thomas. *The Voice Imitator*. Translated by Kenneth Northcott. Chicago: University of Chicago Press, 1997.

Bernhard, Thomas. *Von einer Katastrophe in die andere: 13 Gespräche mit Thomas Bernhard*. Weitra: Bibliothek der Provinz, 1992.
Bernhard, Thomas. *Walking: A Novella*. Translated by Kenneth Northcott, preface by Brian Evenson. Chicago and London: University of Chicago Press, 2015.
Bernhard, Thomas. *Werke in 22 Bänden: Band 1: Frost*. Edited by Martin Huber and Wendelin Schmidt-Dengler. Frankfurt am Main: Suhrkamp, 2003.
Bernhard, Thomas. *Werke in 22 Bänden: Band 2: Verstörung*. Edited by Martin Huber and Wendelin Schmidt-Dengler. Frankfurt am Main: Suhrkamp, 2003.
Bernhard, Thomas. *Werke in 22 Bänden: Band 3: Das Kalkwerk. Roman*. Edited by Renate Langer. Frankfurt am Main: Suhrkamp, 2004.
Bernhard, Thomas. *Werke in 22 Bänden: Band 4: Korrektur*. Edited by Martin Huber and Wendelin Schmidt-Dengler. Frankfurt am Main: Suhrkamp, 2005.
Bernhard, Thomas. *Werke in 22 Bänden: Band 5: Beton*. Edited by Martin Huber and Wendelin Schmidt-Dengler. Frankfurt am Main: Suhrkamp, 2006.
Bernhard, Thomas. *Werke in 22 Bänden: Band 9: Auslöschung*. Edited by Hans Höller. Frankfurt am Main: Suhrkamp, 2009.
Bernhard, Thomas. *Werke in 22 Bänden: Band 10: Die Autobiographie*. Edited by Martin Huber and Manfred Mittermayer. 2nd ed. Frankfurt am Main: Suhrkamp, 2004.
Bernhard, Thomas. *Werke in 22 Bänden: Band 11: Erzählungen I*. Edited by Martin Huber and Wendelin Schmidt-Dengler. 2nd ed. Frankfurt am Main: Suhrkamp, 2004.
Bernhard, Thomas. *Werke in 22 Bänden: Band 12: Erzählungen II*. Edited by Hans Höller and Manfred Mittermayer. 1st ed. Frankfurt am Main: Suhrkamp, 2006.
Bernhard, Thomas. *Werke in 22 Bänden: Band 13: Erzählungen III*. Edited by Hans Höller and Manfred Mittermayer. 1st ed. Frankfurt am Main: Suhrkamp, 2008.
Bernhard, Thomas. *Werke in 22 Bänden: Band 14: Erzählungen. Kurzprosa*. Edited by Manfred Mittermayer, Martin Huber, and Hans Höller. 4th ed. Frankfurt am Main: Suhrkamp, 2003.
Bernhard, Thomas. *Werke in 22 Bänden: Band 15: Dramen I*. Edited by Manfred Mittermayer and Jean-Marie Winkler. 1st ed. Frankfurt am Main: Suhrkamp, 2004.
Bernhard, Thomas. *Werke in 22 Bänden: Band 16: Dramen II*. Edited by Manfred Mittermayer and Jean-Marie Winkler. 1st ed. Frankfurt am Main: Suhrkamp, 2005.
Bernhard, Thomas. *Werke in 22 Bänden: Band 17: Dramen III*. Edited by Martin Huber and Bernhard Judex. 1st ed. Frankfurt am Main: Suhrkamp, 2010.
Bernhard, Thomas. *Werke in 22 Bänden: Band 19: Dramen V*. Edited by Martin Huber, Bernhard Judex, and Manfred Mittermayer. Frankfurt am Main: Suhrkamp, 2011.
Bernhard, Thomas. *Werke in 22 Bänden: Band 20: Dramen VI*. Edited by Martin Huber and Wendelin Schmidt-Dengler. Frankfurt am Main: Suhrkamp, 2012.
Bernhard, Thomas. *Werke in 22 Bänden: Band 21: Gedichte*. Edited by Raimund Fellinger. Frankfurt am Main: Suhrkamp, 2015.
Bernhard, Thomas. *Werke in 22 Bänden: Band 22: Journalistisches Reden Interviews*. Edited by Wolfram Bayer, Martin Huber, and Manfred Mittermayer. Frankfurt am Main: Suhrkamp, 2015.
Bernhard, Thomas. *Wittgenstein's Nephew*. Translated by David McLintock. New York: Vintage, 2009.

Bernhard, Thomas. *Woodcutters*. Translated by David McLintock. New York: Vintage, 2010.
Bernhard, Thomas. *Yes*. Translated by Ewald Osers. London: Quartet Books, 1991.
Bernhard, Thomas, and Krista Fleischmann. "Die Ursache bin ich selbst. Madrid 1986." *Thomas Bernhard. Eine Begegnung. Gespräche mit Krista Fleischmann*. Frankfurt am Main: Suhrkamp, 2007.
Bernhard, Thomas, and Rita Cirio. "Austriacus infelix." In *Von einer Katastrophe in die andere. 13 Gespräche mit Thomas Bernhard*, edited by Sepp Dreissinger. Weitra: Bibliothek der Provinz, 1992. [Originally in *L'Espresso*, November 7, 1982.]
Bernhard, Thomas, and Siegfried Unseld. *Der Briefwechsel Thomas Bernhard/Siegfried Unseld*. Berlin: Suhrkamp, 2009.
Berwald, Olaf. "Against Aboutness: The Corpse That Almost Got Away." In *The Scofield* 1.4 (Spring 2016): Special Issue: Max Frisch & Identity, 196–97.
Betz, Uwe, and Manfred Mittermayer. "Wirkung auf andere Autoren und Autorinnen." In *Bernhard Handbuch: Leben – Werk – Wirkung*, edited by Martin Huber and Manfred Mittermayer, 512–19. Würzburg: Metzler, 2018.
Bloom, Harold. *The Anxiety of Influence: A Theory of Poetry*. New York: Oxford University Press, 1997.
Bloom, Harold. *The Western Canon: The Books and School of the Ages*. London: Macmillan, 1995.
Bottlong, René. "À Glenn Gould à cent pour cent." In *Thomas Bernhard et les siens*, edited by Gemma Salem, 196–202. Paris: La Table Ronde, 1993.
Bullaro, Grace Russo, and Stephanie V. Love, eds. *The Works of Elena Ferrante: Reconfiguring the Margins*. New York: Palgrave Macmillan, 2016.
Calasso, Roberto. *The Art of the Publisher*. Translated by Richard Dixon. New York: Farrar, Straus and Giroux, 2013.
Calvino, Italo. *If on a Winter's Night a Traveler*. Translated by William Weaver. New York: Harcourt Brace, 1981.
Calvino, Italo. *La strada di San Giovanni*. Edited by Cesare Garboli. Milan: Oscar Mondadori, 2011.
Calvino, Italo. *Lettere 1940–1985*. Milano: Mondadori Italian, 2000.
Calvino, Italo. *Lezioni americane: Sei proposte per il prossimo millennio*. Milan: Mondadori, 2002.
Calvino, Italo. "Dall'opaco." In *Adelphiana 1971*, 299–312. Milan: Adelphi, 1971.
Calvino, Italo. *Se una notte d'inverno un viaggiatore*. Milan: Mondadori, 2002.
Calvino, Italo. *Six Memos for the Next Millennium*. Translated by Patrick Creagh. New York: Vintage Books, 1993.
Calvino, Italo. *Sono nato in America: Interviste 1951–1985*. Edited by Luca Baranelli and Mario Barenghi. Milan: Mondadori, 2012.
Calvino, Italo. *The Road to San Giovanni*. Toronto: Vintage Canada, 1995.
Calvino, Italo, and Michael Wood. *Italo Calvino: Letters, 1941–1985. Updated Edition*. Translated by Martin McLaughlin. Revised edition. Princeton: Princeton University Press, 2014.
Castellanos Moya, Horacio. *El asco: Thomas Bernhard en San Salvador*. San Salvador: Arcoiris, 1997.
Castellanos Moya, Horacio. *Revulsion: Thomas Bernhard in San Salvador*. Translated by Lee Klein. New York: New Direction Books, 2016.
Celan, Paul. *The Meridian: Final Version—Drafts—Materials*. Edited by Bernhard Böschenstein and Heino Schmull and translated by Pierre Joris. Stanford: Stanford University Press, 2011.

Bibliography 237

"Charleston County Public Library." Accessed November 23, 2019. https://www.ccpl.org/eds/detail?db=edsglr&an=edsgcl.87460084&isbn=edsglr.

Chiusano, Italo Alighiero. *Literatur: Scrittori e libri tedeschi*. Milan: Rusconi, 1984.

Cole, Teju. "Memories of Things Unseen." *The New York Times*, October 14, 2015, sec. Magazine. https://www.nytimes.com/2015/10/18/magazine/memories-of-things-unseen.html.

Connolly, Andy. *Philip Roth and the American Liberal Tradition*. Lanham, MD: Lexington, 2017.

Couling, Della. "Champagner mit einer Prize Strychnin. Bernhards Theaterstücke in England." In *Kontinent Bernhard. Zur Thomas-Bernhard-Rezeption in Europa*, edited by Wolfram Bayer, 423–29. Vienna: Böhlau, 1995.

Cousineau, Thomas J. *Three-Part Inventions: The Novels of Thomas Bernhard*. Newark: University of Delaware Press, 2008.

Daviau, Donald G. "The Reception of Thomas Bernhard in the United States." *Modern Austrian Literature* 21.3/4 (1988): 243–76.

Dowden, Stephen D. "A Testament Betrayed: Bernhard and His Legacy." In *A Companion to the Works of Thomas Bernhard*, edited by Matthias Konzett, 51–68. Rochester, NY: Camden House, 1998.

Dowden, Stephen D. *Understanding Thomas Bernhard*. Columbia: University of South Carolina Press, 1991.

Driver, Tom. "Beckett by the Madeleine." *Columbia University Forum* 4 (1961): 21–25.

Dyer, Geoff. "D. H. Lawrence: *Sons and Lovers*." In *Otherwise Known as the Human Condition: Selected Essays and Reviews, 1989–2010*, 123–28. Minneapolis: Graywolf, 2011.

Dyer, Geoff. *Otherwise Known as the Human Condition: Selected Essays and Reviews*. Minneapolis: Graywolf Press, 2011.

Dyer, Geoff. *Out of Sheer Rage: Wrestling with D. H. Lawrence*. London: Picador, 2009.

Eickhoff, Hajo. "Die Stufen der Disziplinierung: Thomas Bernhards Geistesmensch." In *Thomas Bernhard: Die Zurichtung des Menschen*, edited by Alexander Honold and Markus Joch, 155–62. Würzburg: Königshausen & Neumann, 1999.

"Ein übersetztes Buch ist wie eine Leiche": Übersetzer antworten Thomas Bernhard. Mattighofen: Korrektur Verlag, 2017.

Eliraz, Israel. *Chez Thomas Bernhard à Steinhof*. Paris: José Corti, 2006.

Eshel, Amir. *Poetic Thinking Today*. Stanford: Stanford University Press, 2020.

Federmair, Leo. "Als ich *Das Kalkwerk* von Thomas Bernhard las." *Literatur und Kritik* 385/386 (2004): 46–60.

Félix, Brigitte, ed. *Reading William Gaddis*. Orléans: Presses Universitaires d'Oréans, 2007.

Felski, Rita. *The Limits of Critique*. Chicago: University of Chicago Press, 2015.

Ferrante, Elena. *Frantumaglia: A Writer's Journey*. Translated by Ann Goldstein. New York: Europa Editions, 2016.

Ferrante, Elena. "I'm tired of fiction, I no longer see a reason to go hunting for anecdotes." *The Guardian*, February 17, 2018. Translated by Ann Goldstein. https://www.theguardian.com/lifeandstyle/2018/feb/17/elena-ferrante-im-tired-of-fiction-i-no-longer-see-a-reason-to-go-hunting-for-anecdotes.

Ferrante, Elena. *L'amica geniale*. Rome: Edizioni e/o, 2011.

Ferrante, Elena. *L'amore molesto*. Rome: Edizioni e/o, 1992.

Ferrante, Elena. *L'invenzione occasionale*. Rome: Edizioni e/o, 2019.

Ferrante, Elena. *My Brilliant Friend*. Translated by Ann Goldstein. New York: Europa Editions, 2012.

Ferrante, Elena. *Troubling Love*. Translated by Ann Goldstein. New York: Europa Editions, 2006.

Fetz, Bernhard, Klaus Kastberger, Österreichisches Literaturarchiv, Deutsches Literaturarchiv, and Österreichische Nationalbibliothek, eds. *Die Teile und das Ganze: Bausteine der literarische Moderne in Österreich*. Profile (Vienna, Austria), vol. 10. Vienna: Zsolnay, 2003.

Finkelstein, Norman G. *The Holocaust Industry: Reflections on the Exploitation of Jewish Suffering*. London: Verso, 2015.

Fludernik, Monika. *Echoes and Mirrorings: Gabriel Josipovici's Creative Oeuvre*. Frankfurt am Main and New York: Peter Lang, 2000.

Frantzen, Mikkel. "The Demonic Comedy of Thomas Bernhard." *Journal of Austrian Studies* 50 (2018), 89–108.

Friedrich, Otto. *Glenn Gould: A Life and Variations*. New York: Random House, 1989.

Gadamer, Hans-Georg. *Wahrheit und Methode. Grundzüge einer philosophischen Hermeneutik. Vol. 1 of Gesammelte Werke*. Tübingen: J.C.B. Mohr (Paul Siebeck), 1990.

Gadamer, Hans-Georg. *Truth and Method*. 2nd revised ed. Translation revised by Joel Weinsheimer and Donald G. Marshall. New York: Continuum, 1995.

Gaddis, William. *Agapē Agape*. New York: Viking, 2002.

Gaddis, William. *Agapē Agape*. Introduction by Sven Birkerts, Afterword by Joseph Tabbi. London: Penguin, 2003.

Gaddis, William. *Das mechanische Klavier*. Translated by Marcus Ingendaay. Munich: Goldmann, 2003.

Gaddis, William. *J R*. New York: Penguin, 1993.

Gaddis, William. *The Letters of William Gaddis*, ed. Steven Moore. Champaign, Ill., London, and Dublin: Dalkey Archive, 2013.

Gaddis, William. Letter to Gregory Comnes. http://www.williamgaddis.org/agape/wordsruin.shtml.

Gaddis, William. "Stop Player. Joke No. 4." In *The Rush for Second Place*, ed. Joseph Tabbi. New York: Penguin, 2002.

Gaddis, William. *Torschlußpanik*. Read by Ignaz Kirchner. Co-Production by Deutschlandfunk, Bayerischer Rundfunk, and Westdeutscher Rundfunk, 1999.

Gaede, Friedrich, Patrick O'Neill, and Ulrich Scheck, eds. *Hinter dem schwarzen Vorhang. Die Katastrophe und die epische Tradition: Festschrift für Anthony W. Riley*. Tübingen: Francke, 1994.

Gargani, Aldo Giorgio. "'Thomas Bernhard's Infinite Phrase': A Summary." *Argumentation* 6 (1993): 445–59.

Gargani, Aldo Giorgio. *La frase infinita: Thomas Bernhard e la cultura austriaca*. Roma-Bari: Laterza, 1990.

Gargani, Aldo Giorgio. ed. *La crisi della ragione*. Turin: Einaudi, 1979.

Gass, William H. "The Art of Fiction 16." Interviewed by Thomas LeClair. *Paris Review* 70 (Summer 1977): 61–94.

Glaser, Jennifer. "The Jew in the Canon: Reading Race and Literary History in Philip Roth's *The Human Stain*." *PMLA* 123.5 (2008): 1465–78.

Glover, Douglas. "A Scrupulous Fidelity: Thomas Bernhard's The Loser." In *Attack of the Copula Spiders and Other Essays on Writing*. Windsor, Ont.: Biblioasis, 2012.

Gooblar, David. *The Major Phases of Philip Roth*. New York: Continuum, 2011.

Gößling, Andreas. "Auslöschung." In *Bernhard-Handbuch, Leben – Werk – Wirkung*, edited by Bernhard Judex and Manfred Mittermayer, 88–96. Stuttgart: J. B. Metzler, 2018.
Götze, Clemens. "Der geehrte Autor und die Kunst der Invektive. Zu Thomas Bernhards 'Meine Preise'." *Studia Austriaca* 20 (2012): 55–84.
Gray, Richard T. "Fabulation and Metahistory: W. G. Sebald and Contemporary German Holocaust Fiction." Edited by Christoph Zeller. *Literarische Experimente: Medien, Kunst, Texte Seit 1950*, Beiträge zur neueren Literaturgeschichte: 296, no. 433 (2012): 271–301.
Guibert, Hervé. *A l'ami qui ne m'a pas sauvé la vie*. Paris: Gallimard, 1990.
Guibert, Hervé. *To the Friend Who Did Not Save My Life*. Translated by Linda Coverdale. New York: Atheneum, 1991
Haas, Franz. "In Italien." In *Blick von Aussen: Österreichische Literatur im internationalen Kontext*, edited by Franz Haas, Hermann Schlösser, and Klaus Zeyringer, 144–82. Innsbruck: Haymon, 2003.
Handke, Peter. "Als ich *Verstörung* von Thomas Bernhard las." In *Meine Ortstafeln, Meine Zeittafeln, 1967–2007*, 283–88. Frankfurt: Suhrkamp, 2007.
Handke, Peter. *Meine Ortstafeln - Meine Zeittafeln: 1967–2007*. Frankfurt am Main: Suhrkamp, 2007.
Hayes, Patrick. *Philip Roth: Fiction and Power*. Oxford: Oxford University Press, 2014.
Heidelberger-Leonard, Irene. "Auschwitz als Pflichtfach für Schriftsteller." In *Anti-autobiografie. Thomas Bernhards Auslöschung*, edited by Irene Heidelberger-Leonard and Hans Höller, 181–96. Frankfurt am Main: Suhrkamp, 1995.
Hirsch, Marianne. *The Generation of Postmemory: Writing and Visual Culture After the Holocaust*. New York: Columbia University Press, 2012.
Hoell, J., A. Honold, and K. Luehrs-Kaiser. *Thomas Bernhard–Eine Einschärfung*. Berlin: Verlag Vorwerk 8, 1998.
Höller, Hans. "Rekonstruktion des Romans im Spektrum der Zeitungsrezensionen." In *Anti-autobiografie. Thomas Bernhards Auslöschung*, edited by Irene Heidelberger-Leonard and Hans Höller, 53–69. Frankfurt am Main: Suhrkamp, 1995.
Hofmann, Kurt. *Aus Gesprächen mit Thomas Bernhard*. Vienna: Locker, 1988.
Hofmannsthal, Hugo von. *The Lord Chandos Letter and Other Writings*. Translated by Joel Rotenberg. New York: New York Review of Books, 2005.
Honegger, Gitta. *Thomas Bernhard: The Making of an Austrian*. New Haven: Yale University Press, 2001.
Honold, Alexander. *Thomas Bernhard: die Zurichtung des Menschen*. Würzburg: Königshausen und Neumann, 1999.
Huber, Martin. "'Gedächtnisarbeit': Robert Schindels Roman *Der Kalte*." In *Die Rampe—Porträt Robert Schindel*, edited by Bernhard Judex, 166-176. Linz: Trauner, 2018.
Huber, Martin, and Manfred Mittermayer, eds. *Bernhard-Handbuch: Leben – Werk – Wirkung*. 1. Aufl. 2018 edition. Stuttgart: J. B. Metzler, 2018.
Huizinga, Johan. *Dutch Civilisation in the Seventeenth Century and other Essays*. Translated by Arnold J. Pomerans. New York: Ungar, 1968.
Huizinga, Johan. *Homo Ludens. A Study of the Play-Element in Culture*. London: Routledge and Kegan Paul, 1955.
Huizinga, Johan. *Homo Ludens. Proeve eener Bepaling van het Spel-Element der Cultuur*. Haarlemz H. D. Tjeenk Willink & Zoon, 1938.
Huot, Cyril. *Le rire triomphant des perdants (Journal de guerre)*. Paris: Tinbad, 2016a.

Huot, Cyril. *Le spectre de Thomas Bernhard*. Paris: Tinbad, 2016b.
Huston, Nancy. "L'Asphyxie: Thomas Bernhard." In *Professeurs de Désespoir*, 177–206. Arles: Actes Sud, 2004.
Huston, Nancy. "Femmes teintées de noir: Sarah Kane, Christine Angot, Linda Lê," in *Professeurs de Désespoir*, 305–33. Arles: Actes Sud, 2004.
Hutcheon, Linda. *A Theory of Adaptation*. London and New York: Routledge, 2012.
Ibsch, Elrud. "From Hypothesis to Korrektur: Refutation as a Component of Postmodernist Discourse." In *Approaching Postmodernism*, edited by Douwe Fokkema and Hans Bertens, 119–34. Amsterdam: John Benjamins Publishing Company, 1986.
Jahrbuch der Thomas-Bernhard-Privatstiftung. In Kooperation mit dem Österreichischen Literaturarchiv: Thomas Bernhard Jahrbuch 2007/2008: 5. Erscheinungsort nicht ermittelbar, 2009.
Jelinek, Elfriede. *Das Lebewohl: 3 kl. Dramen*. Berlin: Berlin Verlag, 2000.
Josipovici, Gabriel. *Contre-Jour: A Triptych after Pierre Bonnard*. Manchester: Carcanet, 1986.
Josipovici, Gabriel. *Moo Pak*. Manchester: Carcanet, 1994.
Josipovici, Gabriel. "The Big Glass: A Note." *Salmagundi*, 88/89 (1990): 333–38.
Josipovici, Gabriel. *What Ever Happened to Modernism?* New Haven and London: Yale University Press, 2010.
Josipovici, Gabriel. "Wittgenstein's Awkward Nephew." *New Statesman America*, January 13, 2011.
Josipovici, Gabriel. *Infinity: The Story of a Moment*. Manchester: Carcanet, 2013.
Josipovici, Gabriel. "Interview with Gabriel Josipovici." *BookBlast*. April 24, 2018.
Judex, Bernhard. "Werke Thomas Bernhards." In *Bernhard Handbuch: Leben – Werk – Wirkung*, edited by Martin Huber and Manfred Mittermayer, 531–35. Würzburg: Metzler, 2018.
Kertész, Imre. *Galeerentagebuch: Roman*. Translated by Kristin Schwamm. Reinbek: Rowohlt, 1999.
Kertész, Imre. *Eine gedankenlange Stille, während das Erscheißungskommando neu lädt*. Translated by Kristin Schwamm et al. Reinbek: Rowohlt, 1999.
Kertész, Imre. "Language in Exile." Translated by Lewis P. Hinchman. *Hannah Arendt Newsletter* 4 (2001): 5–11.
Kertész, Imre. *Kaddish for an Unborn Child*. Translated by Tim Wilkinson. New York: Vintage International, 2004.
Kertész, Imre. *Briefe an Eva Haldimann*. Translated by Kristin Schwamm. Reinbek: Rowohlt, 2009.
Kimmage, Michael. "Philip Roth, Thomas Mann and the Other Other Europe." *Philip Roth Studies* 11.1 (2015): 91–104.
Kirchmayr, Raoul. "La via Di Fuga. Immagini Dell'infanzia Nell'autobiografia Di Thomas Bernhard." *Cultura Tedesca* 32 (2007): 115–30.
Knape, Joachim, and Olaf Kramer. *Rhetorik und Sprachkunst bei Thomas Bernhard*. Würzburg: Königshausen und Neumann, 2011.
Koestenbaum, Wayne. "Thomas Bernhard's Virtues." *Review of Contemporary Fiction*, 31.1 (2011): 53–55.
Konzett, Matthias, ed. *A Companion to the Works of Thomas Bernhard*. Rochester, NY: Camden House, 2002.
Körte, Mona. *Essbare Lettern, brennendes Buch: Schriftvernichtung in der Literatur der Neuzeit*. Munich: Wilhelm Fink Verlag, 2012.

Krylova, Katya. "'Eine den Menschen zerzausende Landschaft': Psychotopography and the Alpine Landscape in Thomas Bernhard's *Frost*." *Austrian Studies* 18 (2010): 74–88.

Krylova, Katya. *Walking Through History: Topography and Identity in the Works of Ingeborg Bachmann and Thomas Bernhard*. Bern and Oxford: Peter Lang, 2013.

Krylova, Katya. *The Long Shadow of the Past: Contemporary Austrian Literature, Film, and Culture*. Rochester: Camden House, 2020.

Krylova, Katya, ed. *New Perspectives on Contemporary Austrian Literature and Culture*. Oxford: Peter Lang, 2018.

Kuhn, Gudrun. "Eingedenken. Imre Kertész im Dialog mit Thomas Bernhard." In *Thomas Bernhard Jahrbuch 2007/2008*, edited by Martin Huber, Bernhard Judex, Manfred Mittermayer, Wendelin Schmidt-Dengler, 37–51. Vienna, Cologne, Weimar: Böhlau, 2009.

LaCapra, Dominick. *Writing History, Writing Trauma*. Reprint edition. Baltimore: Johns Hopkins University Press, 2014.

Lahayne, Olaf. *Beschimpft Österreich! Der Skandal um die Staatspreisrede Thomas Bernhards im März 1968*. Göttingen: V&R, 2016.

Lê, Linda. *Les dits d'un idiot*. Paris: Bourgois, 1995.

Lê, Linda. *Voix: Une crise*. Paris: Bourgois, 1998.

Lê, Linda. *Tu écriras sur le bonheur*. Paris: Bourgois, 1999.

Lê, Linda. *Les Aubes* (Paris: Bourgois, 2000).

Lê, Linda. *Au fond de l'inconnu pour trouver du nouveau*. Paris: Bourgois, 2009.

Lê, Linda. *Oeuvres Vives*. Paris: Bourgois, 2014.

Lê, Linda. *Par Ailleurs (Exils)*. Paris: Bourgois, 2014.

LeClair, Thomas. "William Gass, The Art of Fiction No. 65." *The Paris Review*. Accessed November 23, 2019. https://www.theparisreview.org/interviews/3576/william-gass-the-art-of-fiction-no-65-william-gass.

Lindemann, Tobias. "Robert Schindel - Interview zu seinem Roman 'Der Kalte' über die Waldheim-Jahre in Österreich." *freie-radios.net*, June 26, 2013, http://www.freie-radios.net/56812.

Long, J. J. *W. G. Sebald: Image, Archive, Modernity*. New York: Columbia University Press, 2007.

Lorenz, Dagmar. "The Established Outsider: Thomas Bernhard." *A Companion to the Works of Thomas Bernhard*, ed. Matthias Konzett, 29–50. Rochester: Camden House, 2002.

Magris, Claudio. *Blameless*. Translated by Anne Milano Appel. New Haven: Yale University Press, 2017.

Magris, Claudio. *Danube*. Translated by Patrick Creagh. New York: Farrar, Straus and Giroux, 1990.

Magris, Claudio. *Danubio*. Milan: Garzanti, 2003.

Magris, Claudio. *Il mito absburgico nella letteratura austrica moderna*. Turin: G. Einaudi, 1988.

Magris, Claudio. *Non luogo a procedere*. Milan: Garzanti, 2015.

Magris, Claudio. "Perturbazione." In *Il romanzo tedesco del Novecento*, edited by Giuliano Baioni, Giuseppe Bevilacqua, Cesare Cases, and Claudio Magris, 553–66. Turin: Einaudi, 1973.

Magris, Claudio. *Se non siamo innocenti: Marco Alloni dialoga con Claudio Magris*. Rome: Aliberti editore, 2011.

Magris, Claudio. "Tenebra e geometria." In *Dietro le parole*, 285–90. Milan: Garzanti, 2002.

Marquard, Odo. "Inkompetenzkompensationskompetenz? Über Kompetenz und Inkompetenz der Philosophie." In *Abschied vom Prinzipiellen: Philosophische Studien*, by Odo Marquard, 23–38. Stuttgart: Reclam, 1981.
Martin, Charles W. *The Nihilism of Thomas Bernhard. The Portrayal of Existential and Social Problems in His Prose Works*. Amsterdam: Brill Rodopi, 1995.
Mathews, Harry, and Alastair Brotchie. *Oulipo Compendium*. London: Atlas, 1998.
Mittermayer, Manfred. "Antworten auf Thomas Bernhard aus der internationalen Literatur." *Cultura tedesca* 32, January–June (2007): 159–79.
Mittermayer, Manfred. "Lächerlich, charakterlos, furchterregend. Zu Thomas Bernhards Rhetorik der Bezichtigung." In *Rhetorik und Sprachkunst bei Thomas Bernhard*, edited by Joachim Knape and Olaf Kramer, 25–44. Würzburg: Königshausen & Neumann, 2011.
Mittermayer, Manfred. *Thomas Bernhard. Eine Biografie*. Frankfurt am Main: Suhrkamp, 2015.
Mittermayer, Manfred. "Von Montaigne zu Jean-Paul Sartre. Vermutungen zur Intertexualität in Bernhards Auslöschung." In *Thomas Bernhard: Traditionen und Trabanten*, edited by Joachim Hoell and Kai Luehrs-Kaiser, 159–76. Würzburg: Königshausen und Neumann, 1999.
Moore, Steven. *William Gaddis*. Expanded edition. New York and London: Bloomsbury, 2015.
Morachielli, Elena. "Il triangolo dell'assoluto nei romanza: Un altro mare di Claudio Magris e Il soccombente di Thomas Bernhard." *Nuova antologia* 572 (January–March 1994): 480–500.
Moser, Joseph. "Blurring Fiction with Reality: Robert Schindel's comédie humaine of 1980s Vienna in *Gebürtig* and *Der Kalte*." In *New Perspectives on Contemporary Austrian Literature and Culture*, edited by Katya Krylova, 373–91. Oxford: Peter Lang, 2018.
Moser, Joseph. "Crime in Thomas Bernhard's Novels: A Critique of the Fathers." Edited by Rebecca S. Thomas. *Crime and Madness in Modern Austria: Myth, Metaphor and Cultural Realities*, 388–402. Newcastle, UK: Cambridge Scholars Publishing, 2008.
Moya, Horacio. Castellanos. *El asco*. Buenos Aires: Tusquets, 2014.
Moya, Horacio. *Revulsion: Thomas Bernhard in San Salvador*. Translated by Lee Klein. New York: New Directions, 2016.
Mueller, Agnes C. *The Inability to Love: Jews, Gender, and America in Recent German Literature*. Evanston, IL: Northwestern University Press, 2014.
Mulitzer, Thomas. *Tau*. Vienna: Kremayr & Scheriau, 2017.
Naqvi, Fatima. "Dialectic at a Standstill: The Discourse of Victimhood in Thomas Bernhard's Heldenplatz." *German Quarterly* 77.4 (2002): 408–21.
Neumeyer, Harald. "'Experimentalsätze' und 'Lebensversicherungen'. Thomas Bernhards *Kalkwerk* und die Methode des Viktor Urbantschitsch." *Politik und Medien bei Thomas Bernhard*, edited by Franziska Schößler and Ingeborg Villinger, 4–29. Würzburg: Königshausen & Neumann, 2002.
O'Connor, Flannery. *Collected Works*. New York: Library of America, 1988.
O'Neill, Patrick. "Endgame Variations: Narrative and Noise in Thomas Bernhard's Das Kalkwerk." *Hinter dem schwarzen Vorhang: Die Katastrophe und die epische Tradition. Festschrift für Anthony W. Riley*, edited by Friedrich Gaede, Patrick O'Neill, and Ulrich Scheck, 231–41. Marburg: Francke, 1994.
Page, Tim, ed. *The Glenn Gould Reader*. New York: Knopf, 1984.
Parks, Tim. *The Novel: A Survival Skill*. Oxford, UK: Oxford University Press, 2015.

Parks, Tim. *Translating Style: A Literary Approach to Translation - A Translation Approach to Literature*. London and New York: Routledge, 2016.
"Novels." http://tim-parks.com/novels/.
Parmegiani, Sandra. "Remembering War: Memory and History in Claudio Magris's Blameless." In *Transmissions of Memory: Echoes, Traumas, and Nostalgia in Post-World War II Italian Culture*, edited by Patrizia Sambuco, 91–107. Vancouver/Madison: Fairleigh Dickinson University Press, 2018.
Peck, Dale. "*My Prizes* and *Prose* by Thomas Bernhard." *The New York Times*, December 24, 2010, sec. Sunday Book Review. https://www.nytimes.com/2010/12/26/books/review/Peck-t.html.
Plunka, Gene A. *Holocaust Drama: The Theater of Atrocity*. Cambridge, UK: Cambridge University Press, 2009.
Porcell, Claude. "Die Verklärung des heiligen Bernhard. Zur Rezeption der Erzählprosa in Frankreich." In Wolfram Bayer, ed., *Kontinent Bernhard. Zur Thomas-Bernhard-Rezeption in Europa*, 241–68. Vienna/Cologne/Weimar: Böhlau, 1995.
Proctor, Minna Zallman. *Landslide: True Stories*. New York: Catapult, 2017.
Puckett, Yana, and Abdullah A. Bokhari, "Prednisone". *StatPearls* [Internet]. Treasure Island, FL: StatPearls Publishing, 2019.
Purdon, James. "What Ever Happened to Modernism?" *The Observer*, October 2, 2010.
Quattrocchi, Luigi. "Thomas Bernhard in Italia." *Cultura e scuola* 26. 103 (1987): 46–58.
Re, Lucia. "Pasolini vs. Calvino, One More Time: The Debate on the Role of Intellectuals and Postmodernism in Italy Today." *MLN* 129.1 (2014): 99–117.
Reiterer, Reinhold. "Oft weit weg von der Originalfigur." *Kleine Zeitung*, April 8, 2013, https://www.kleinezeitung.at/kultur/4040095/Oft-weit-weg-von-der-Originalfigur.
Ricciardi, Alessia. *After La Dolce Vita: A Cultural Prehistory of Berlusconi's Italy*. Stanford: Stanford University Press, 2012.
Richter, Sandra. *Eine Weltgeschichte der deutschsprachigen Literatur*. Munich: C. Bertelsmann, 2017.
Rieff, David. *Swimming in a Sea of Death: A Son's Memoir*. New York: Simon and Schuster, 2008.
Roberts, John P. L., ed. *The Art of Glenn Gould*. Toronto: Malcolm Lester Books, 1999.
Rodogni, Davide. "Italiani brava gente? Fascist Italy's Policy Toward the Jews in the Balkans, April 1941–July 1943." *European History Quarterly* 35.2 (2005): 213–40.
Roth, Gerhard. *Orkus: Reise zu den Toten*. Frankfurt am Main: Fischer, 2011.
Roth, Philip.*Exit Ghost*. London: Vintage, 2016.
Roth, Philip. *Reading Myself and Others*. London: Vintage, 2010.
Roth, Philip. *The Counterlife*. London: Vintage, 2016.
Roth, Philip. *The Human Stain*. London: Vintage, 2016.
Roth, Philip. *Philip Roth: Why Write?* New York: Library of America, 2017.
Roth, Philip. *Sabbath's Theater*. New York: Vintage, 1996.
Ruhe, Cornelia. "Wenn Ränder Mitte Werden: Zivilisation, Literatur und Sprache im Interkulturellen Kontext. Festschrift für F. Peter Kirsch zum 60. Geburtstag, Wien: WUV-Universitätsverlag, 2001." Augsburg: Wißner, 2003.
Salem, Gemma. *Lettre à l'ermite autrichien*. Paris: La Table Ronde, 1989.
Salem, Gemma. *L'Artiste*. Paris: La Table Ronde, 1991.

Salem, Gemma. (ed.). *Thomas Bernhard et les siens*. Paris: La Table Ronde, 1993.
Salem, Gemma. *La Rhumba à Beethoven*. Paris: Roux, 2014.
Sauer, Jörg Uwe. *Uniklinik*. Salzburg: Residenz, 1999.
Schäfer, Andreas. "Sein Schreibstil war ein Virus." *Die Zeit*, June 2, 2014.
Schimmelbusch, Alexander. *Die Murau Identität*. Berlin: Metrolit, 2014.
Schindel, Robert. *Der Kalte*. Berlin: Suhrkamp, 2013.
Schmidt-Dengler, Wendelin. "Der Tod als Naturwissenschaft neben dem Leben, Leben." In *Über Thomas Bernhard*, edited by Anneliese Botond, 34–41. Frankfurt am Main: Suhrkamp, 1970.
Schmidt-Dengler, Wendelin. "Den ganzen Erdball überstrahlend. Thomas Bernhard, Österreich und Europa." In *Wenn Ränder Mitte werden. Zivilisation, Literatur und Sprache im interkulturellen Kontext*, edited by Chantal Adobati, Maria Aldouri-Lauber, Manuela Hager, and Reinhart Hosch, 706–20. Vienna: Facultas, 2001.
Schmidt-Dengler, Wendelin. *Der Übertreibungskünstler: Studien zu Thomas Bernhard*. Vienna: Sonderzahl, 2010.
Schössler, Franziska, and Ingeborg Villinger, eds. *Politik und Medien bei Thomas Bernhard*. Würzburg: Königshausen u. Neumann, 2002.
Schütte, Uwe. In *Thomas Bernhard. Gesellschaftliche und Politische Bedeutung der Literatur*, edited by Johann Lughofer, 303–19. Vienna: Böhlau, 2012.
Schütte, Uwe, and Johann Lughofer. "Ein Lehrer. Über W. G. Sebald und Thomas Bernhard." In *Thomas Bernhard: Gesellschaftliche und Politische Bedeutung der Literatur*, 303–19. Vienna and Cologne: Böhlau, 2012.
Schwartz, Alexandra. "The 'Unmasking' of Elena Ferrante," *The New Yorker*, October 3, 2016. https://www.newyorker.com/culture/cultural-comment/the-unmasking-of-elena-ferrante.
Sebald, W. G. "Wo die Dunkelheit den Strick zuzieht: Zu Thomas Bernhard." In *Die Beschreibung des Unglücks. Zur österreichischen Literatur von Stifter bis Handke*, 103–14. Frankfurt am Main: Fischer, 2012 [1985].
Sebald, W. G. *Austerlitz*. Reinbek: Rowohlt, 2003.
Silverblatt, Michael. "A Poem of an Invisible Subject." In *The Emergence of Memory: Conversations with W. G. Sebald*, ed. Sharon Lynn Schwartz, 77–86. New York: Seven Stories Press, 2007.
Simon, John. "The Sun Never Rises on Rudolf," *New York Times*, July 1, 1984.
Sontag, Susan. *Against Interpretation and Other Essays*. New York: Farrar, Straus & Giroux, 1966.
Sontag, Susan. *The Way We Live Now*. New York: Noonday, 1991.
Sontag, Susan. "The Art of Fiction," *Paris Review* 137 (1995): 175–208.
Sontag, Susan. *Conversations with Susan Sontag*. Edited by Leland Poague. Jackson: University of Mississippi Press, 1995.
Sontag, Susan. *At the Same Time: Essays and Speeches*. Edited by Paolo Dilonardo and Anne Jump, with a foreword by David Rieff. New York: Farrar, Straus & Giroux, 2007.
Sontag, Susan. *On Photography*. New York: Farrar, Straus & Giroux, 2001.
Stakhovitch, Nicolas. *Les Aphorismes de Gralph*. Paris: Nadeau, 1991.
Steiner, George. "Black Danube." In *George Steiner at the New Yorker*, edited by Robert Boyers, 117–27. New York: New Directions, 2009.
Sullam, Simon Levi. *The Italian Executioners: The Genocide of the Jews of Italy*. Translated by Oona Smith with Claudia Patane. Princeton: Princeton University Press, 2018.

Tabah, Mireille. "Gedächtnis und Performanz. W. G. Sebald's *Austerlitz* versus Thomas Bernhard's *Auslöschung*." In *W. G. Sebald: Intertextualität und Topographie*, edited by Irene Heidelberger-Leonhard and Mireille Tabah, 125–39. Münster: LIT Verlag, 2008.

Tani, Stefano. "La Giovane Narrativa: Emerging Italian Novelists in the Eighties." In *Postmodern Fiction in Europe and the Americas*, edited by Theo D'Haen and Hans Bertens, 161–92. Amsterdam: Rodopi, 1988.

Thomas, Rebecca S. "Elfriede Jelinek's *Die Liebhaberinnen*: On the (Re)-Production Line." In *Modern Austrian Prose: Interpretations and Insights*, edited by Paul F. Dvorak, 59–85. Riverside: Ariadne, 2001.

Thornton, Megan. "A Postwar Perversion of Testimonio in Horacio Castellanos Moya's *El asco*." *Hispania* 97.2 (2014): 207–19.

Thuswaldner, Gregor. "Skandale und Erregungen." In *Bernhard Handbuch: Leben – Werk – Wirkung*, edited by Martin Huber and Manfred Mittermayer, 470–77. Stuttgart: Metzler, 2018.

Tinkler, Alan. "Italo Calvino." *The Review of Contemporary Fiction* 22.1 (Spring 2002): 59–94.

Trevisan, Vitaliano. *Il ponte. Un crollo*. Turin: Einaudi, 2007.

Updike, John. "Studies in Post-Hitlerian Self-Condemnation in Austria and West Germany." In *Odd Jobs*, 620–29. London: Penguin, 1992.

Verondini, Isabella Berthier. "Trilogia dell'intellettuale: *Frost, Verstörung, Das Kalkwerk* di Thomas Bernhard." *Studi Germanici* 12.1 (February 1974): 69–97.

Wagner, Karl. "Holzfällen. Eine Erregung." In *Bernhard Handbuch: Leben – Werk – Wirkung*, edited by Martin Huber and Manfred Mittermayer, 74–79. Stuttgart: Metzler, 2018.

Webber, Andrew. "Costume Drama: Performance and Identity in Bernhard." In *A Companion to the Works of Thomas Bernhard*, edited by Matthias Konzett, 149–68. Rochester, NY: Camden House, 2002.

Weinmann, Ute. *Thomas Bernhard, L'Autriche et la France. Histoire d'une reception littéraire*. Paris: L'Harmattan, 2000.

Weinmann, Ute. "La réception de Thomas Bernhard en France." In *Thomas Bernhard*, eds. Pierre Chabert and Barbara Hutt, 165–73. Paris: Minerve, 2002.

Weinmann, Ute. "Rezeption in den romanischsprachigen Ländern: Frankreich." In *Thomas Bernhard Handbuch: Leben – Werk – Wirkung*, edited by Martin Huber and Manfred Mittermayer, 491–94. Stuttgart: J. B. Metzler, 2018.

Weinzierl, Ulrich. "Bernhard als Erzieher: Thomas Bernhards *Auslöschung*." *German Quarterly* 63.3–4 (1990): 455–61.

Wiggershaus, Renate. "Adorno in Shorts." *Neue Zürcher Zeitung*, October 30, 2010.

Winkler, Jean-Marie. "Todesengel, Nihilist und Prophet. Die Rezeption der Bühnenwerke in Frankreich 1986–1991." In *Kontinent Bernhard. Zur Thomas-Bernhard-Rezeption in Europa*, edited by Wolfram Bayer, 269–96. Vienna/Cologne/Weimar: Böhlau, 1995.

Zima, Peter V. *Modern/Postmodern: Society, Philosophy, Literature*. London and New York: Continuum, 2010.

Zweig, Stefan. *Die Welt von Gestern: Erinnerungen eines Europäers*. Frankfurt am Main: Fischer, [1944] 2001.

Contributors

Olaf Berwald is Chair of the Department of Foreign Languages and Professor of German at Kennesaw State University. His book publications include the edited volumes, *Timescapes of Waiting: Spaces of Stasis, Delay and Deferral*, with Christoph Singer and Robert Wirth (2019), *A Companion to the Works of Max Frisch* (2013), *La globalización y sus espejismos: Encuentros y desencuentros interculturales vistos desde el Sur y el Norte*, with Michael Handelsman (2009), *Der untote Gott: Religion und Ästhetik in der deutschen und österreichischen Literatur des 20. Jahrhunderts*, with Gregor Thuswaldner (2007), and the monographs, *An Introduction to the Works of Peter Weiss* (2003) and *Philipp Melanchthons Sicht der Rhetorik* (1994).

Stephen Dowden is a professor of German language and literature at Brandeis University. Among his books is *Understanding Thomas Bernhard* (1991). Recently he has completed a book manuscript entitled *Mimesis and Modernism: Fiction, Painting, Music, and Poetry* (2021). He is currently at work on a new book to be entitled *Critique of Erotic Reason*. His most recent scholarly collection, coedited with Thomas P. Quinn, is *Tragedy and the Tragic in German Literature, Art, and Thought* (2015).

Kata Gellen is Associate Professor of German at Duke University. Her main areas of research are German literary modernism, German-Jewish studies, Austrian literature, Weimar film, and sound studies. Her book *Kafka and Noise: The Discovery of Cinematic Sound in Literary Modernism* (2019) is an intermedial study of the numerous strange, unsettling sounds in Franz Kafka's literary and personal writings. She has also published articles on Joseph Roth, Robert Musil, Fritz Lang, Thomas Bernhard, and others. Her current project, tentatively titled *Shtetl Modern: The Literature Imagination of Jewish Futures in World War II Europe*, explores a series of German-Jewish novels that depict traditional Jewish life at a time of crisis, upheaval, and confrontation with modernity.

Contributors 247

Martin Klebes is Associate Professor of German at the University of Oregon and the current editor of the digital interdisciplinary German Studies journal *Konturen* (http://konturen.uoregon.edu). He is the author of *Wittgenstein's Novels* (2006) and the translator of Ernst-Wilhelm Händler's *City with Houses* (2002). His more recent article publications have treated the relationship of Hermann Broch's work to Enlightenment thought and to the figuration of "the jew" in modernity; Hannah Arendt's conception of active reading; and intertextuality in the work of W. G. Sebald. He has also written on philosophers including Kant, Kierkegaard, and David Lewis.

Katya Krylova is Lecturer in German, Film and Visual Culture at the University of Aberdeen. She studied German and Italian at Churchill College, Cambridge, where she then completed a PhD in German Literature in 2011. Her first monograph, *Walking Through History: Topography and Identity in the Works of Ingeborg Bachmann and Thomas Bernhard* (2013), won the 2011 Peter Lang Young Scholars Competition in German Studies. Her second monograph, *The Long Shadow of the Past: Contemporary Austrian Literature, Film, and Culture* (2017), won the 2018 CHOICE Outstanding Academic Title Award. She is also editor of the multiauthored volume *New Perspectives on Contemporary Austrian Literature and Culture* (2018).

Agnes Mueller is the College of Arts & Sciences Distinguished Professor of the Humanities at the University of South Carolina, where she serves also as Director of the university's Program in Global Studies. Her most recently published book is *The Inability to Love: Jews, Gender, and America in Recent German Literature* (2015). It has been translated into German as *Die Unfähigkeit zu lieben: Juden und Antisemitismus in der Gegenwartsliteratur* (2017). Among her varied books and essays is also a recent volume, coedited with Katja Garloff, *German Jewish Literature after 1990* (2018). Currently Professor Mueller is at work on a new project tentatively entitled *Holocaust Migration: Jewish Fiction in Today's Germany*. In it, she identifies, explores, and analyzes how the new, multiethnic Germany—a plural society into which past trauma has been dispersed—negotiates its unprecedented challenges.

Heike Scharm is Associate Professor of Spanish literature and culture at the University of South Florida at Tampa Bay. She is the author of *El tiempo y el ser en Javier Marías* (2013) and of the edited volume *Postnational Perspectives on Contemporary Hispanic Literature* (2017). She has published articles and chapters on ecocriticism and transatlantism, and is currently preparing a book manuscript titled *Transcorporeality, the Anthropocene, and the Post-Human*, which offers an ecocritical reading of recent Spanish novels in dialogue with the literary production of other countries. Besides ecocriticism, her main research interests are globalization, science fiction, philosophy, and identity politics, as well as cross-cultural and postnational approaches to European and Latin American literatures.

Byron Spring is a stipendiary lecturer in German at Lincoln College, University of Oxford, where he teaches a range of papers in modern German literature and translation in the Oxford undergraduate course. His research, funded by the Arts and Humanities Research Council in the United Kingdom, explores what it means to consider Thomas Bernhard as a world author, examining the significance of Bernhard's prose and dramatic works to late twentieth-century literature and aesthetics beyond their existing international receptions.

Gregor Thuswaldner is Provost and Executive Vice President at Whitworth University in Spokane, Washington. He has written on Austrian and German literature, culture, politics, history, religion, literary theory, linguistics, film, and higher education. His latest book publications include the coedited volumes *The Hermeneutics of Hell: Visions and Representations of the Devil in World Literature* (2017) and *Making Sacrifices: Visions of Sacrifice in European and American Cultures* (2016). Thuswaldner currently serves as President of the Austrian Studies Association. He is an elected member of the European Academy of Sciences and Arts, Pen American Center, Pen Austria, as well as a Fellow of the Royal Historical Society, and the Royal Society of Arts.

Juliane Werner is a postdoctoral assistant and lecturer in the Department of Comparative Literature at the University of Vienna. Her primary research interests are franco-germanophone cultural transfer in the nineteenth and twentieth centuries, philosophical fiction, word and music studies, spatial theory, transgression narratives, and medical humanities. In 2019, she was Artist in Residence of the International Thomas Bernhard Society in Ottnang, Upper Austria. She is the author of a book on the relationship between Thomas Bernhard and Jean-Paul Sartre entitled *Thomas Bernhard und Jean-Paul Sartre* (2016), as well as a forthcoming book on French existentialism in Austria called *Existentialismus in Österreich: Kultureller Transfer und literarische Resonanz* (2020).

Saskia Elizabeth Ziolkowski is Assistant Professor of Romance Studies at Duke University. She is the author of *Kafka's Italian Progeny* (2020), which explores Franz Kafka's sometimes surprising connections with key writers—from Massimo Bontempelli, Lalla Romano, and Italo Calvino to Antonio Tabucchi, Paola Capriolo, and Elena Ferrante—who have shaped Italy's literary landscape. Because she works on Italian literature from a comparative perspective, her articles often focus on pairs of authors, including Italo Svevo and William Shakespeare, Primo Levi and Franz Kafka, Scipio Slataper and Rainer Maria Rilke, and Pier Antonio Quarantotti Gambini and Joseph Roth.

Index

abulia in literature 145
Adelphi Press 185
Adorno, Theodor 90
AIDS virus 71, 82, 159, 210
Améry, Jean 1, 15
Anderson, Mark M. 193
anti-Semitism 18–19, 28, 109, 112, 201–5
Arendt, Hannah 12, 89
Arnim, Bettina von 161
artists 11
Auschwitz 6, 14–18, 79, 91–4
"Auslöschung" concept 35 see *also* Bernhard, Thomas: works by: *Extinction*
Austria 1–2, 8–9, 14, 18, 21, 25–31, 34, 42, 142–4, 192–203
  Ministry of Culture and Art 198
Austro-Hungarian Empire 196
authorial agency 135, 192
Azúa, Félix 6, 137–41, 153

Bach, J. S. 125–30, 133
Bachmann, Ingeborg 29, 158, 167, 197–8
Bahr, Hermann 193
barbarism 12
Baroja, Pío 6–7, 140, 145–54
  The Tree of Knowledge 147–53
Bayer, Wolfram 115
Beckett, Samuel 2–4, 10, 13, 17, 181, 222
Beethoven, L. van 90, 179

Benjamin, Walter 12, 126–7, 225
Bernhard, Thomas
  autobiographical works by 138, 140, 182, 199
  biographical writing on 141, 147
  character and behavior of 2–3, 8–11, 15, 90, 139, 180–1, 187
  compendia of works 23
  ill-health experienced by 1, 87, 153, 167, 176
  impact of 2, 4, 6, 21, 72, 80, 84–5, 137, 207–9
  literary style of 1–4, 6–7, 13, 20–1, 81–7, 100, 140, 142, 158, 164, 175, 189
  musicality and musical style of 8, 138, 179
  new understanding of 4
  plays by 24–9
  poetic thinking of 13
  political views of 138
  popularity and unpopularity of 144, 181
  relations with the media 181
  status of 1–3, 23–8, 31, 42, 137, 170, 183–5, 189, 192, 198, 207
  studies by 170
  things *not* said by 18
  views of: as an exaggeration artist 9–10, 13, 19–20, 29; as a mentor and model 5; as a one-trick pony 84; as a

truth-teller 95; as a "writer's writer" 207
works by: *Blameless (Non luogo a procedere)* 184, 203–6; *Concrete (Beton)* 5, 118–23, 176, 191, 204, 209, 223; *Extinction (Auslöschung)* 3, 5, 9, 19, 21, 32, 95, 97–8, 105–15, 174–5, 207, 211–13, 222–3, 226, 230, 232; *Frost* 1–3, 10–11, 24–5, 36–41, 90, 140–1, 145, 147, 150–3, 177, 207; *Gargoyles (Ver-störung)* 18, 23, 32, 138, 145, 200; *Heldenplatz* 19, 24, 26, 95, 201–6, 226; *The Italian (Der Italianer)* 197–8; *The Lime Works (Das Kalkwerk)* 5, 10, 13, 48, 63, 82, 87, 189; *The Loser (Der Untergeher)* 5, 10, 18, 118, 143; *Old Masters (Alte Meister)* 3, 190, 192; *Woodcutters (Holzfällen)* 27–32, 182; *Yes* 21, 215
Berwald, Olaf 7, 246; *co-editor and author of Chapter 8*
"blocked" writers 5
Bloom, Harold 115, 209–10
Borowski, Tadeusz 15
Bottlang, René 160–1
Broch, Hermann 82–3, 89–90
"B" sides of records 46

Calasso, Roberto 195, 198
Calles, José María 146
Calvino, Italo 7, 184–9, 195
Camus, Albert 92–3, 222
Canetti, Elias 90
Castellanos Moya, Horacio 7, 207, 212, 217–18, 224–31
Catholicism 141–2, 217–18
Cela, Camilio José 152
Celan, Paul 10, 13, 166
Chamacoco people 203

Chardin, Philippe 145
Clinton, Bill 99, 101
Cole, Teju 73–4, 78
Comnes, Gregory 134
conspicuous consumption 3
cosmopolitan writers 6
Couling, Della 115
counterfeiting 133
Cousineau, Thomas 205
critical distance 51

Dante Alighieri 181
Daviau, Donald 98–9
Demand, Thomas 73–4
democracy, disenchantment with 138–9
Derrida, Jacques 127
Descartes, René 220
Desselbrunn 144
Dostoevsky, Fyodor 11
Dowden, Stephen 138, 144–5, 192, 246; *co-editor, author of Introduction and Chapter 4*
Drawert, Kurt 117
Duchamp, Marcel 171–2, 182
Dupin, Jacques 158, 166
Dyer, Geoff 5, 45–8, 52–69

Eastwood 62
Einaudi (publisher) 183–4
Eliraz, Israel 7, 158, 166–7
L'Éphémère (magazine) 166–7
Eshel, Amir 12

Fabjan, Peter 221
families, representation of 190
fascism 2, 18–19, 141–2, 201–2
Faulkner, William 85
Felski, Rita 49–51
Ferrante, Elena 7, 184, 190–4
Fialik, Maria 142
film 83
Fleischmann, Krista 35, 142
Florence 197

Index

Florencio, Rafael Núñez 149
Fludernik, Monika 173, 178
Foer, Jonathan Safran 79
Fosse, Jon 207, 210–11
Foucauldian theory 49
Francophone writers 157–8, 166
Frankfurt School 195
Freud, Sigmund (and Freudian theory) 49–50
Freunbichler, Johannes 170–1
Friedrich, Otto 129
friendship 147

Gadamer, Hans-Georg 125–7
Gaddis, William 5, 117–35, 207, 209
  Agapē Agape 117–19, 134
Gargani, Aldo Giorgio 195
Gass, William H. 189
Gellen, Kata 5, 10, 246–7; *author of Chapter 2*
German fiction 84–5
German language 79–80, 191, 198–9
Goethe, J.W. von 90, 109–10, 118
Gould, Glenn 118, 127–34, 160
Goya, Francisco 143
Guibert, Hervé 7, 158–9, 210
Gulbransen Co. 131–2

Haas, Franz 195
Habsburg Empire 199
Haldimann, Eva 93
Hals, Franz 196
Händel, G. F. 143
Hardy, Thomas 52, 68
Hemingway, Ernest 17
Hirsch, Marianne 79
Hitler, Adolf 19, 26, 78, 202
HIV infection *see* AIDS
Hofmann, Gert 117
Hofmannsthal, Hugo von 1, 193–4
Holocaust, the 14–15, 72–80, 202
Horowitz, Vladimir 127–8

Hrdlicka, Alfred 26, 28
Huizinga, Johan 123–30
human condition, the 8
Huntemann, Willi 161, 169
Huot, Cyril 7, 158, 163–6

imitative texts 210–11
Italy 7, 143, 184–5, 189, 193–9, 202, 216–18

James, Henry 172
Jelinek, Elfriede 117, 171
Josipovici, Gabriel 7, 17, 169–75, 178–81, 207, 209
Joyce, James 172

Kafka, Franz 1–2, 4, 10, 13, 29, 75, 92–5, 99, 181, 196
Kant, Immanuel 129, 152, 220
Karajan, Herbert von 133
Kertész, Imre 5–6, 14–15, 91–5, 207, 210
Kierkegaard, Søren 3–4, 11, 220–1
Klebes, Martin 5, 10, 247; *author of Chapter 6*
Knirps, Josef 170
Koestenbaum, Wayne 45
Körte, Mona 78
Kraus, Karl 4
Krömer, Wolfram 137
Krylova, Katya 4, 9, 247; *author of Chapter 1*

LaCapra, Dominick 75–6
Lachprogramm 151–2
Lampersberg, Gerhard 27
language as an approximation to the truth 6
Latini, Micaela 184
Lawrence, D. H. 5, 45–6, 52–5, 61–70
Lê, Linda 7, 58, 161–3
Lenin, V. I. 9

Lernet-Holenia, Alexander 195
Lewinsky, Monica 99, 101
Lish, Gordon 208–9
Liszt, Franz 179
literary scholarship 47–52
literature as knowledge 82–3
Littell, Jonathan 79
Long, J. J. 72, 110

Mach, Ernst 193
McLintock, David 122
Madland, Helga Stipa 146
Magris, Claudio 7, 183–4, 199–206
Mallorca 142
Mann, Thomas 93–4, 99, 103, 200
Marías, Javier 6, 137–40, 152
Marković, Barbi 208, 210
medical profession and medical procedures 153–4
Mendelssohn-Bartholdy, Felix 118–19, 121
Meyer, E. Y. 208
mimetic writing 13
Mittner, Ladislao 200
Montaigne, Michel de 221
Moritz, Herbert 27
Moser, Joseph 25
Mozart, W. A. (and "Mozartization") 34
Mueller, Agnes 5, 19, 21, 247; *author of Chapter 3*
Mulitzer, Thomas 4, 24–5, 36–43
Müller, Herta 200
Murphy, Muriel Oxenberg 134
musicality 8, 179
Mussolini, Benito 202

Nabokov, Vladimir 83
Nadeau, Maurice 158–9
Naipaul, V. S. 178
Naples 192–4
narrative structures 75
Nazism 18, 25, 85, 97, 112, 140–1, 201, 203, 206

negation in Bernhard's work 13
neoconservatives 101
Nestroy, Johann Nepomuk 4, 171
New York Times 122
Nietzsche, Friedrich 127, 146
Nobel Prizes 92, 184–5
novels
  form of 17, 64
  secret power of 17

O'Connor, Flannery 1–4, 10, 13
Ortega y Gasset, José 146, 148
Oulipo group 121
outtakes from films 46

"paisajismo" technique
Paradase Lost 86
Parks, Tim 7, 157, 207, 211–18, 228
Pascal, Blaise 221
Paz, Octavio 182
Perec, Georges 172
Perlentaucher (online magazine) 169
Peymann, Claus 26
photography 71–80, 225
piano playing and player pianos 117–22, 127–33
Piglia, Ricardo 209
Pinter, Harold 171–2
Pisa 196
plagiarism 121–2, 127, 131, 208
play, concept and properties of 124–5
postmodernism 189, 195
prednisolone and *prednisone* 122–3
Proust, Marcel 170

Qualtinger, Helmut 33–4
Quattrocchi, Luigi 185

Rabelais, François 4, 14
Rachmaninov, Sergei 179
Raimund, Ferdinand 28

Raja, Anita 184
recording technology 130–3
repetition in fiction 189
Rieff, David 88
Risiera San Sabba 201
Rogers, Edith 152
Rome 197
Rossini, Giacchino 143
Roth, Gerhard 4, 24, 29–31, 42–3
Roth, Joseph 1, 29, 195
Roth, Philip 5, 14, 98–101, 105, 108, 111, 115–16
Rotstein, Jason 172
Rushdie, Salman 34

Sáenz, Miguel 140–2, 147
Salem, Gemma 7, 158–62
Salzburg 15–16
San Salvador 227–8
Sauer, Jörg Uwe 208–9
Scelsi, Giacinto 182
Schäfer, Andreas 209
Scharm, Heike 6–7, 21, 248
   author of Chapter 7
Schiller, Friedrich 126
Schimek, Otto 203
Schimmelbusch, Alexander 4, 24, 31–8, 42–3, 208
Schindel, Robert 4, 24–31, 42–3
Schnitzler, Arthur 195
Schoenberg, Arnold 92
Schopenhauer, Arthur 145–6, 152, 154, 219–21
Scriabin, A. N. 179
Sebald, W. G. 4–5, 19–20, 71–80, 84–5, 90
Second World War 202
Shakespeare, William 110
Shaw, D. L. 152
Shaw, Donald 145
Shoah, the 3, 18, 72, 74, 80, 202–3
Sisto, Michele 184
Skakhovitch, Nicolas 158–9
"smarginatura" 194

sociability of art works 50
Sontag, Susan 5–6, 17, 50–1, 71, 81–91
Spain 6, 137–56
   Bernhard's emigration to 143
   relevance of Bernhard's writing to 139–47, 152, 156
Spanish language 147
Spiel, Hilde 142
Spielberg, Steven 91
Spring, Byron 5, 14, 248; *author of Chapter 5*
Stakhovitch, Nicolas 7
Steiner, George 115
Stendhal 148
Studi austriaci (journal) 195
Suhrkamp (publisher) 7, 169, 182
Sullam, Simon Levis 202
Swift, Jonathan 4, 14, 181

Tani, Stefano 189
Thomas, Rebecca S. 202
Thuswaldner, Gregor 7, 12, 248;
   co-editor and author of Chapter 9
Tinkler, Alan 188
Tintoretto 192
tonality and atonality 15
transcendence 191–2, 206
translations of Bernhard's works 211–12
trauma narratives 75, 79
Trevisan, Vitaliano 7, 207, 212–23
Trieste 203

Unseld, Siegfried 23, 32, 207–8, 226–30
Updike, John 98

Valle-Inclán, Ramón María 140–1, 145, 152
van Gogh, Vincent 16
van Meegeren Han 130
Velázquez, Diego de Silva y 143

Vienna 26–30, 43, 88–9, 93, 143, 146, 180, 192, 217
"village literature" 200
virus infection 160; see *also* AIDS

Wagner, Otto 32
Waldheim, Kurt 24–8, 31, 43, 97
walking 177
Weininger, Otto 1
Weiß, Ernst 1
Werner, Juliane 7, 21, 248–9; *author of Chapter 11*
Wibrow, Patricia Cifre 140
Wiggershaus, Renate 169–70
Wittgenstein, Ludwig 109, 165, 178, 194, 221

Woolf, Virginia 193
World Literature, recognition as 115, 231
writing
 failure in 45–6, 54–64, 67–70, 121
 relationship to life 186
Wylie, Andrew 34–5

Zambrano, María 137
Ziolkowski, Saskia Elizabeth 7, 18–19, 249; *author of Chapter 10*

www.ingramcontent.com/pod-product-compliance
Lightning Source LLC
Chambersburg PA
CBHW072138290426
44111CB00012B/1909